Dragon Knights

ALSO AVAILABLE FROM TOKYOPOP®

MANGA

*INDICATES 100% AUTHENTIC MANGA (RIGHT-TO-LEFT FORMAT)

ANGELIC LAYER*
BABY BIRTH* (September 2003)
BATTLE ROYALE*
BRAIN POWERED* (June 2003)
BRIGADOON* (August 2003)
CARDCAPTOR SAKURA
CARDCAPTOR SAKURA: MASTER OF THE CLOW*
CLAMP SCHOOL DETECTIVES*
CHOBITS*
CHRONICLES OF THE CURSED SWORD (July 2003)
CLOVER
CONFIDENTIAL CONFESSIONS* (July 2003)
CORRECTOR YUI
COWBOY BEBOP*
COWBOY BEBOP: SHOOTING STAR* (June 2003)
DEMON DIARY (May 2003)
DIGIMON
DRAGON HUNTER (June 2003)
DRAGON KNIGHTS*
DUKLYON: CLAMP SCHOOL DEFENDERS* (September 2003)
ERIKA SAKURAZAWA* (May 2003)
ESCAFLOWNE* (July 2003)
FAKE*(May 2003)
FLCL* (September 2003)
FORBIDDEN DANCE* (August 2003)
GATE KEEPERS*
G-GUNDAM* (June 2003)
GRAVITATION* (June 2003)
GTO*
GUNDAM WING
GUNDAM WING: ENDLESS WALTZ*
GUNDAM: THE LAST OUTPOST*
HAPPY MANIA*
HARLEM BEAT
INITIAL D*
I.N.V.U.
ISLAND
JING: KING OF BANDITS* (June 2003)
JULINE
KARE KANO*
KINDAICHI CASEFILES* (June 2003)
KING OF HELL (June 2003)

KODOCHA*
LOVE HINA*
LUPIN III*
MAGIC KNIGHT RAYEARTH* (August 2003)
MAN OF MANY FACES* (May 2003)
MARMALADE BOY*
MARS*
MIRACLE GIRLS
MIYUKI-CHAN IN WONDERLAND* (October 2003)
MONSTERS, INC.
NIEA_7* (August 2003)
PARADISE KISS*
PARASYTE
PEACH GIRL
PEACH GIRL: CHANGE OF HEART*
PET SHOP OF HORRORS* (June 2003)
PLANET LADDER*
PLANETS* (October 2003)
PRIEST
RAGNAROK
RAVE*
REAL BOUT HIGH SCHOOL*
REALITY CHECK
REBIRTH
REBOUND*
SABER MARIONETTE J* (July 2003)
SAILOR MOON
SAINT TAIL
SAMURAI DEEPER KYO* (June 2003)
SCRYED*
SHAOLIN SISTERS*
SHIRAHIME-SYO* (December 2003)
THE SKULL MAN*
SORCERER HUNTERS
TOKYO MEW MEW*
UNDER THE GLASS MOON (June 2003)
VAMPIRE GAME* (June 2003)
WILD ACT* (July 2003)
WISH*
X-DAY* (August 2003)
ZODIAC P.I.* (July 2003)

CINE-MANGA™

AKIRA*
CARDCAPTORS
FAIRLY ODD PARENTS (COMING SOON)
JIMMY NEUTRON (COMING SOON)
KIM POSSIBLE
LIZZIE McGUIRE
SPONGEBOB SQUAREPANTS (COMING SOON)
SPY KIDS 2

NOVELS

SAILOR MOON

TOKYOPOP KIDS

STRAY SHEEP (September 2003)

ART BOOKS

CARDCAPTOR SAKURA*
MAGIC KNIGHT RAYEARTH*

ANIME GUIDES

GUNDAM TECHNICAL MANUALS
COWBOY BEBOP
SAILOR MOON SCOUT GUIDES

Dragon Knights

Written and Illustrated by
Mineko Ohkami

Volume 7

Los Angeles • Tokyo

Translator - Agnes Yoshida
English Adaption - Stephanie Sheh
Retouch and Lettering - Paul Tanck
Cover Layout - Anna Kernbaum

Senior Editor - Luis Reyes
Managing Editor - Jill Freshney
Production Coordinator - Antonio DePietro
Production Manager - Jennifer Miller
Art Director - Matthew Alford
Director of Editorial - Jeremy Ross
VP of Production & Manufacturing - Ron Klamert
President & C.O.O. - John Parker
Publisher - Stuart Levy

Email: editor@TOKYOPOP.com
Come visit us online at www.TOKYOPOP.com

A **TOKYOPOP** Manga

TOKYOPOP® is an imprint of Mixx Entertainment, Inc.,
5900 Wilshire Blvd. Suite 2000, Los Angeles, CA 90036

ISBN: 1-59182-111-8

First TOKYOPOP® printing: April 2003

10 9 8 7 6 5 4 3 2 1

Printed in the USA

From the Chronicles of Dusis, the West Continent...

The Beginnings: Nadil and Lord Lykouleon

When the Yokai Nadil, the leader of the Demon Forces, kidnapped the Dragon Queen Raseleane, the Dragon Lord Lykouleon ventured to the Demon Realm to rescue her. He defeated Nadil by cutting off his head, but not before the demon leader rendered Raseleane barren, unable to give Lykouleon a child... and the Dragon Kingdom an heir. Now, the demon and Yokai forces, under the command of Shydeman and Shyrendora, plot to attack Draqueen, the Dragon Kingdom, and retrieve their leader's head in the hopes of reviving him. But other shady characters such as Master Kharl the Alchemist and the rogue Yokai Bierrez have also entered the contest for the control of all Dusis. The Dragon Officers and Lord Lykouleon desperately try to ready the Dragon Palace to repel an assault by the Demon Forces.

The Dragon Knights: A Motley Trio

The Dragon Knights are three specially-chosen warriors granted the power of the various elemental dragons for the protection of the Dragon Realm. They have been dispatched on three separate missions. The human/demon Rath is the Dragon Knight of Fire and has gone out of his way to accompany the fortuneteller Cesia to Mt. Mfartha. However, his reluctance to be entirely forthcoming about his motives may be a point of concern. Thatz, a human thief, is the Dragon Knight of Earth and is currently engaged in a search for the mysterious Three Treasures. The elfin prince Rune, the Dragon Knight of Water, has left the Dragon Palace to investigate reports that the Faerie Realm, his home, has been destroyed.

Rath and Cesia

Now partners, these two have always had a strained relationship, primarily because each doesn't trust the fact that the other is part demon. But they care about each other tremendously. When Cesia-prone to curses as she is-finds herself the victim of dark magic, it is Rath who helps her through each crisis. And when Rath becomes consumed with anger-as he is prone to do-it is Cesia that coaxes him back into calm. On their way to Mt. Mfartha, the two have been distracted by other callings, but these tangential adventures may very well lead to surprising revelations about themselves.

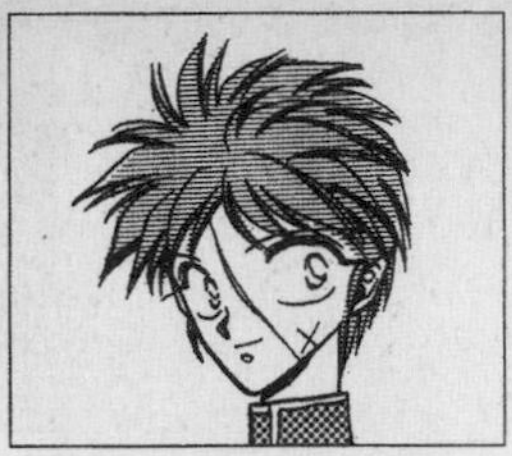

Thatz - Ex-thief turned Dragon Knight of Earth who has an insatiable appetite for food, drink and gold.

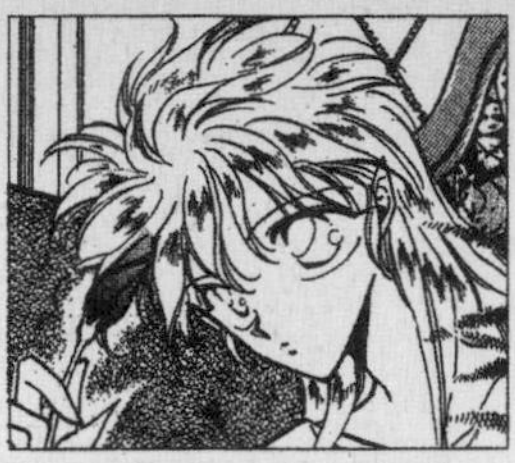

Rune - Dragon Knight of Water who longs to regain his elfin healing powers and save his faerie brood.

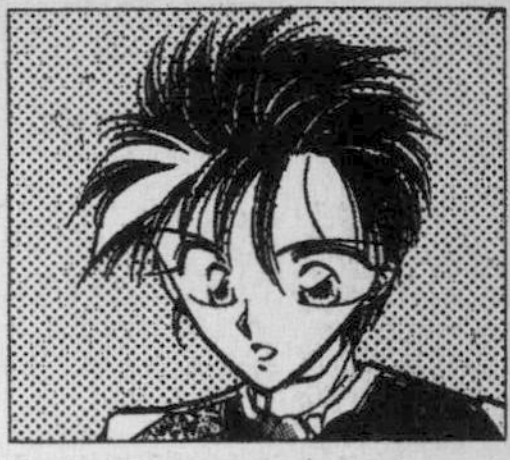

Rath Illuser - Dragon Knight of Fire who, though part demon, is obsessed with demon-hunting.

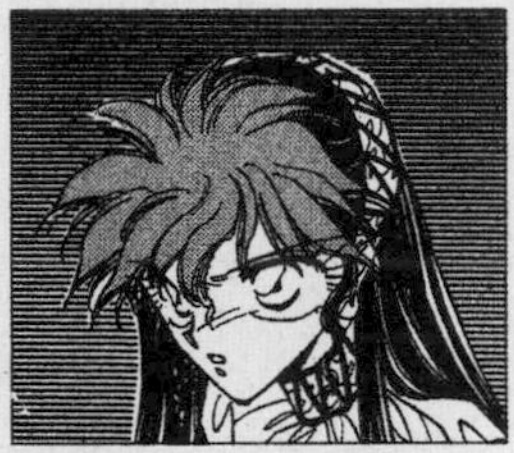

Cesia - A Yokai, raised by a witch, whose mysterious powers are sought after by many.

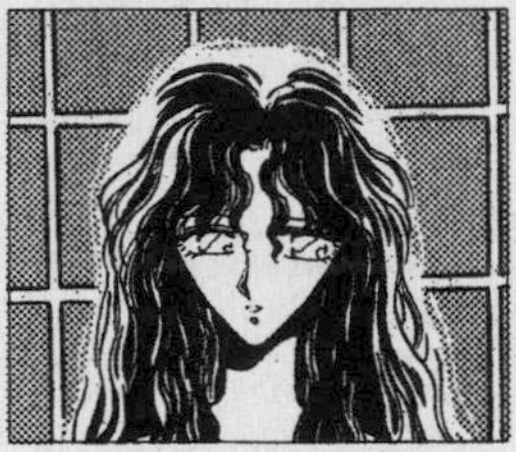

Raseleane - The Dragon Queen who has been made barren by the now deceased Lord Nadil.

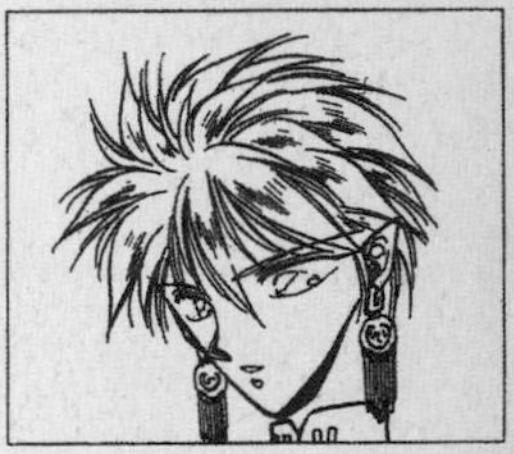

Lykouleon - The Dragon Lord who, with his Dragon of Light, leads the Dragon Tribe.

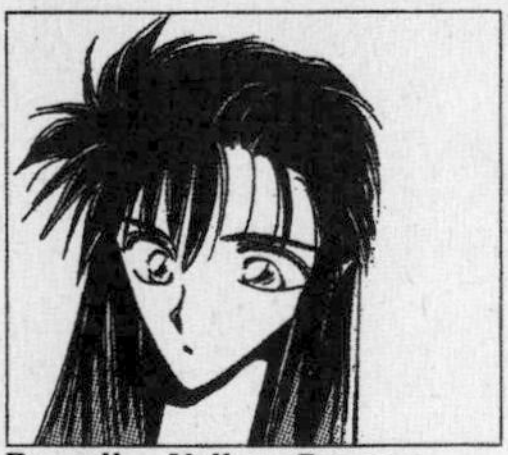

Ruwalk - Yellow Dragon Officer and Secretary of State. Assumes command when the Lord is away.

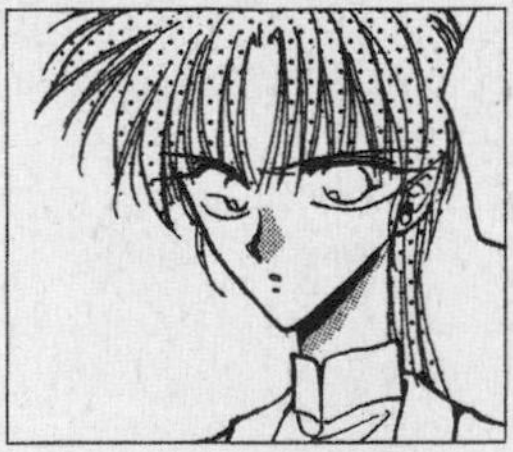

Alfeegi - White Dragon Officer and Chief Secretary. Oversees operations in the Dragon Castle.

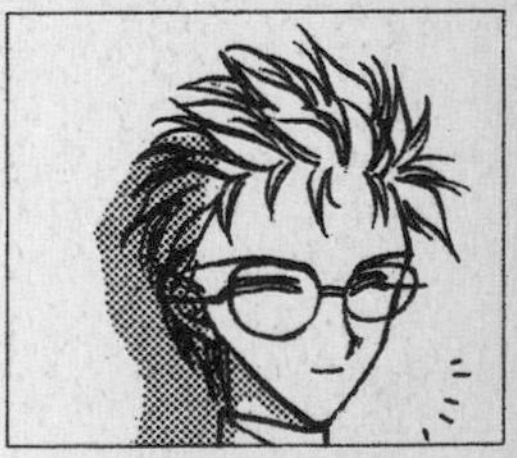

Kai-stern - Blue Dragon Officer and Secretary of Foreign Affairs. A close friend to Rath.

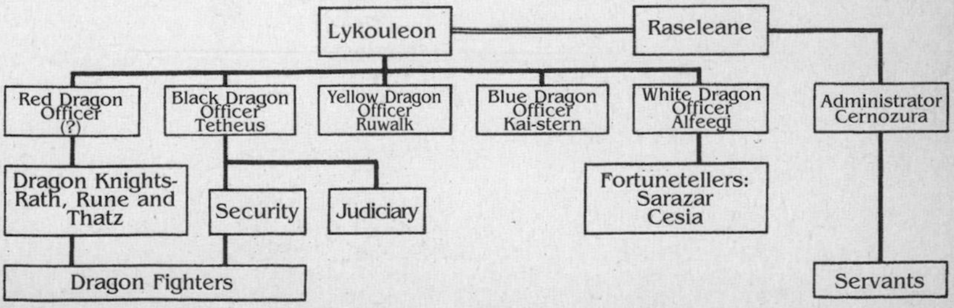
Lykouleon
Raseleane
Red Dragon Officer (?)
Black Dragon Officer Tetheus
Yellow Dragon Officer Ruwalk
Blue Dragon Officer Kai-stern
White Dragon Officer Alfeegi
Administrator Cernozura
Dragon Knights- Rath, Rune and Thatz
Security
Judiciary
Fortunetellers: Sarazar Cesia
Dragon Fighters
Servants

Tintlet - Elfin princess and protector of the Faerie Forest. Trapped in a magic seal.

Cernozura - Dragon Castle Administrator. Attendant to Queen Raseleane and the giver of hearty meals.

Tetheus - Black Dragon Officer and Secretary of Security. A paternal force for the young Dragon Knights.

Kharl - A famous Yokai alchemist and sorcerer. Author of the legendary "Demon Bible."

Kitchel - Thief and former rival to Thatz. Searching for pieces of a map for the Dragon Lord.

Zoma - Yokai in love with Cesia. Unable to use his legs without the help of a magical bird.

Nadil - King of the demons who was beheaded. His head is coveted by the Demon Army.

Shydeman & Shyrendora - Nadil's chief officers. In defacto command of the demon army.

Bierrez - Yokai in Nadil's army and the only demon who can penetrate the shield of the Dragon Castle.

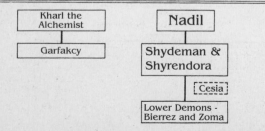

Kharl the Alchemist
Garfakcy

Nadil
Shydeman & Shyrendora
Cesia
Lower Demons - Bierrez and Zoma

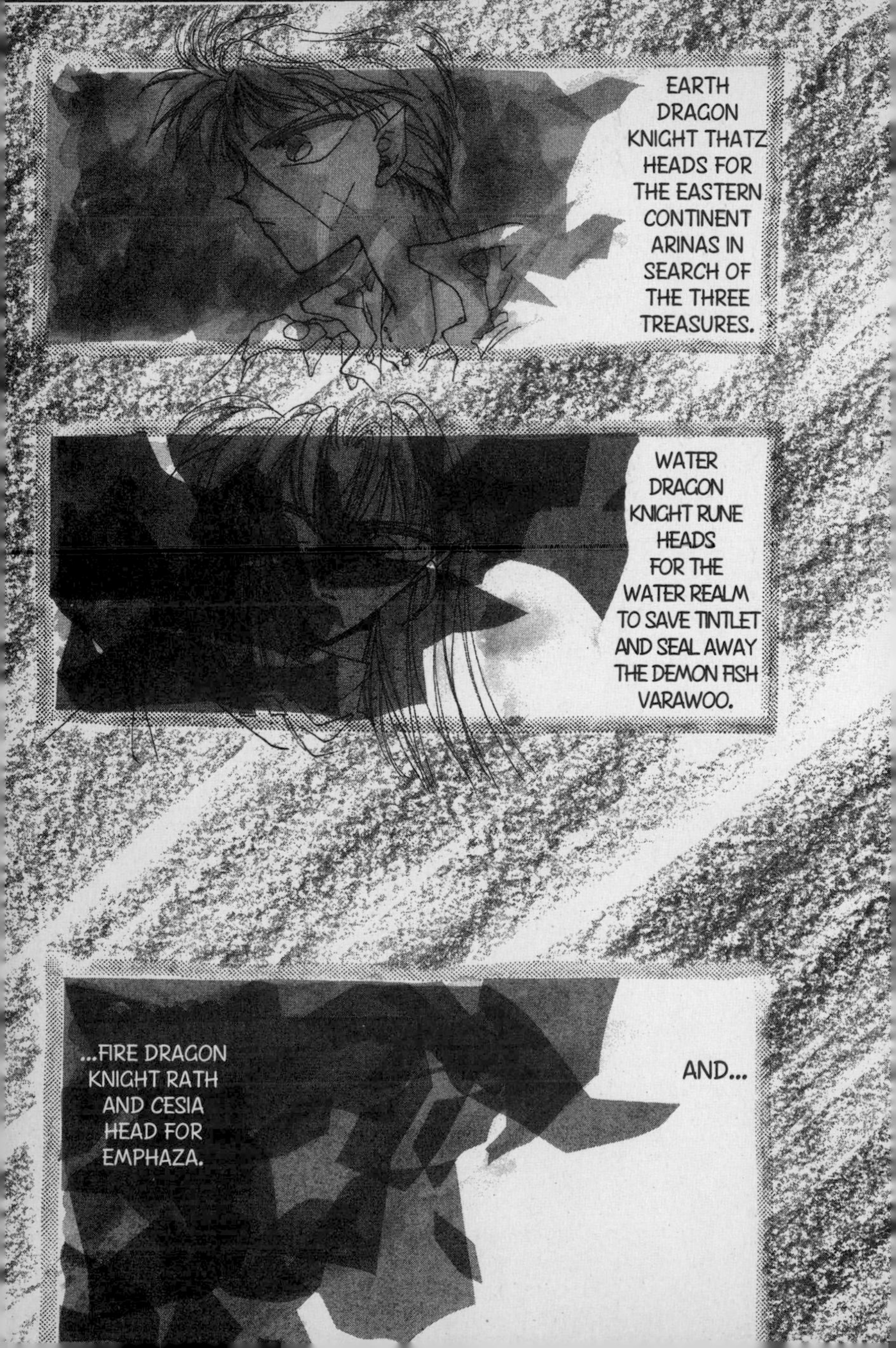
EARTH DRAGON KNIGHT THATZ HEADS FOR THE EASTERN CONTINENT ARINAS IN SEARCH OF THE THREE TREASURES.
WATER DRAGON KNIGHT RUNE HEADS FOR THE WATER REALM TO SAVE TINTLET AND SEAL AWAY THE DEMON FISH VARAWOO.
AND...
...FIRE DRAGON KNIGHT RATH AND CESIA HEAD FOR EMPHAZA.

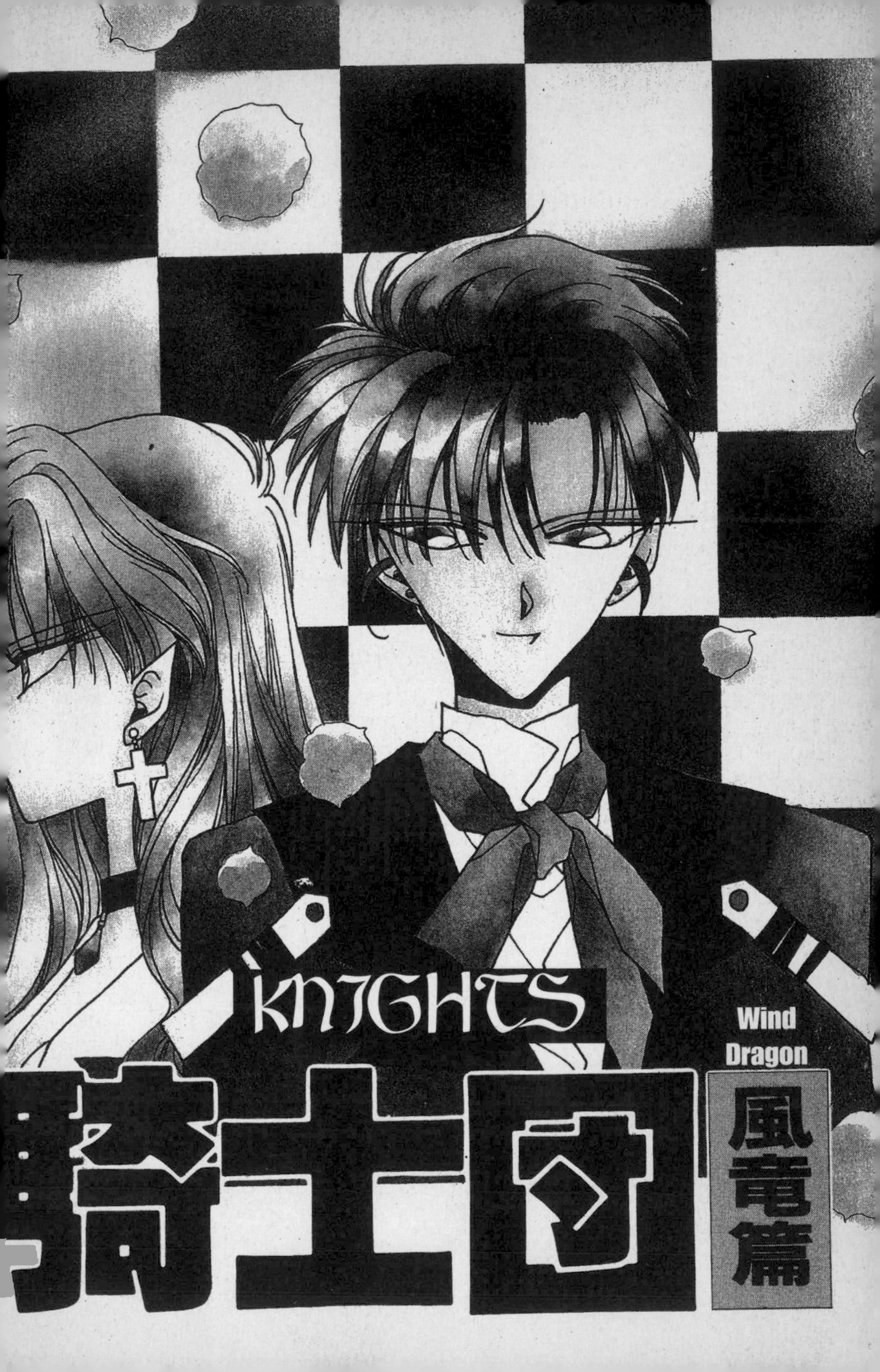

KNIGHTS
騎士団
Wind Dragon
風竜篇

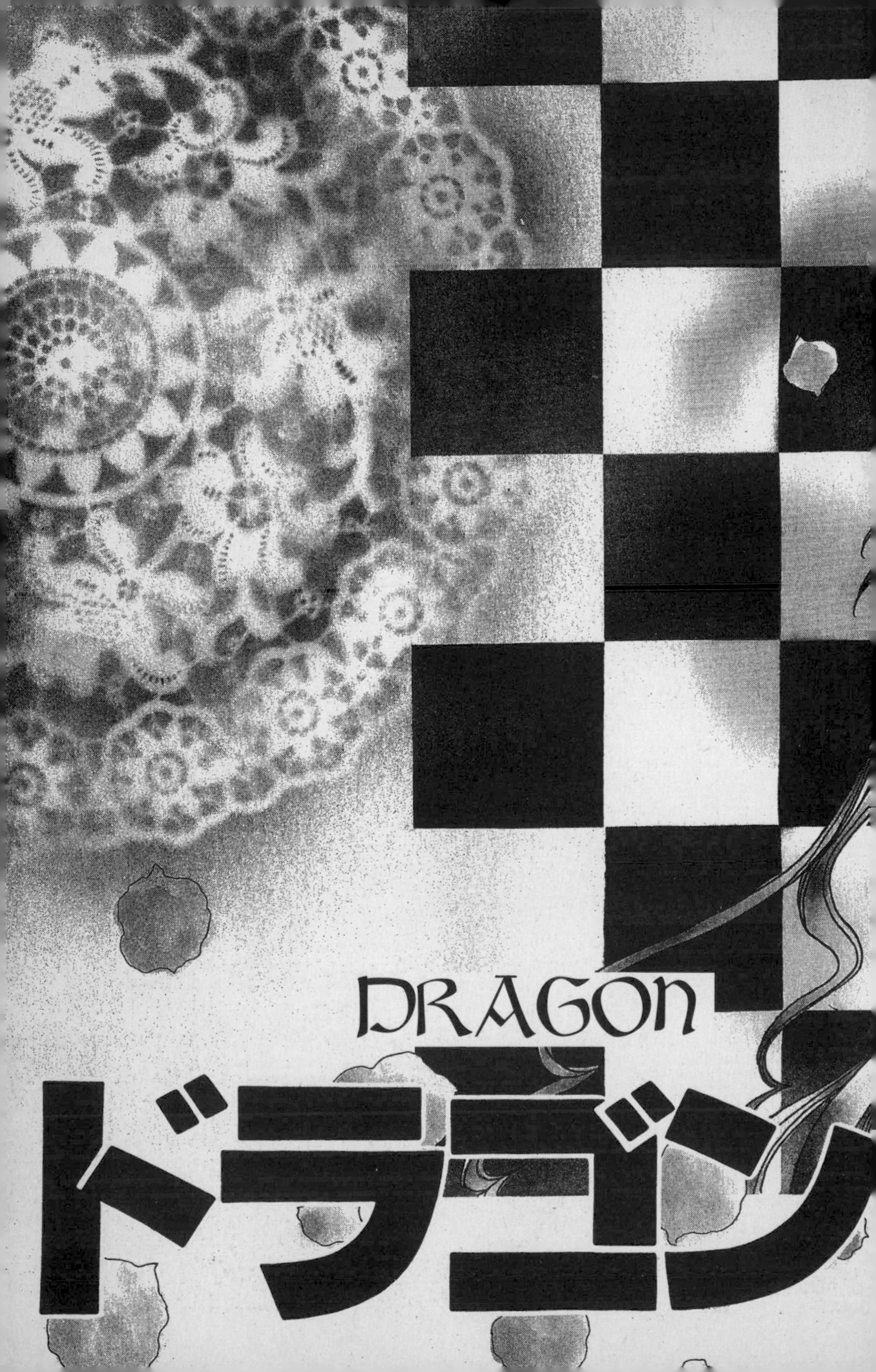
DRAGON
ドラゴン

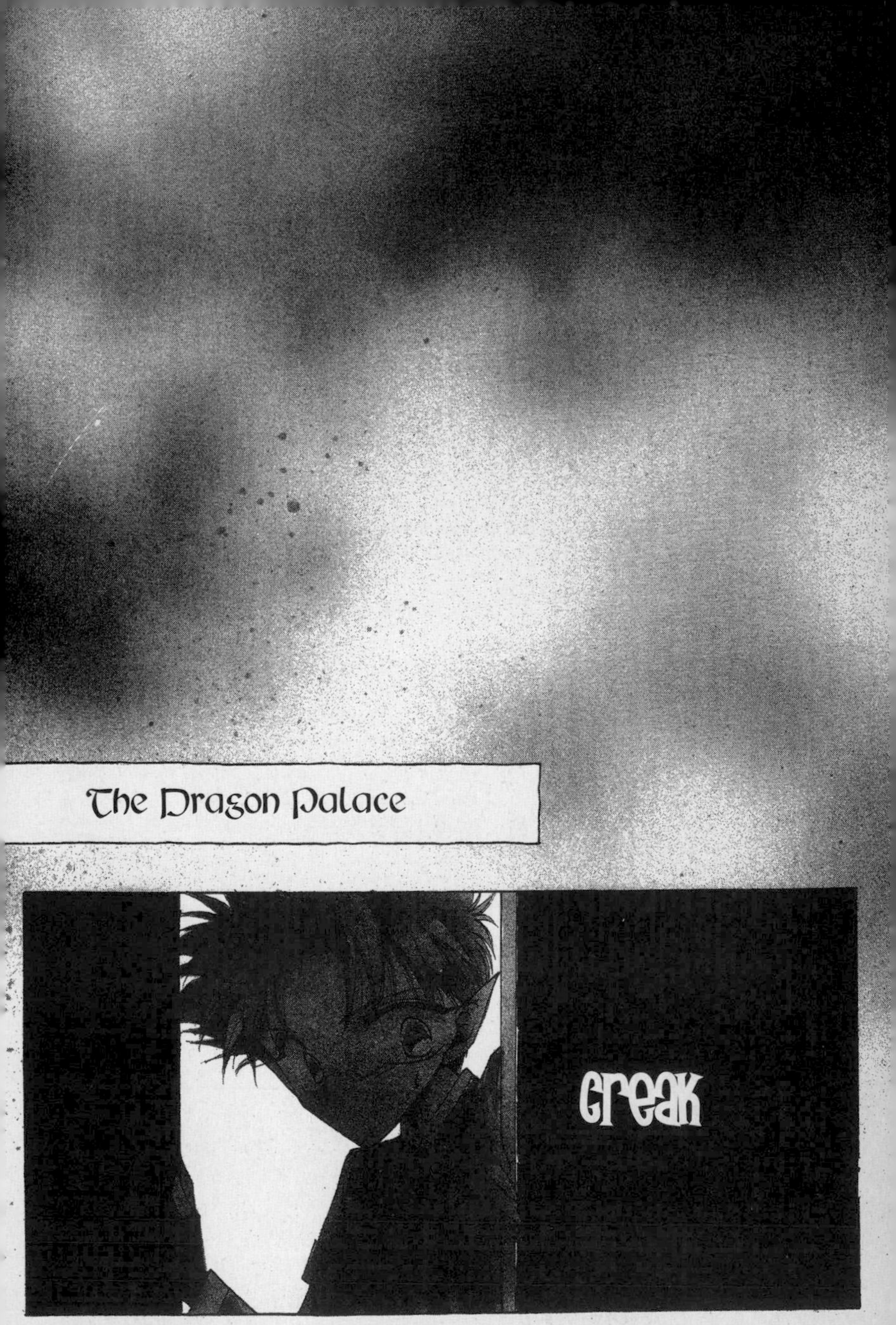
The Dragon Palace
creak

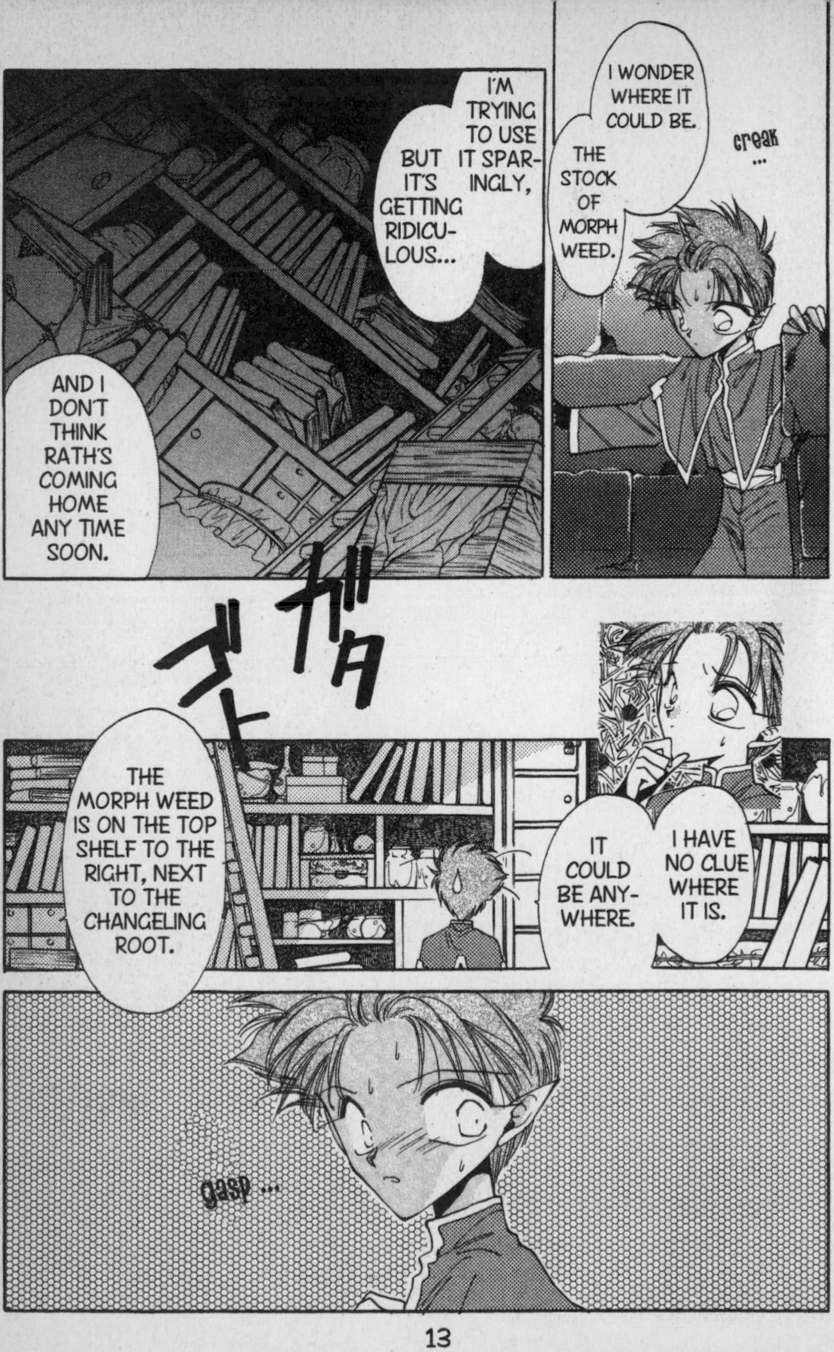
I WONDER WHERE IT COULD BE.
THE STOCK OF MORPH WEED.
creak ...
I'M TRYING TO USE IT SPARINGLY,
BUT IT'S GETTING RIDICULOUS...
AND I DON'T THINK RATH'S COMING HOME ANY TIME SOON.
ガタ
ゴト
I HAVE NO CLUE WHERE IT IS.
IT COULD BE ANYWHERE.
THE MORPH WEED IS ON THE TOP SHELF TO THE RIGHT, NEXT TO THE CHANGELING ROOT.
gasp ...

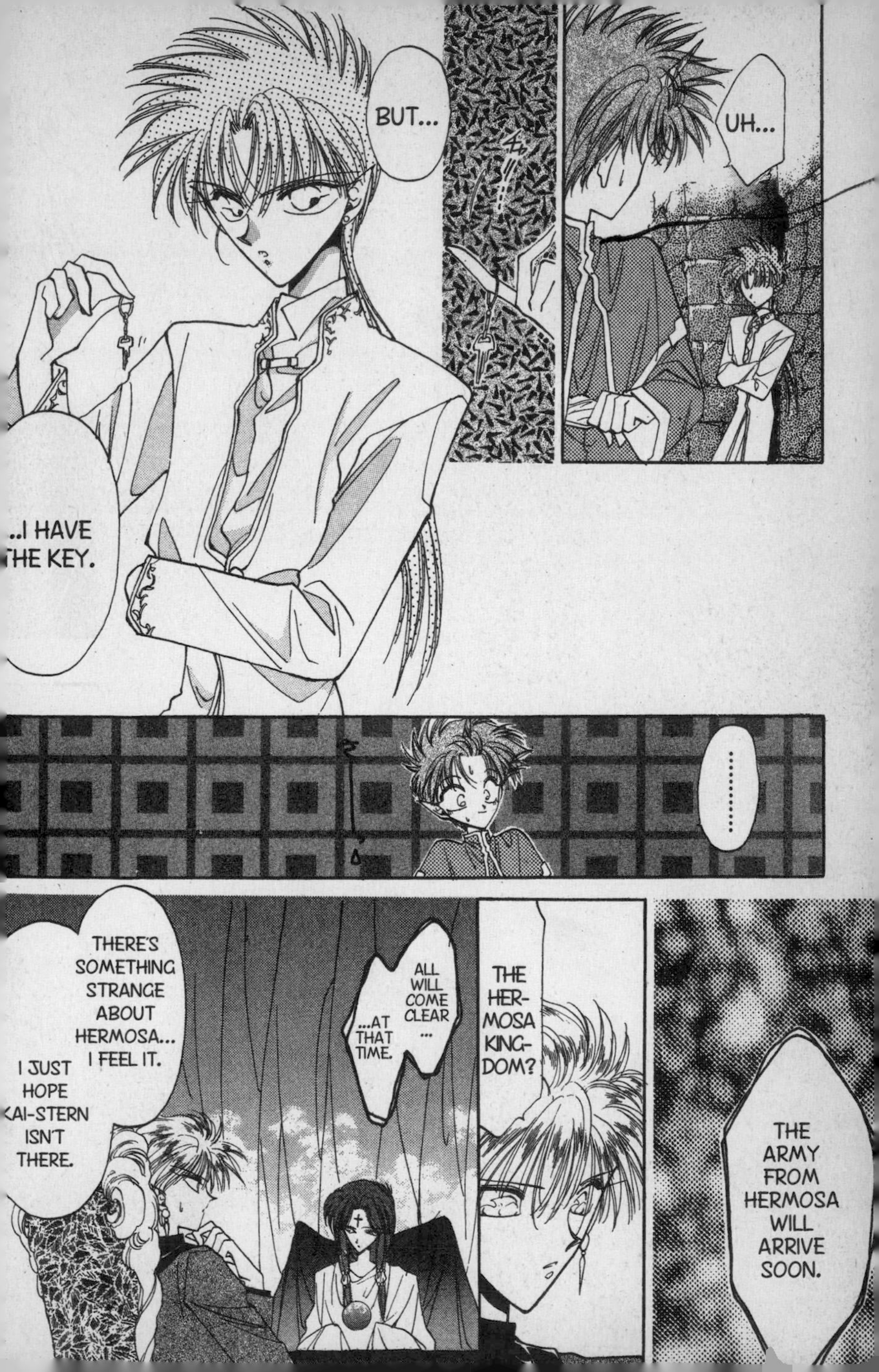
UH...
BUT...
..I HAVE THE KEY.
......
THE ARMY FROM HERMOSA WILL ARRIVE SOON.
THE HER-MOSA KING-DOM?
ALL WILL COME CLEAR ...
...AT THAT TIME.
THERE'S SOMETHING STRANGE ABOUT HERMOSA... I FEEL IT.
I JUST HOPE KAI-STERN ISN'T THERE.

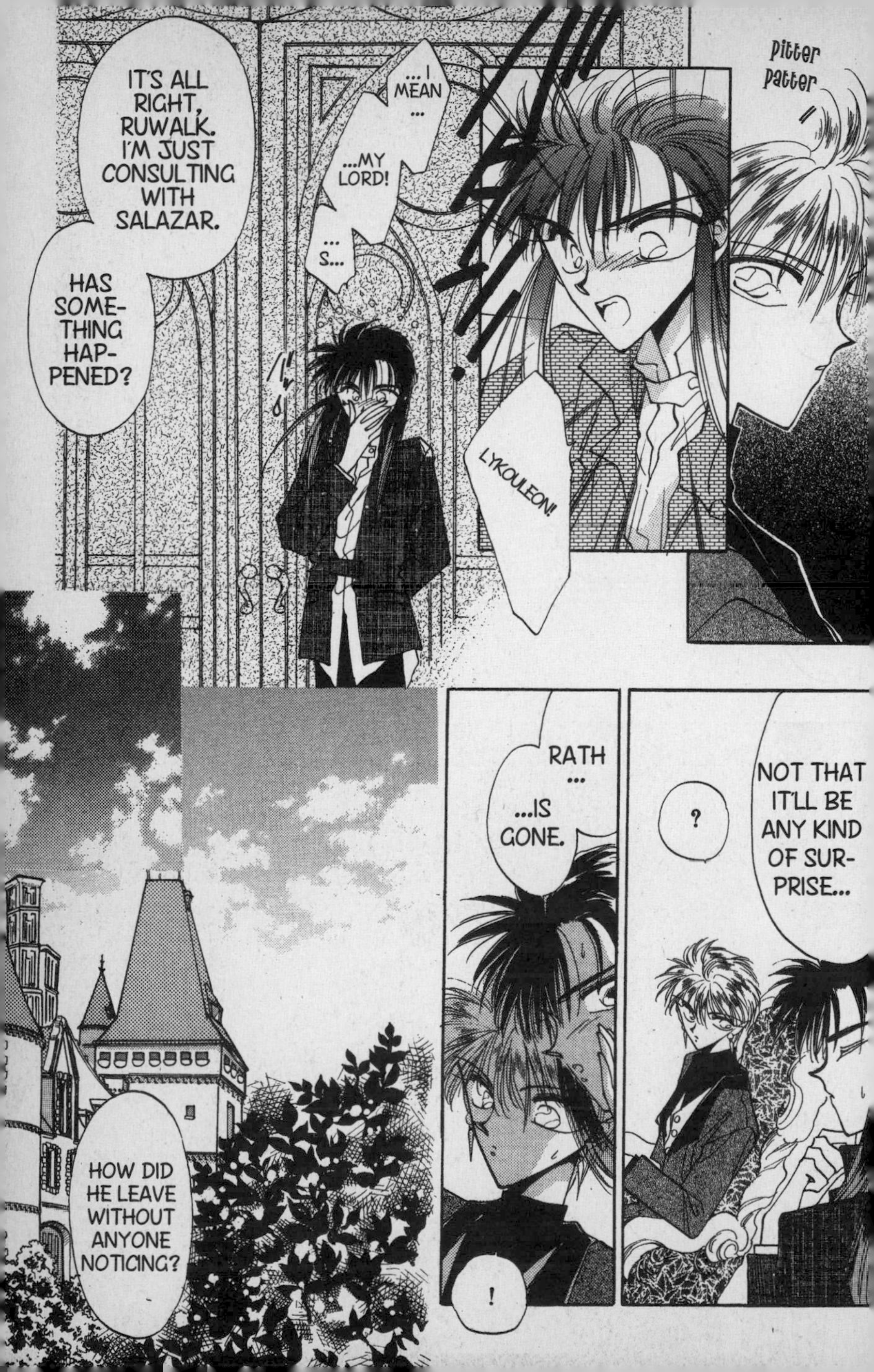
pitter patter
LYKOULEON!
...I MEAN...
...MY LORD!
...S...
IT'S ALL RIGHT, RUWALK. I'M JUST CONSULTING WITH SALAZAR.
HAS SOMETHING HAPPENED?
NOT THAT IT'LL BE ANY KIND OF SURPRISE...
?
RATH...
...IS GONE.
!
HOW DID HE LEAVE WITHOUT ANYONE NOTICING?

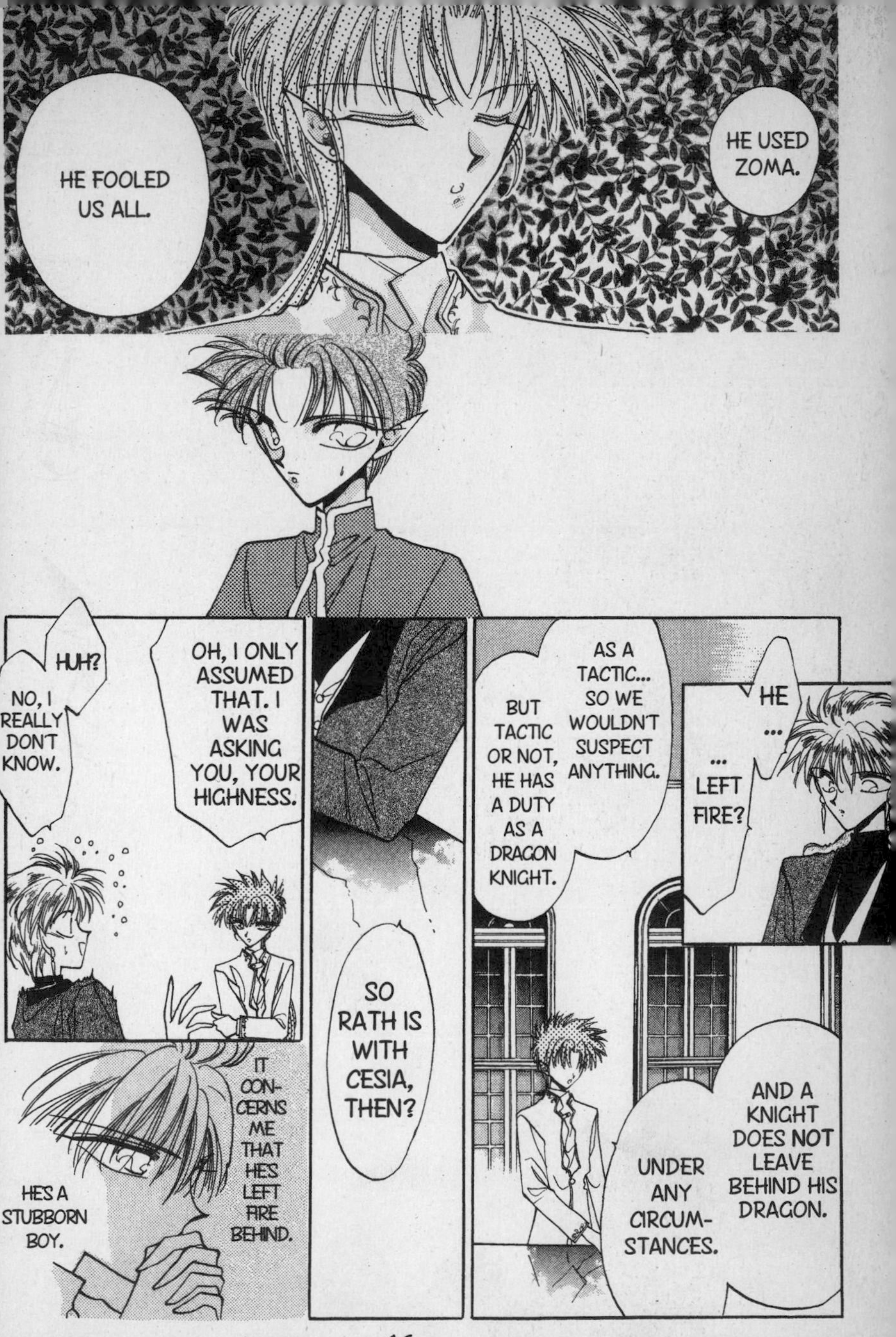
HE USED ZOMA.
HE FOOLED US ALL.
HE ... ... LEFT FIRE?
AS A TACTIC... SO WE WOULDN'T SUSPECT ANYTHING.
BUT TACTIC OR NOT, HE HAS A DUTY AS A DRAGON KNIGHT.
AND A KNIGHT DOES NOT LEAVE BEHIND HIS DRAGON.
UNDER ANY CIRCUM-STANCES.
SO RATH IS WITH CESIA, THEN?
OH, I ONLY ASSUMED THAT. I WAS ASKING YOU, YOUR HIGHNESS.
HUH?
NO, I REALLY DONT KNOW.
IT CON-CERNS ME THAT HES LEFT FIRE BEHIND.
HES A STUBBORN BOY.

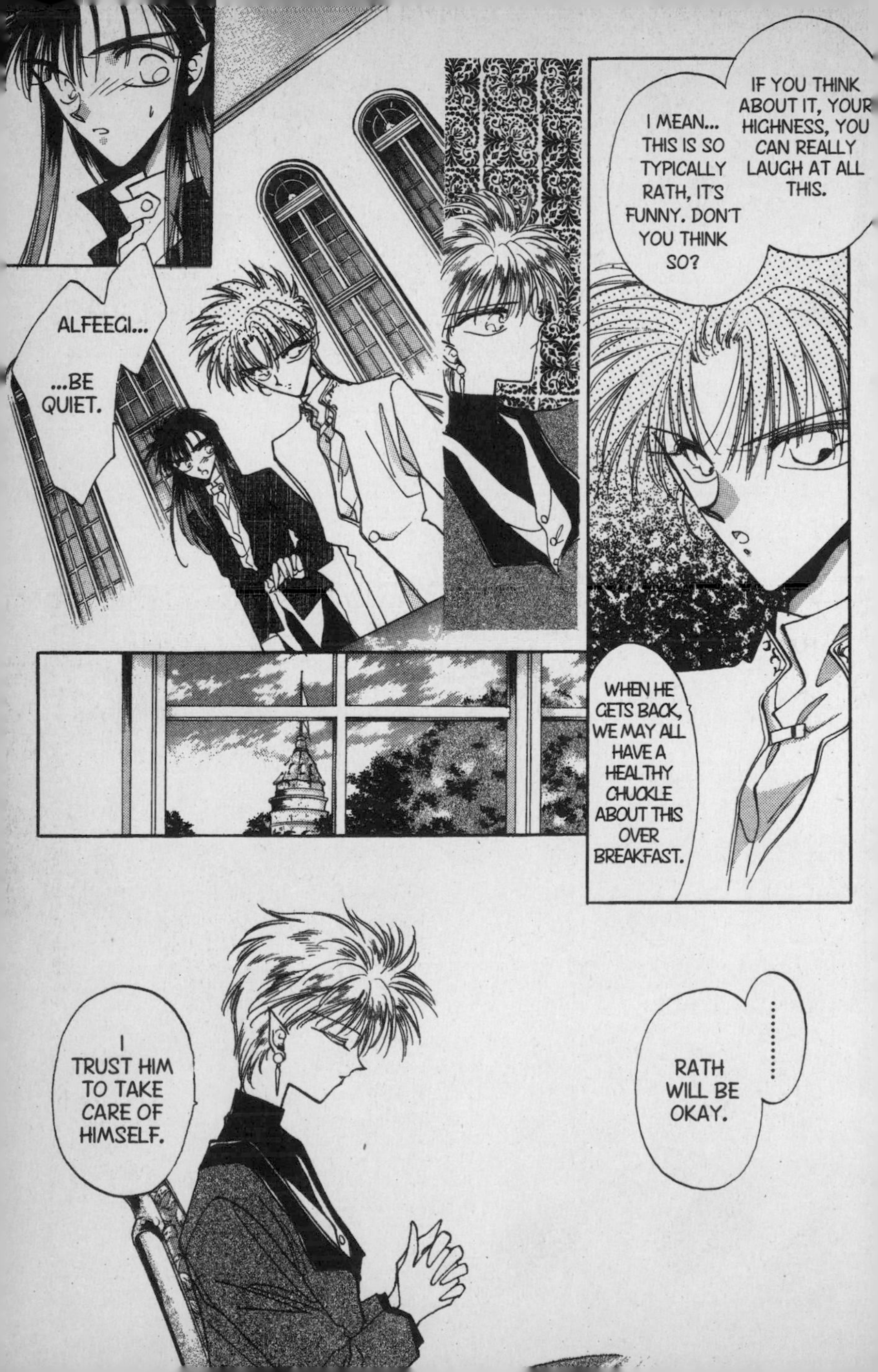
IF YOU THINK ABOUT IT, YOUR HIGHNESS, YOU CAN REALLY LAUGH AT ALL THIS.
I MEAN... THIS IS SO TYPICALLY RATH, IT'S FUNNY. DON'T YOU THINK SO?
WHEN HE GETS BACK, WE MAY ALL HAVE A HEALTHY CHUCKLE ABOUT THIS OVER BREAKFAST.
ALFEEGI...
...BE QUIET.
......
RATH WILL BE OKAY.
I TRUST HIM TO TAKE CARE OF HIMSELF.

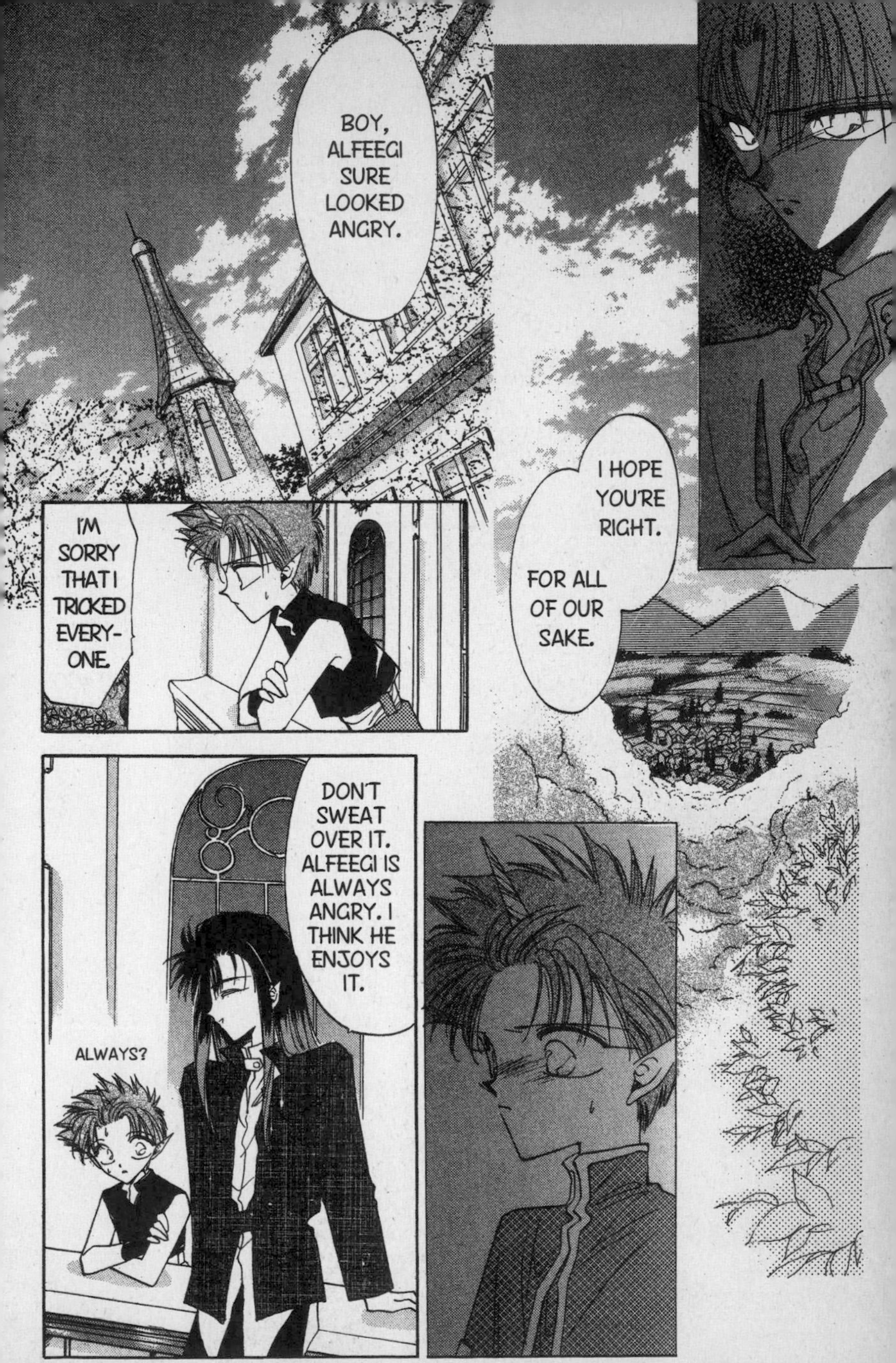
BOY, ALFEEGI SURE LOOKED ANGRY.
I'M SORRY THAT I TRICKED EVERY-ONE.
DON'T SWEAT OVER IT. ALFEEGI IS ALWAYS ANGRY. I THINK HE ENJOYS IT.
ALWAYS?
I HOPE YOU'RE RIGHT.
FOR ALL OF OUR SAKE.

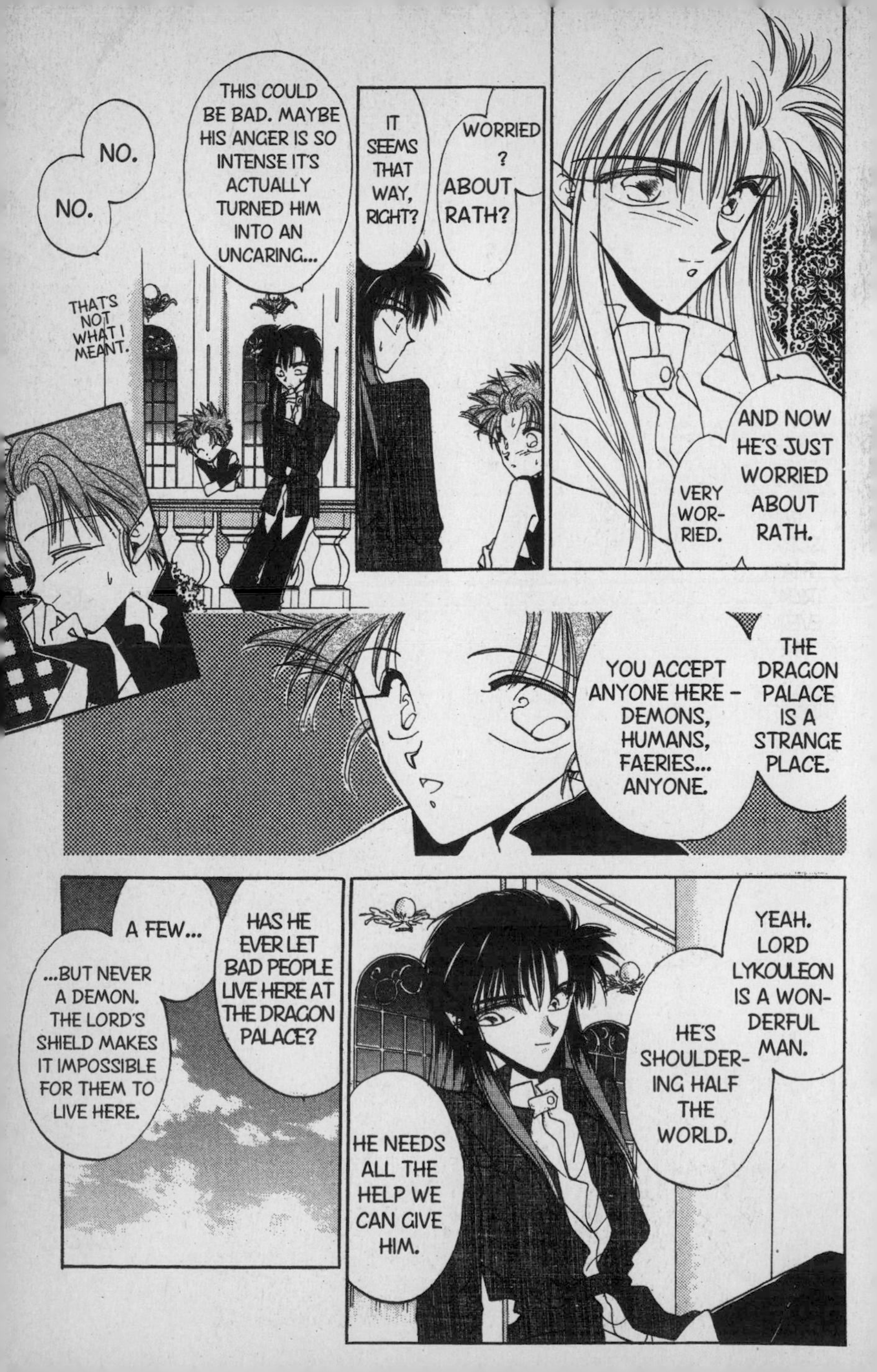
AND NOW HE'S JUST WORRIED ABOUT RATH.
VERY WORRIED.
WORRIED? ABOUT RATH?
IT SEEMS THAT WAY, RIGHT?
THIS COULD BE BAD. MAYBE HIS ANGER IS SO INTENSE IT'S ACTUALLY TURNED HIM INTO AN UNCARING...
NO.
NO.
THAT'S NOT WHAT I MEANT.
THE DRAGON PALACE IS A STRANGE PLACE.
YOU ACCEPT ANYONE HERE – DEMONS, HUMANS, FAERIES... ANYONE.
YEAH. LORD LYKOULEON IS A WONDERFUL MAN.
HE'S SHOULDERING HALF THE WORLD.
HE NEEDS ALL THE HELP WE CAN GIVE HIM.
HAS HE EVER LET BAD PEOPLE LIVE HERE AT THE DRAGON PALACE?
A FEW...
...BUT NEVER A DEMON. THE LORD'S SHIELD MAKES IT IMPOSSIBLE FOR THEM TO LIVE HERE.

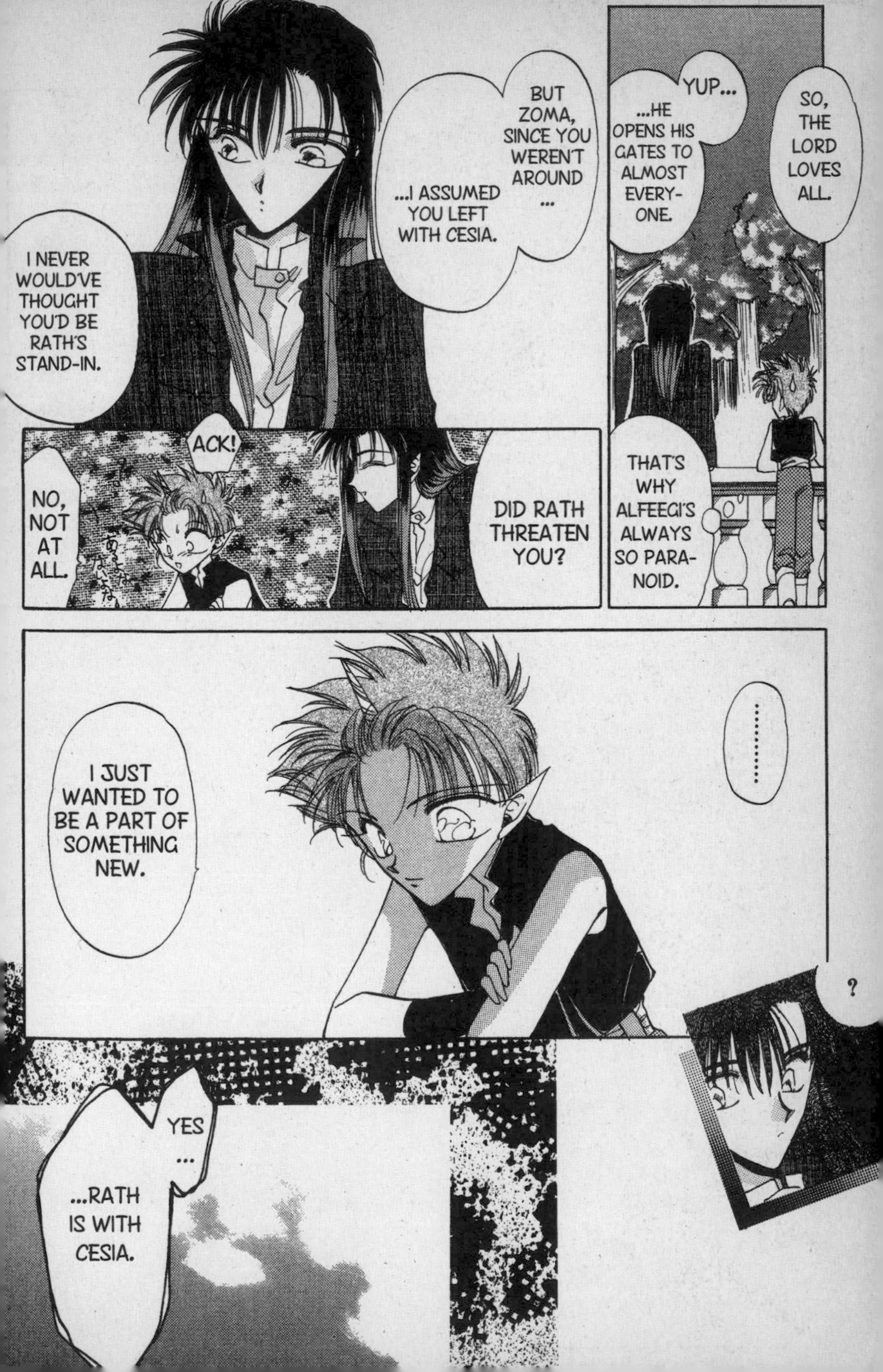
SO, THE LORD LOVES ALL.
YUP...
...HE OPENS HIS GATES TO ALMOST EVERY-ONE.
THAT'S WHY ALFEEGI'S ALWAYS SO PARA-NOID.
BUT ZOMA, SINCE YOU WEREN'T AROUND...
...I ASSUMED YOU LEFT WITH CESIA.
I NEVER WOULD'VE THOUGHT YOU'D BE RATH'S STAND-IN.
DID RATH THREATEN YOU?
ACK!
NO, NOT AT ALL.
......
I JUST WANTED TO BE A PART OF SOMETHING NEW.
?
YES...
...RATH IS WITH CESIA.

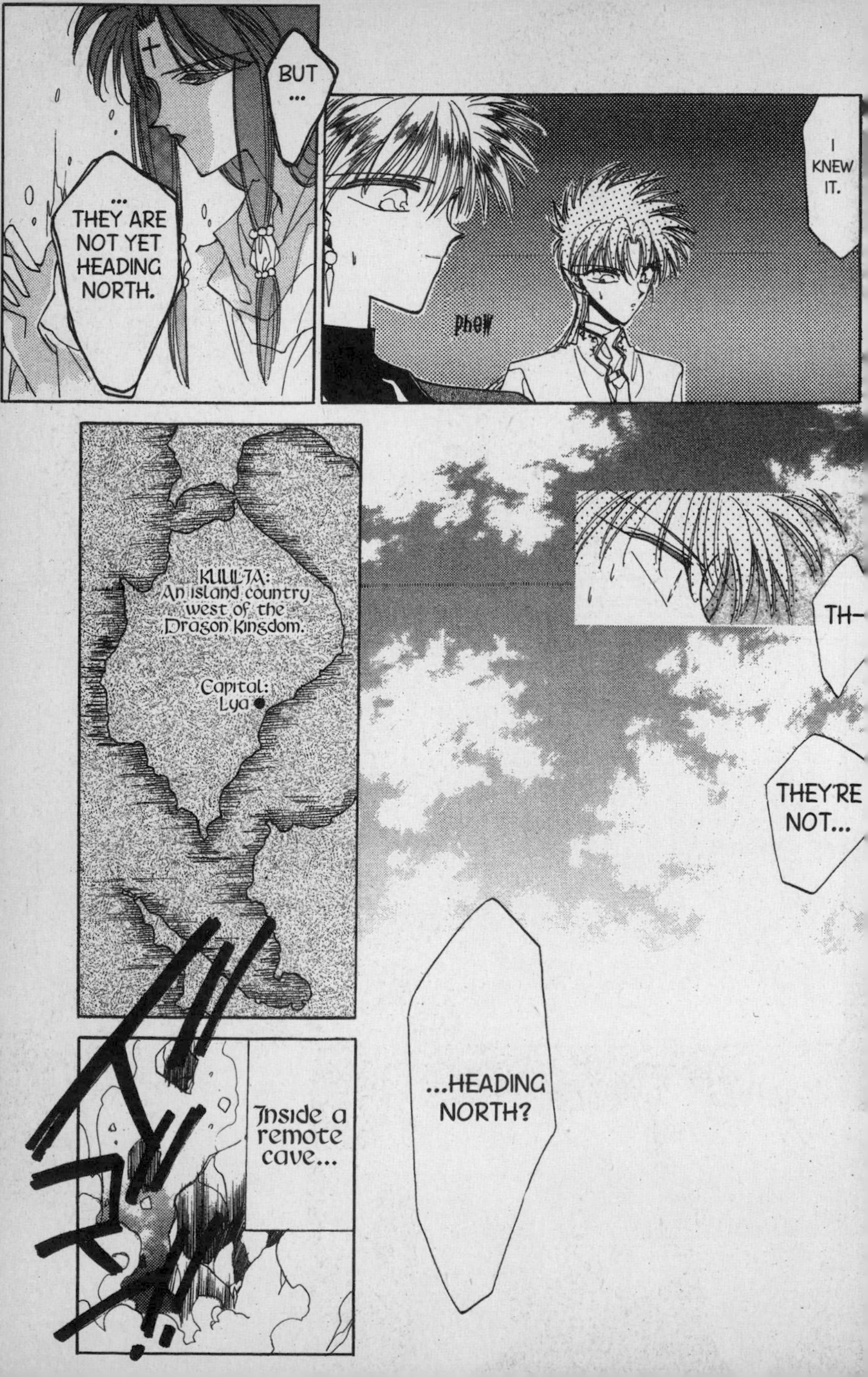
I KNEW IT.
phew
BUT ...
... THEY ARE NOT YET HEADING NORTH.
TH—
THEY'RE NOT...
...HEADING NORTH?
KUULJA: An island country west of the Dragon Kingdom.
Capital: Lya
Inside a remote cave...

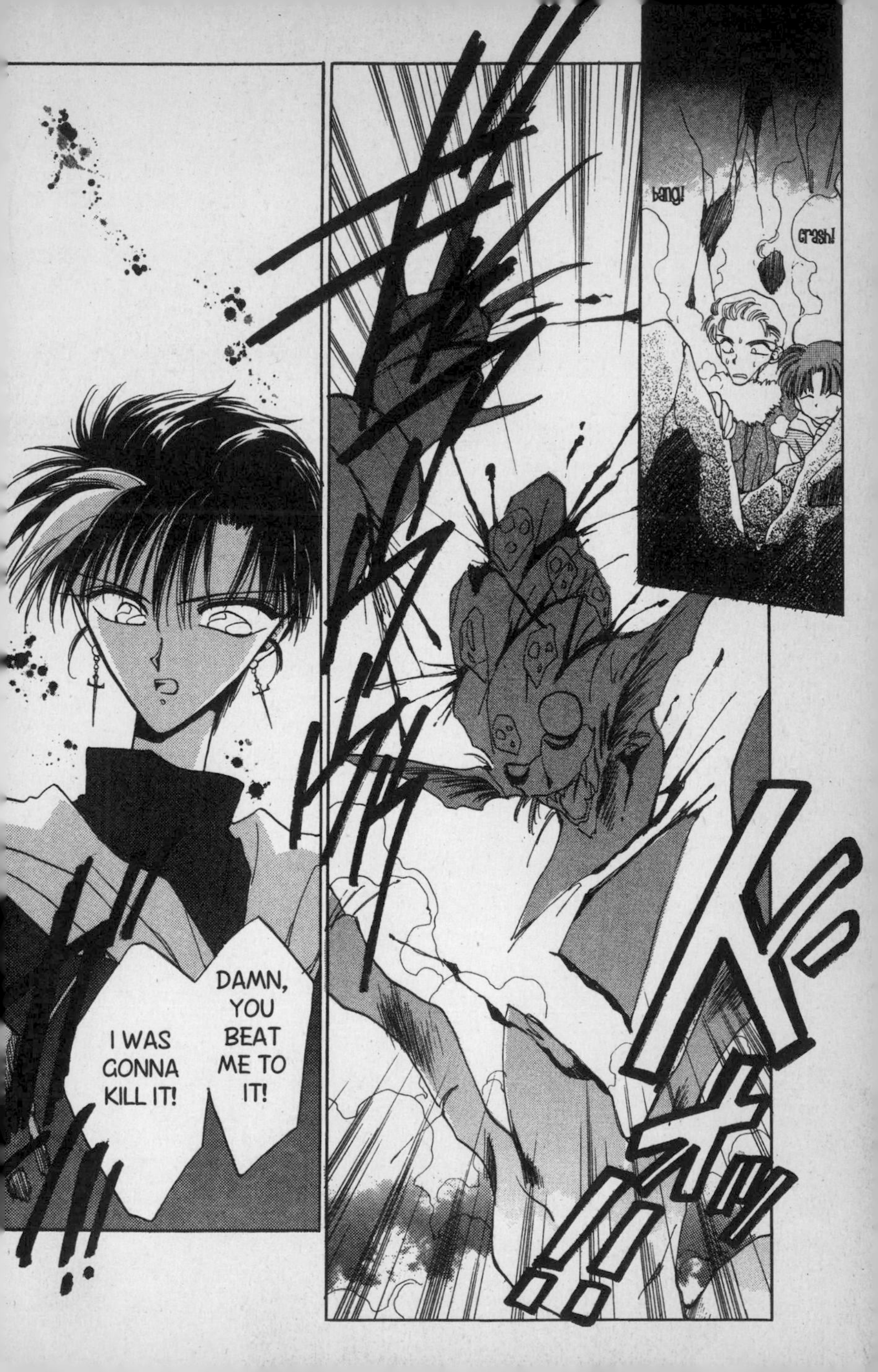
Bang!
Crash!
DAMN, YOU BEAT ME TO IT!
I WAS GONNA KILL IT!

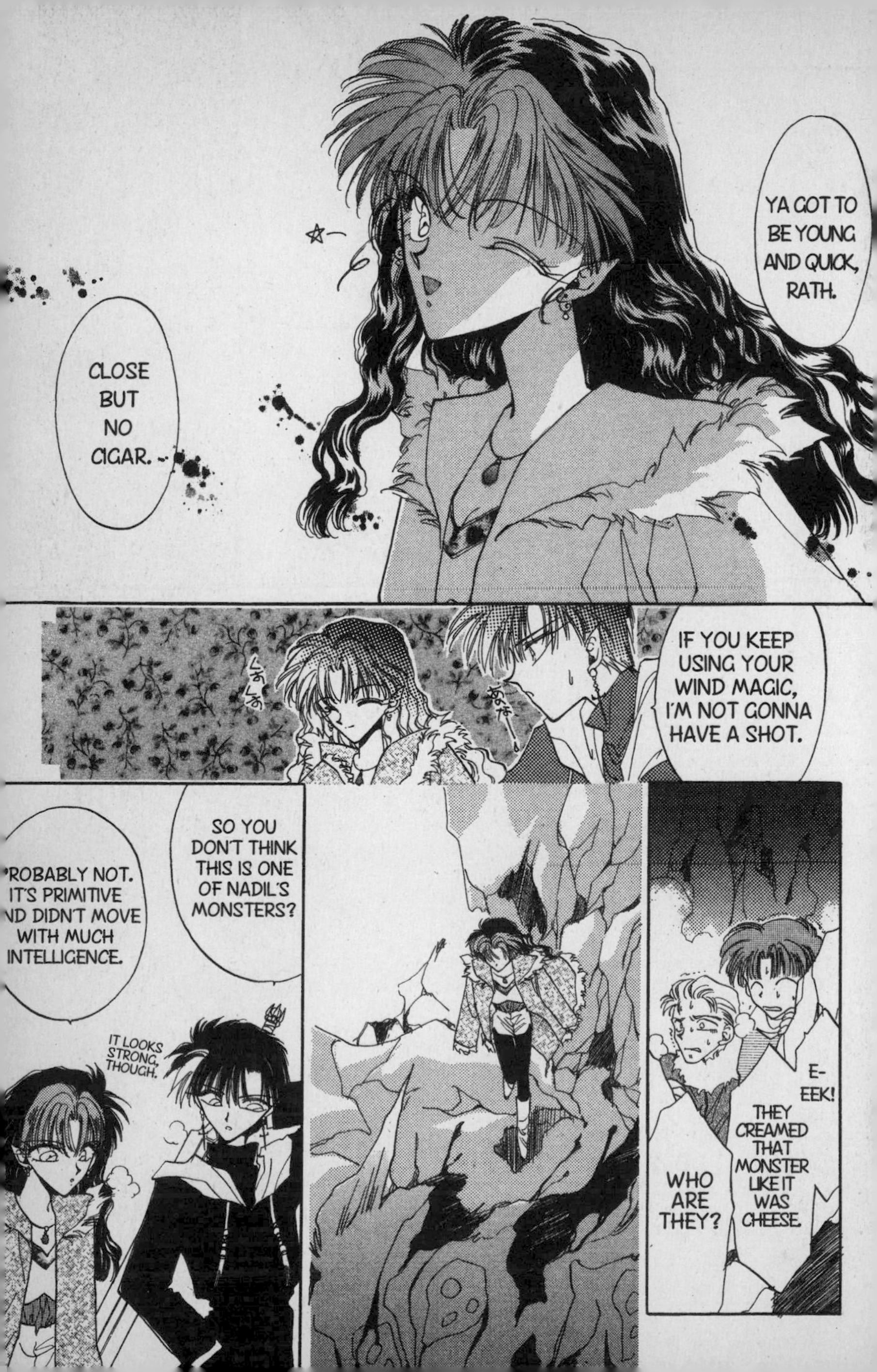
YA GOT TO BE YOUNG AND QUICK, RATH.
CLOSE BUT NO CIGAR.
IF YOU KEEP USING YOUR WIND MAGIC, I'M NOT GONNA HAVE A SHOT.
E-EEK!
THEY CREAMED THAT MONSTER LIKE IT WAS CHEESE.
WHO ARE THEY?
SO YOU DON'T THINK THIS IS ONE OF NADIL'S MONSTERS?
'ROBABLY NOT. IT'S PRIMITIVE ND DIDN'T MOVE WITH MUCH INTELLIGENCE.
IT LOOKS STRONG, THOUGH.

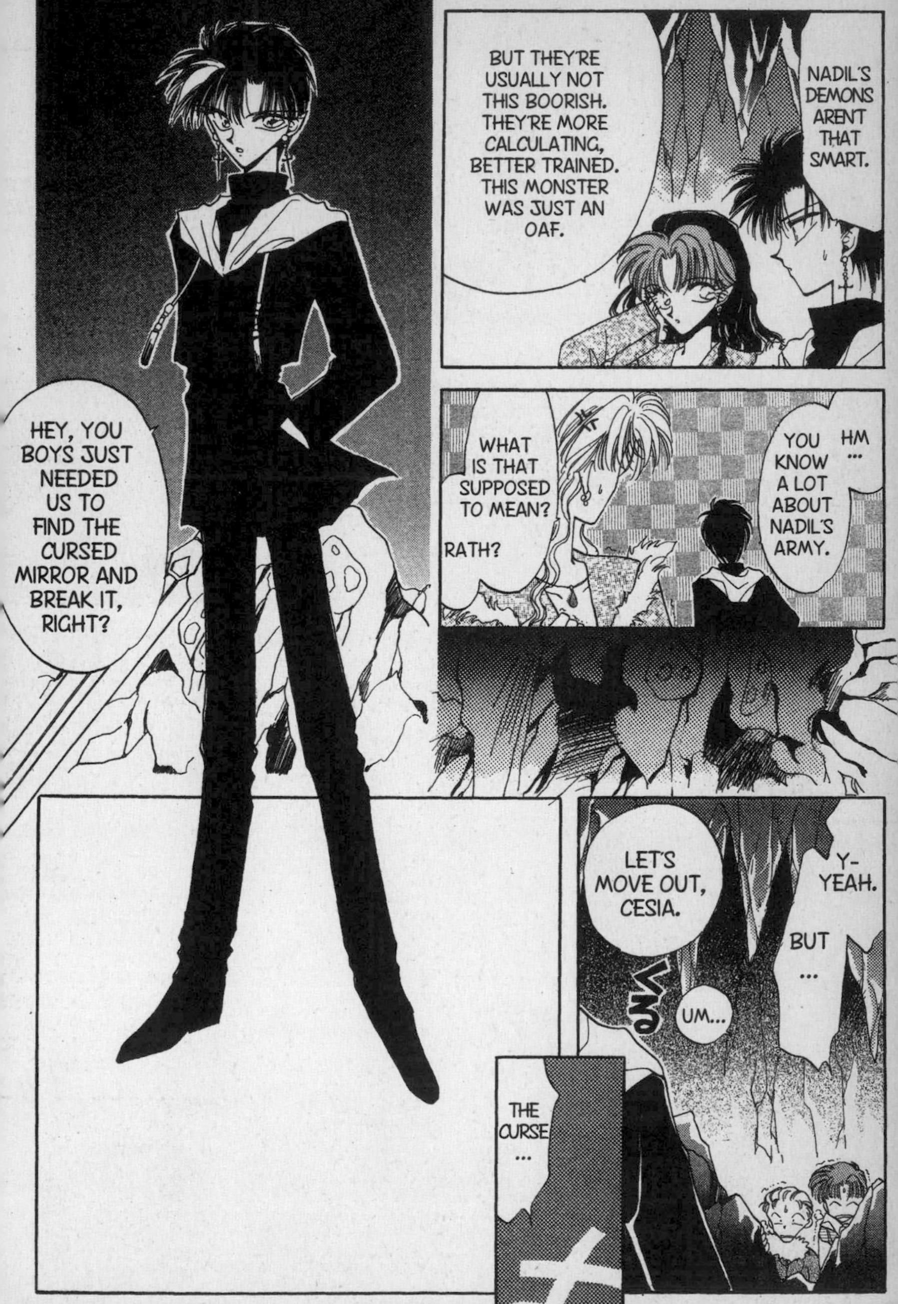
NADIL'S DEMONS ARENT THAT SMART.
BUT THEY'RE USUALLY NOT THIS BOORISH. THEY'RE MORE CALCULATING, BETTER TRAINED. THIS MONSTER WAS JUST AN OAF.
HM...
YOU KNOW A LOT ABOUT NADIL'S ARMY.
WHAT IS THAT SUPPOSED TO MEAN?
RATH?
HEY, YOU BOYS JUST NEEDED US TO FIND THE CURSED MIRROR AND BREAK IT, RIGHT?
Y-YEAH.
BUT...
LET'S MOVE OUT, CESIA.
UM...
THE CURSE...

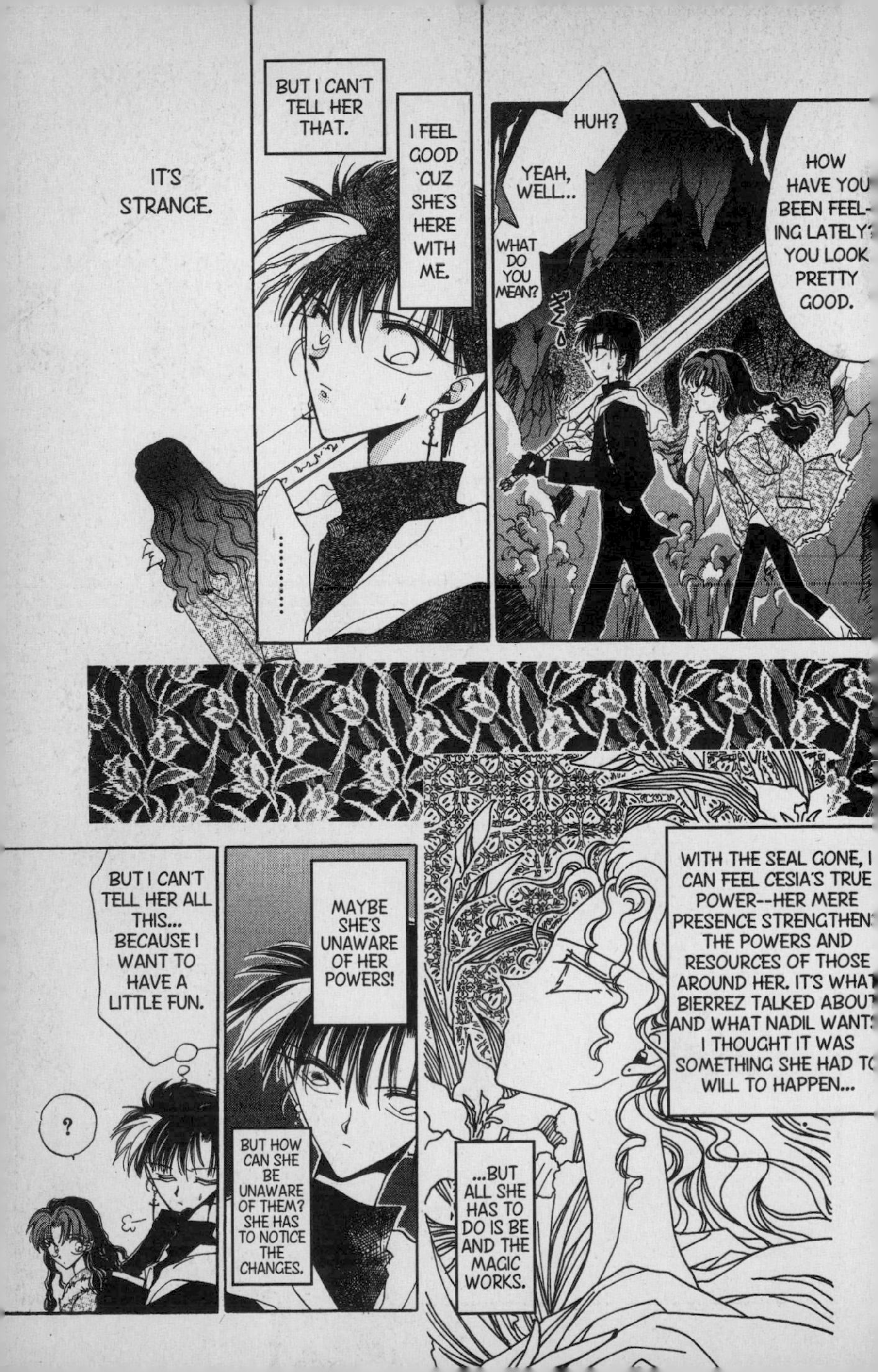
HOW HAVE YOU BEEN FEEL-ING LATELY? YOU LOOK PRETTY GOOD.
HUH?
YEAH, WELL...
WHAT DO YOU MEAN?
I FEEL GOOD 'CUZ SHE'S HERE WITH ME.
BUT I CAN'T TELL HER THAT.
......
IT'S STRANGE.
WITH THE SEAL GONE, I CAN FEEL CESIA'S TRUE POWER--HER MERE PRESENCE STRENGTHEN THE POWERS AND RESOURCES OF THOSE AROUND HER. IT'S WHAT BIERREZ TALKED ABOUT AND WHAT NADIL WANT I THOUGHT IT WAS SOMETHING SHE HAD T WILL TO HAPPEN...
...BUT ALL SHE HAS TO DO IS BE AND THE MAGIC WORKS.
MAYBE SHE'S UNAWARE OF HER POWERS!
BUT HOW CAN SHE BE UNAWARE OF THEM? SHE HAS TO NOTICE THE CHANGES.
BUT I CAN'T TELL HER ALL THIS... BECAUSE I WANT TO HAVE A LITTLE FUN.
?

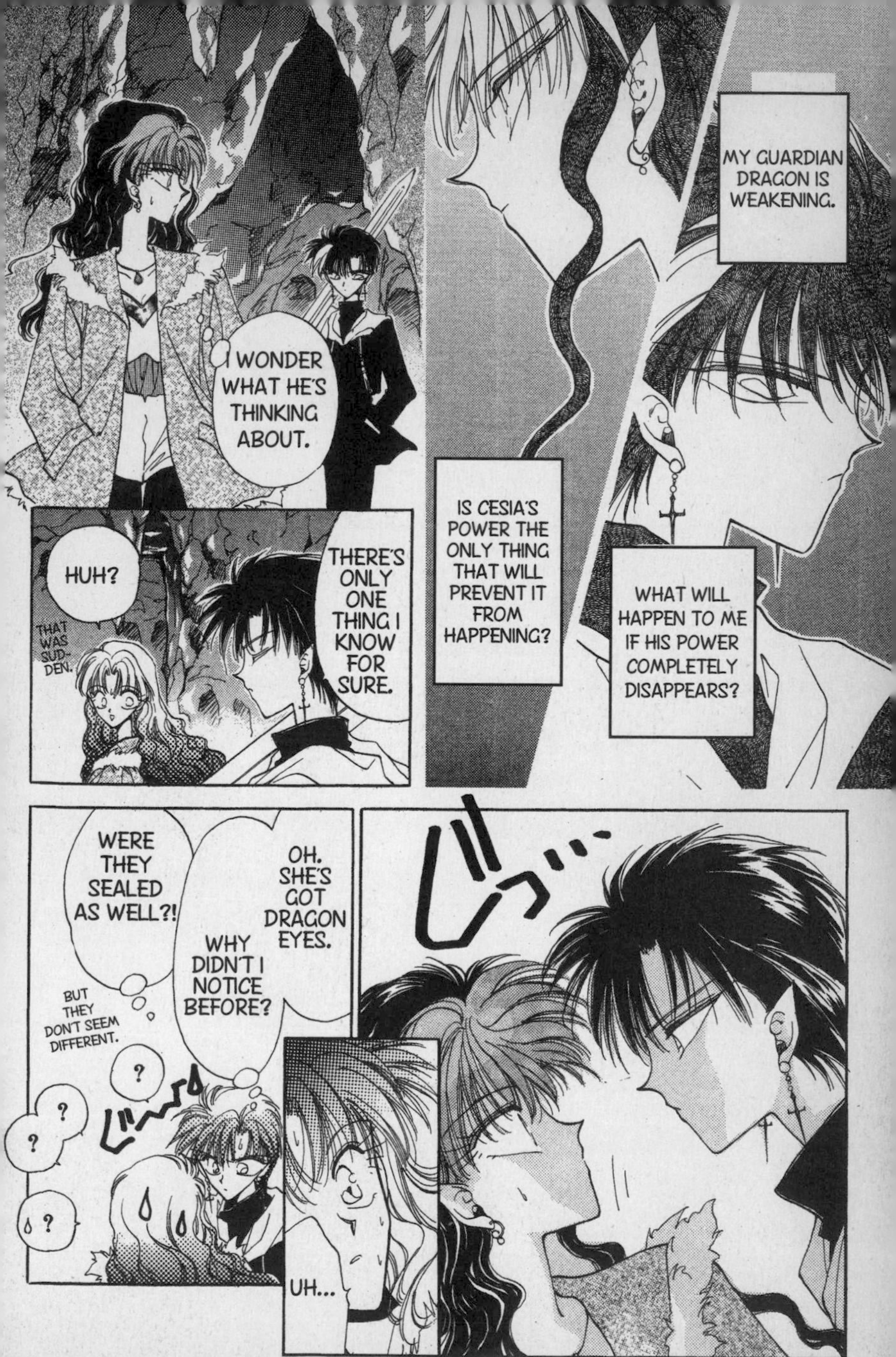

MY GUARDIAN DRAGON IS WEAKENING.
WHAT WILL HAPPEN TO ME IF HIS POWER COMPLETELY DISAPPEARS?
IS CESIA'S POWER THE ONLY THING THAT WILL PREVENT IT FROM HAPPENING?
I WONDER WHAT HE'S THINKING ABOUT.
THERE'S ONLY ONE THING I KNOW FOR SURE.
HUH?
THAT WAS SUD-DEN.
じっ
UH...
OH. SHE'S GOT DRAGON EYES.
WHY DIDN'T I NOTICE BEFORE?
WERE THEY SEALED AS WELL?!
BUT THEY DON'T SEEM DIFFERENT.
?
?
?
?

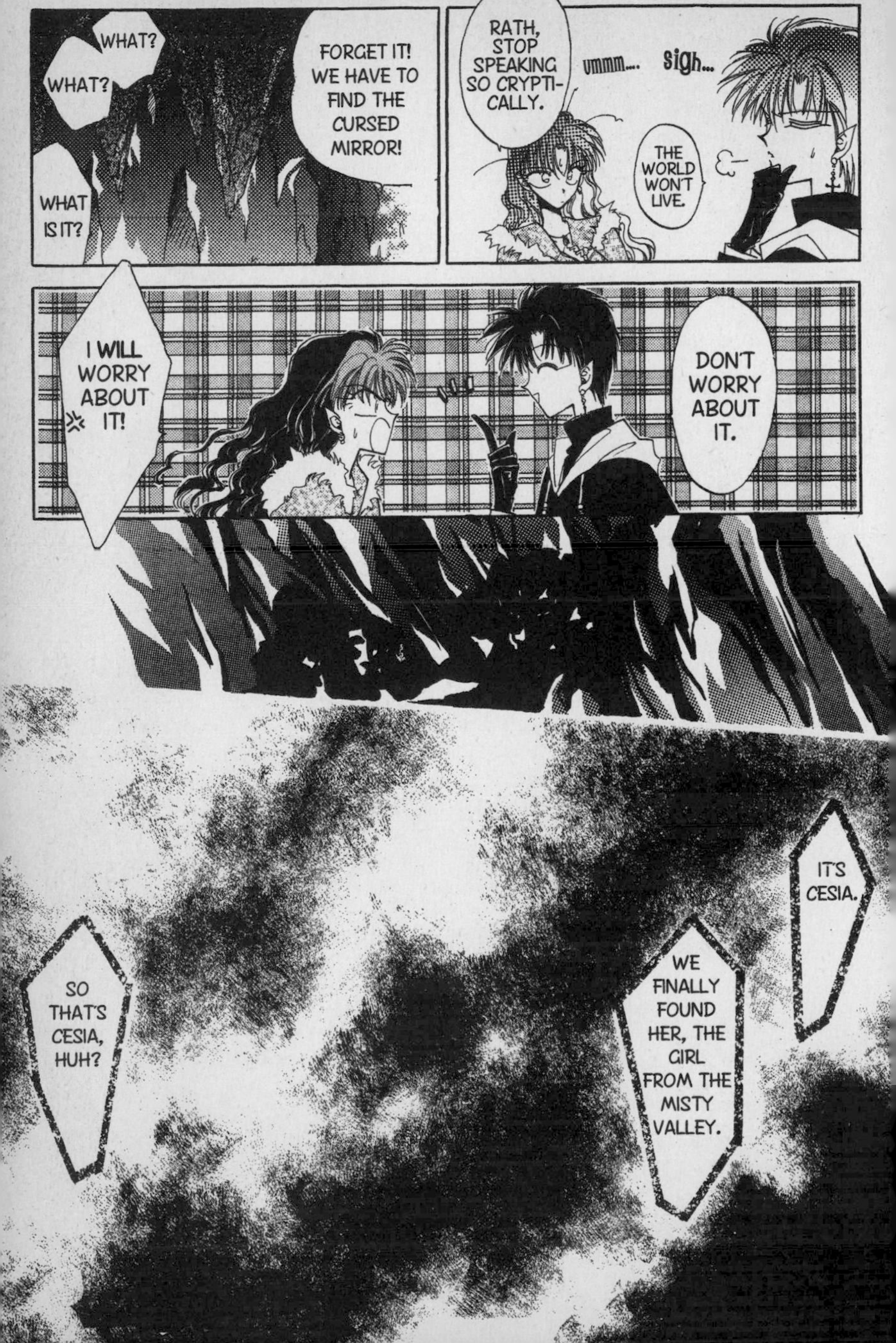
sigh...
ummm....
RATH, STOP SPEAKING SO CRYPTI-CALLY.
THE WORLD WON'T LIVE.
FORGET IT! WE HAVE TO FIND THE CURSED MIRROR!
WHAT?
WHAT?
WHAT IS IT?
DON'T WORRY ABOUT IT.
I WILL WORRY ABOUT IT!
IT'S CESIA.
WE FINALLY FOUND HER, THE GIRL FROM THE MISTY VALLEY.
SO THAT'S CESIA, HUH?

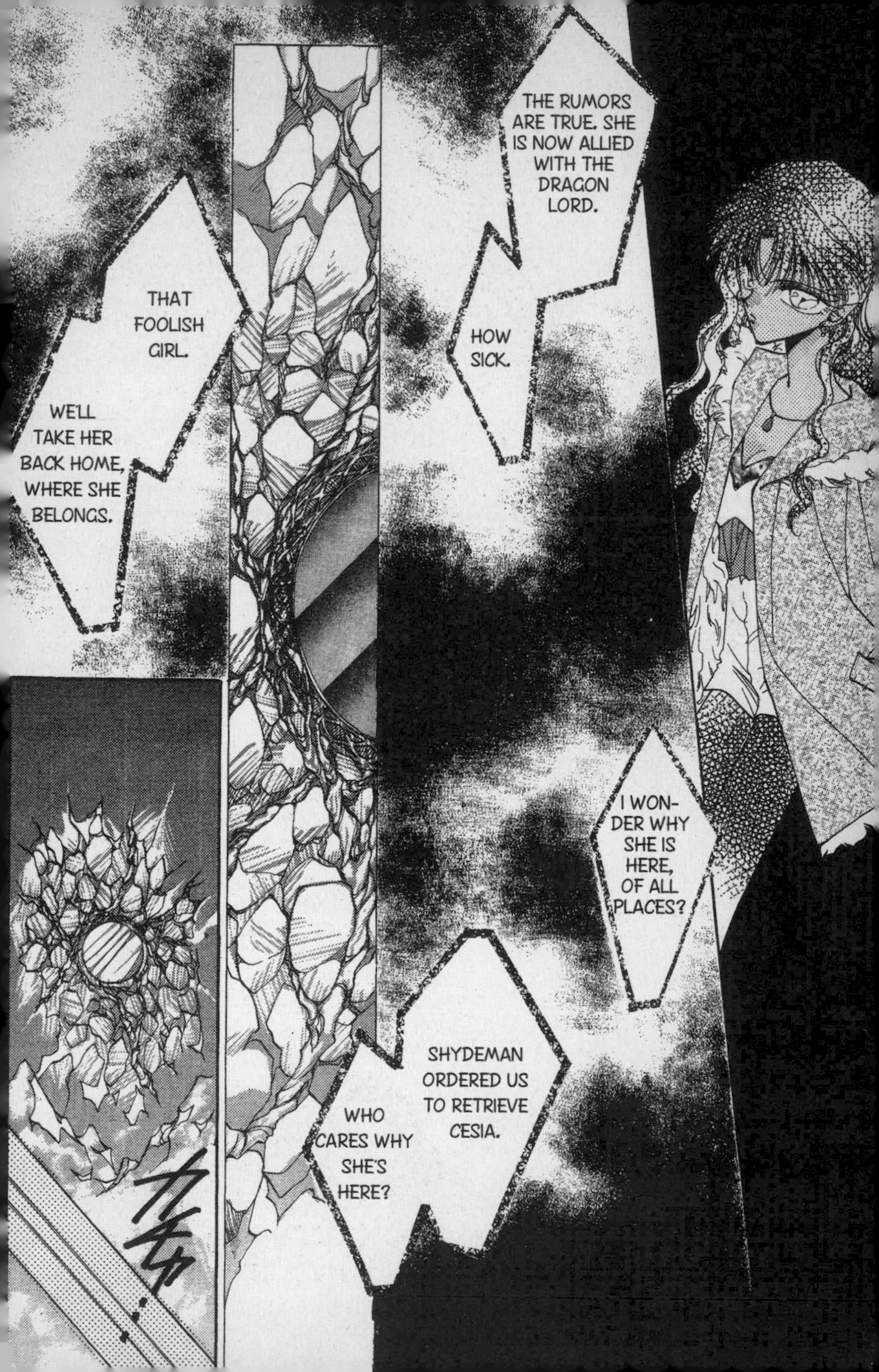
THE RUMORS ARE TRUE. SHE IS NOW ALLIED WITH THE DRAGON LORD.
HOW SICK.
I WON-DER WHY SHE IS HERE, OF ALL PLACES?
SHYDEMAN ORDERED US TO RETRIEVE CESIA.
WHO CARES WHY SHE'S HERE?
THAT FOOLISH GIRL.
WE'LL TAKE HER BACK HOME, WHERE SHE BELONGS.

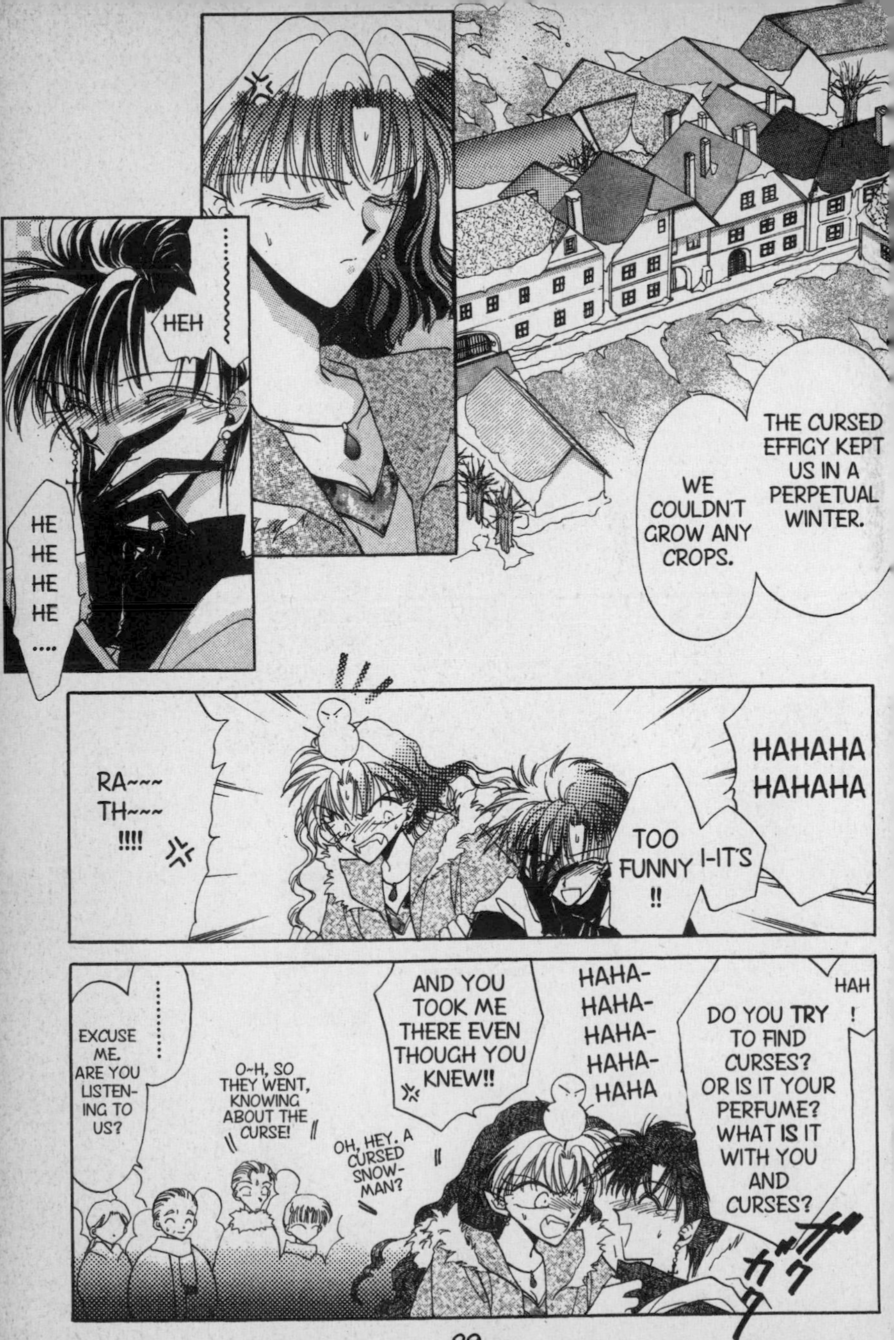
THE CURSED EFFIGY KEPT US IN A PERPETUAL WINTER.
WE COULDN'T GROW ANY CROPS.
......~
HEH
HE HE HE HE ....
HAHAHA HAHAHA
I-IT'S TOO FUNNY !!
RA~~~ TH~~~ !!!!
HAH !
DO YOU TRY TO FIND CURSES? OR IS IT YOUR PERFUME? WHAT IS IT WITH YOU AND CURSES?
HAHA-HAHA-HAHA-HAHA-HAHA
AND YOU TOOK ME THERE EVEN THOUGH YOU KNEW!!
OH, HEY. A CURSED SNOW-MAN?
O~H, SO THEY WENT, KNOWING ABOUT THE CURSE!
....
EXCUSE ME. ARE YOU LISTEN-ING TO US?

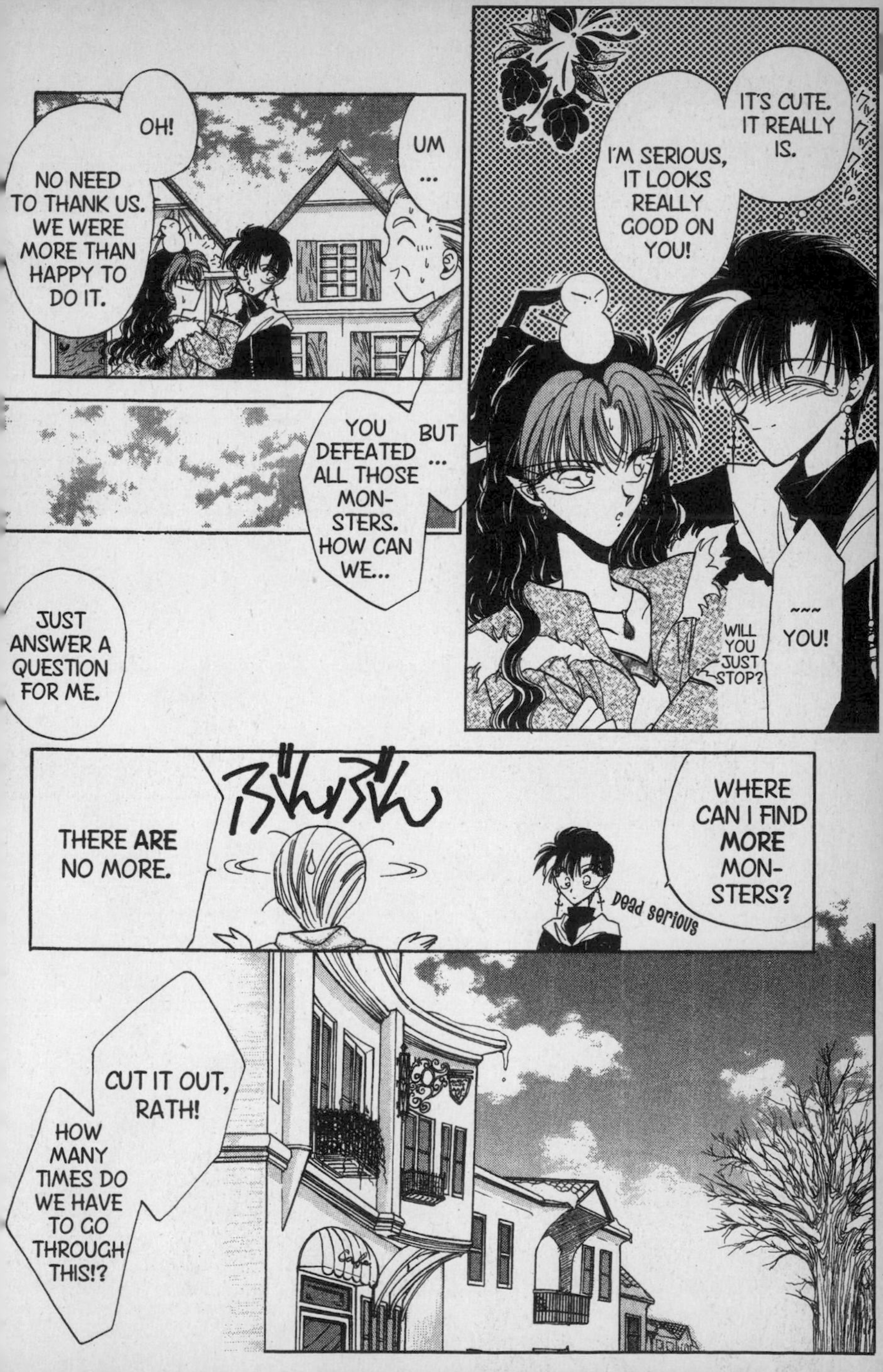
IT'S CUTE. IT REALLY IS.
I'M SERIOUS, IT LOOKS REALLY GOOD ON YOU!
~~~ YOU!
WILL YOU JUST STOP?
UM ...
OH!
NO NEED TO THANK US. WE WERE MORE THAN HAPPY TO DO IT.
BUT ...
YOU DEFEATED ALL THOSE MON-STERS. HOW CAN WE...
JUST ANSWER A QUESTION FOR ME.
WHERE CAN I FIND MORE MON-STERS?
Dead serious
ぶんぶん
THERE ARE NO MORE.
CUT IT OUT, RATH!
HOW MANY TIMES DO WE HAVE TO GO THROUGH THIS!?
~~~

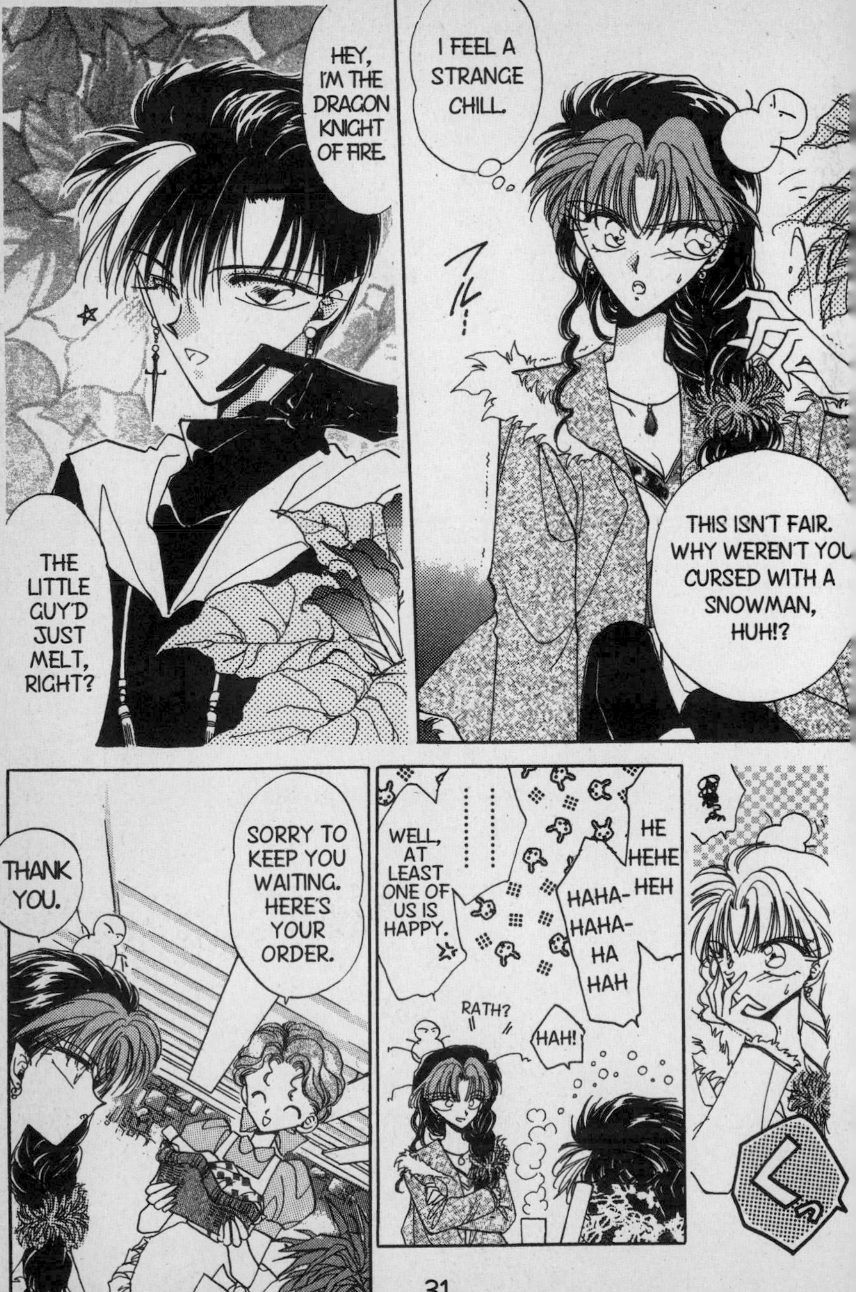
I FEEL A STRANGE CHILL.
THIS ISN'T FAIR. WHY WEREN'T YOU CURSED WITH A SNOWMAN, HUH!?
HEY, I'M THE DRAGON KNIGHT OF FIRE.
THE LITTLE GUY'D JUST MELT, RIGHT?
HE HEHE HEH
HAHA-HAHA-HA HAH
......
WELL, AT LEAST ONE OF US IS HAPPY.
HAH!
RATH?
SORRY TO KEEP YOU WAITING. HERE'S YOUR ORDER.
THANK YOU.

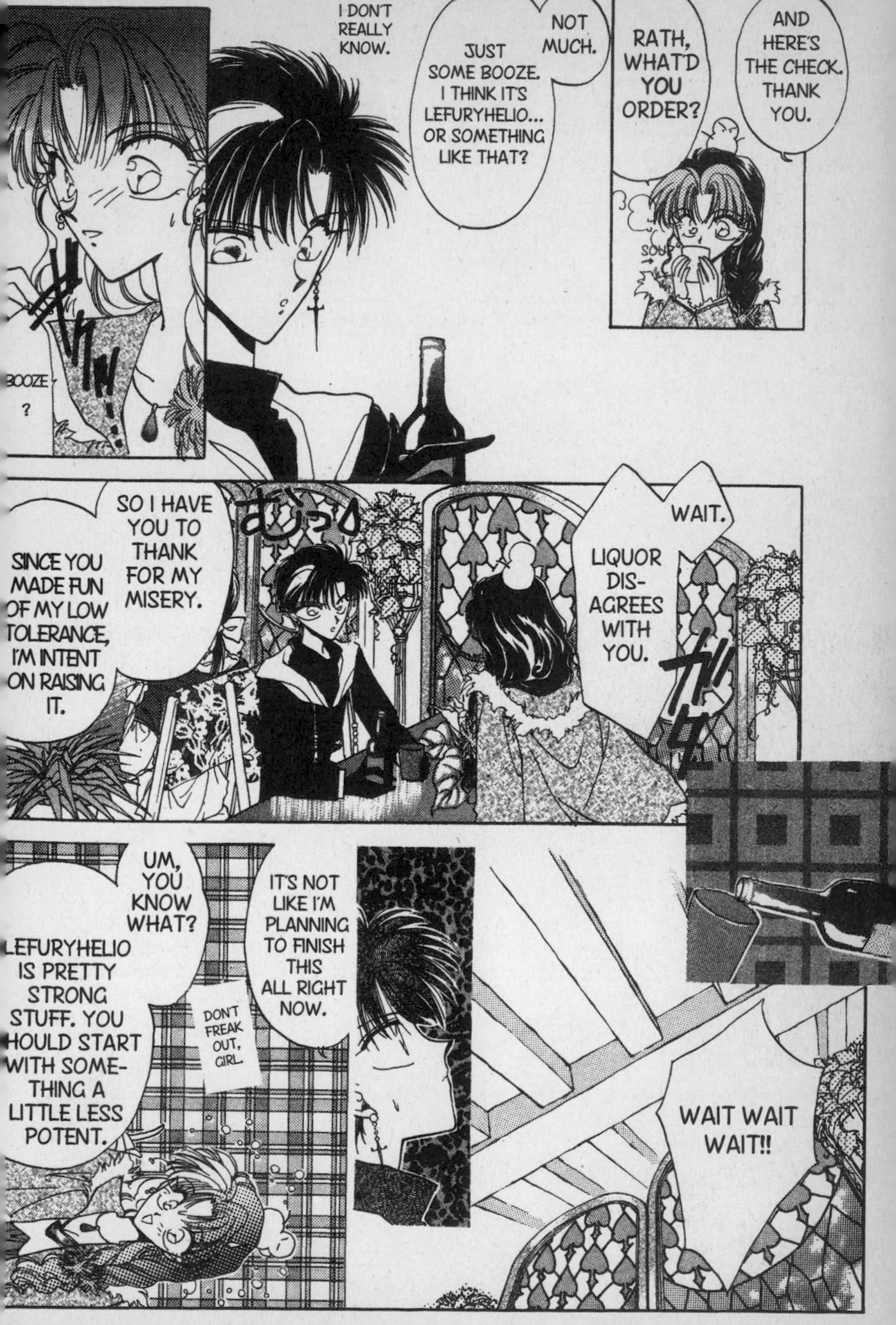
AND HERE'S THE CHECK. THANK YOU.
RATH, WHAT'D YOU ORDER?
SOUP
NOT MUCH.
JUST SOME BOOZE. I THINK IT'S LEFURYHELIO... OR SOMETHING LIKE THAT?
I DON'T REALLY KNOW.
BOOZE ?
WAIT.
LIQUOR DIS-AGREES WITH YOU.
むっ
SO I HAVE YOU TO THANK FOR MY MISERY.
SINCE YOU MADE FUN OF MY LOW TOLERANCE, I'M INTENT ON RAISING IT.
WAIT WAIT WAIT!!
IT'S NOT LIKE I'M PLANNING TO FINISH THIS ALL RIGHT NOW.
UM, YOU KNOW WHAT?
LEFURYHELIO IS PRETTY STRONG STUFF. YOU HOULD START WITH SOME-THING A LITTLE LESS POTENT.
DON'T FREAK OUT, GIRL.

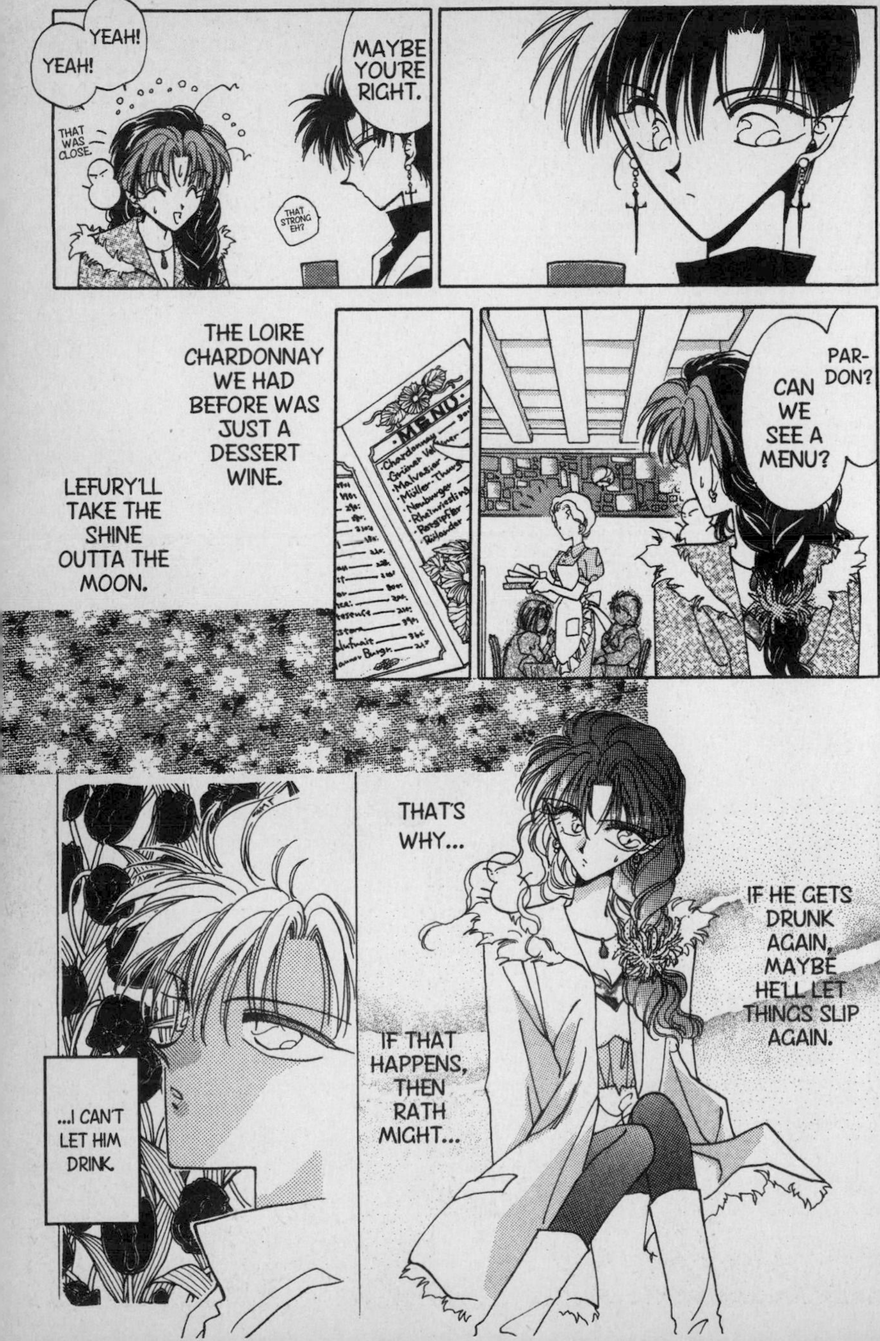
MAYBE YOU'RE RIGHT.
THAT STRONG EH?
YEAH! YEAH!
THAT WAS CLOSE.
PARDON?
CAN WE SEE A MENU?
MENU
THE LOIRE CHARDONNAY WE HAD BEFORE WAS JUST A DESSERT WINE.
LEFURY'LL TAKE THE SHINE OUTTA THE MOON.
THAT'S WHY...
IF HE GETS DRUNK AGAIN, MAYBE HE'LL LET THINGS SLIP AGAIN.
IF THAT HAPPENS, THEN RATH MIGHT...
...I CAN'T LET HIM DRINK.

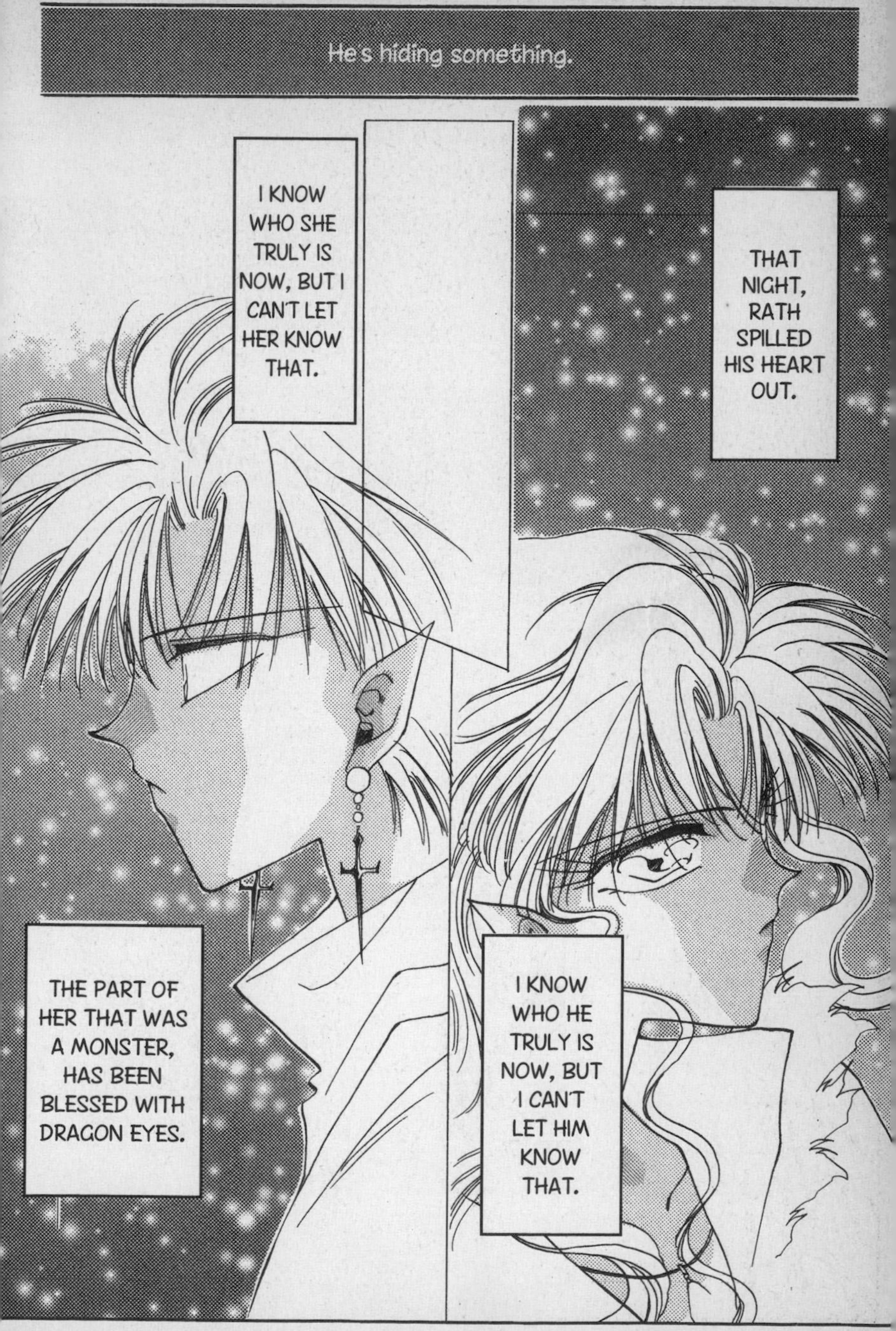
He's hiding something.
THAT NIGHT, RATH SPILLED HIS HEART OUT.
I KNOW WHO HE TRULY IS NOW, BUT I CAN'T LET HIM KNOW THAT.
I KNOW WHO SHE TRULY IS NOW, BUT I CAN'T LET HER KNOW THAT.
THE PART OF HER THAT WAS A MONSTER, HAS BEEN BLESSED WITH DRAGON EYES.

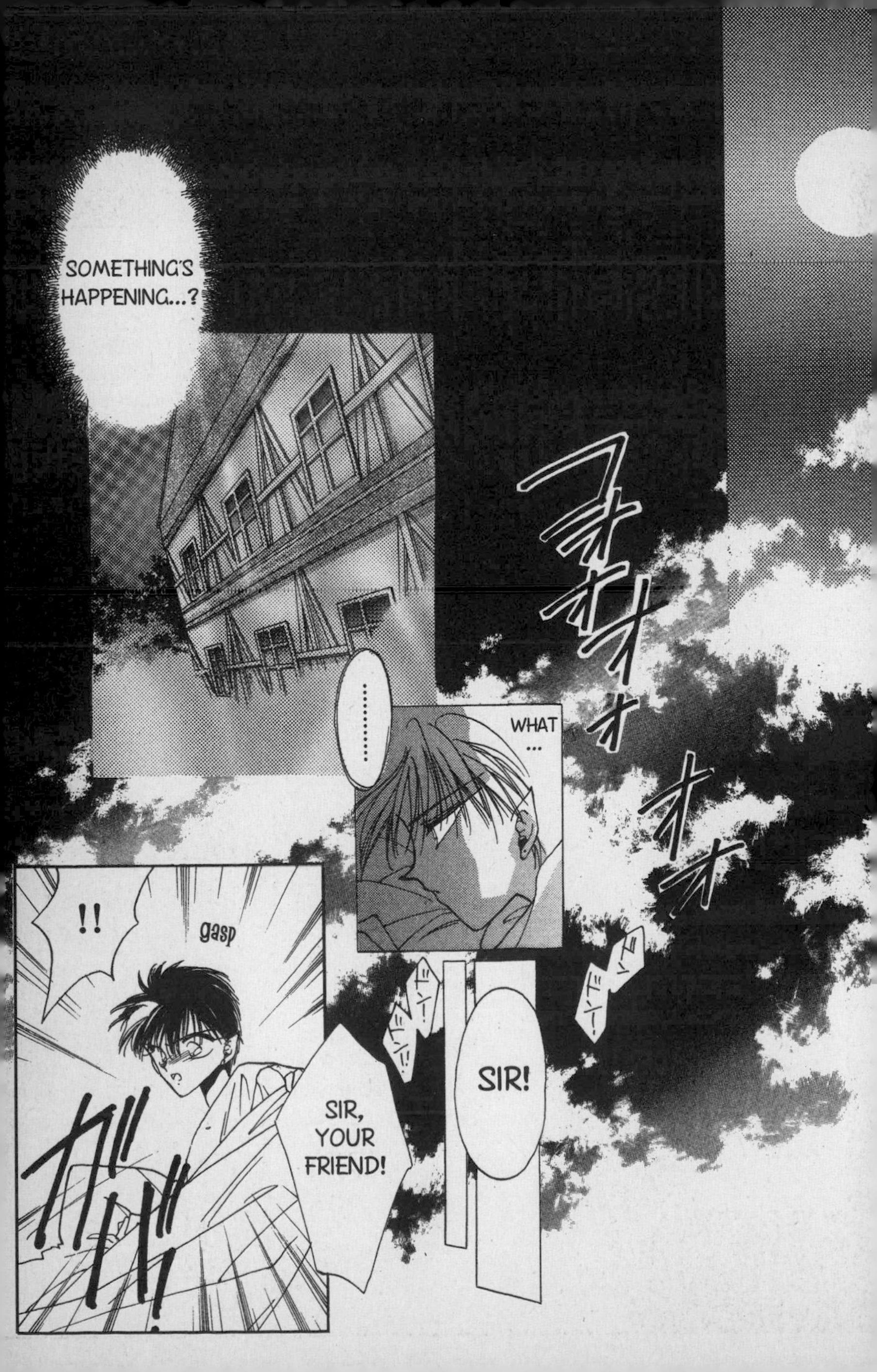
SOMETHING'S HAPPENING...?
......
WHAT ...
SIR!
SIR, YOUR FRIEND!
gasp
!!

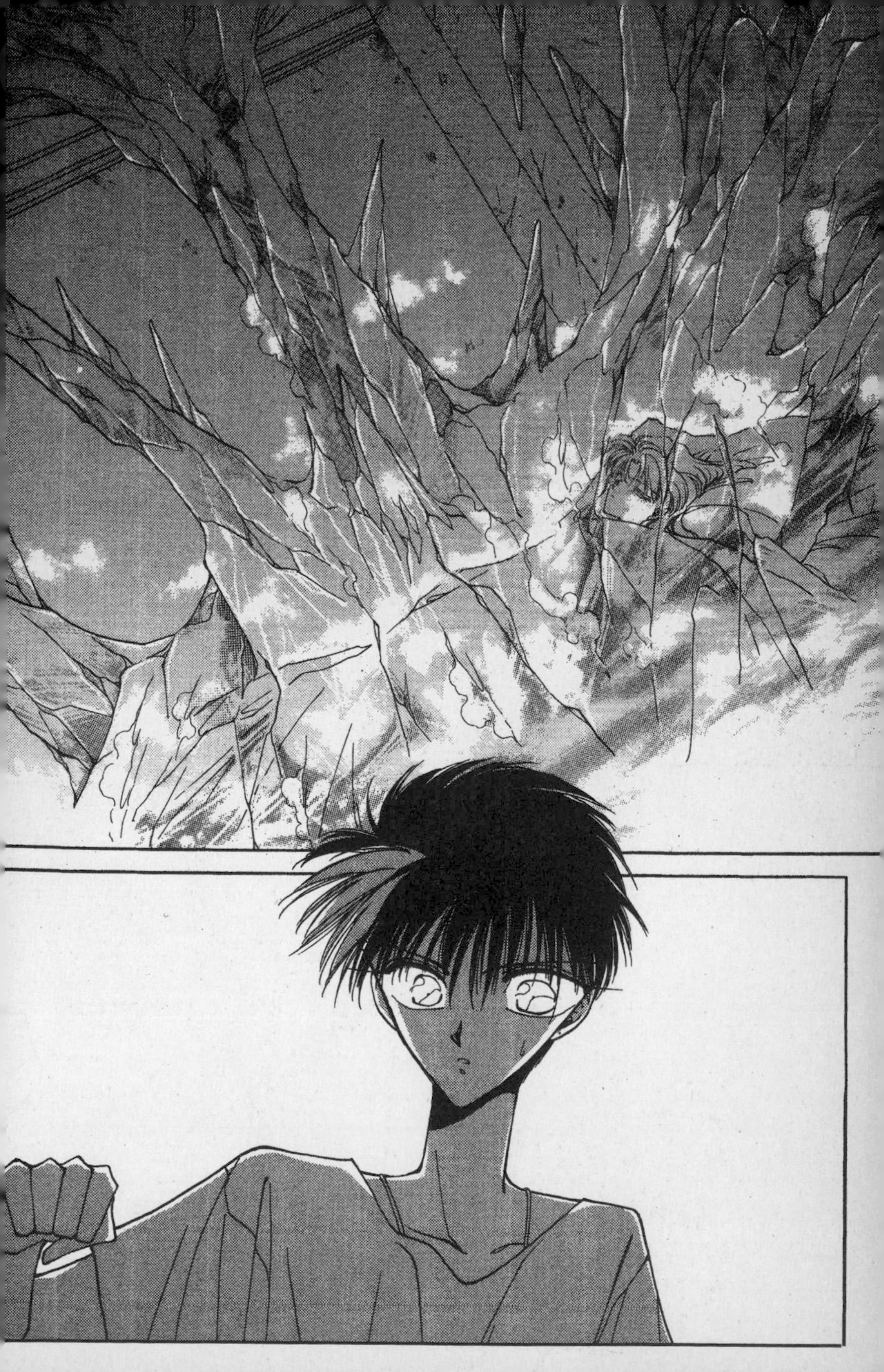

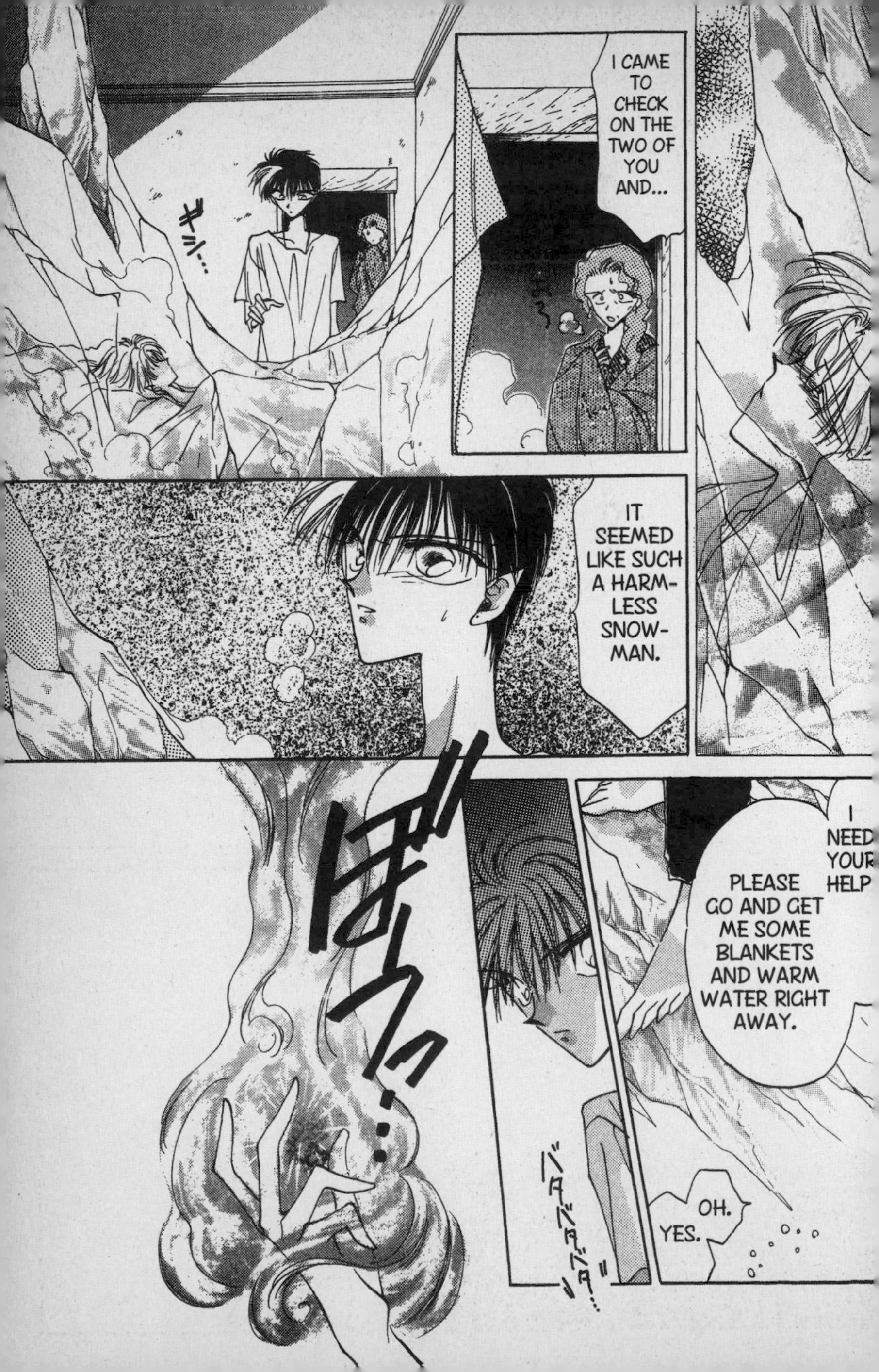
I CAME TO CHECK ON THE TWO OF YOU AND...
ギシ…
IT SEEMED LIKE SUCH A HARMLESS SNOW-MAN.
I NEED YOUR HELP
PLEASE GO AND GET ME SOME BLANKETS AND WARM WATER RIGHT AWAY.
OH. YES.
バタバタバタ…

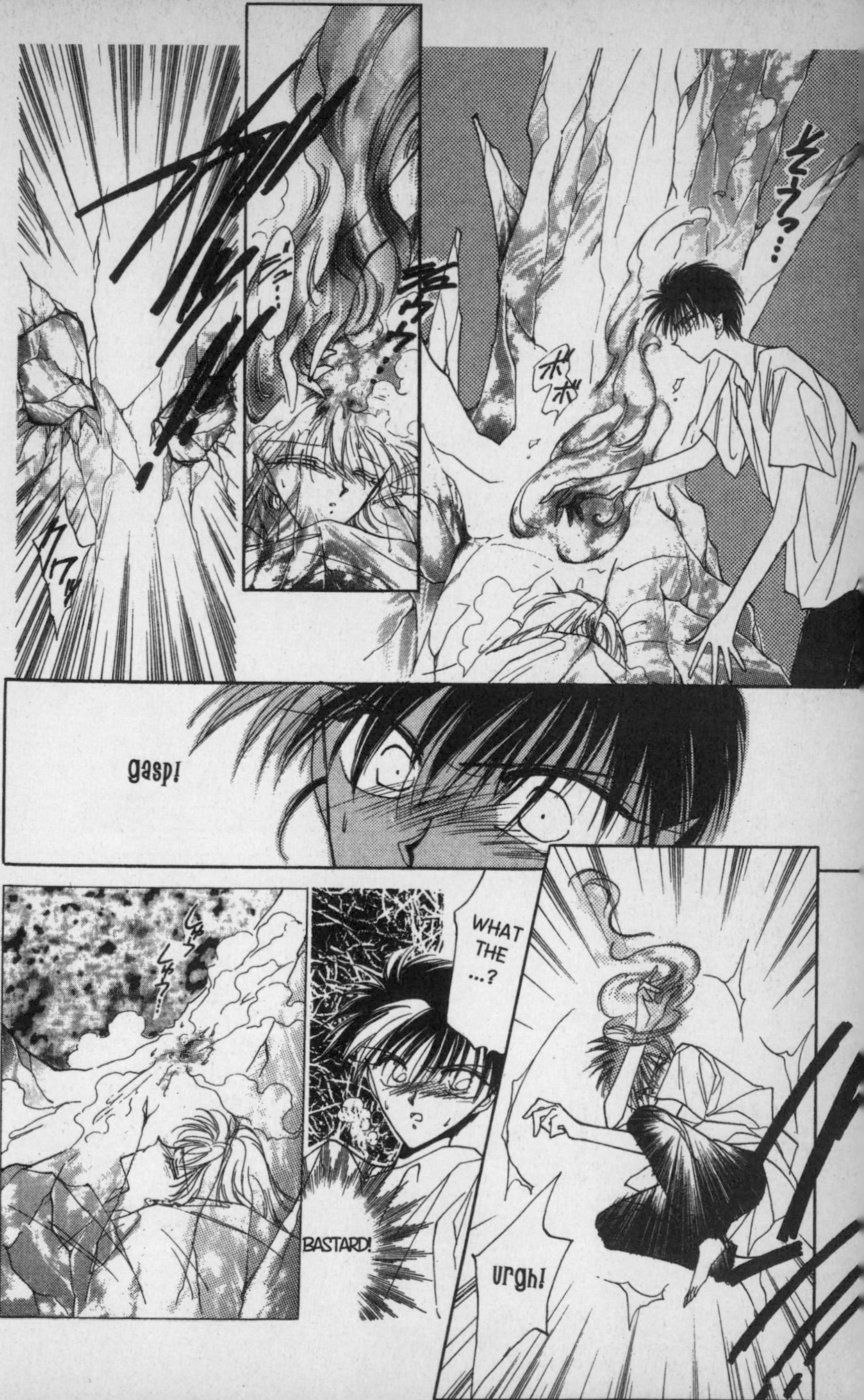
そうっ…
gasp!
Urgh!
WHAT THE ...?
BASTARD!

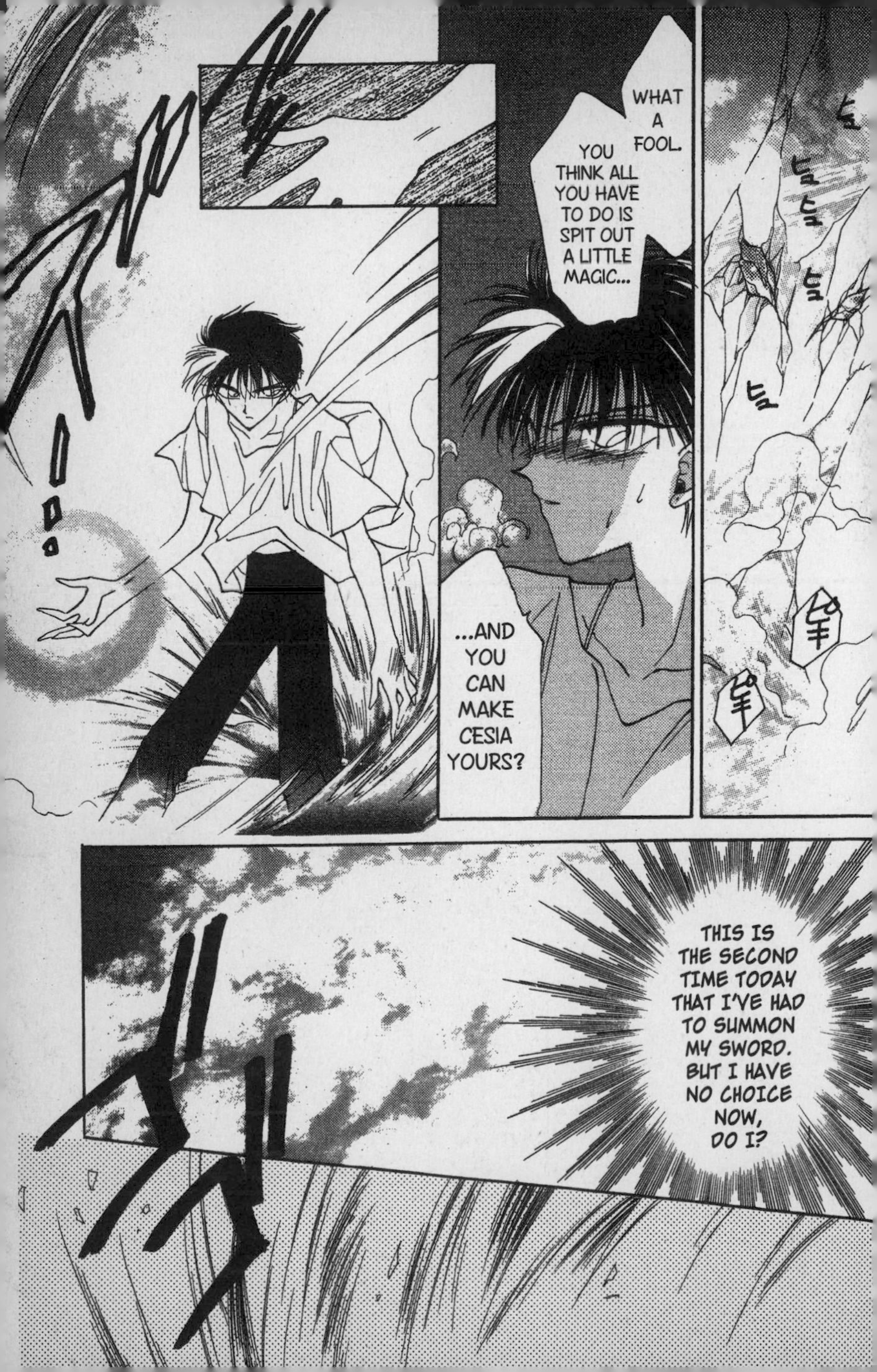
WHAT A FOOL.
YOU THINK ALL YOU HAVE TO DO IS SPIT OUT A LITTLE MAGIC...
...AND YOU CAN MAKE CESIA YOURS?
THIS IS THE SECOND TIME TODAY THAT I'VE HAD TO SUMMON MY SWORD. BUT I HAVE NO CHOICE NOW, DO I?

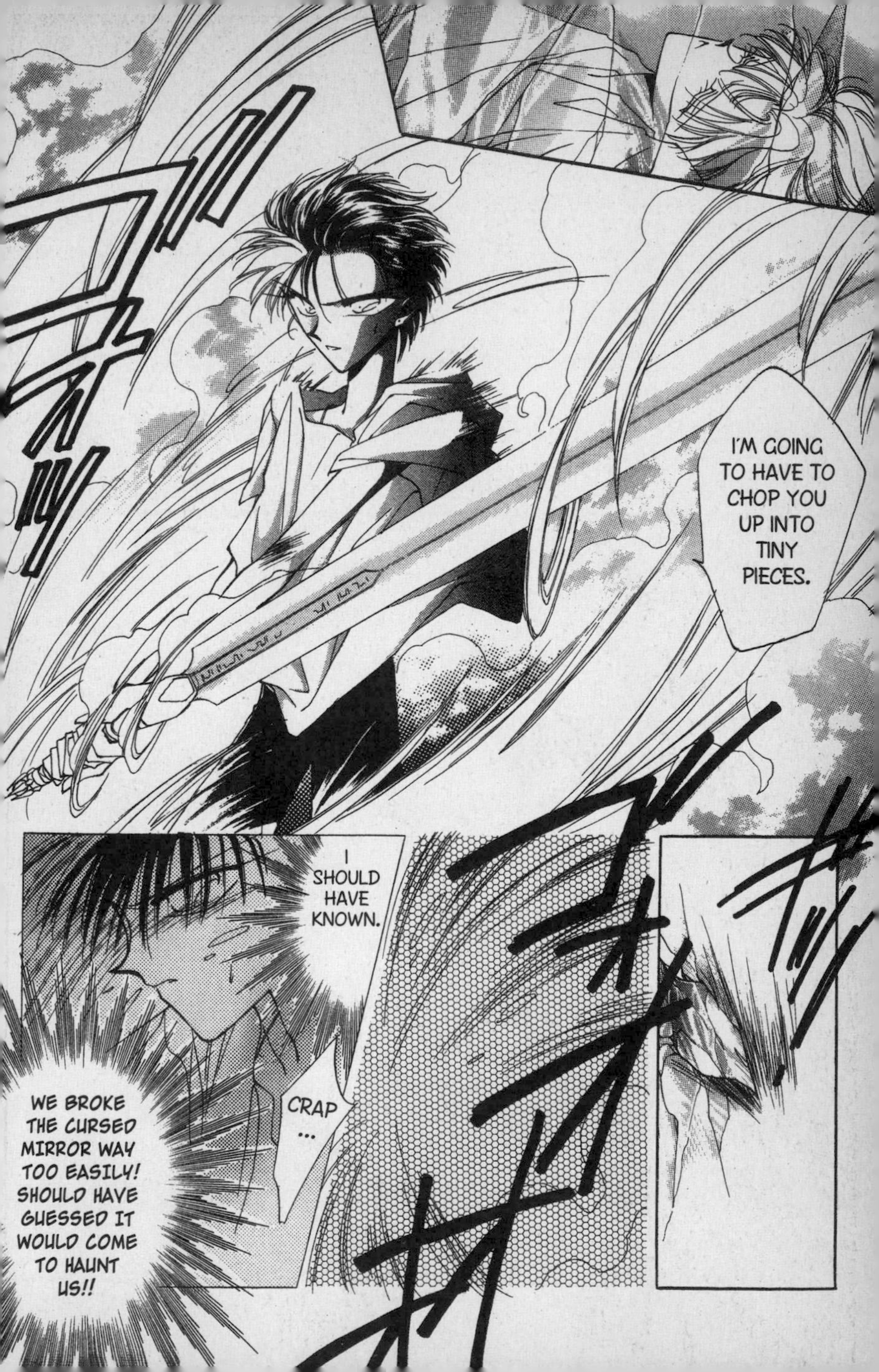
I'M GOING TO HAVE TO CHOP YOU UP INTO TINY PIECES.
I SHOULD HAVE KNOWN.
CRAP ...
WE BROKE THE CURSED MIRROR WAY TOO EASILY! SHOULD HAVE GUESSED IT WOULD COME TO HAUNT US!!

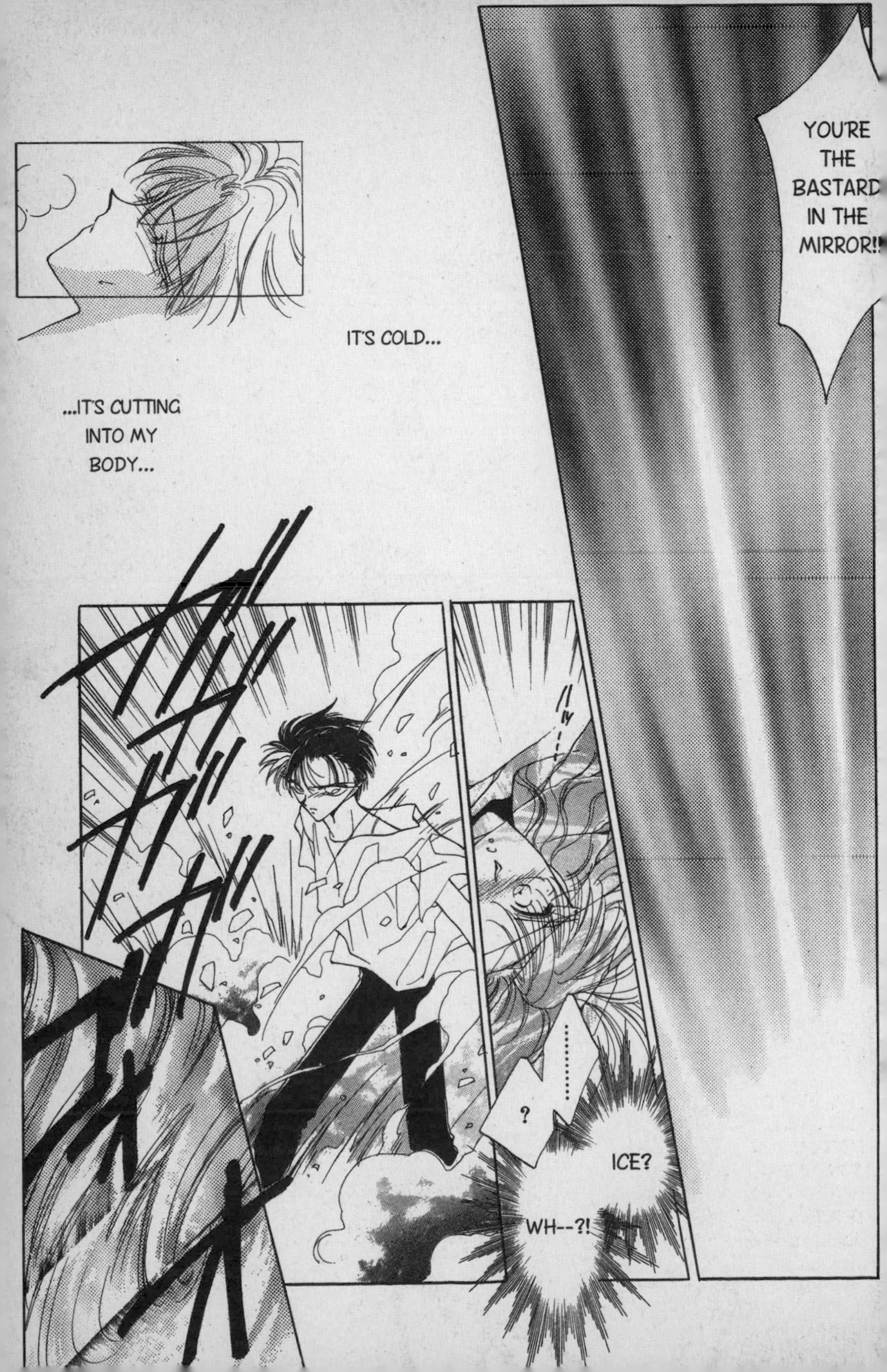
YOU'RE THE BASTARD IN THE MIRROR!!
IT'S COLD...
...IT'S CUTTING INTO MY BODY...
......
?
ICE?
WH--?!

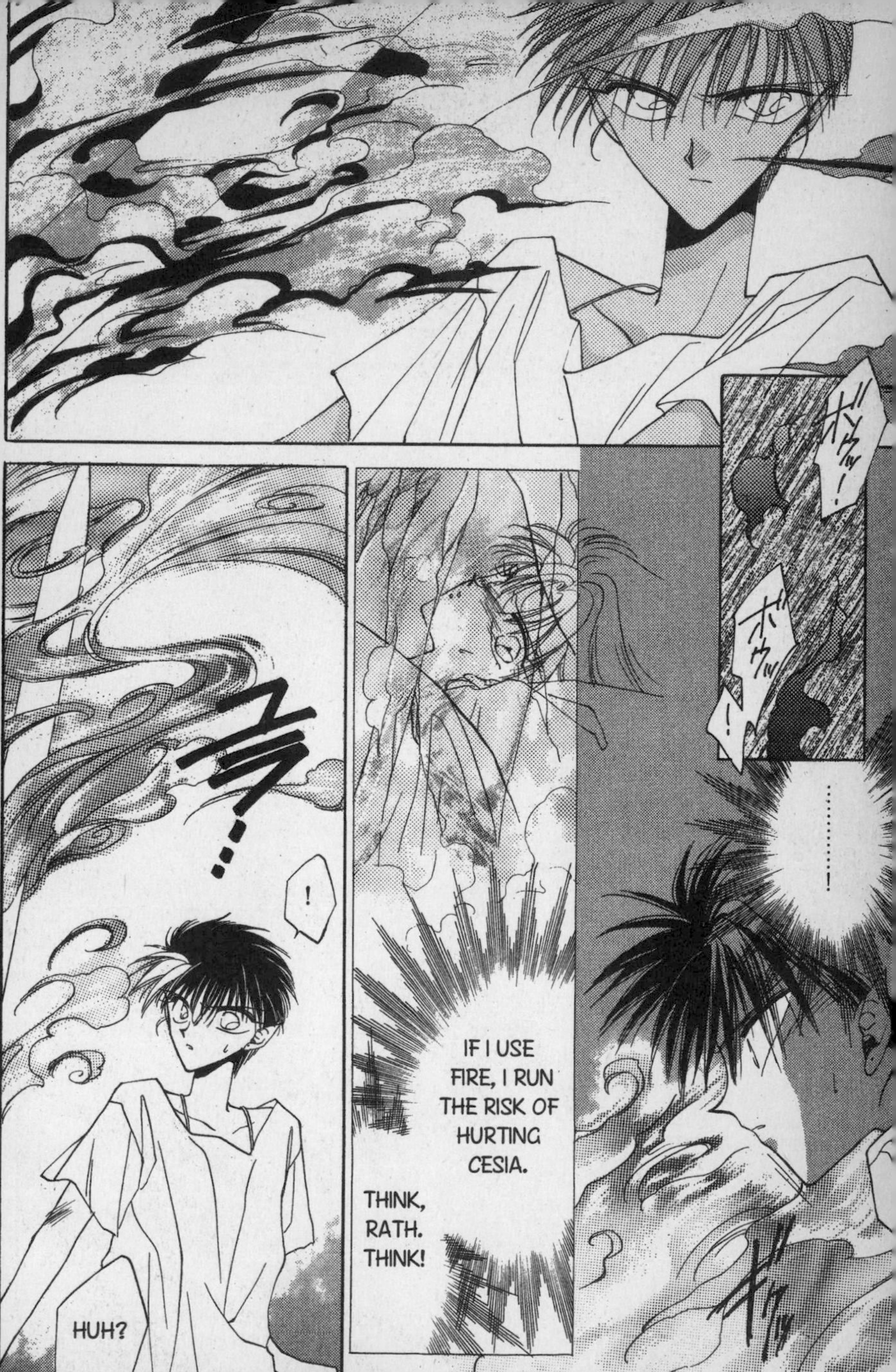
......!
IF I USE FIRE, I RUN THE RISK OF HURTING CESIA.
THINK, RATH. THINK!
!
HUH?

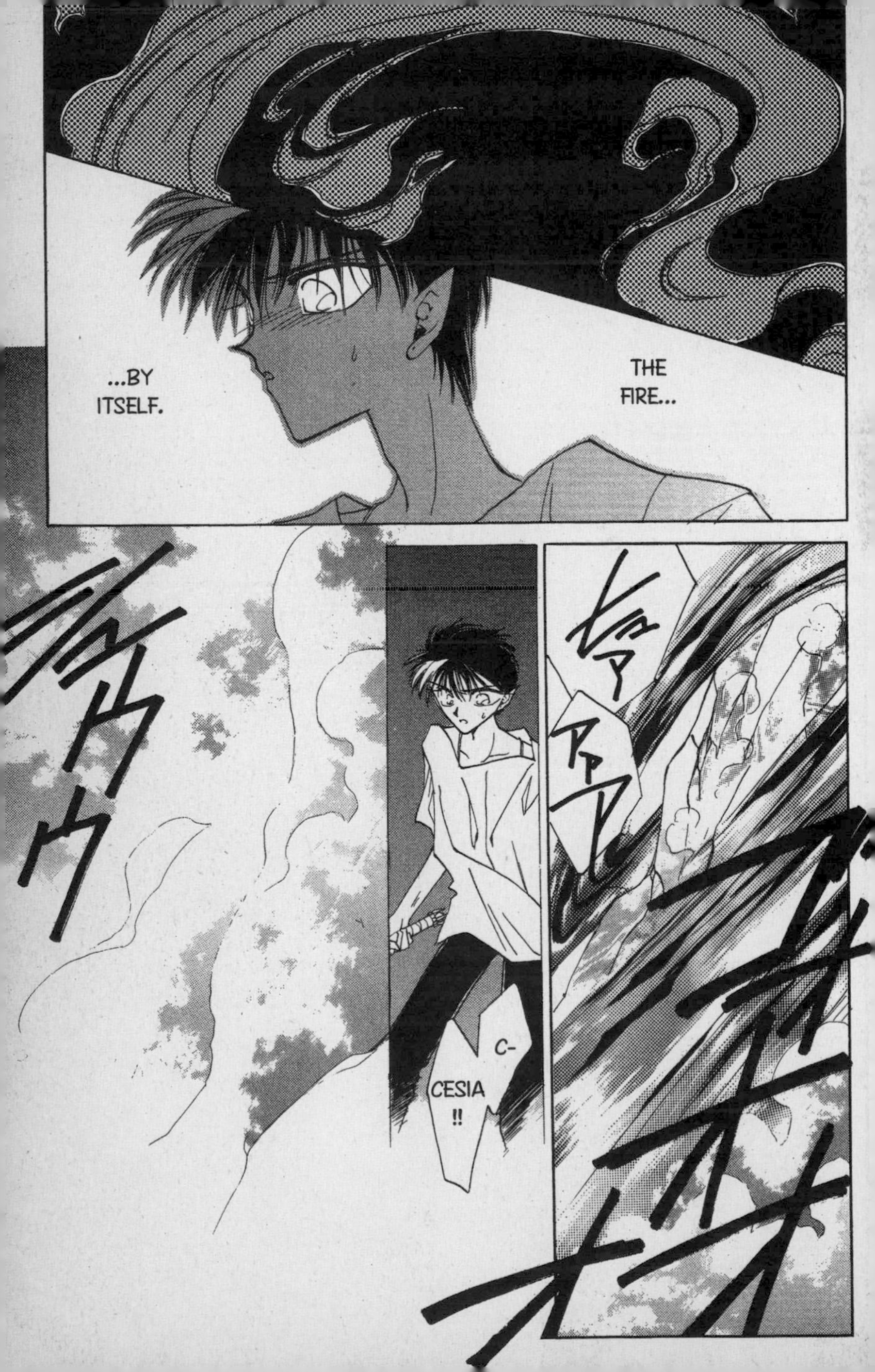
THE FIRE...
...BY ITSELF.
C- CESIA !!

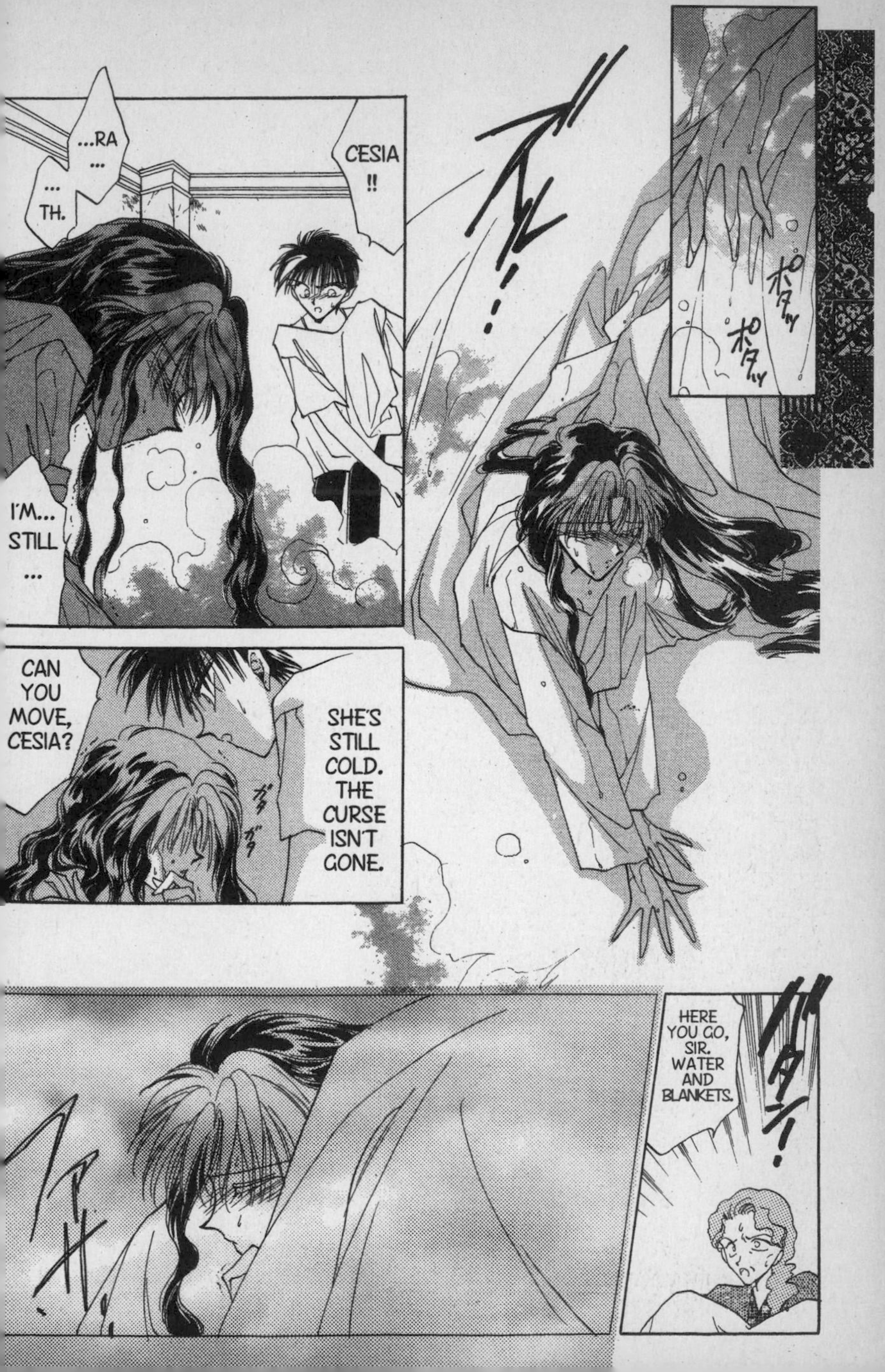
ポタッ
ポタッ
CESIA !!
...RA ... ... TH.
I'M... STILL ...
SHE'S STILL COLD. THE CURSE ISN'T GONE.
CAN YOU MOVE, CESIA?
HERE YOU GO, SIR. WATER AND BLANKETS.

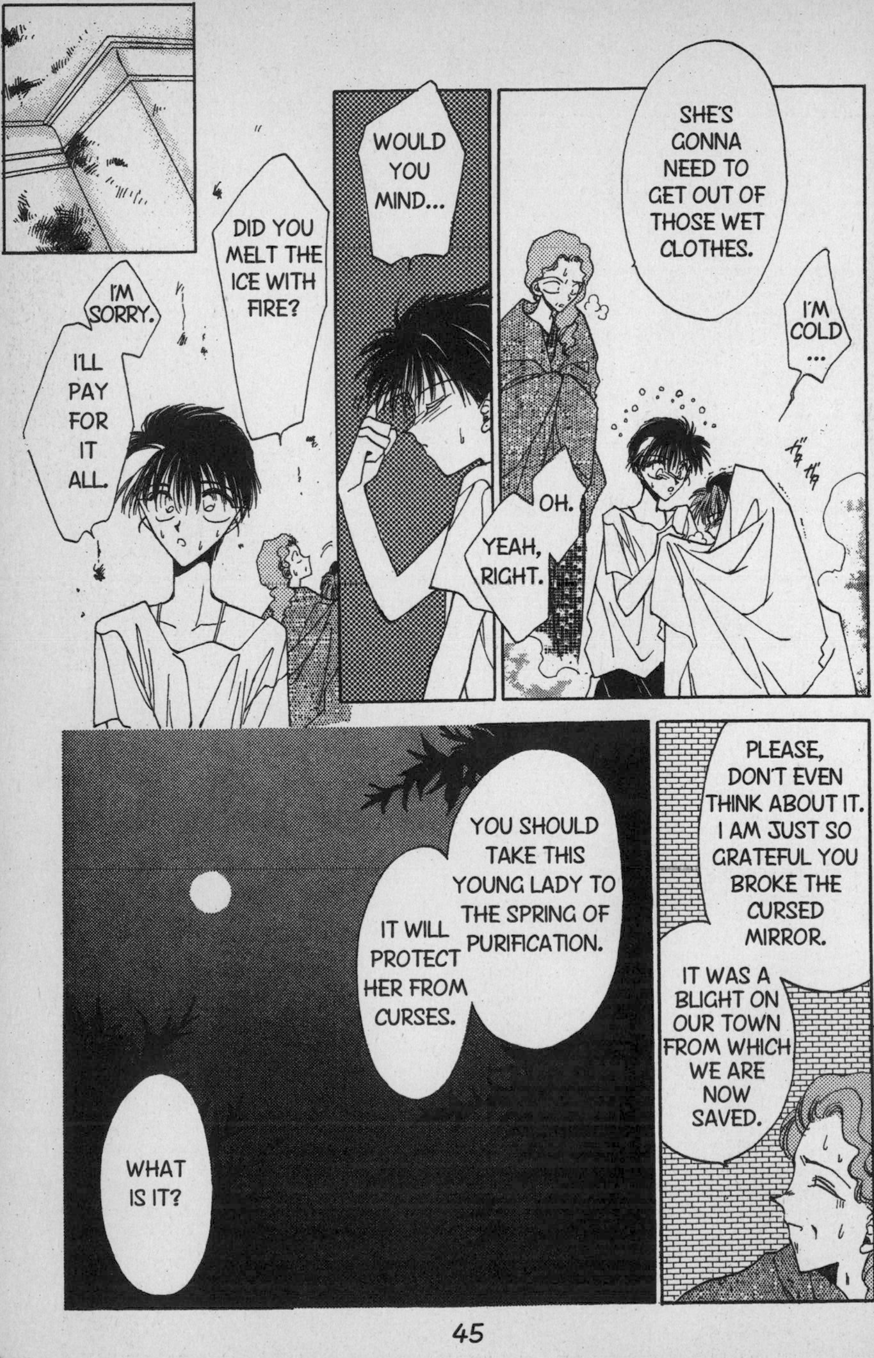
SHE'S GONNA NEED TO GET OUT OF THOSE WET CLOTHES.
I'M COLD ...
WOULD YOU MIND...
OH.
YEAH, RIGHT.
DID YOU MELT THE ICE WITH FIRE?
I'M SORRY.
I'LL PAY FOR IT ALL.
PLEASE, DON'T EVEN THINK ABOUT IT. I AM JUST SO GRATEFUL YOU BROKE THE CURSED MIRROR.
IT WAS A BLIGHT ON OUR TOWN FROM WHICH WE ARE NOW SAVED.
YOU SHOULD TAKE THIS YOUNG LADY TO THE SPRING OF PURIFICATION.
IT WILL PROTECT HER FROM CURSES.
WHAT IS IT?

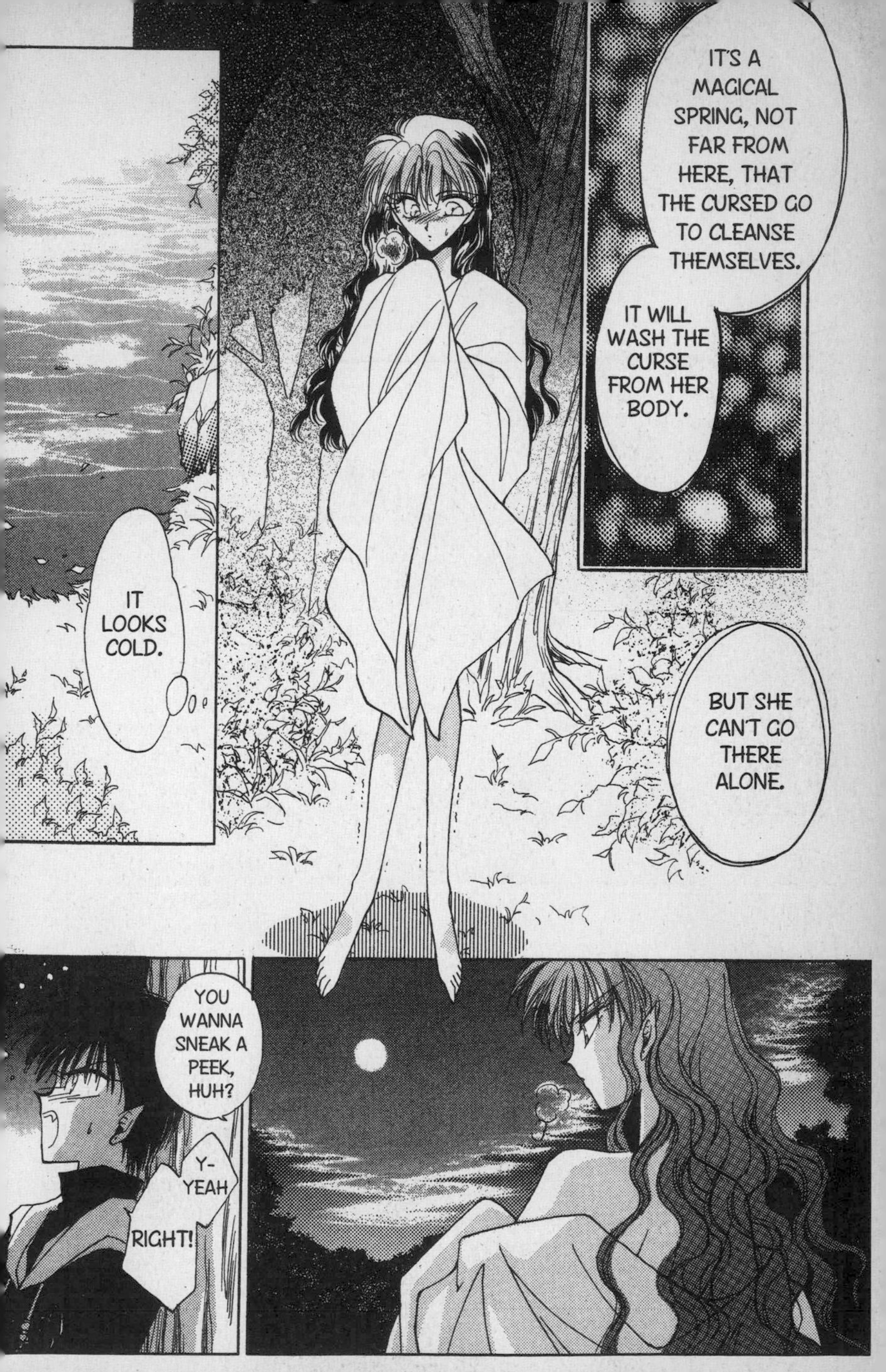
IT'S A MAGICAL SPRING, NOT FAR FROM HERE, THAT THE CURSED GO TO CLEANSE THEMSELVES.
IT WILL WASH THE CURSE FROM HER BODY.
BUT SHE CAN'T GO THERE ALONE.
IT LOOKS COLD.
YOU WANNA SNEAK A PEEK, HUH?
Y-YEAH
RIGHT!

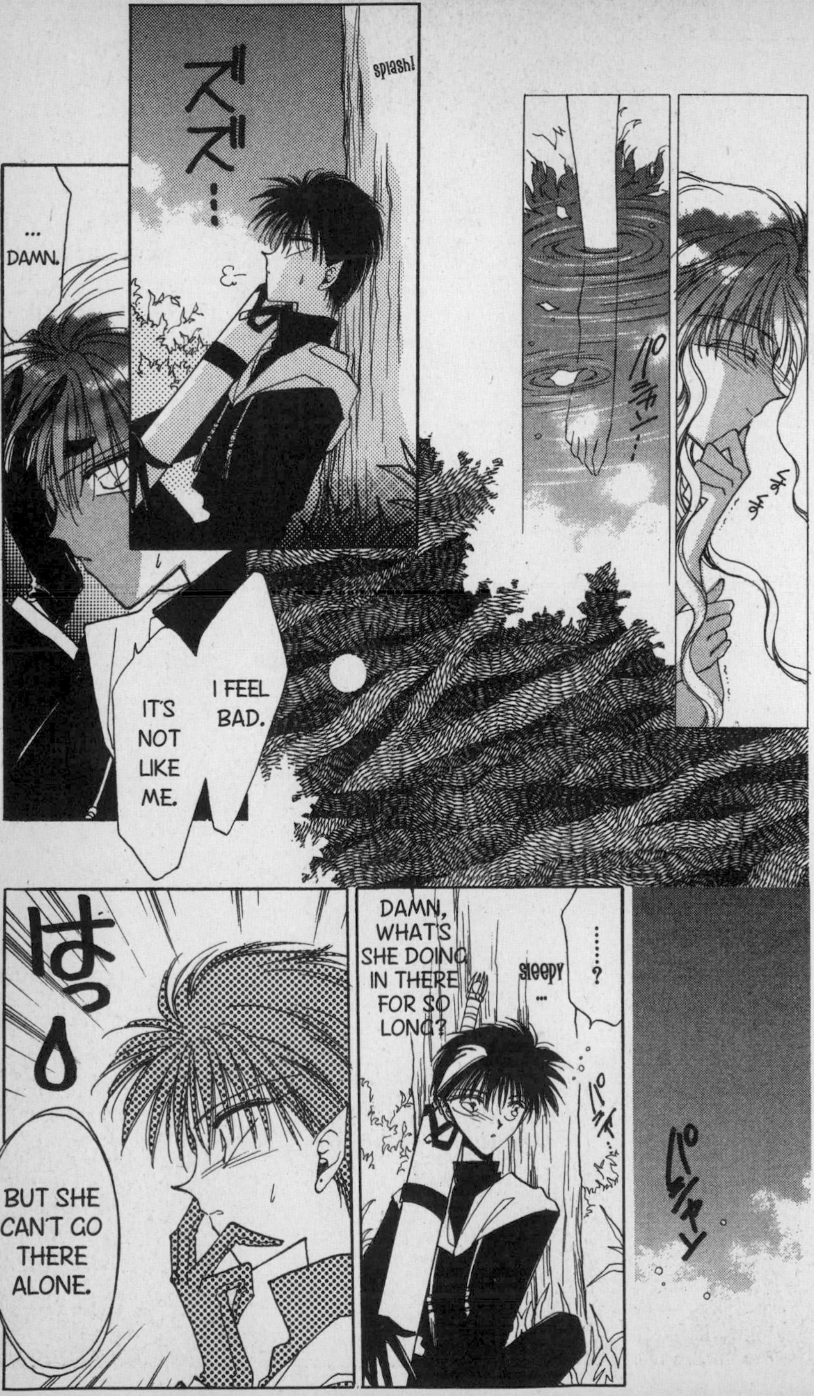
パシャン…
splash!
ズズ…
... DAMN.
I FEEL BAD.
IT'S NOT LIKE ME.
パシャン
......?
sleepy ...
パシャ…
DAMN, WHAT'S SHE DOING IN THERE FOR SO LONG?
はっ
BUT SHE CAN'T GO THERE ALONE.

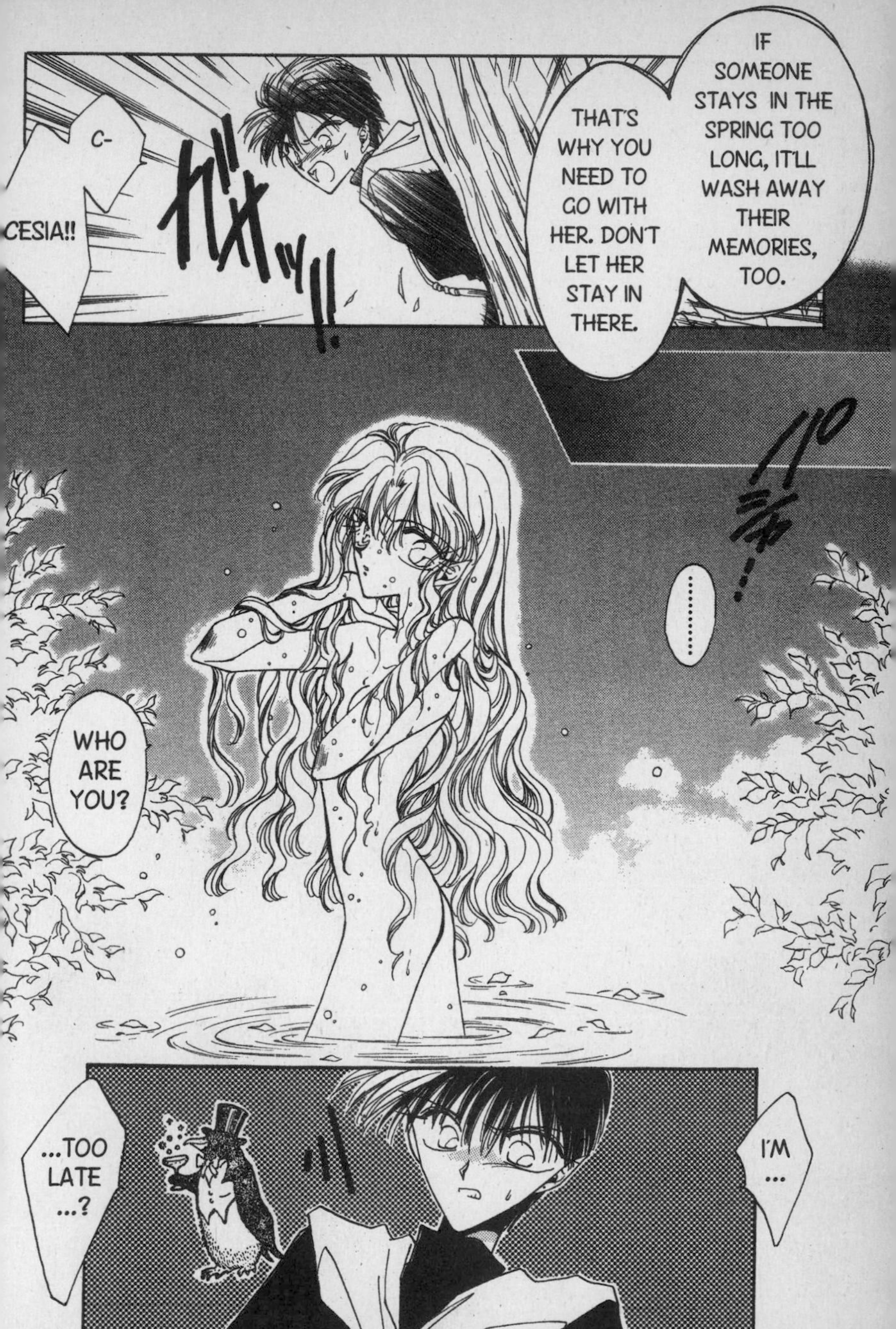
IF SOMEONE STAYS IN THE SPRING TOO LONG, IT'LL WASH AWAY THEIR MEMORIES, TOO.
THAT'S WHY YOU NEED TO GO WITH HER. DON'T LET HER STAY IN THERE.
C-
CESIA!!
....
WHO ARE YOU?
I'M ...
...TOO LATE ...?

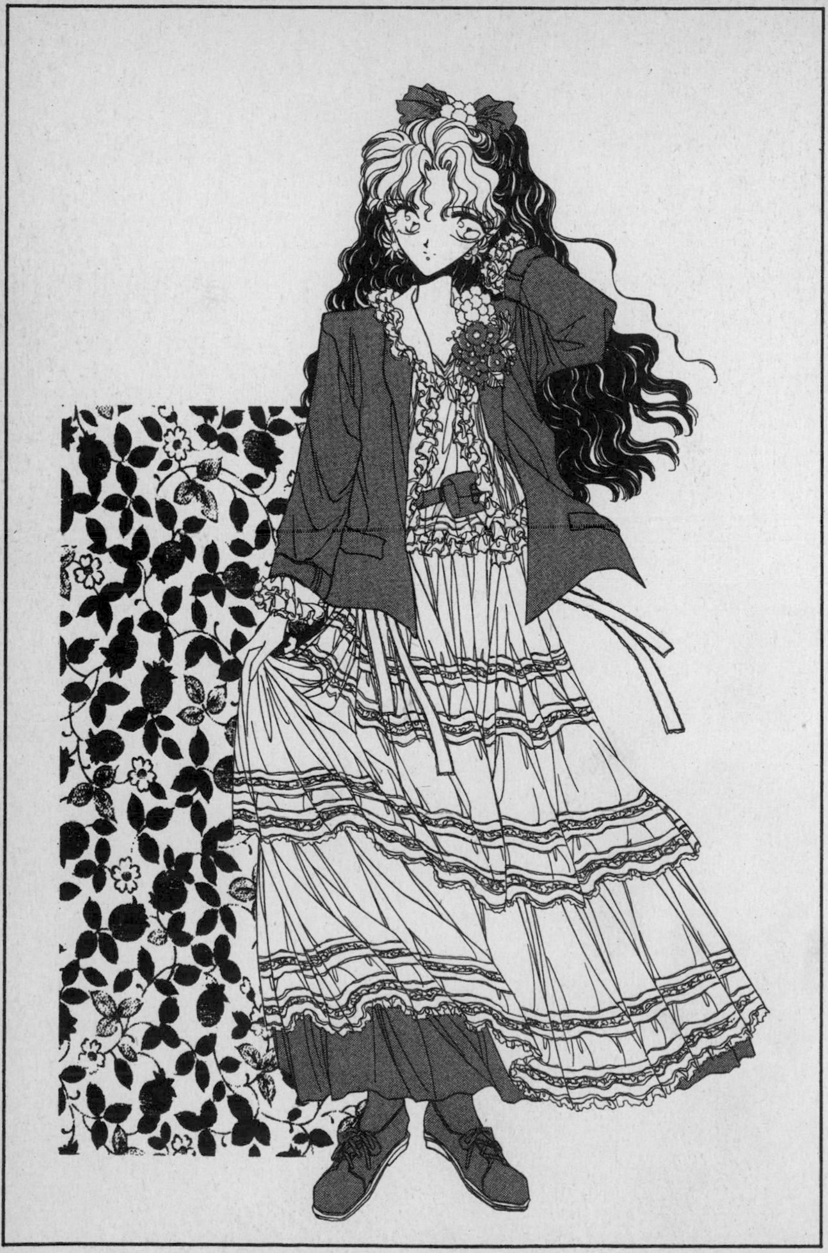

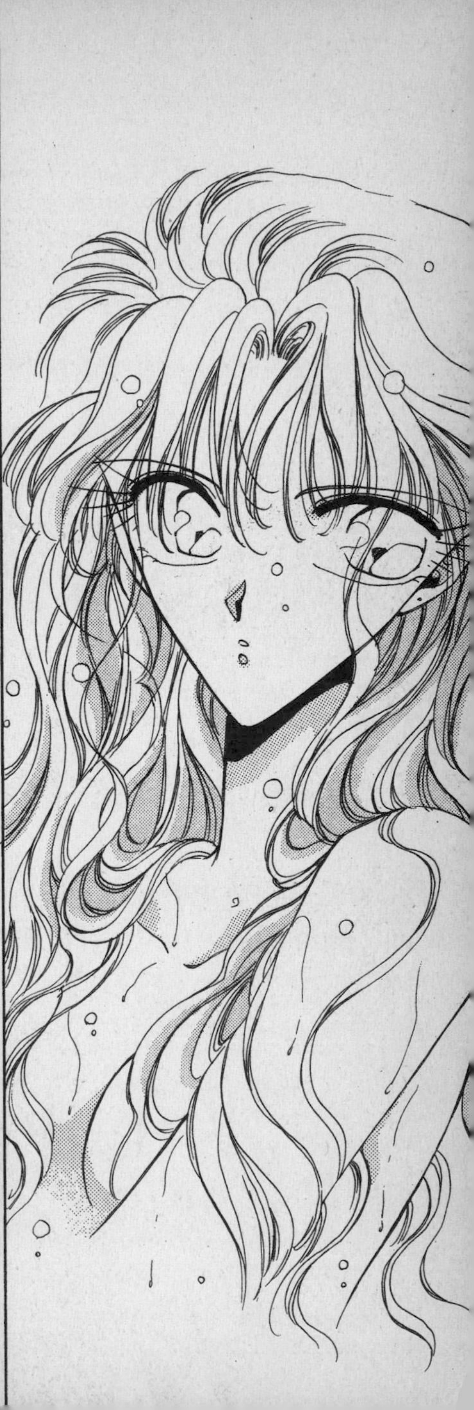

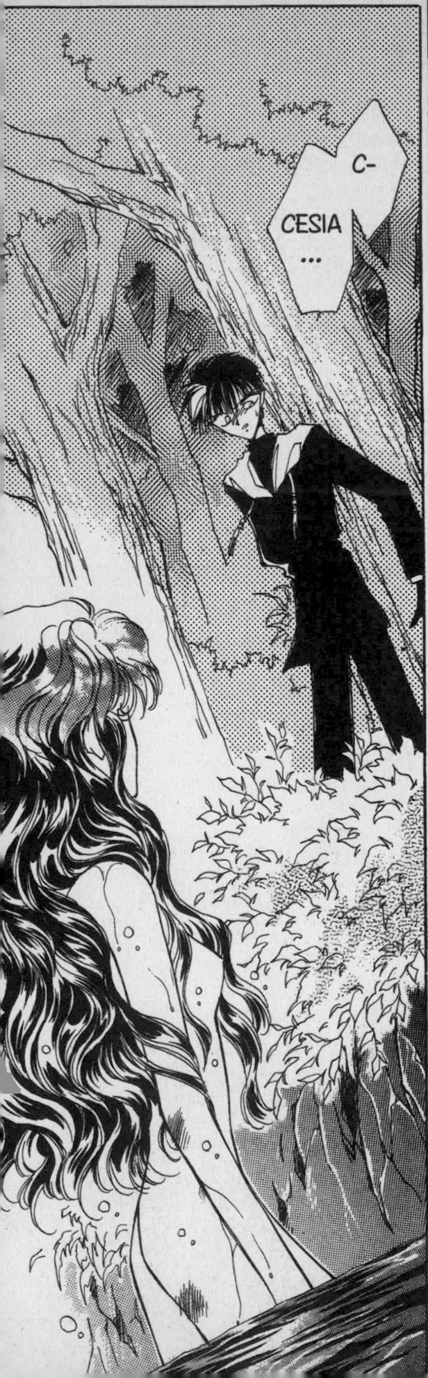
C- CESIA ...

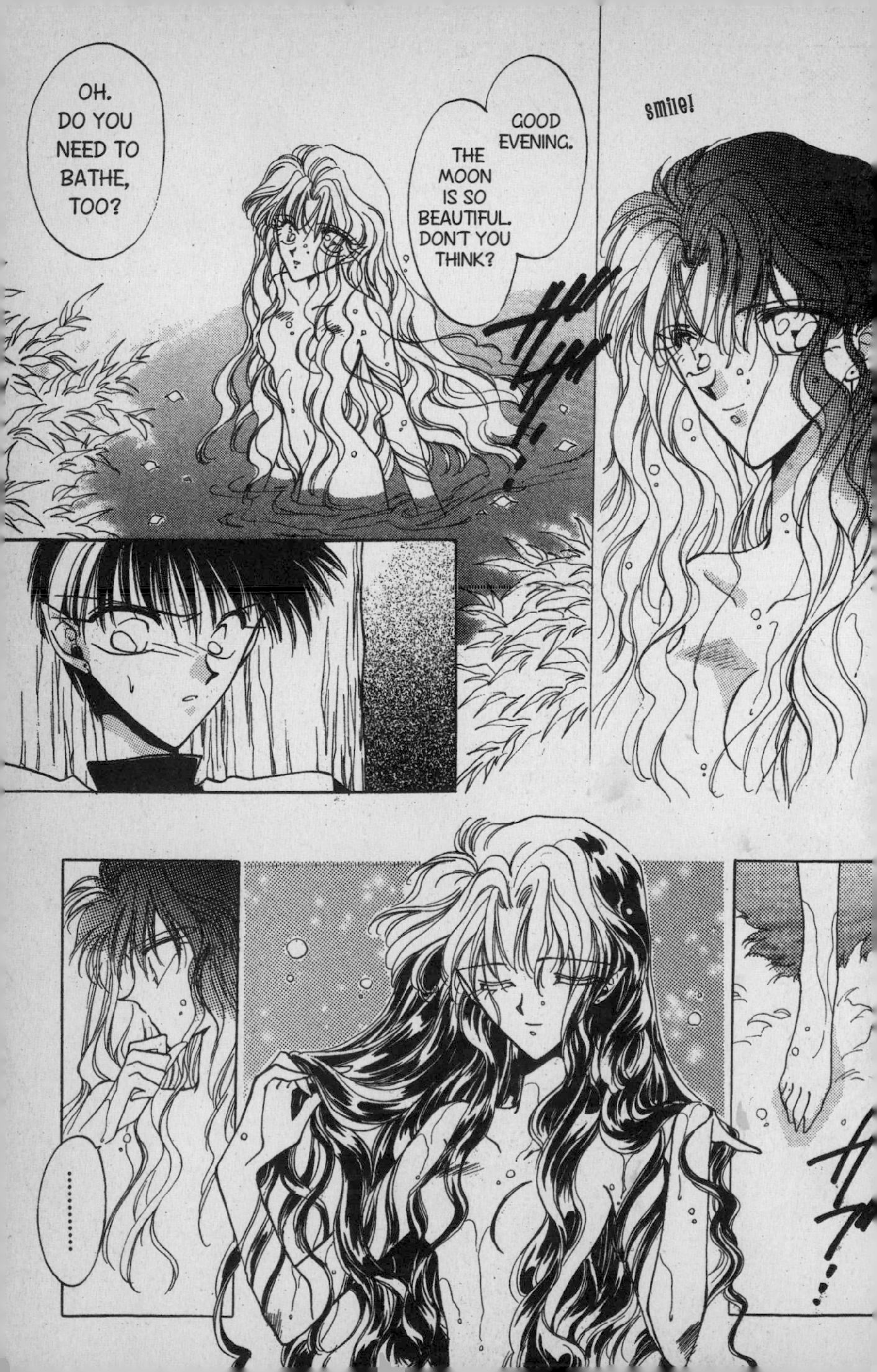
smile!
GOOD EVENING.
THE MOON IS SO BEAUTIFUL. DON'T YOU THINK?
OH. DO YOU NEED TO BATHE, TOO?
....

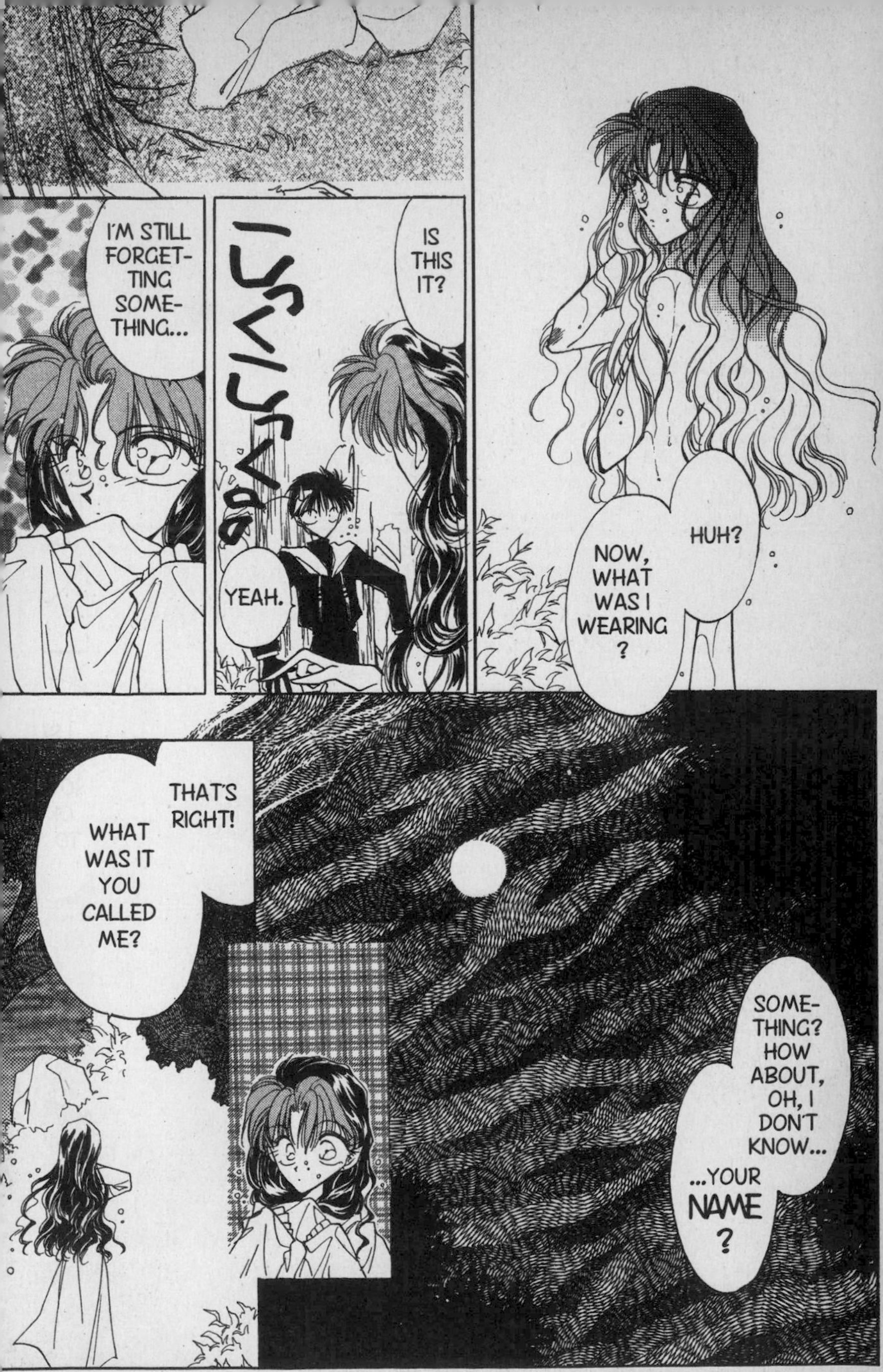
HUH?
NOW, WHAT WAS I WEARING?
IS THIS IT?
YEAH.
I'M STILL FORGET-TING SOME-THING...
SOME-THING? HOW ABOUT, OH, I DON'T KNOW... ...YOUR NAME?
THAT'S RIGHT! WHAT WAS IT YOU CALLED ME?

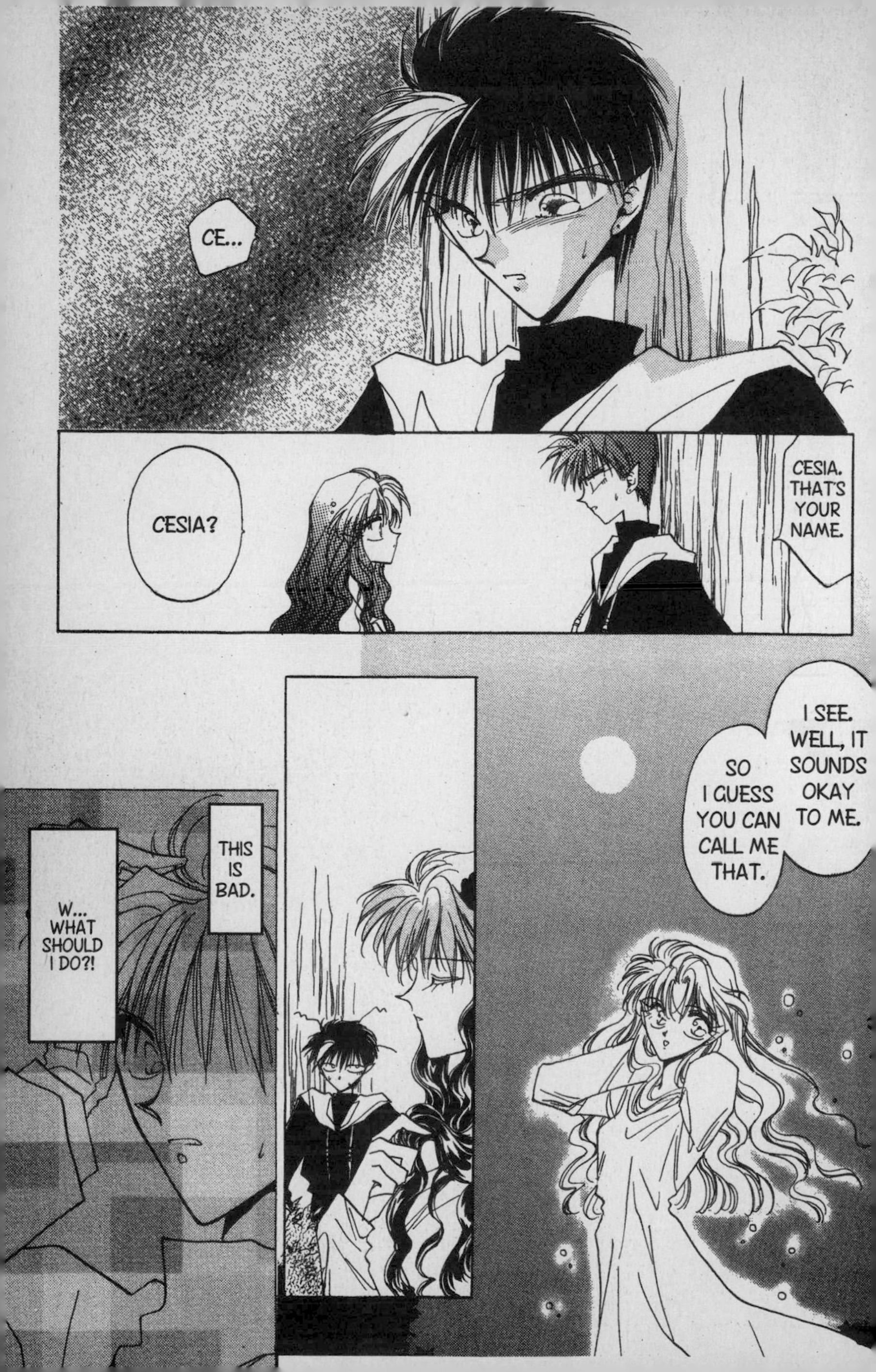
CE...
CESIA. THAT'S YOUR NAME.
CESIA?
I SEE. WELL, IT SOUNDS OKAY TO ME.
SO I GUESS YOU CAN CALL ME THAT.
THIS IS BAD.
W... WHAT SHOULD I DO?!

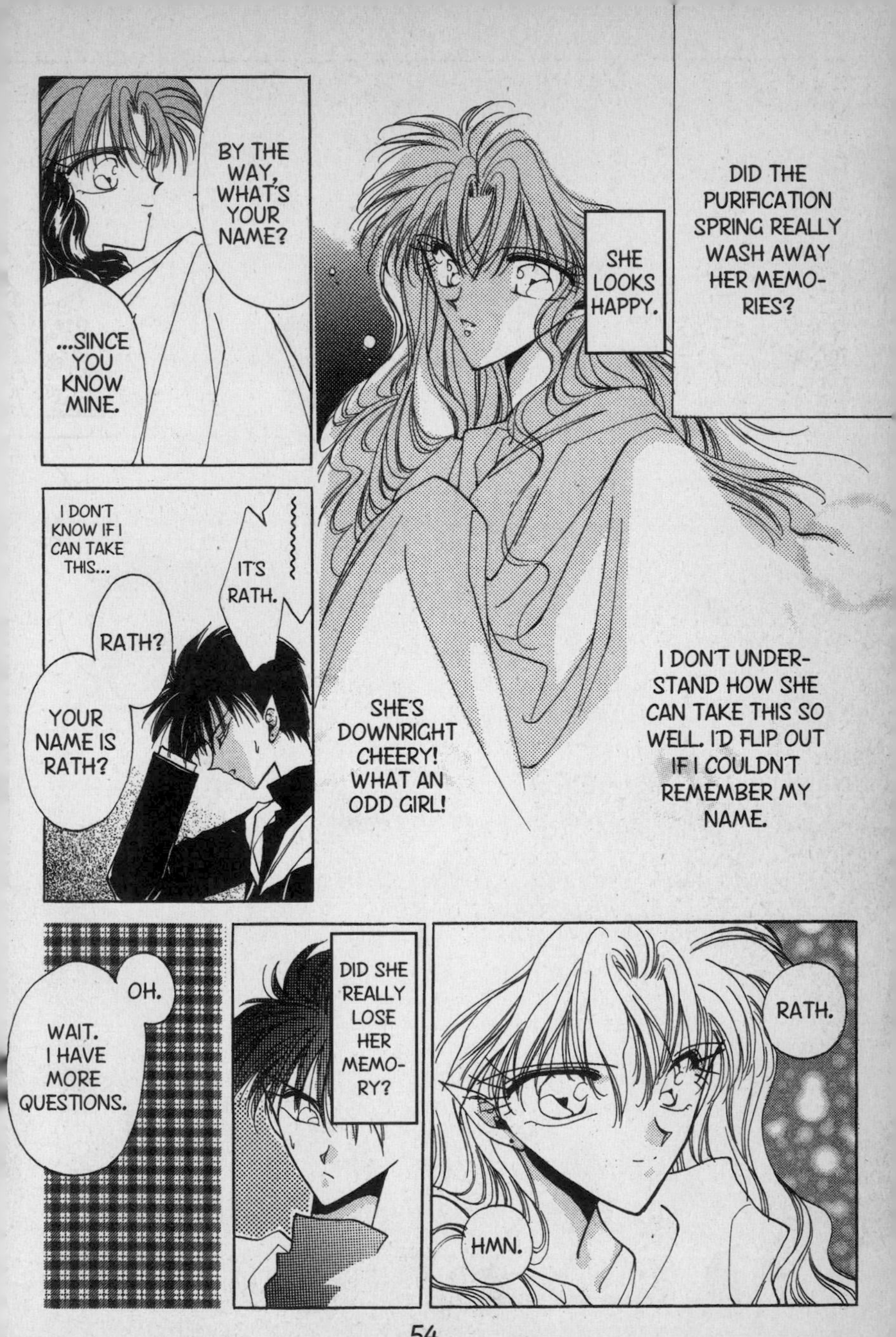
DID THE PURIFICATION SPRING REALLY WASH AWAY HER MEMO-RIES?
SHE LOOKS HAPPY.
I DON'T UNDER-STAND HOW SHE CAN TAKE THIS SO WELL. I'D FLIP OUT IF I COULDN'T REMEMBER MY NAME.
SHE'S DOWNRIGHT CHEERY! WHAT AN ODD GIRL!
BY THE WAY, WHAT'S YOUR NAME?
...SINCE YOU KNOW MINE.
IT'S RATH.
I DON'T KNOW IF I CAN TAKE THIS...
RATH?
YOUR NAME IS RATH?
RATH.
HMN.
DID SHE REALLY LOSE HER MEMO-RY?
OH.
WAIT. I HAVE MORE QUESTIONS.

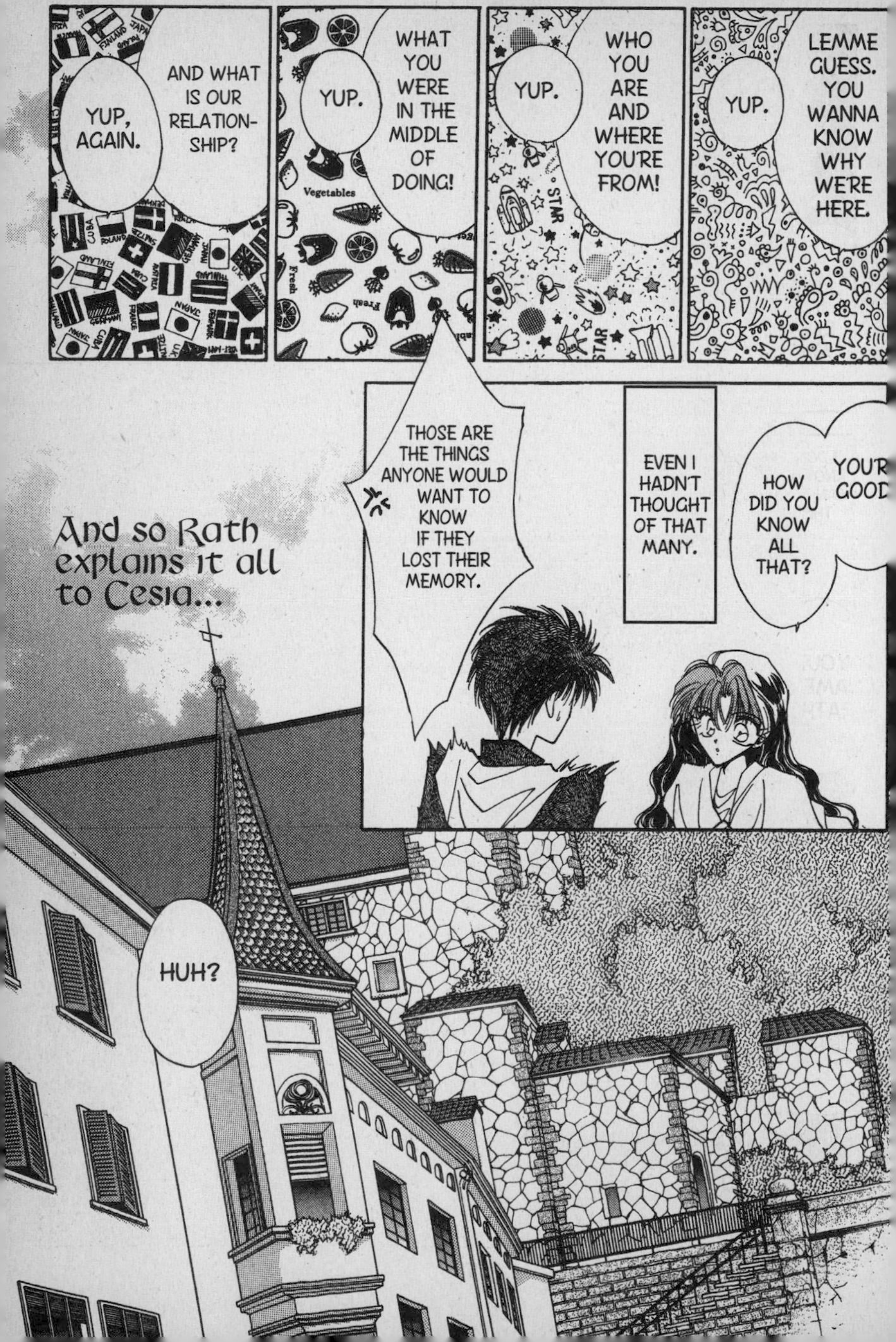
LEMME GUESS. YOU WANNA KNOW WHY WE'RE HERE.
YUP.
WHO YOU ARE AND WHERE YOU'RE FROM!
YUP.
WHAT YOU WERE IN THE MIDDLE OF DOING!
YUP.
AND WHAT IS OUR RELATIONSHIP?
YUP, AGAIN.
YOU'R GOOD
HOW DID YOU KNOW ALL THAT?
EVEN I HADN'T THOUGHT OF THAT MANY.
THOSE ARE THE THINGS ANYONE WOULD WANT TO KNOW IF THEY LOST THEIR MEMORY.
And so Rath explains it all to Cesia...
HUH?

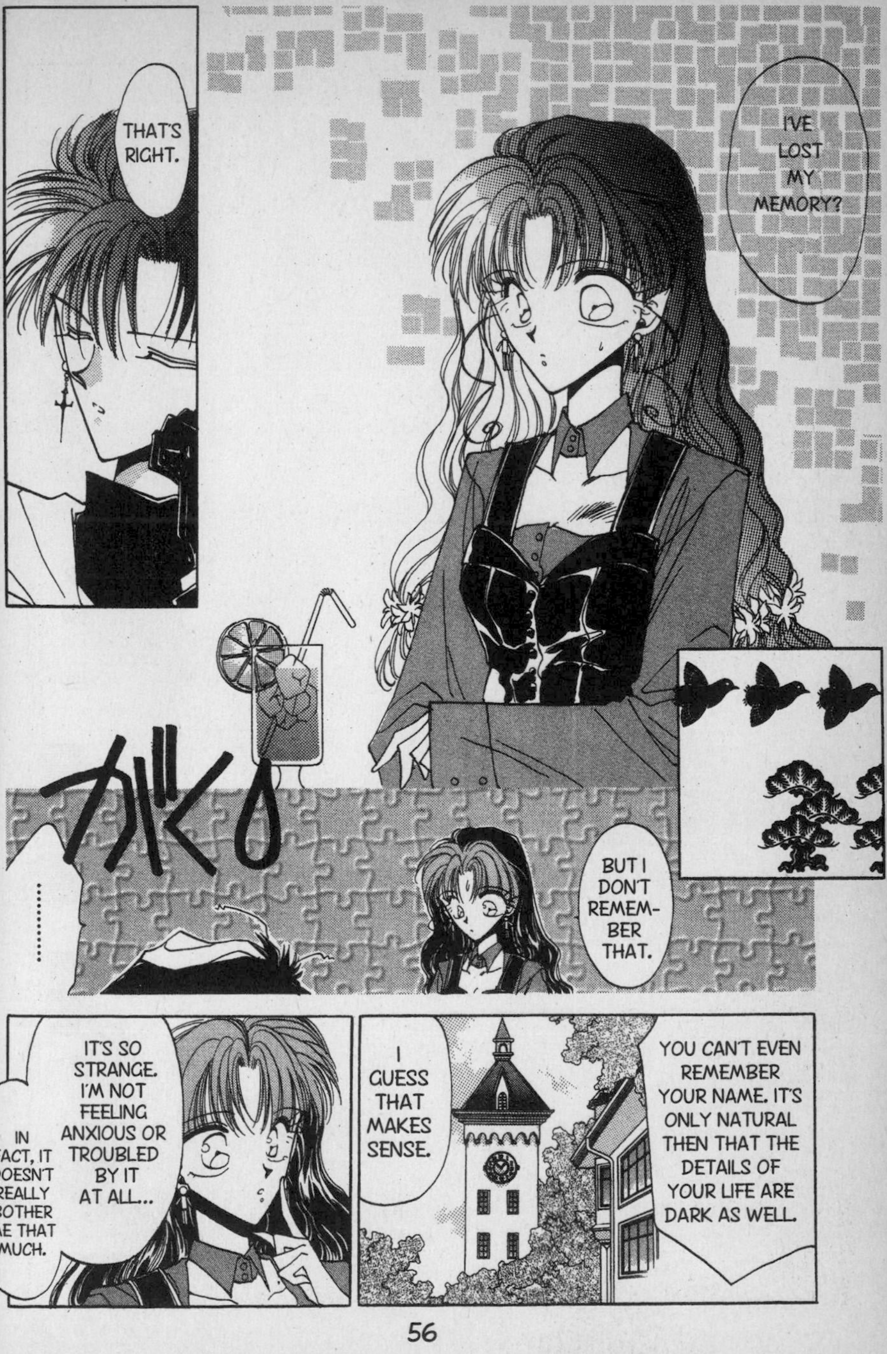
I'VE LOST MY MEMORY?
THAT'S RIGHT.
BUT I DON'T REMEMBER THAT.
がくり
......
YOU CAN'T EVEN REMEMBER YOUR NAME. IT'S ONLY NATURAL THEN THAT THE DETAILS OF YOUR LIFE ARE DARK AS WELL.
I GUESS THAT MAKES SENSE.
IT'S SO STRANGE. I'M NOT FEELING ANXIOUS OR TROUBLED BY IT AT ALL...
IN ACT, IT OESN'T EALLY OTHER E THAT MUCH.

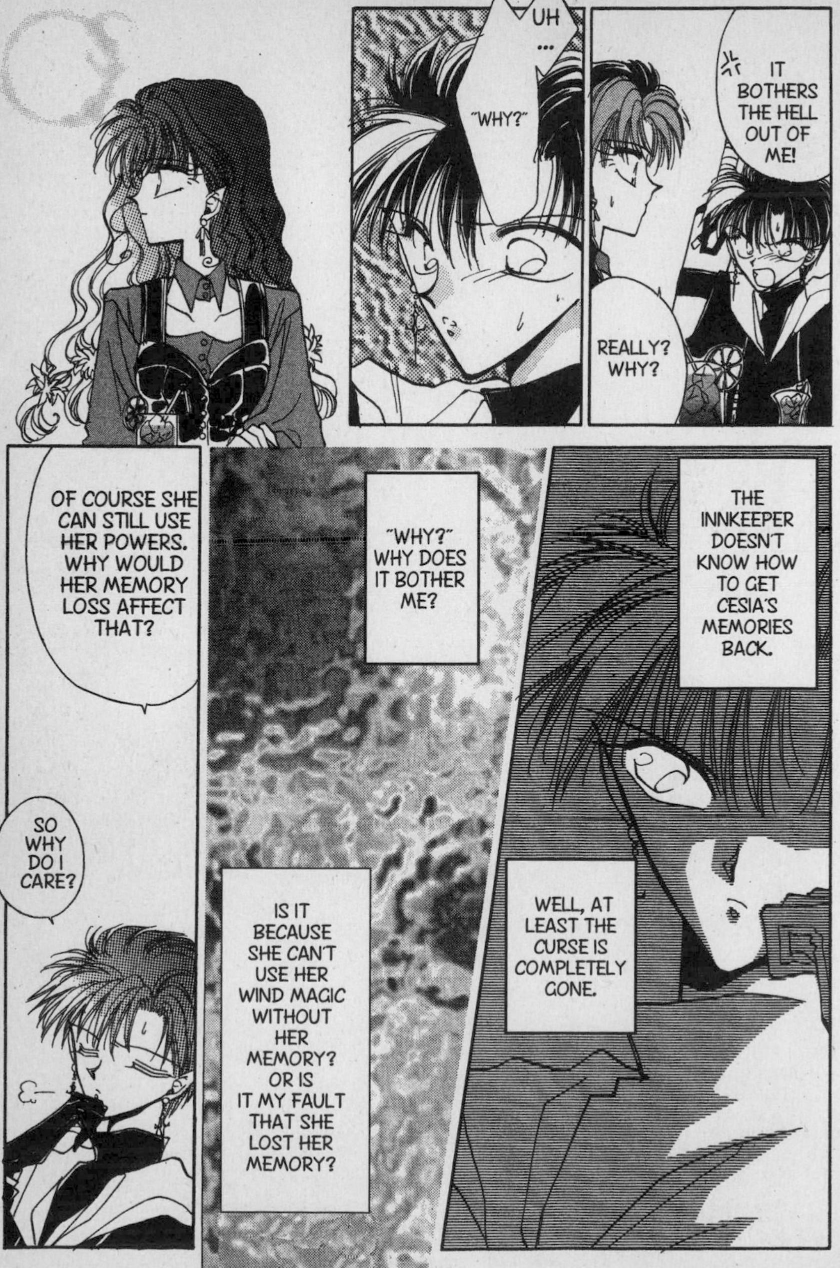
IT BOTHERS THE HELL OUT OF ME!
REALLY? WHY?
UH ...
"WHY?"
THE INNKEEPER DOESN'T KNOW HOW TO GET CESIA'S MEMORIES BACK.
WELL, AT LEAST THE CURSE IS COMPLETELY GONE.
"WHY?" WHY DOES IT BOTHER ME?
IS IT BECAUSE SHE CAN'T USE HER WIND MAGIC WITHOUT HER MEMORY? OR IS IT MY FAULT THAT SHE LOST HER MEMORY?
OF COURSE SHE CAN STILL USE HER POWERS. WHY WOULD HER MEMORY LOSS AFFECT THAT?
SO WHY DO I CARE?

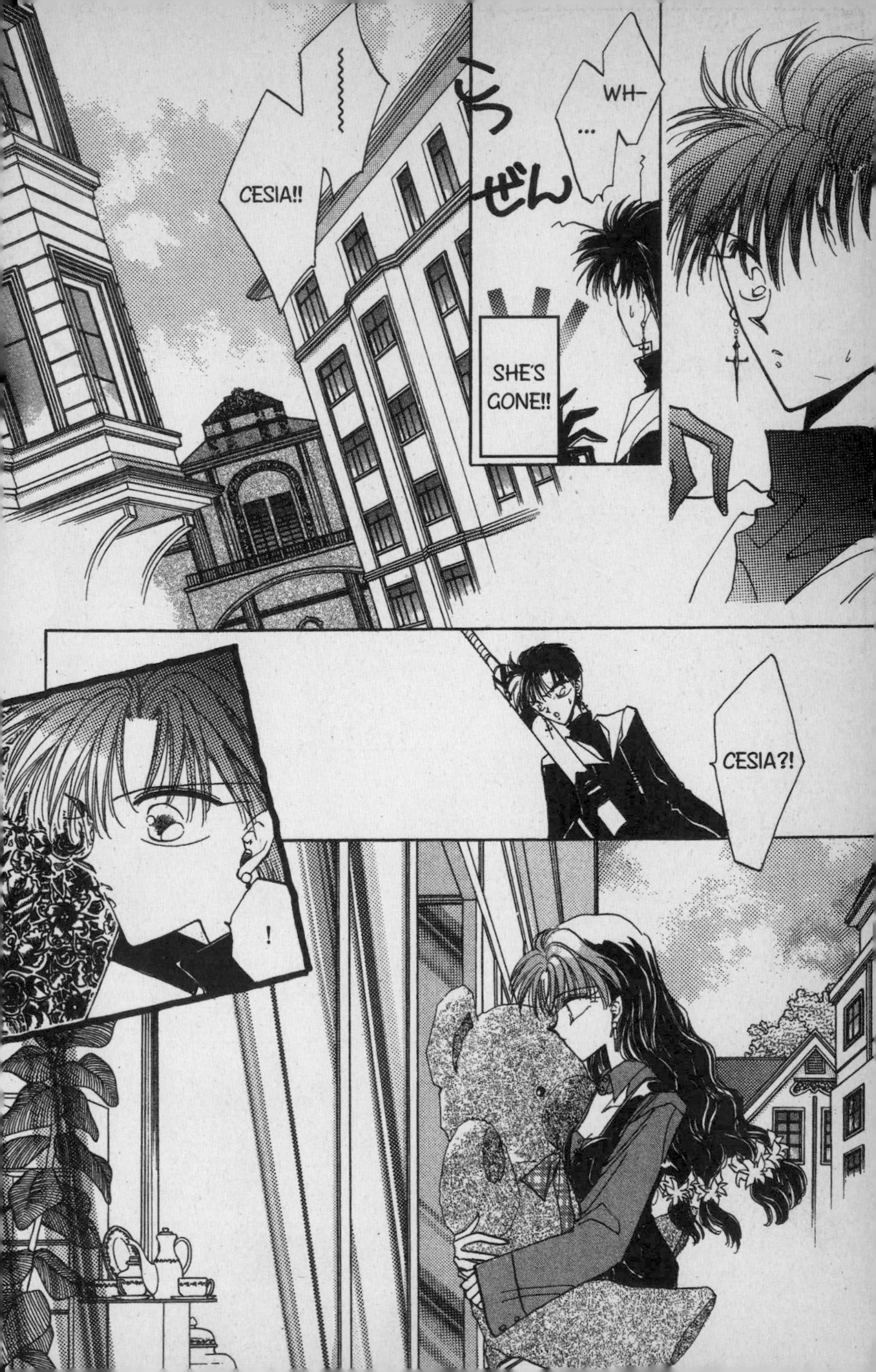
WH-
...
こつぜん
SHE'S GONE!!
CESIA!!
CESIA?!
!

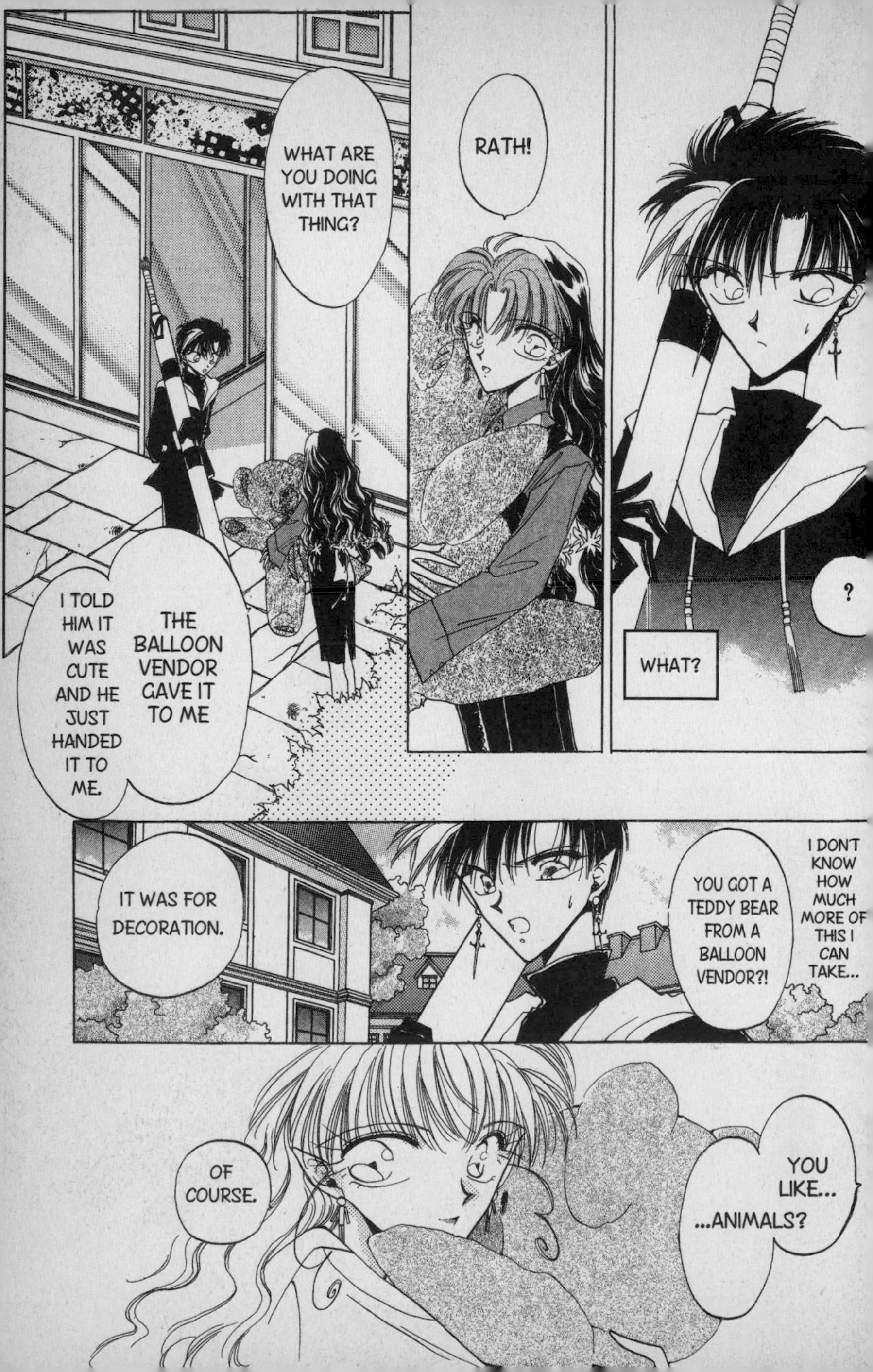
?
WHAT?
RATH!
WHAT ARE YOU DOING WITH THAT THING?
THE BALLOON VENDOR GAVE IT TO ME
I TOLD HIM IT WAS CUTE AND HE JUST HANDED IT TO ME.
I DON'T KNOW HOW MUCH MORE OF THIS I CAN TAKE...
YOU GOT A TEDDY BEAR FROM A BALLOON VENDOR?!
IT WAS FOR DECORATION.
YOU LIKE... ...ANIMALS?
OF COURSE.

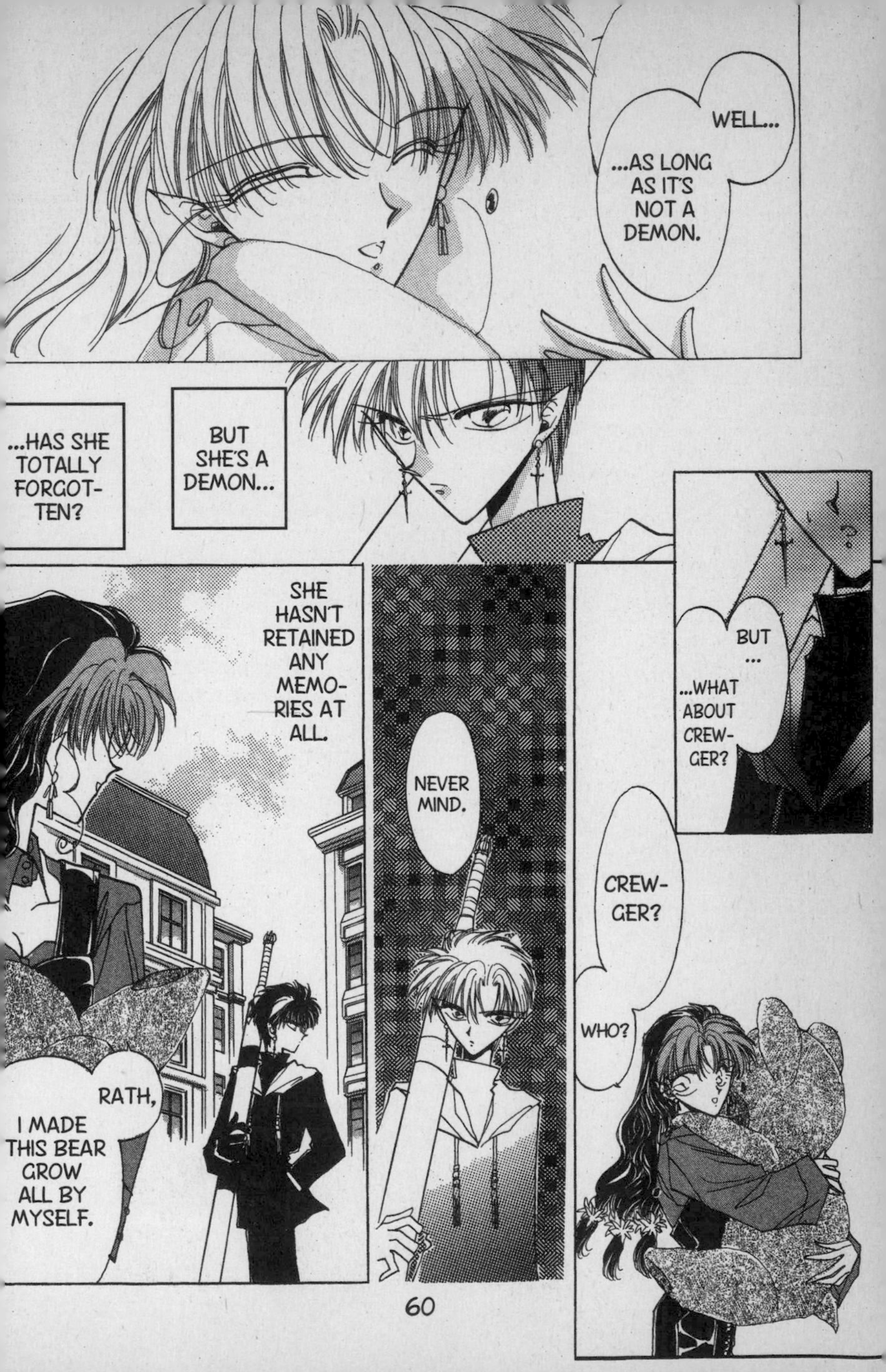
WELL...
...AS LONG AS IT'S NOT A DEMON.
BUT SHE'S A DEMON...
...HAS SHE TOTALLY FORGOT-TEN?
BUT ... ...WHAT ABOUT CREW-GER?
CREW-GER?
WHO?
NEVER MIND.
SHE HASN'T RETAINED ANY MEMO-RIES AT ALL.
RATH, I MADE THIS BEAR GROW ALL BY MYSELF.

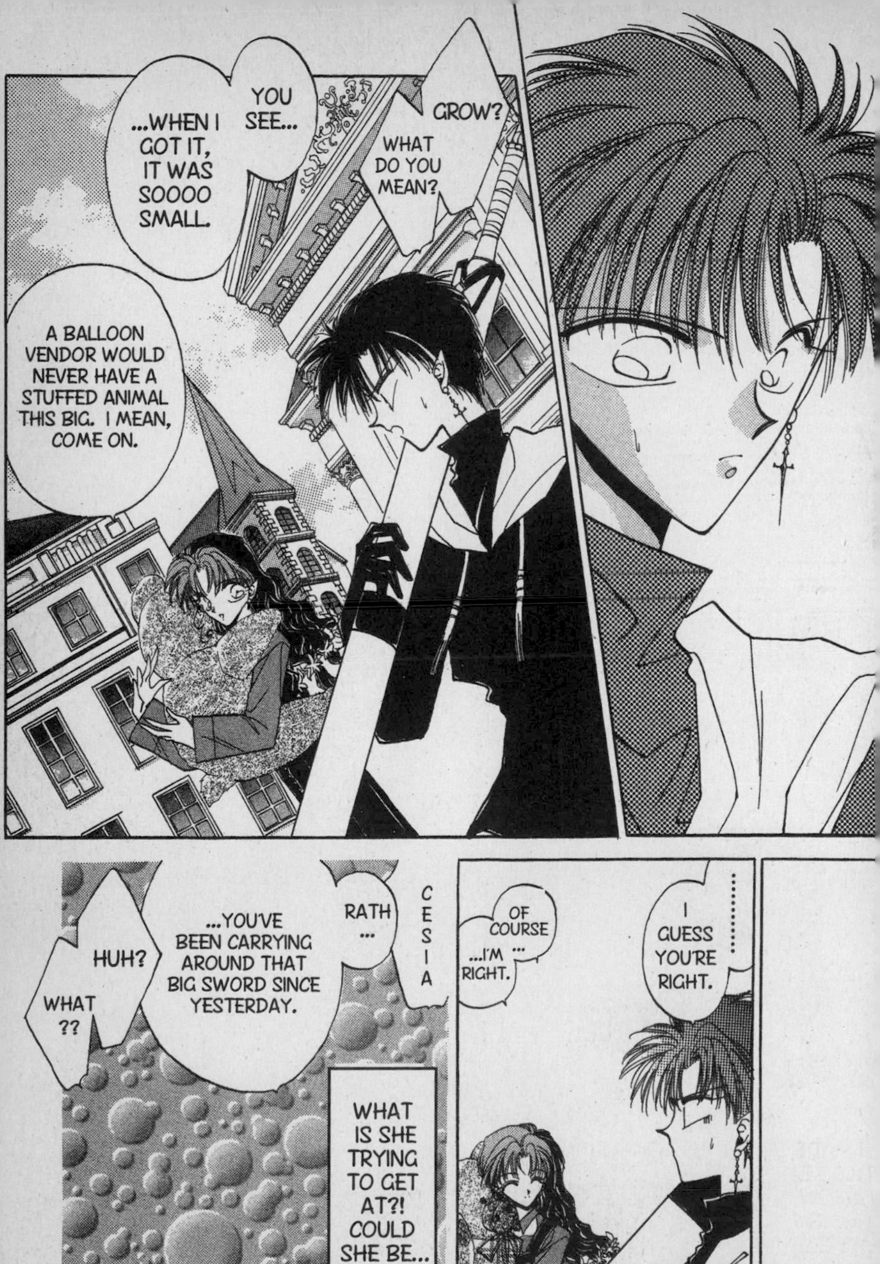
GROW? WHAT DO YOU MEAN?
YOU SEE...
...WHEN I GOT IT, IT WAS SOOOO SMALL.
A BALLOON VENDOR WOULD NEVER HAVE A STUFFED ANIMAL THIS BIG. I MEAN, COME ON.
...... I GUESS YOU'RE RIGHT.
OF COURSE... ...I'M RIGHT.
CESIA
RATH...
...YOU'VE BEEN CARRYING AROUND THAT BIG SWORD SINCE YESTERDAY.
HUH? WHAT??
WHAT IS SHE TRYING TO GET AT?! COULD SHE BE...

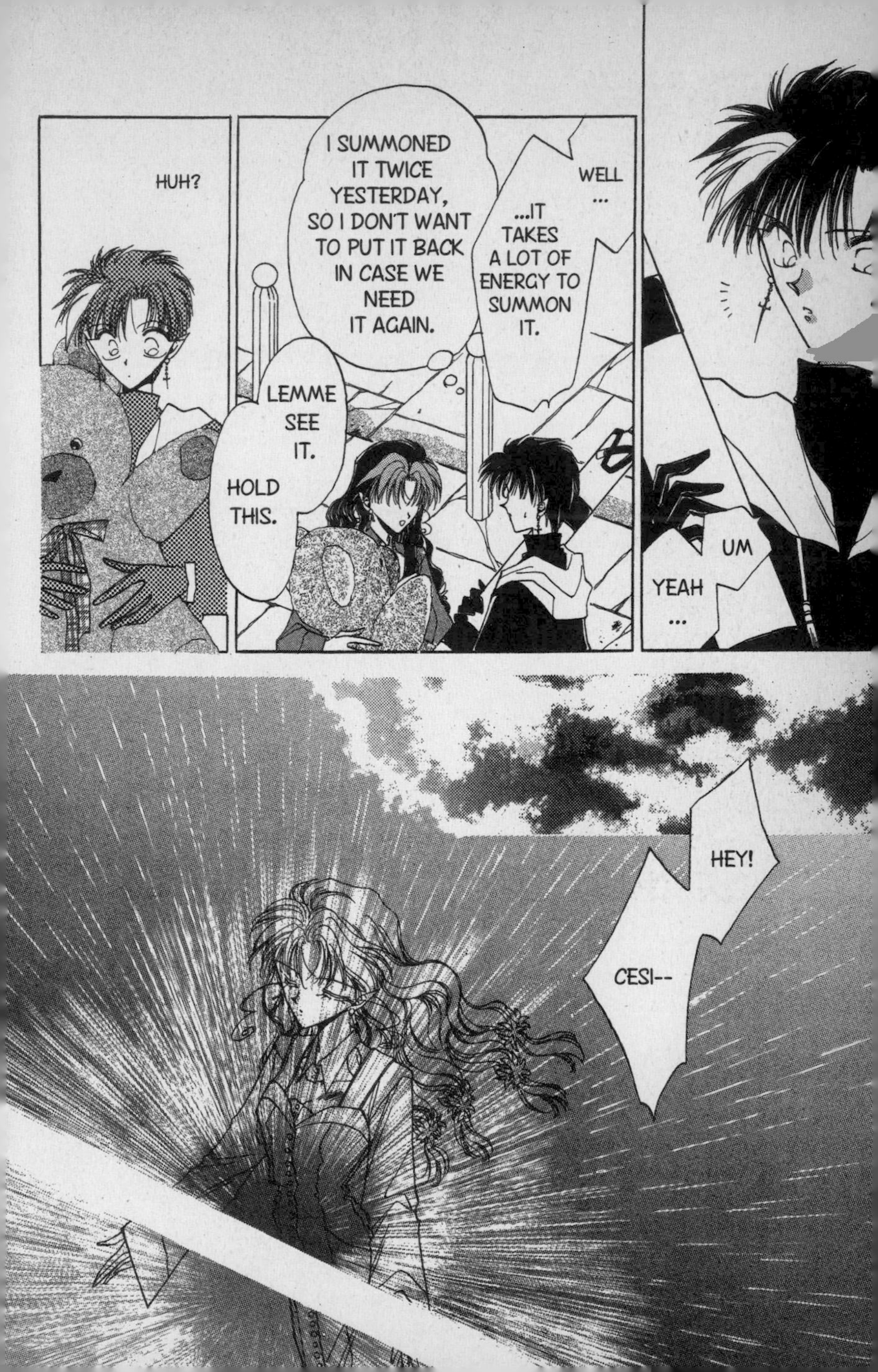
UM
YEAH ...
WELL ...
...IT TAKES A LOT OF ENERGY TO SUMMON IT.
I SUMMONED IT TWICE YESTERDAY, SO I DON'T WANT TO PUT IT BACK IN CASE WE NEED IT AGAIN.
LEMME SEE IT.
HOLD THIS.
HUH?
HEY!
CESI--

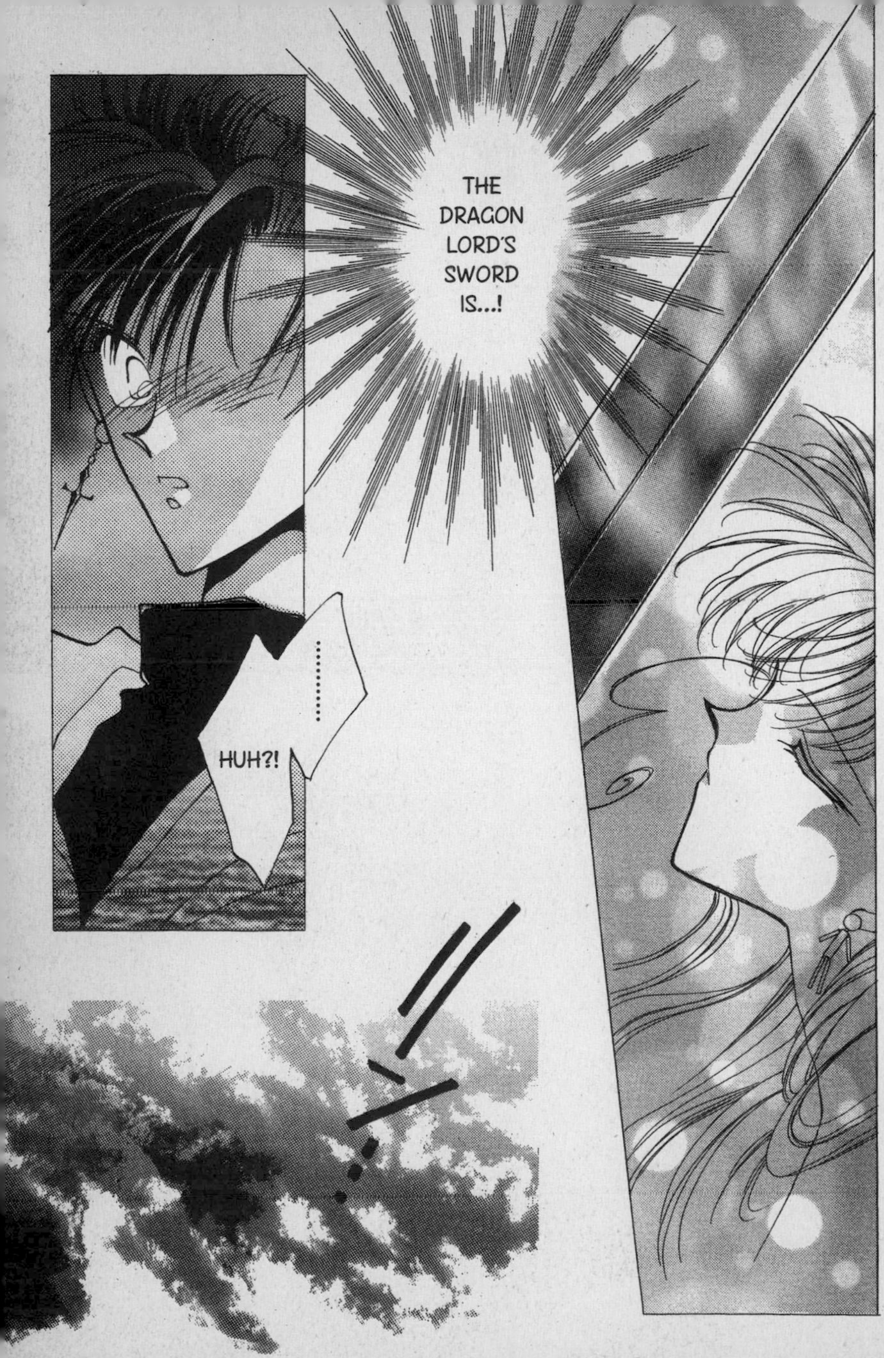
THE DRAGON LORD'S SWORD IS...!
......
HUH?!

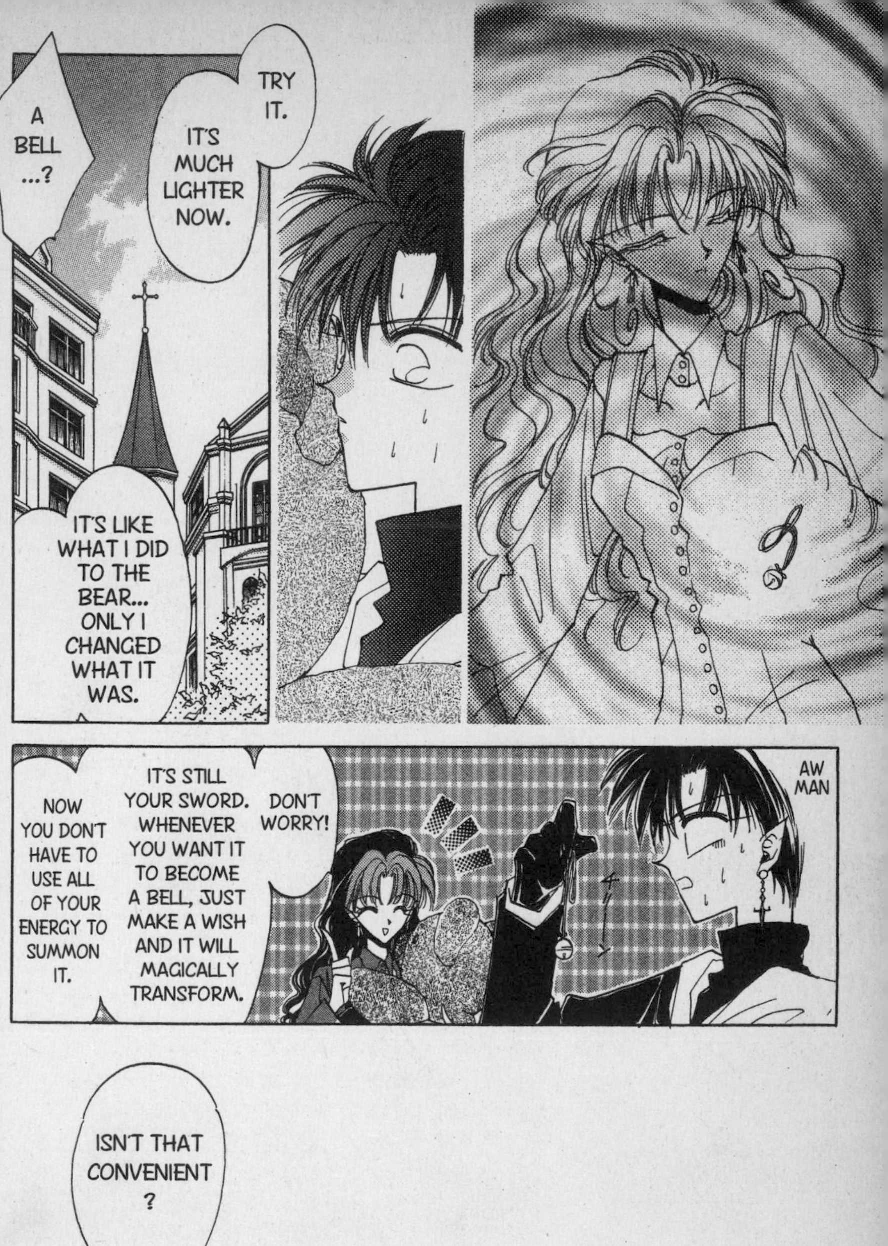
TRY IT.
IT'S MUCH LIGHTER NOW.
A BELL ...?
IT'S LIKE WHAT I DID TO THE BEAR... ONLY I CHANGED WHAT IT WAS.
AW MAN
DON'T WORRY!
IT'S STILL YOUR SWORD. WHENEVER YOU WANT IT TO BECOME A BELL, JUST MAKE A WISH AND IT WILL MAGICALLY TRANSFORM.
NOW YOU DON'T HAVE TO USE ALL OF YOUR ENERGY TO SUMMON IT.
ISN'T THAT CONVENIENT ?

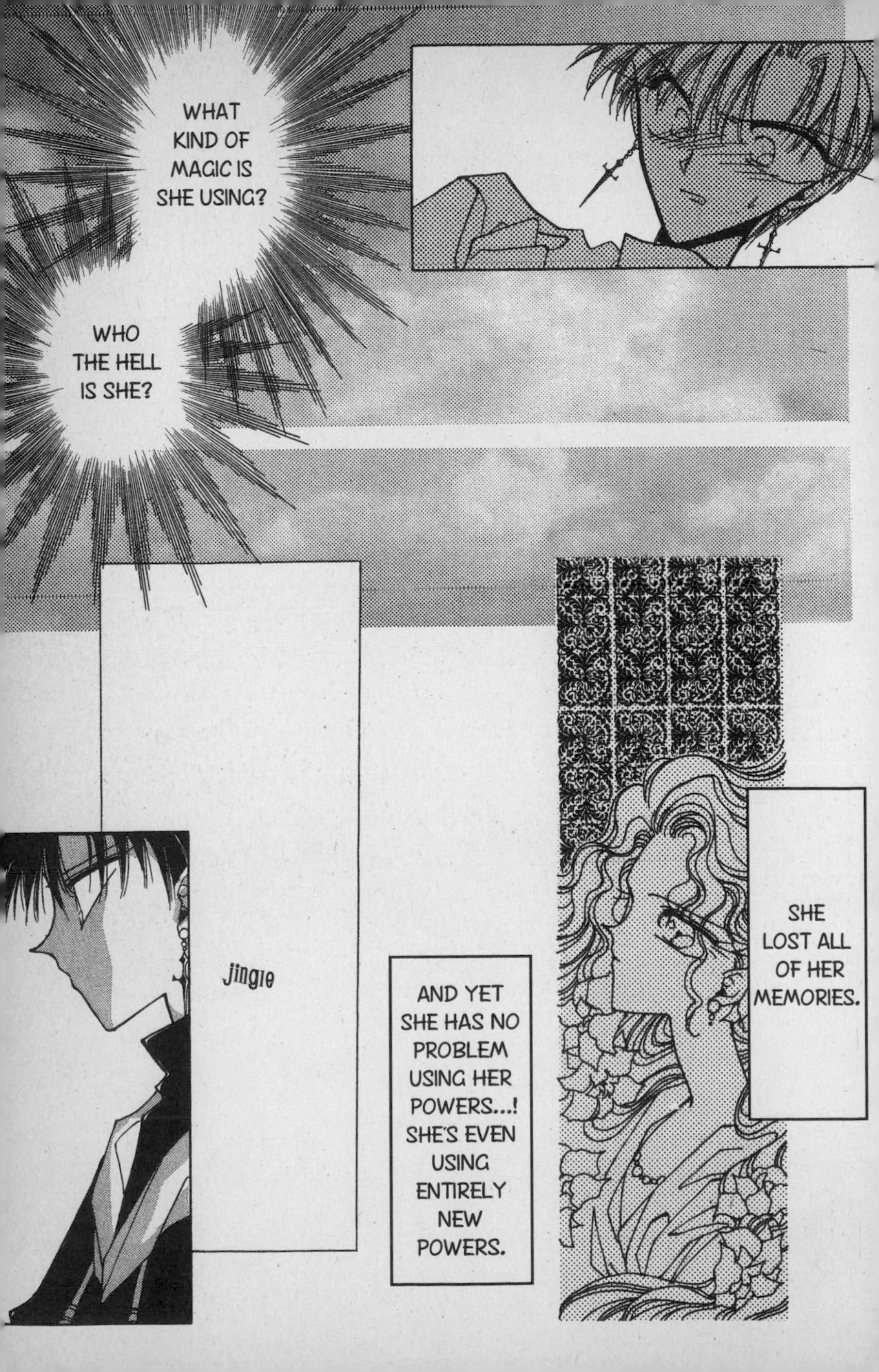
WHAT KIND OF MAGIC IS SHE USING?
WHO THE HELL IS SHE?
SHE LOST ALL OF HER MEMORIES.
AND YET SHE HAS NO PROBLEM USING HER POWERS...! SHE'S EVEN USING ENTIRELY NEW POWERS.
jingle

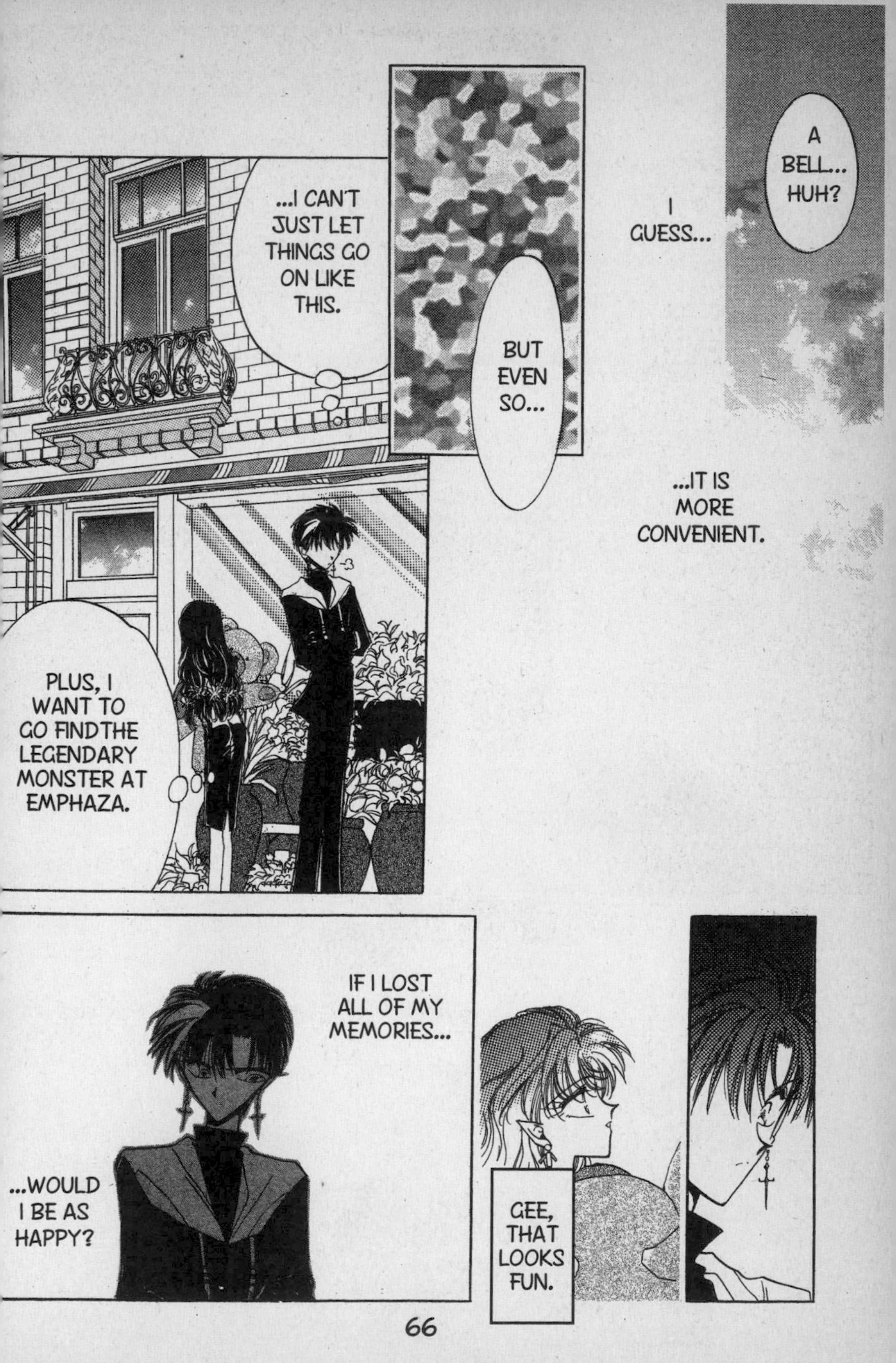
A BELL... HUH?
I GUESS...
...IT IS MORE CONVENIENT.
BUT EVEN SO...
...I CAN'T JUST LET THINGS GO ON LIKE THIS.
PLUS, I WANT TO GO FIND THE LEGENDARY MONSTER AT EMPHAZA.
GEE, THAT LOOKS FUN.
IF I LOST ALL OF MY MEMORIES...
...WOULD I BE AS HAPPY?

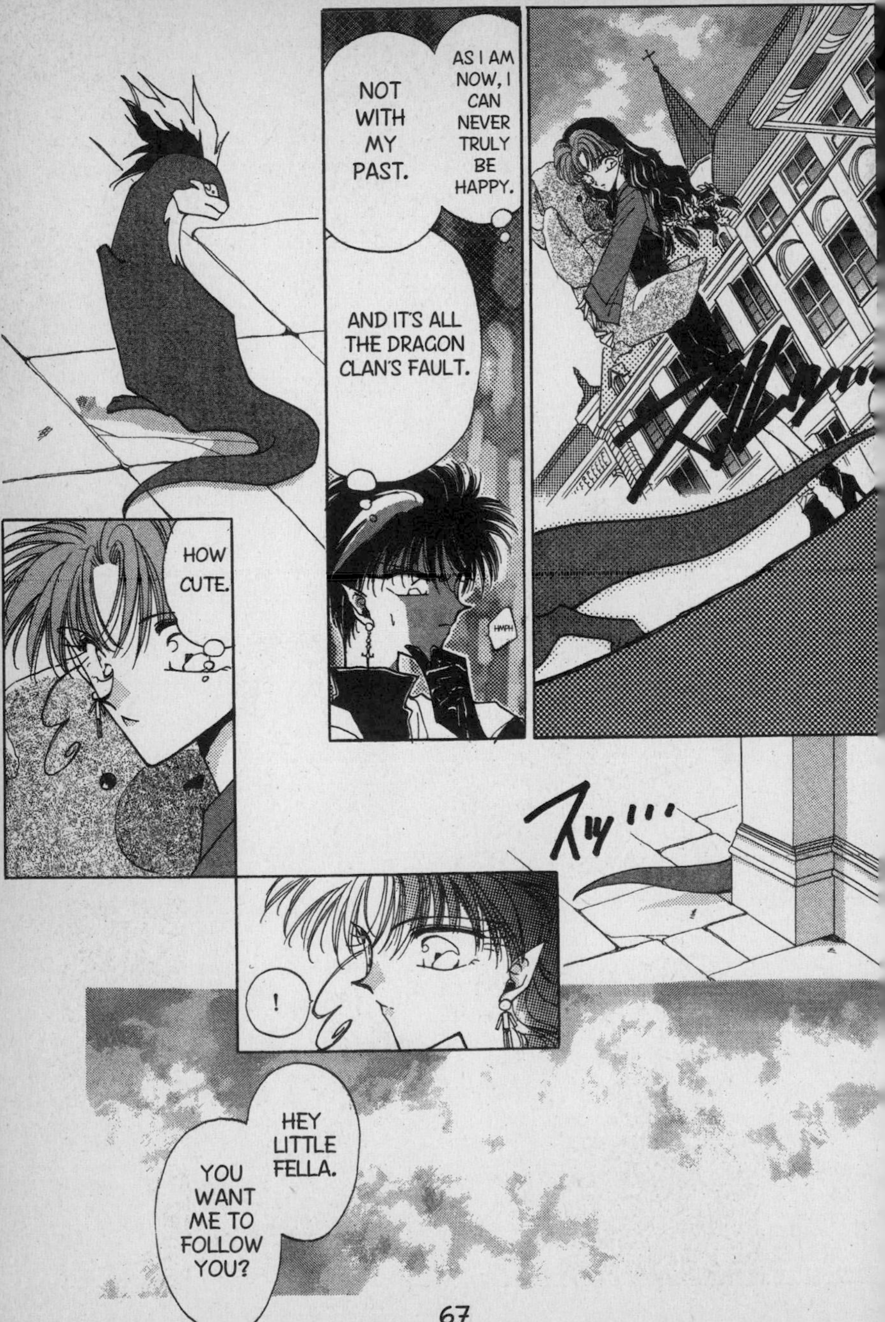
AS I AM NOW, I CAN NEVER TRULY BE HAPPY.
NOT WITH MY PAST.
AND IT'S ALL THE DRAGON CLAN'S FAULT.
HMPH
HOW CUTE.
スッ…
!
HEY LITTLE FELLA.
YOU WANT ME TO FOLLOW YOU?

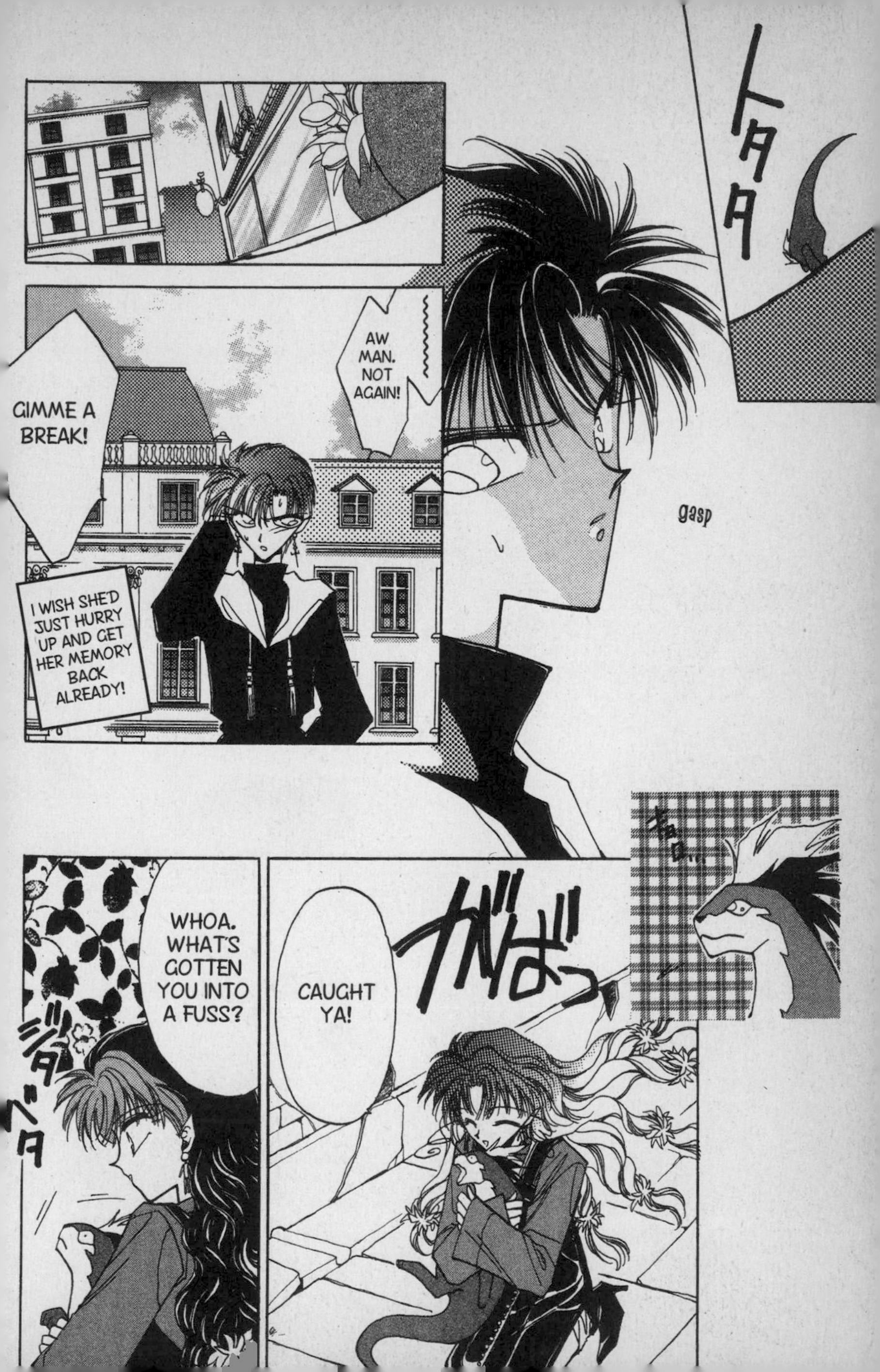

トタタ
gasp
AW MAN. NOT AGAIN!
GIMME A BREAK!
I WISH SHE'D JUST HURRY UP AND GET HER MEMORY BACK ALREADY!
ギロ…
がばっ
CAUGHT YA!
WHOA. WHAT'S GOTTEN YOU INTO A FUSS?
ジタベタ

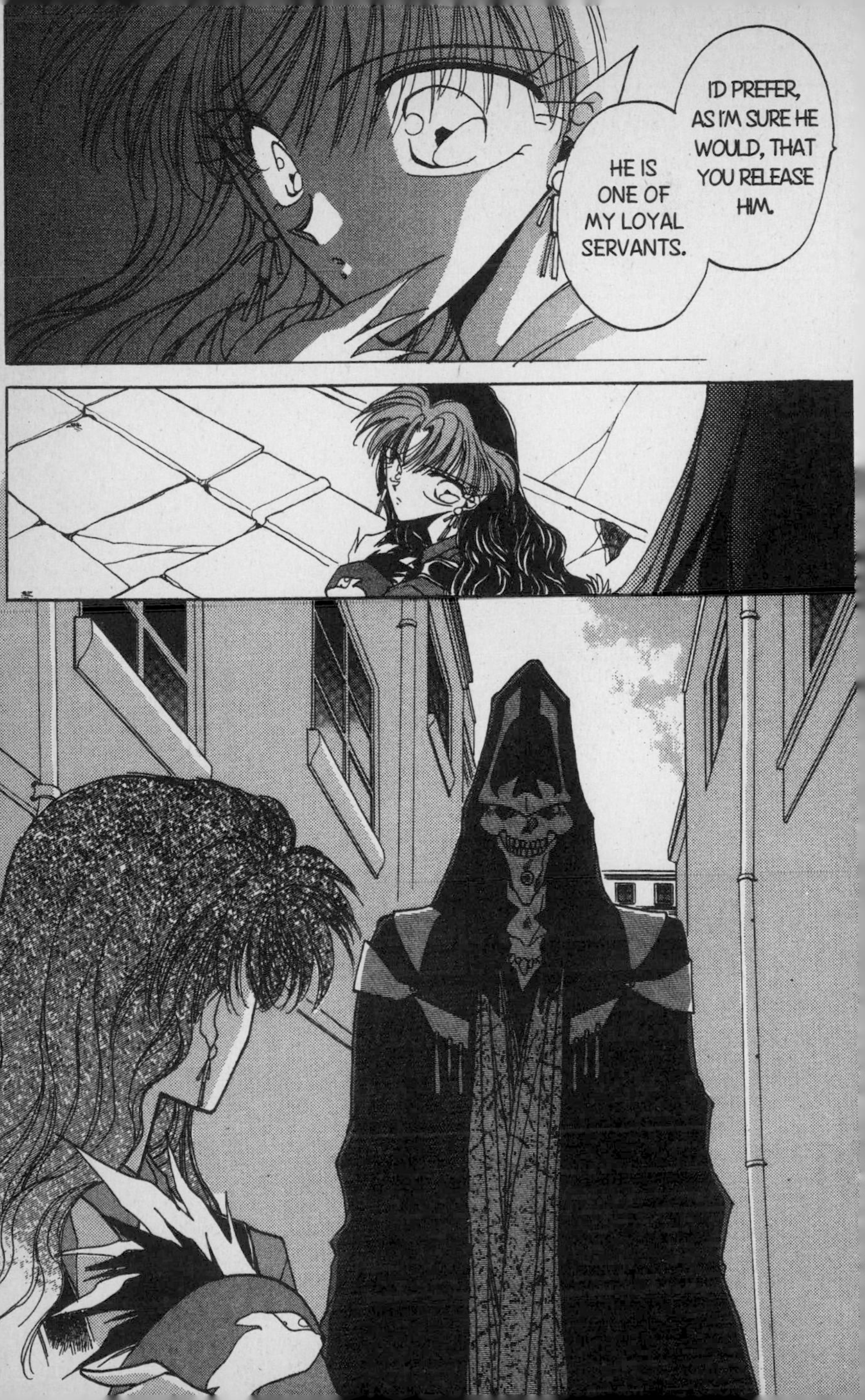
I'D PREFER, AS I'M SURE HE WOULD, THAT YOU RELEASE HIM.
HE IS ONE OF MY LOYAL SERVANTS.

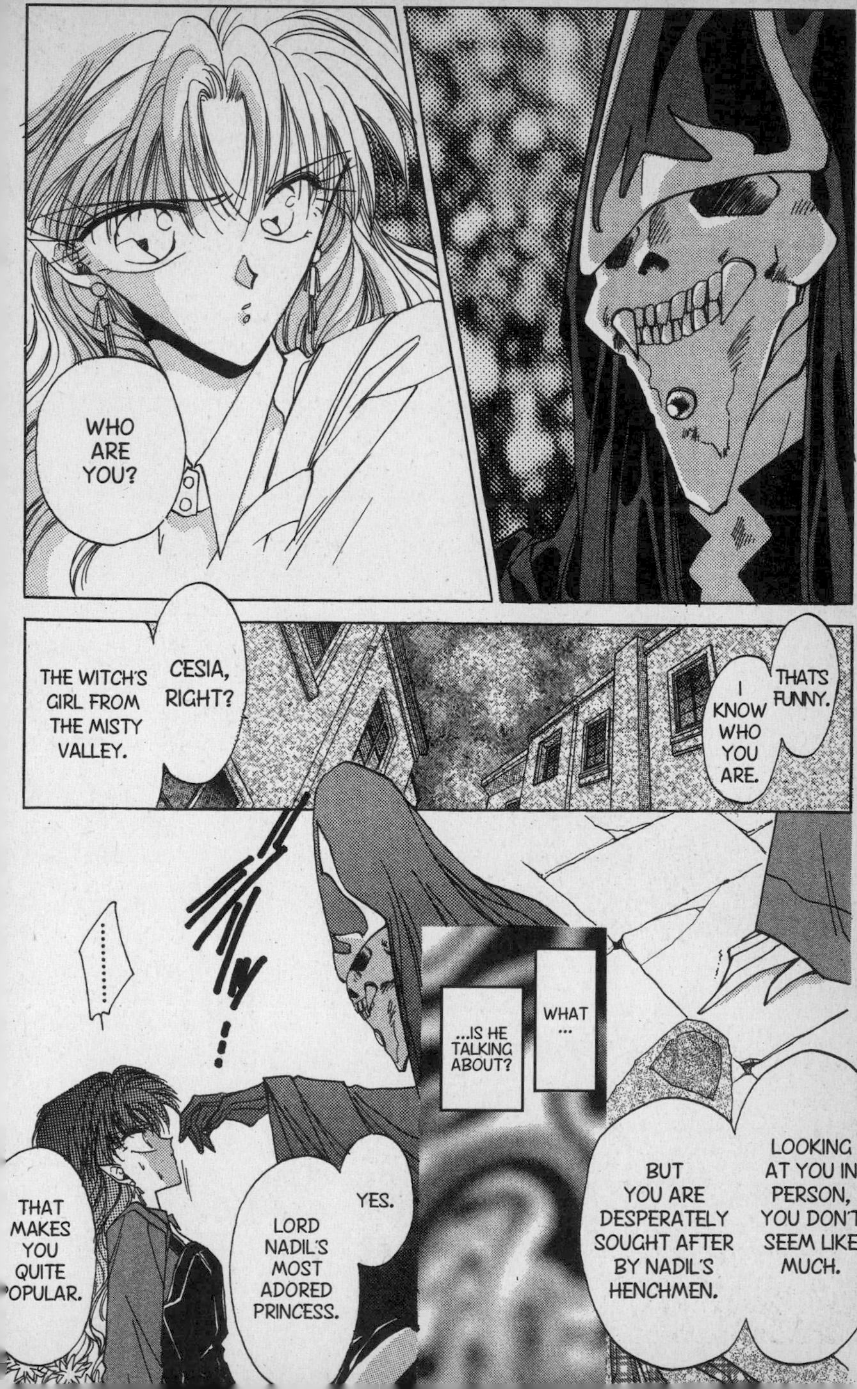
WHO ARE YOU?
THATS FUNNY.
I KNOW WHO YOU ARE.
CESIA, RIGHT?
THE WITCH'S GIRL FROM THE MISTY VALLEY.
LOOKING AT YOU IN PERSON, YOU DON'T SEEM LIKE MUCH.
BUT YOU ARE DESPERATELY SOUGHT AFTER BY NADIL'S HENCHMEN.
WHAT ...
...IS HE TALKING ABOUT?
......
YES.
LORD NADIL'S MOST ADORED PRINCESS.
THAT MAKES YOU QUITE OPULAR.

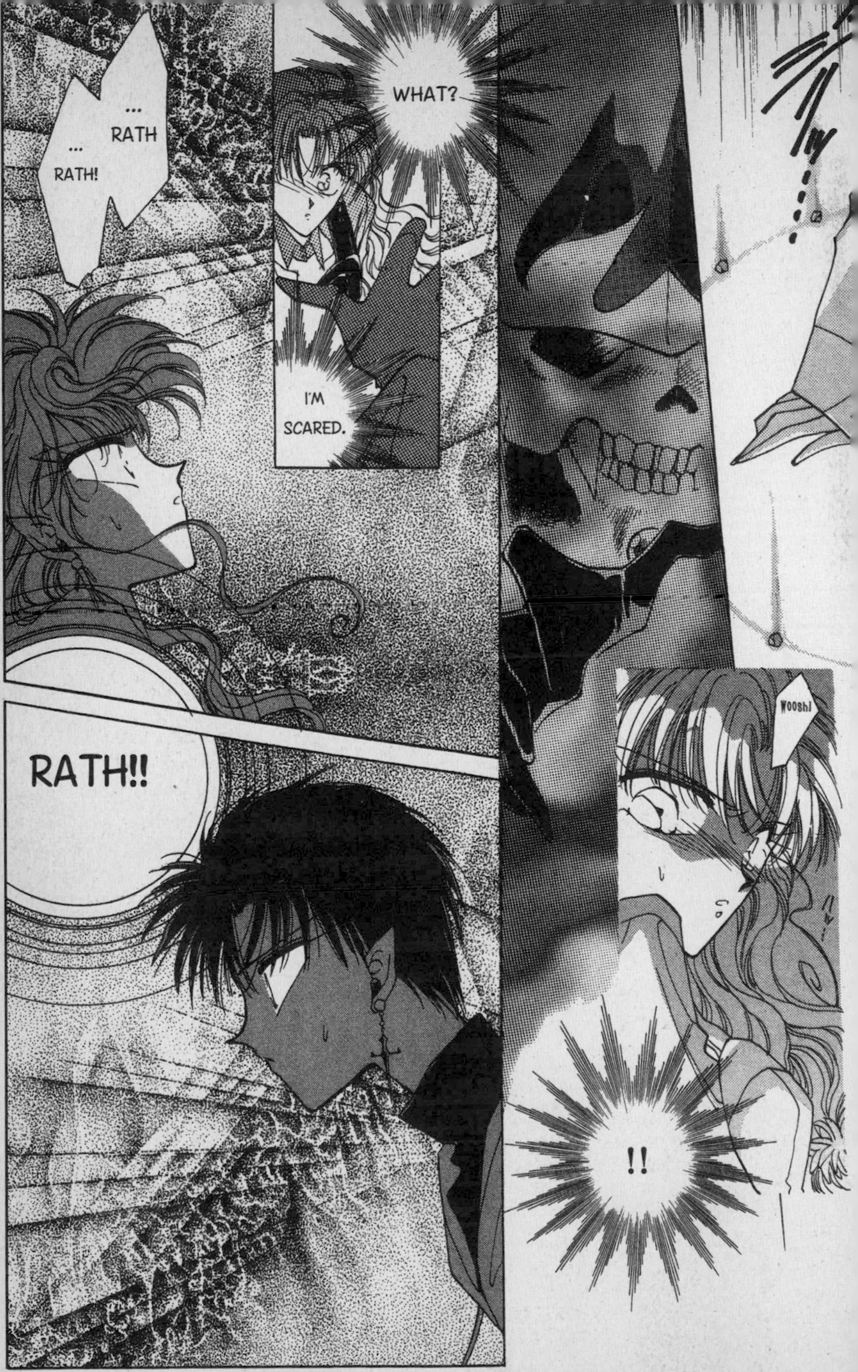
Woosh!
!!
WHAT?
I'M SCARED.
... RATH
... RATH!
RATH!!

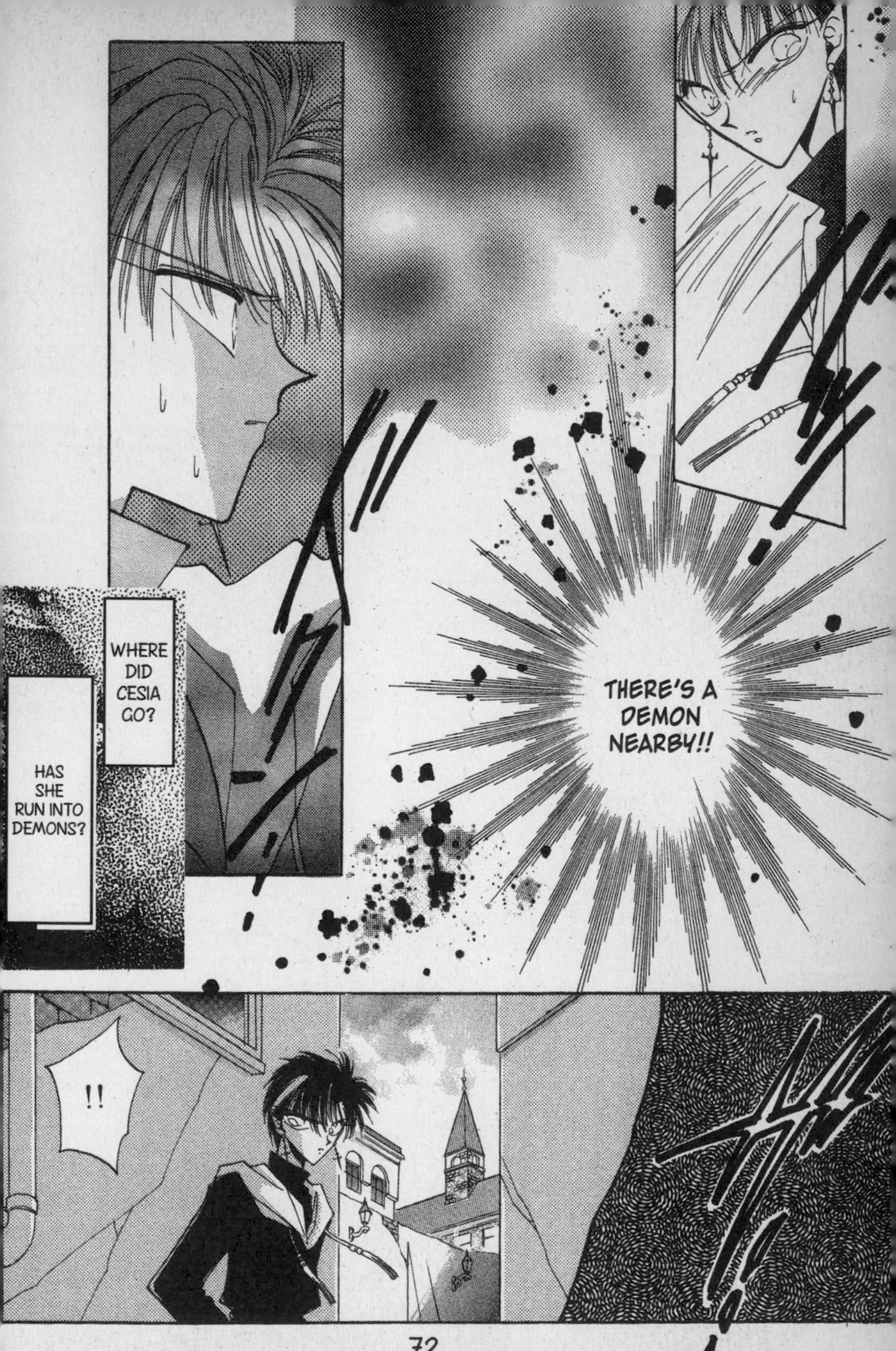
THERE'S A DEMON NEARBY!!
WHERE DID CESIA GO?
HAS SHE RUN INTO DEMONS?
!!

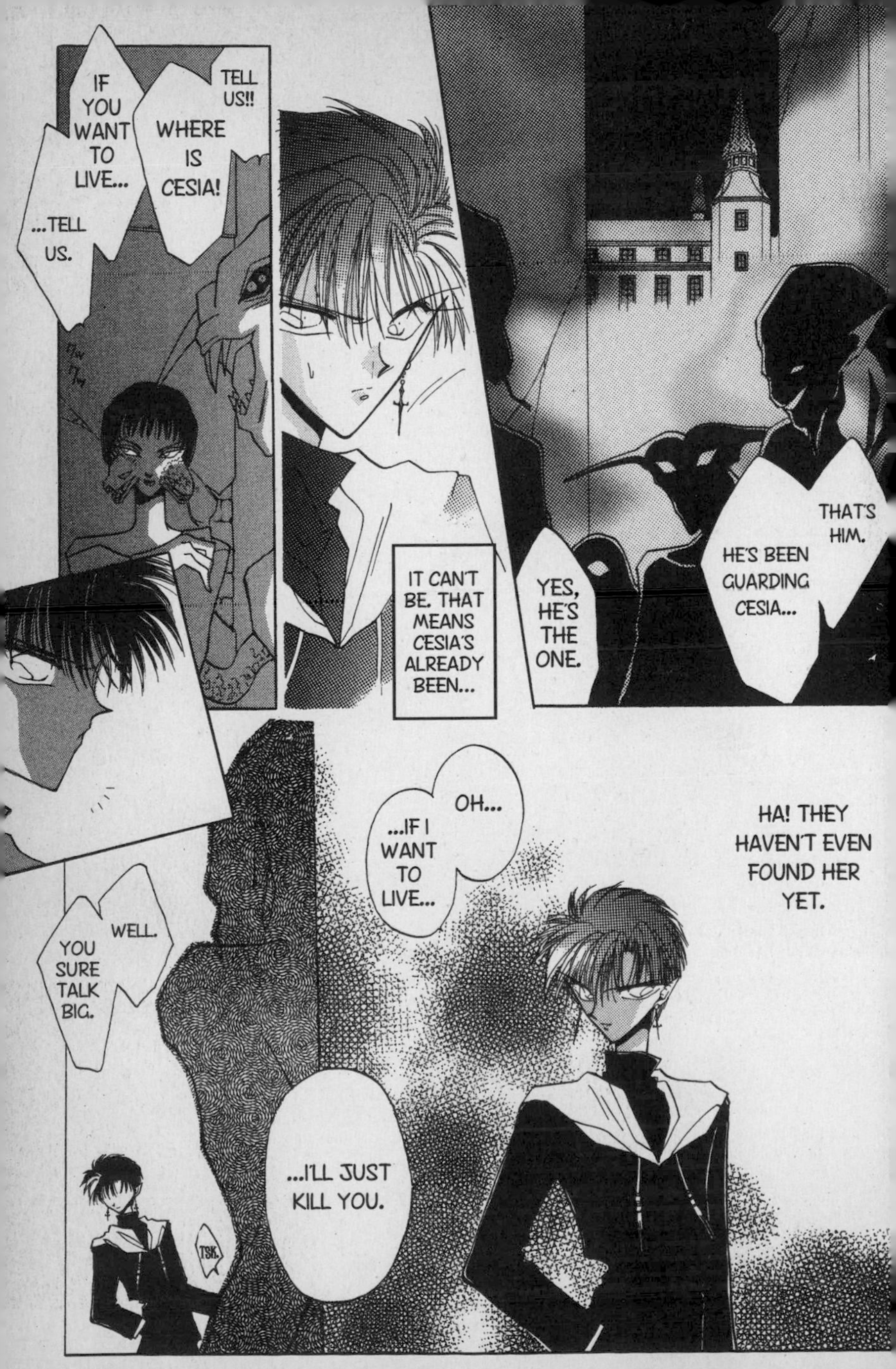
THAT'S HIM.
HE'S BEEN GUARDING CESIA...
YES, HE'S THE ONE.
IT CAN'T BE. THAT MEANS CESIA'S ALREADY BEEN...
TELL US!!
WHERE IS CESIA!
IF YOU WANT TO LIVE...
...TELL US.
HA! THEY HAVEN'T EVEN FOUND HER YET.
OH...
...IF I WANT TO LIVE...
...I'LL JUST KILL YOU.
WELL.
YOU SURE TALK BIG.
TSK.

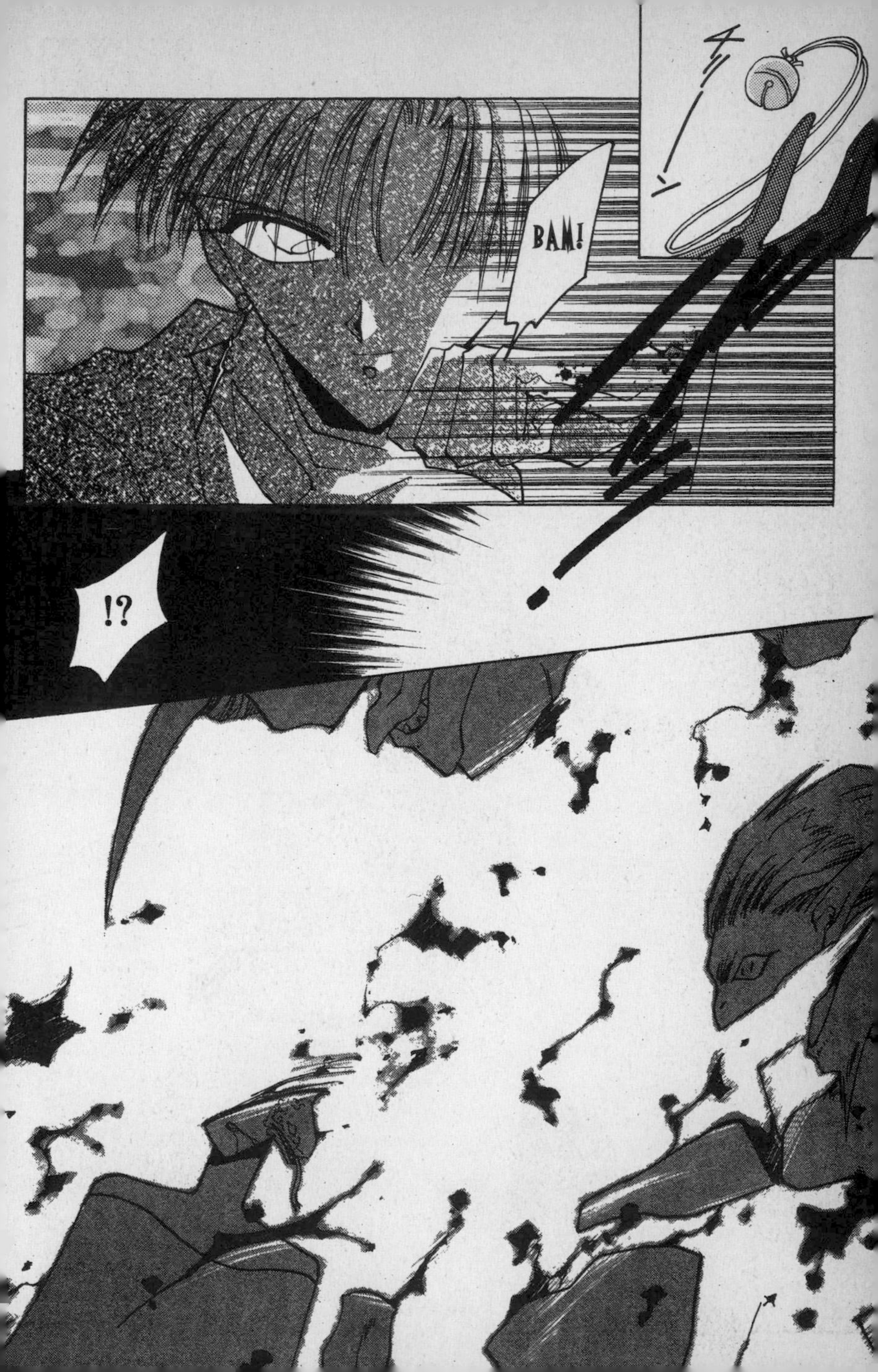
チリーン
BAM!
!?

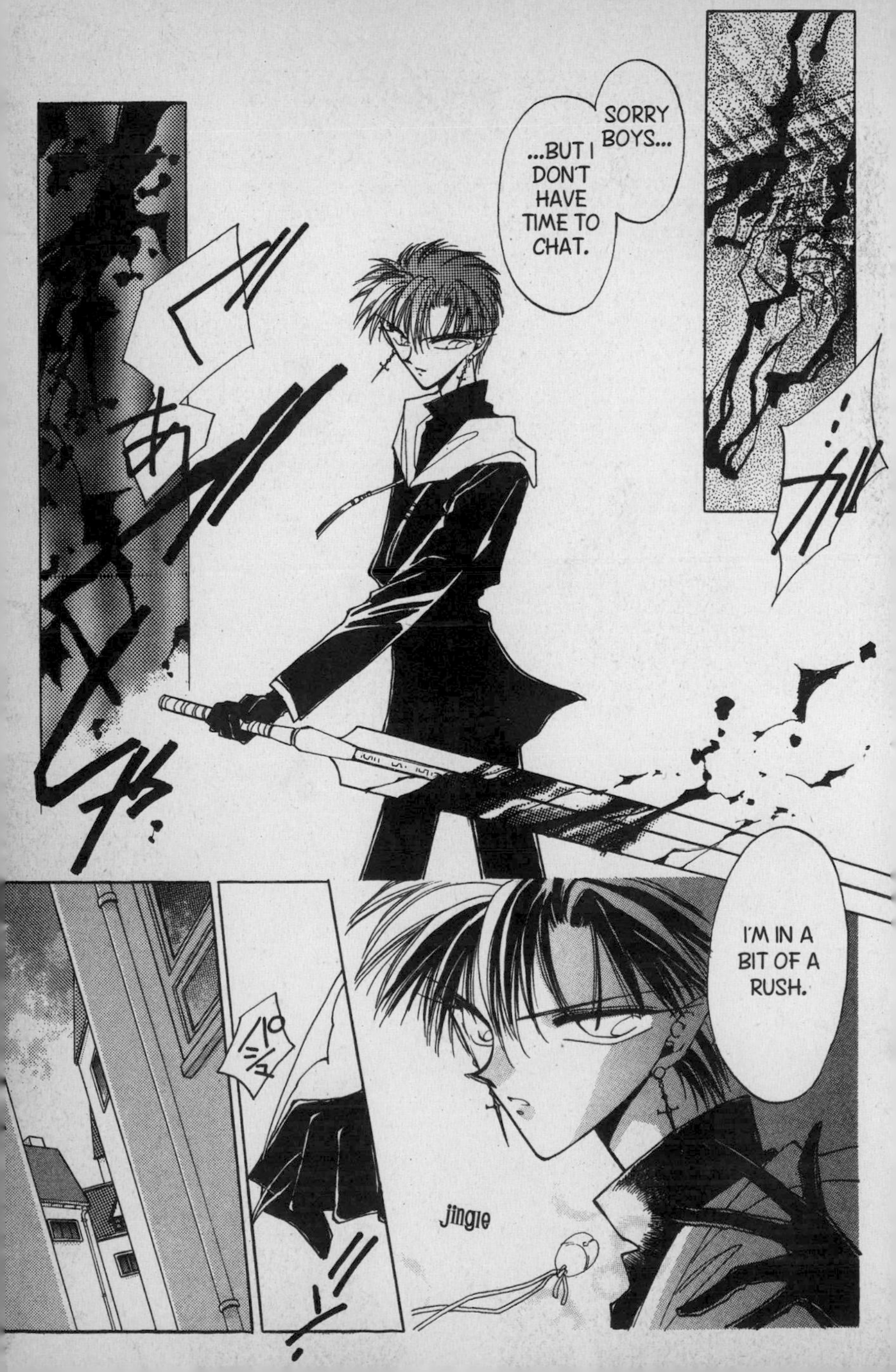
SORRY BOYS...
...BUT I DON'T HAVE TIME TO CHAT.
I'M IN A BIT OF A RUSH.
jingle

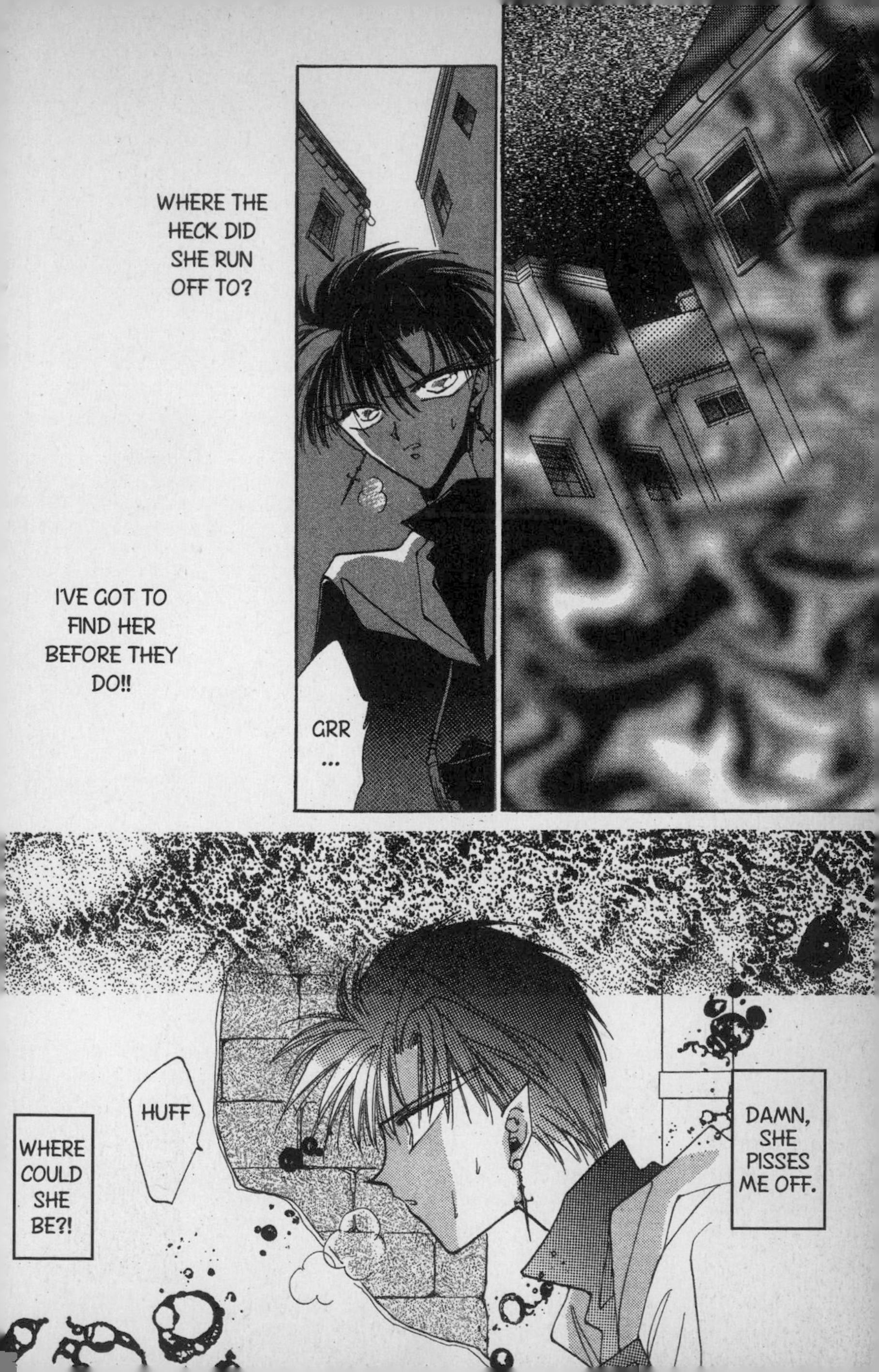
WHERE THE HECK DID SHE RUN OFF TO?
I'VE GOT TO FIND HER BEFORE THEY DO!!
GRR ...
DAMN, SHE PISSES ME OFF.
HUFF
WHERE COULD SHE BE?!

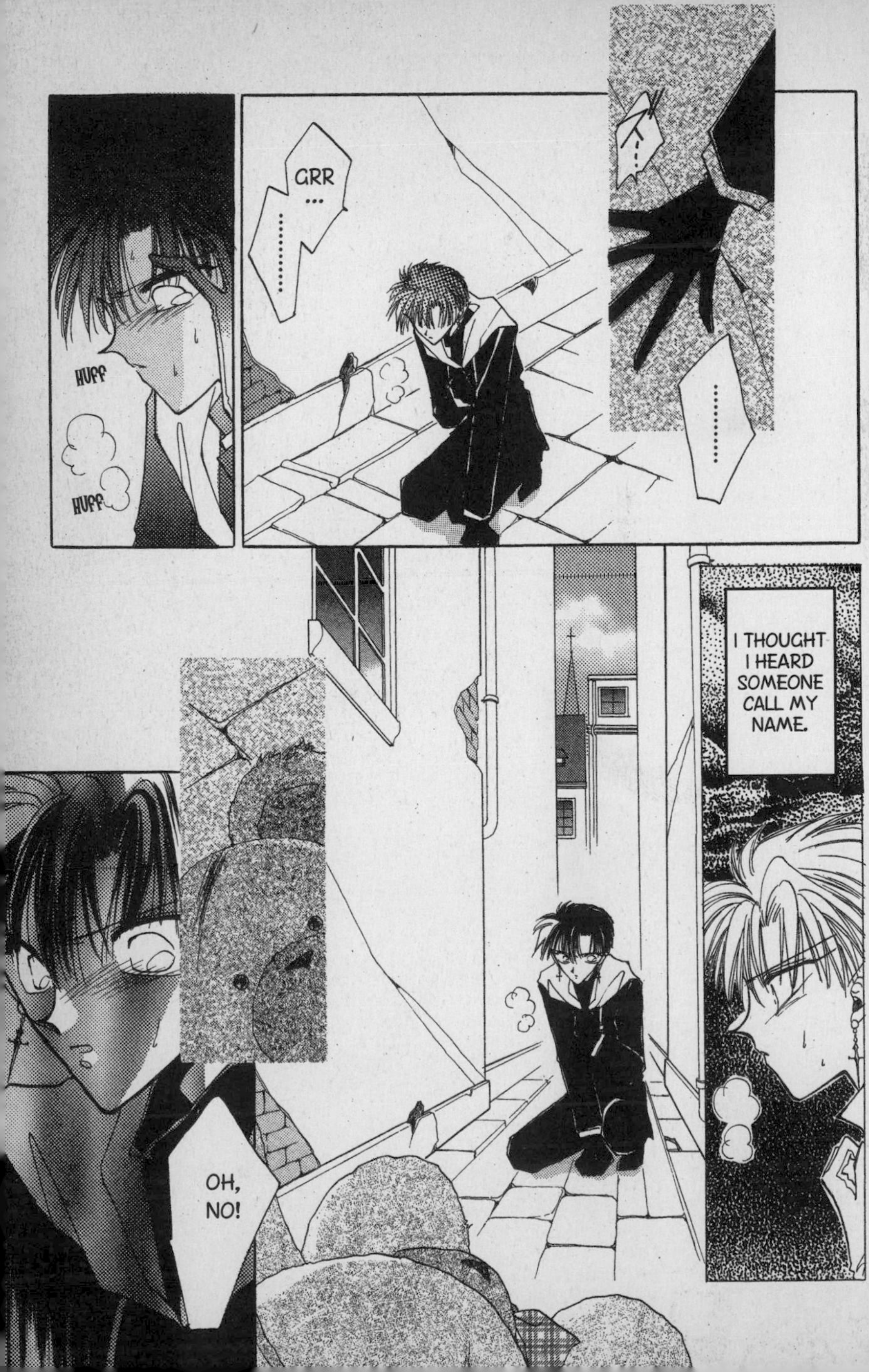
GRR ...
HUFF
HUFF
I THOUGHT I HEARD SOMEONE CALL MY NAME.
OH, NO!

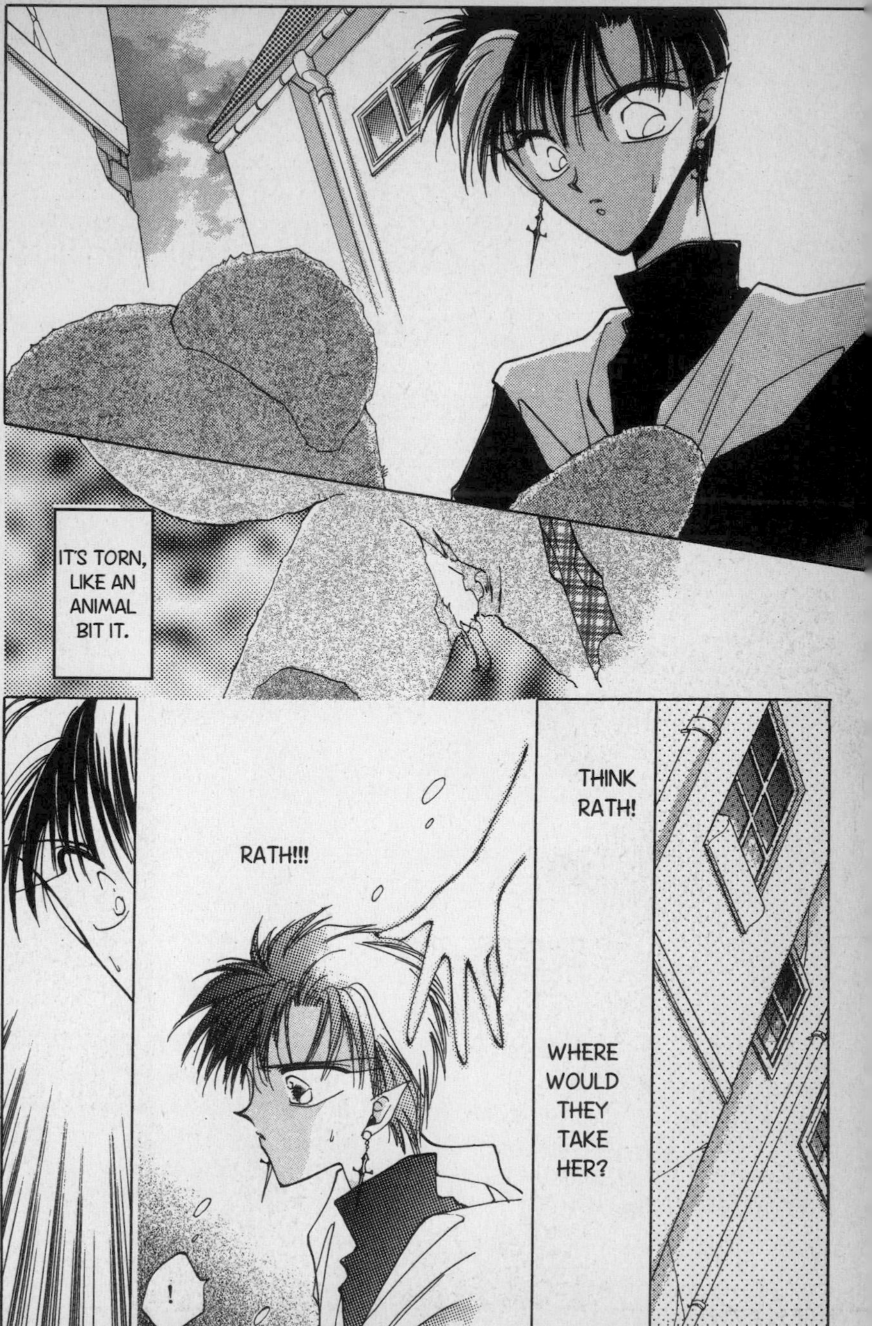
IT'S TORN, LIKE AN ANIMAL BIT IT.
THINK RATH!
WHERE WOULD THEY TAKE HER?
RATH!!!
!

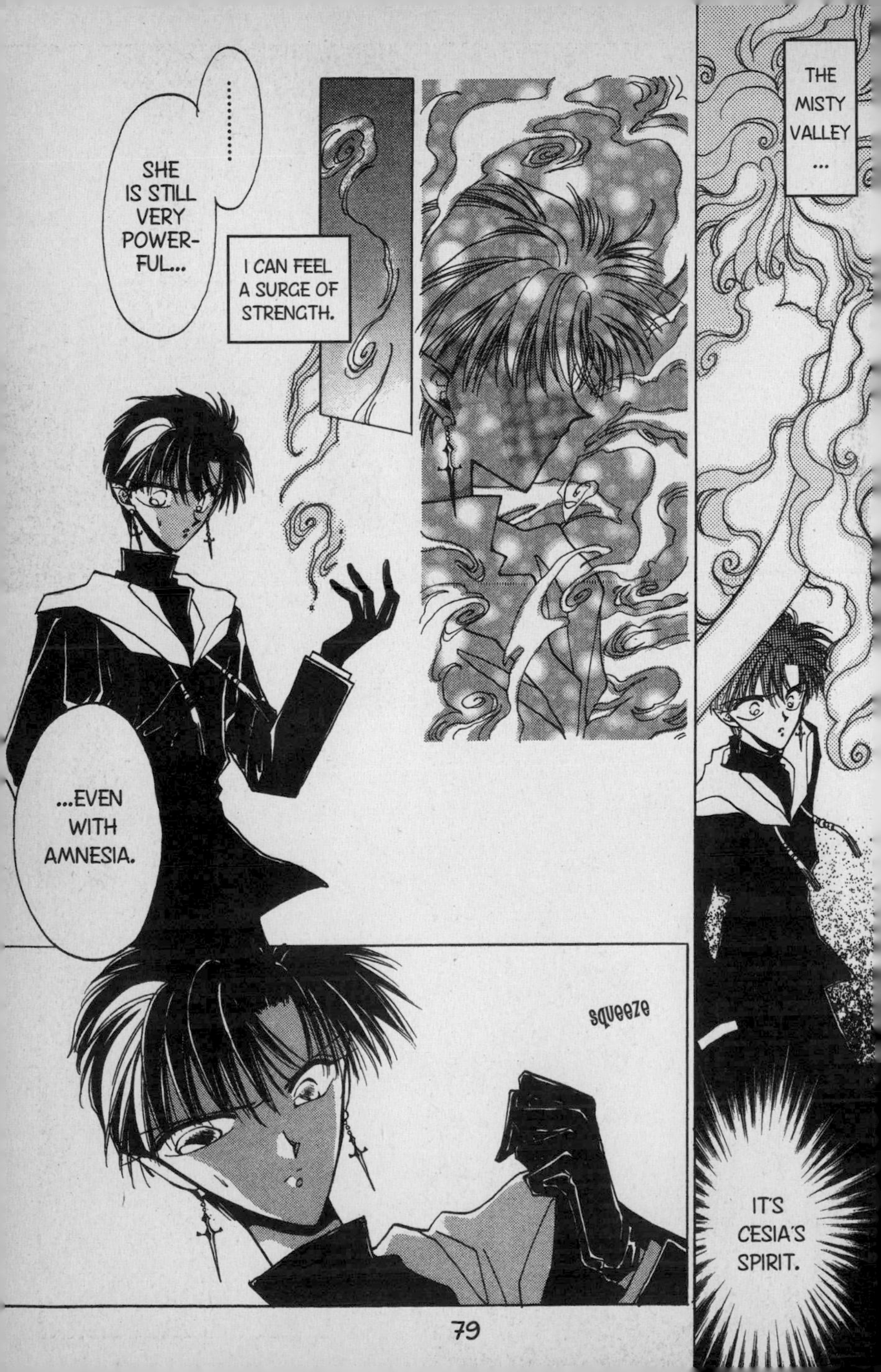
THE MISTY VALLEY ...
IT'S CESIA'S SPIRIT.
......
SHE IS STILL VERY POWER-FUL...
I CAN FEEL A SURGE OF STRENGTH.
...EVEN WITH AMNESIA.
squeeze

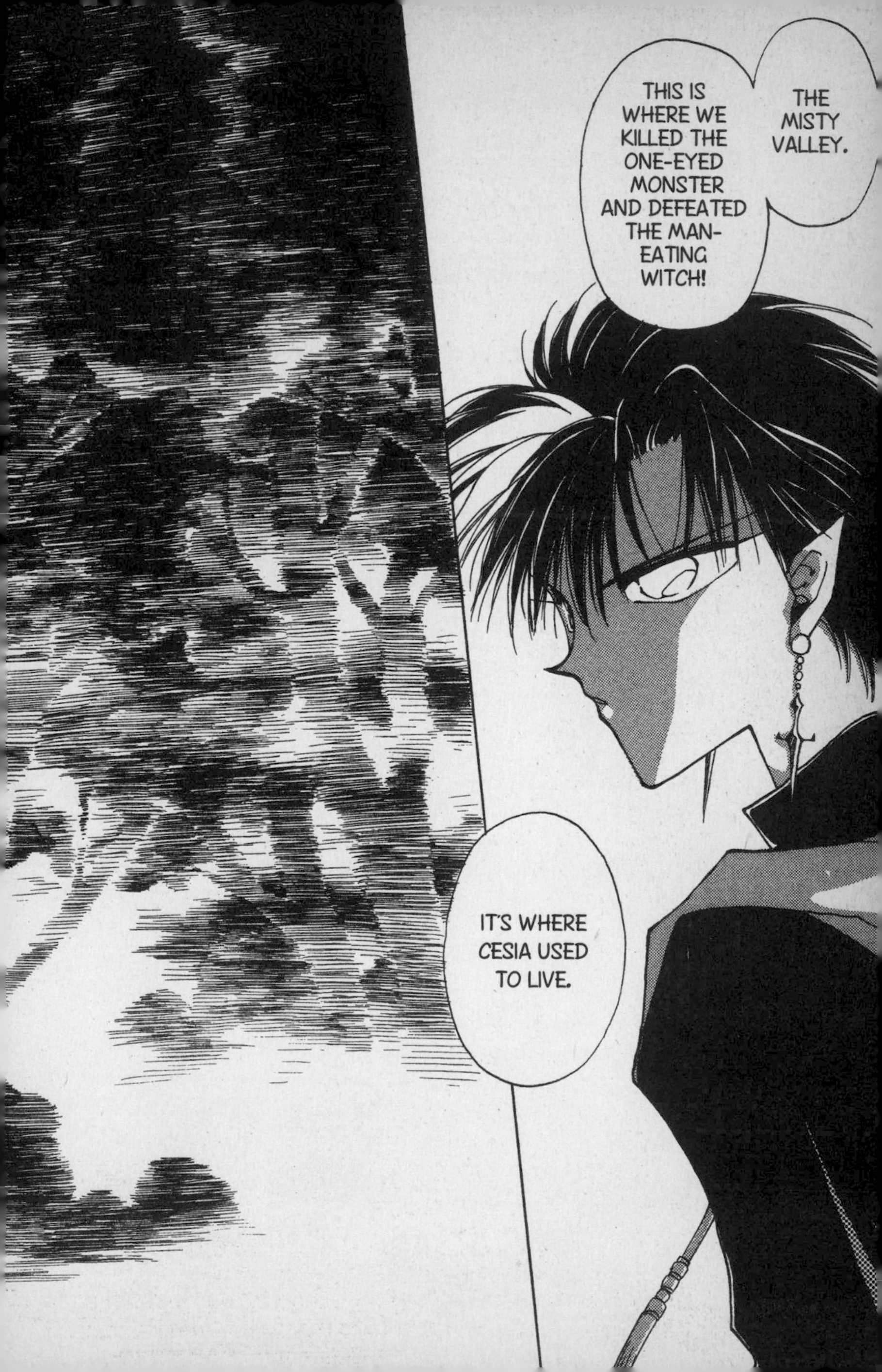
THE MISTY VALLEY.
THIS IS WHERE WE KILLED THE ONE-EYED MONSTER AND DEFEATED THE MAN-EATING WITCH!
IT'S WHERE CESIA USED TO LIVE.

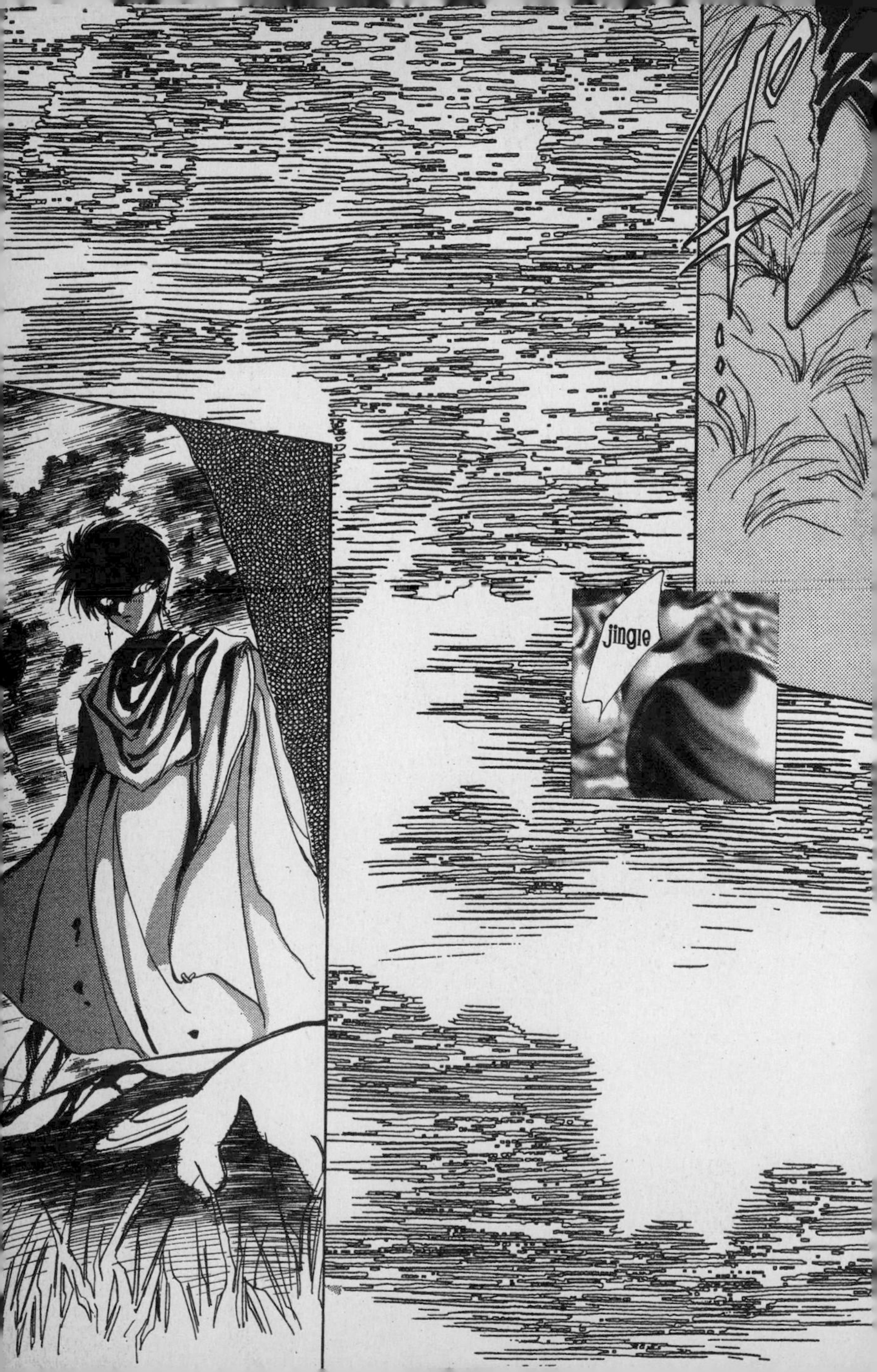
jingle

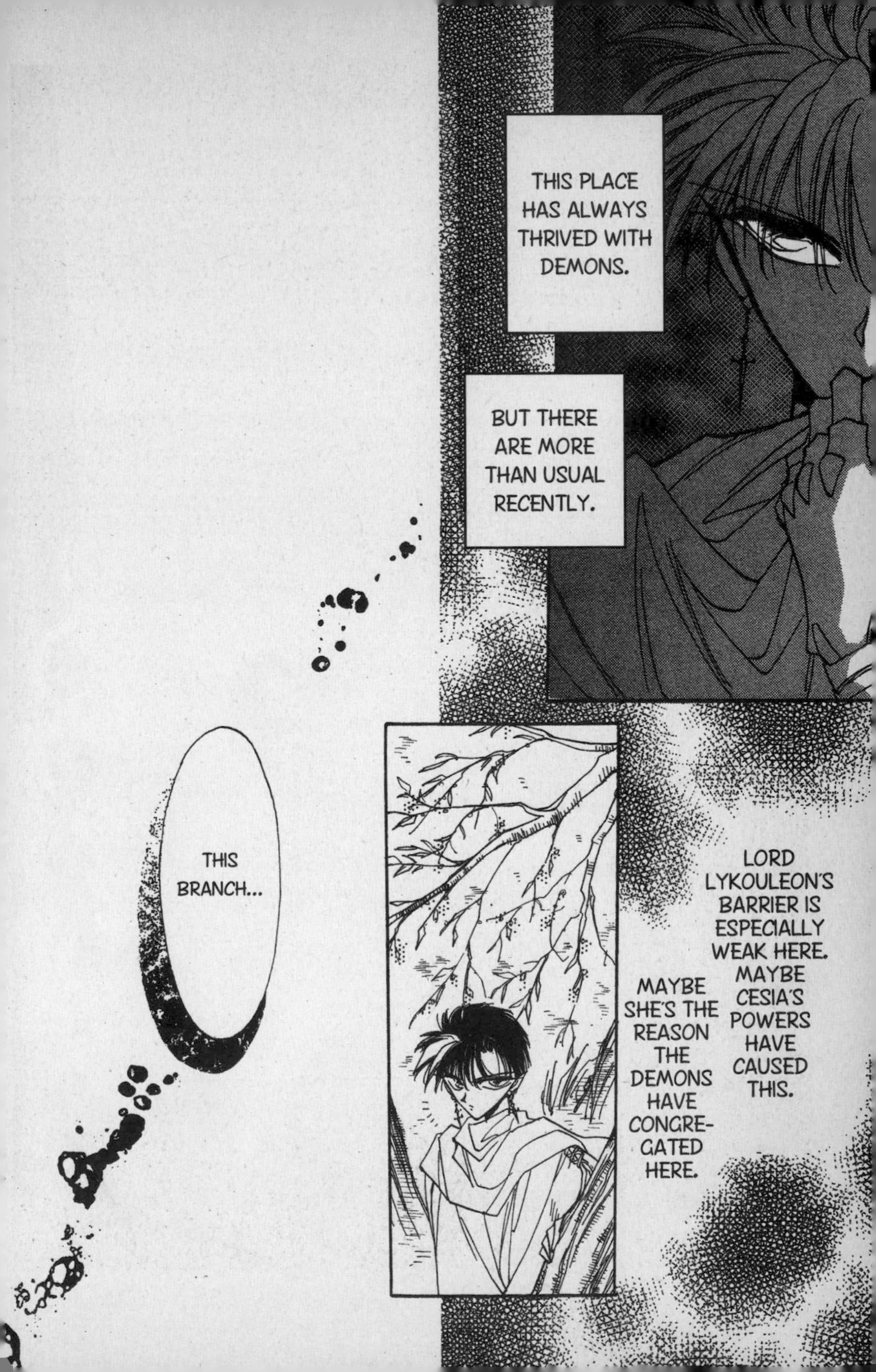
THIS PLACE HAS ALWAYS THRIVED WITH DEMONS.
BUT THERE ARE MORE THAN USUAL RECENTLY.
LORD LYKOULEON'S BARRIER IS ESPECIALLY WEAK HERE. MAYBE CESIA'S POWERS HAVE CAUSED THIS.
MAYBE SHE'S THE REASON THE DEMONS HAVE CONGRE- GATED HERE.
THIS BRANCH...

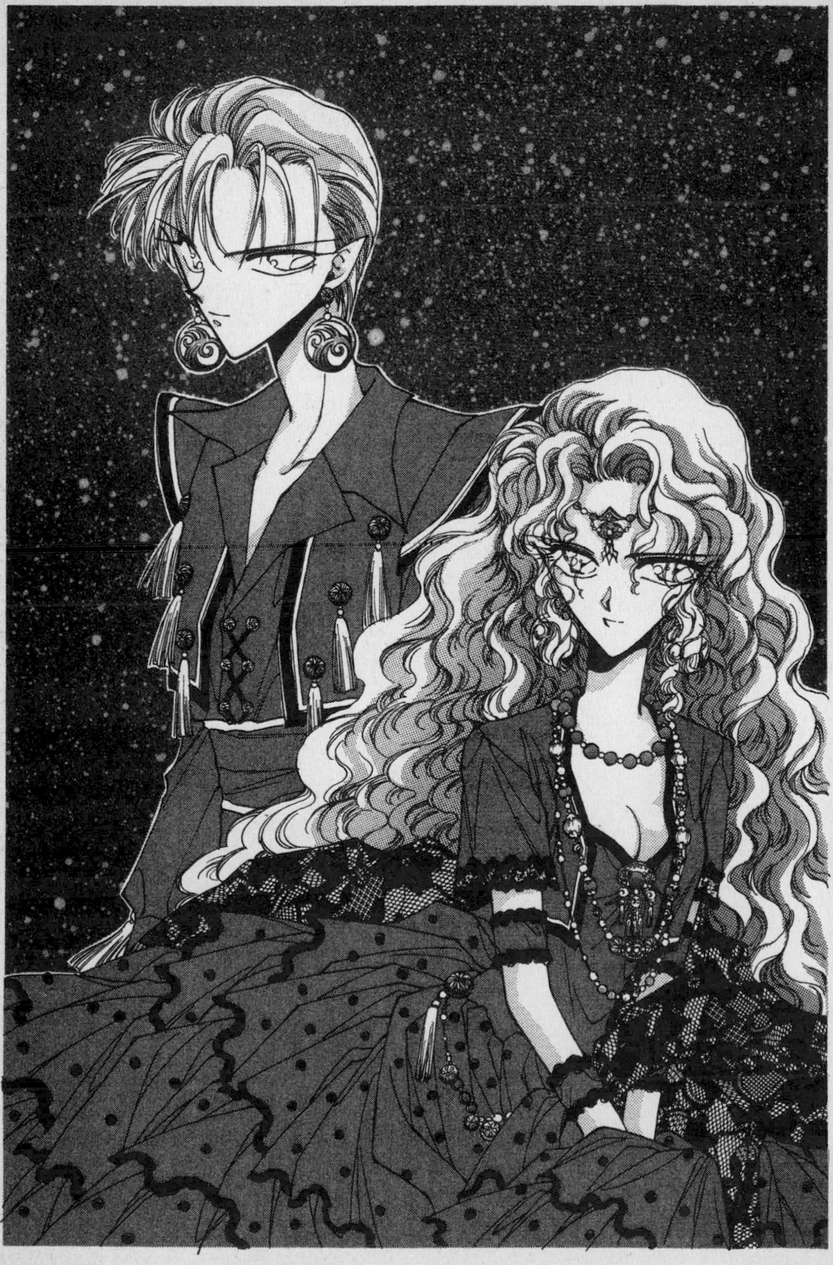

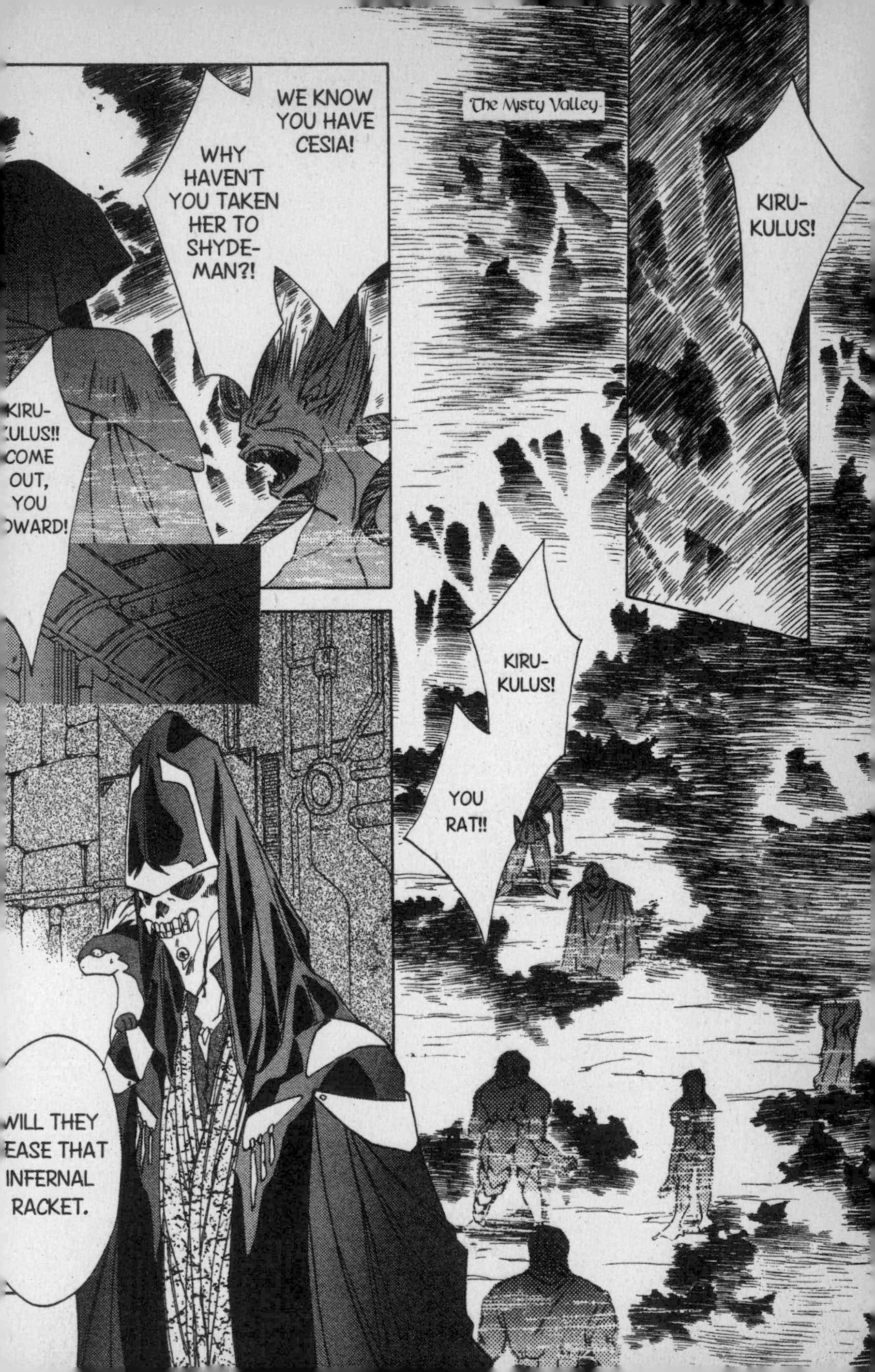
The Misty Valley
KIRU-KULUS!
KIRU-KULUS!
YOU RAT!!
WE KNOW YOU HAVE CESIA!
WHY HAVEN'T YOU TAKEN HER TO SHYDE-MAN?!
KIRU- ULUS!! COME OUT, YOU OWARD!
ILL THEY EASE THAT INFERNAL RACKET.

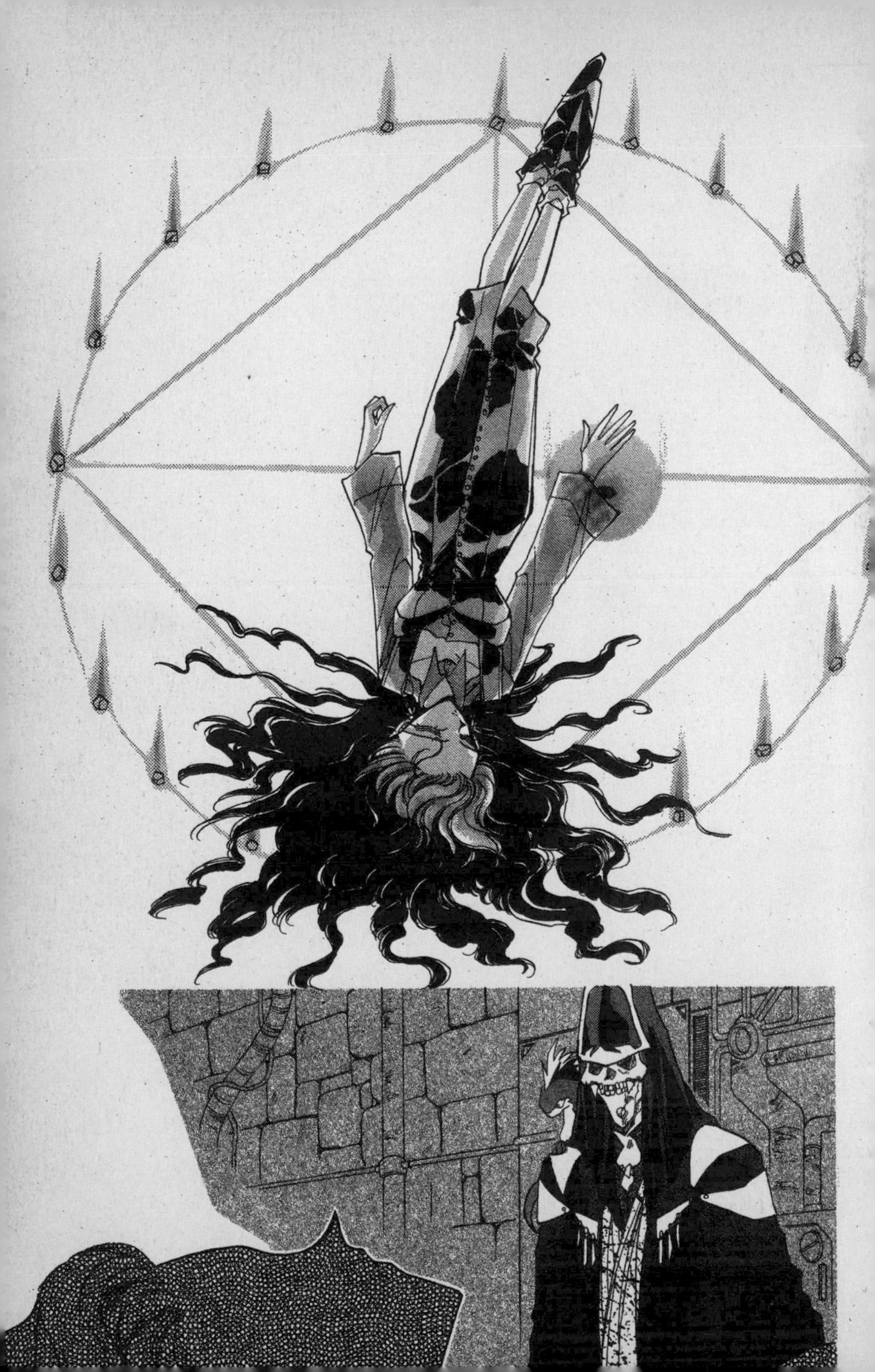

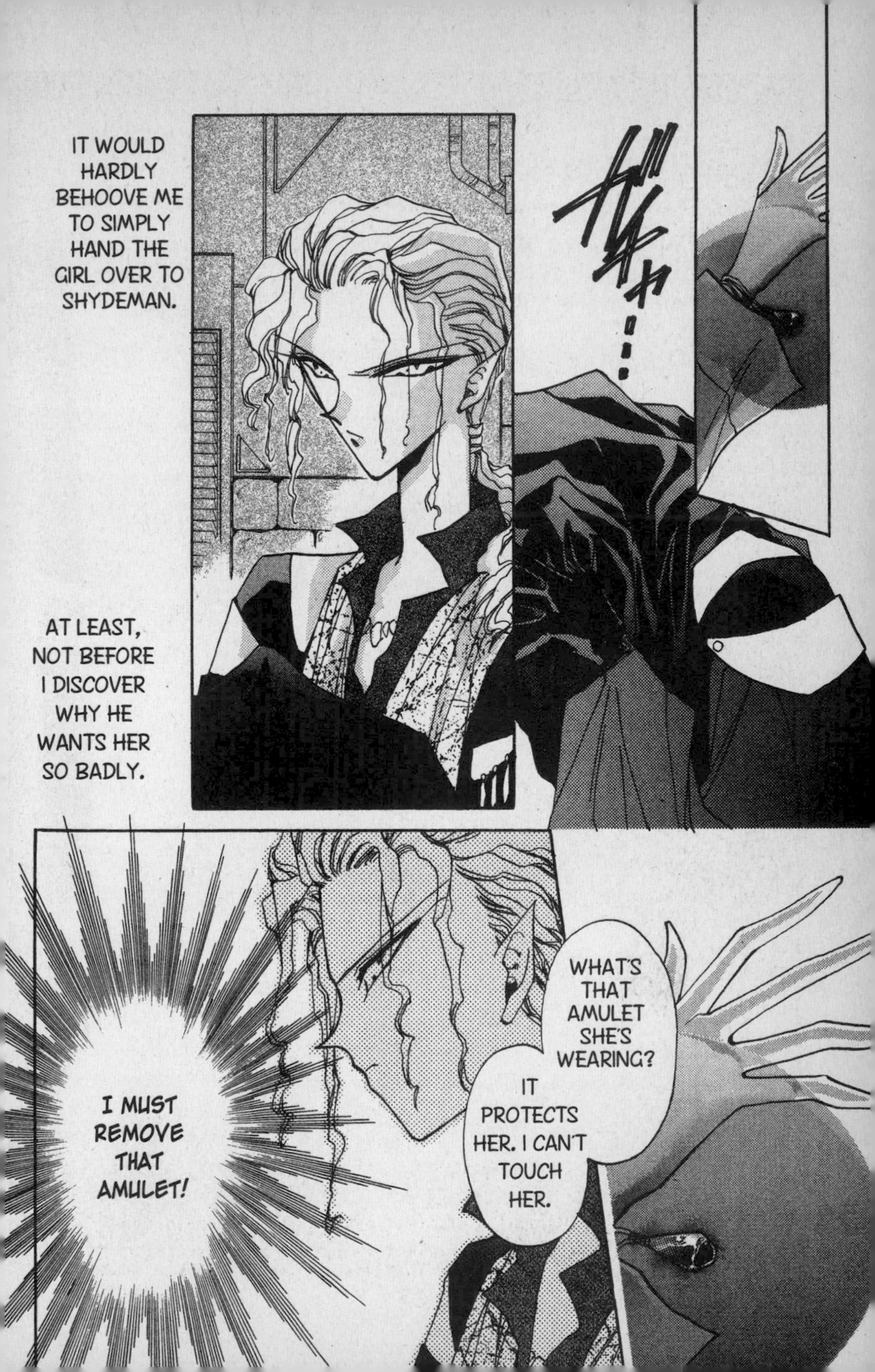
IT WOULD HARDLY BEHOOVE ME TO SIMPLY HAND THE GIRL OVER TO SHYDEMAN.
AT LEAST, NOT BEFORE I DISCOVER WHY HE WANTS HER SO BADLY.
WHAT'S THAT AMULET SHE'S WEARING?
IT PROTECTS HER. I CAN'T TOUCH HER.
I MUST REMOVE THAT AMULET!

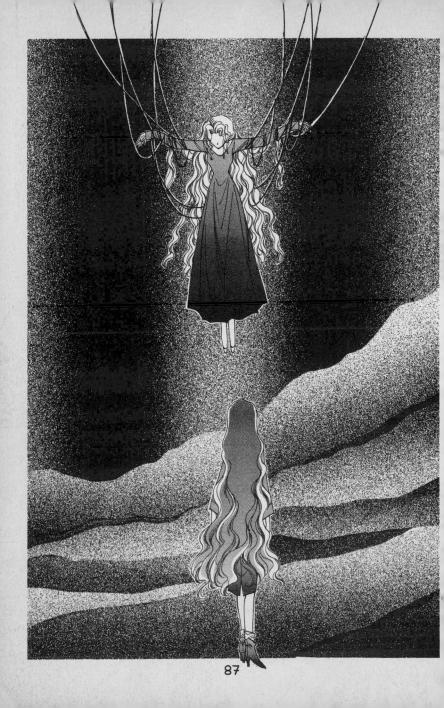

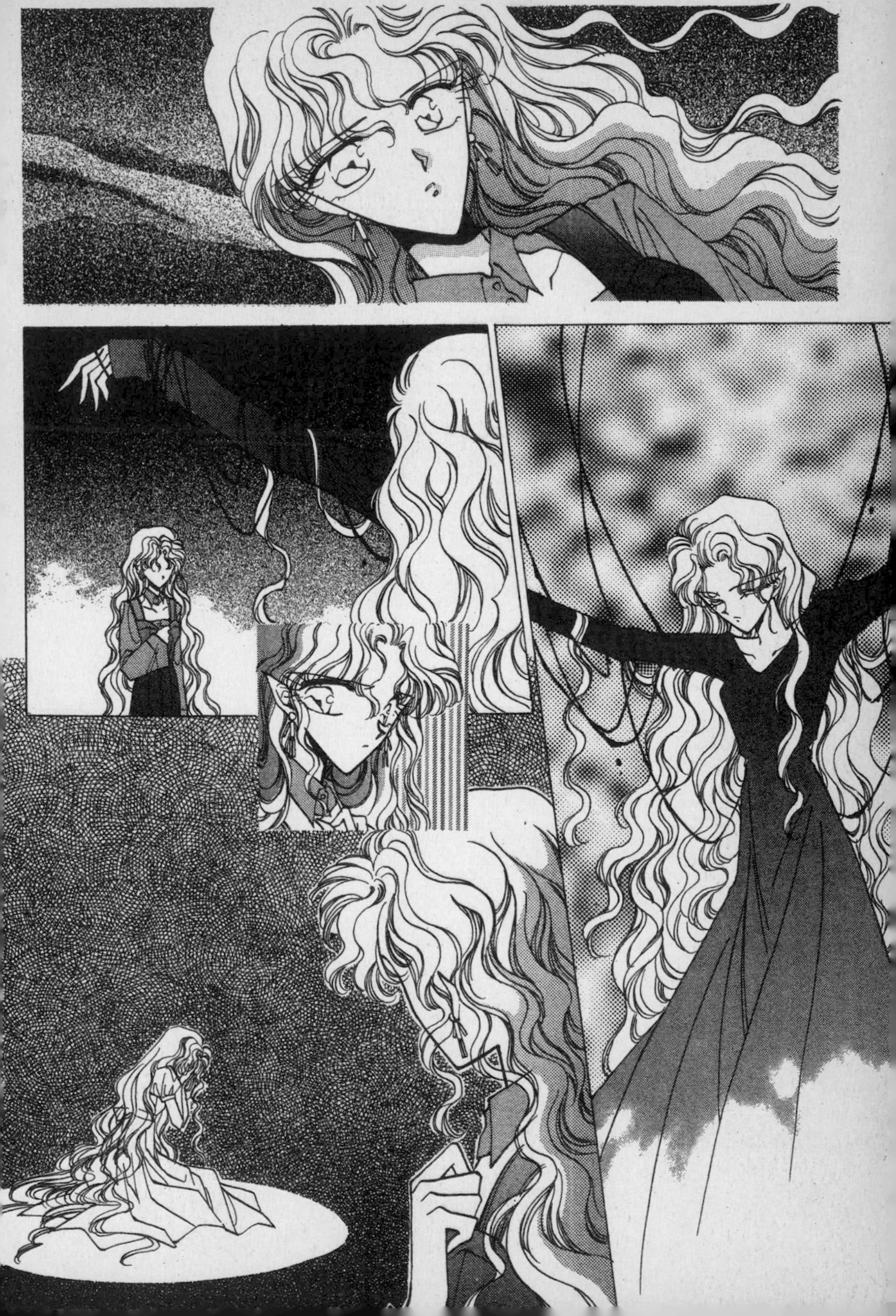

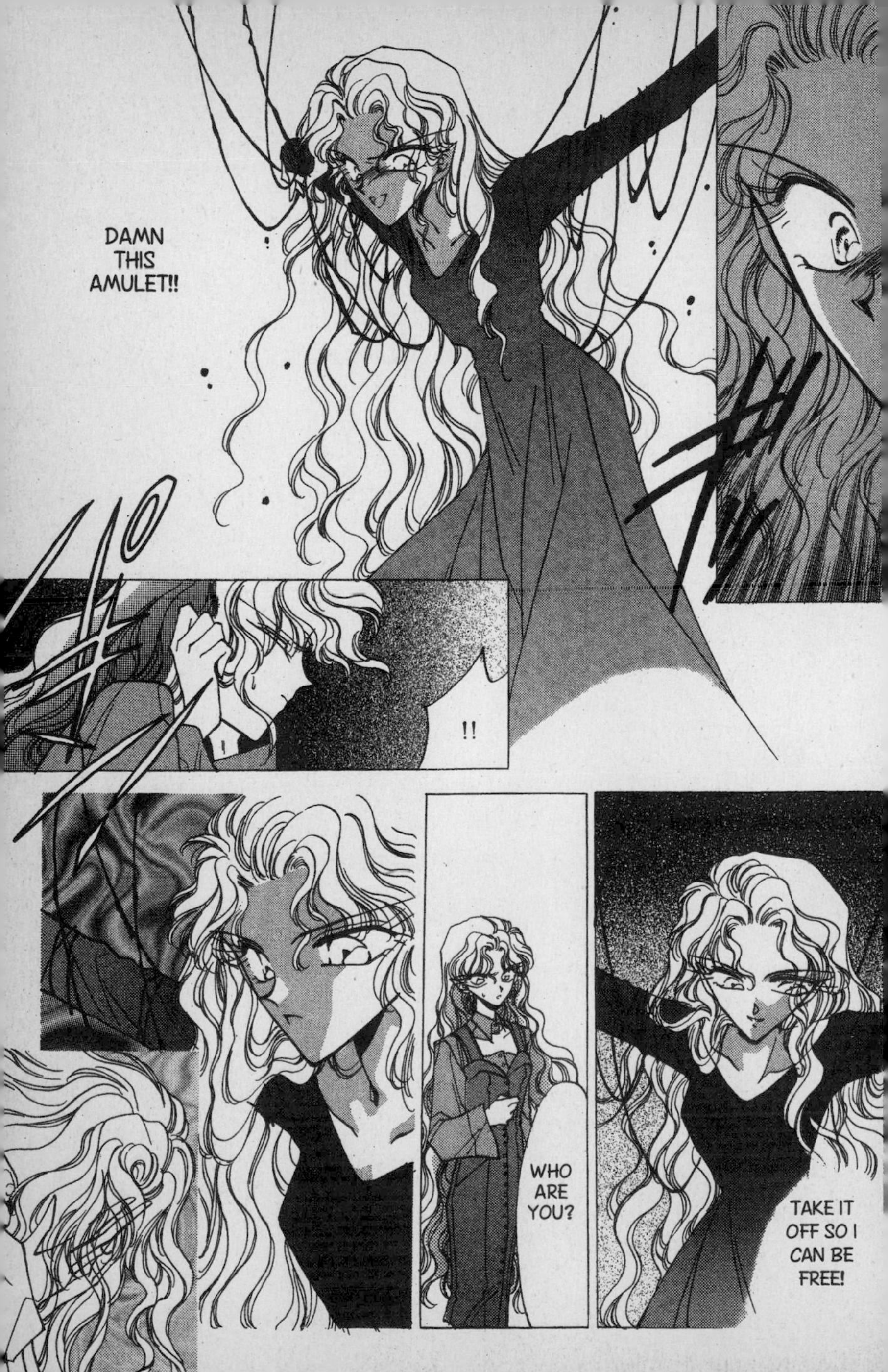
DAMN THIS AMULET!!
!!
TAKE IT OFF SO I CAN BE FREE!
WHO ARE YOU?

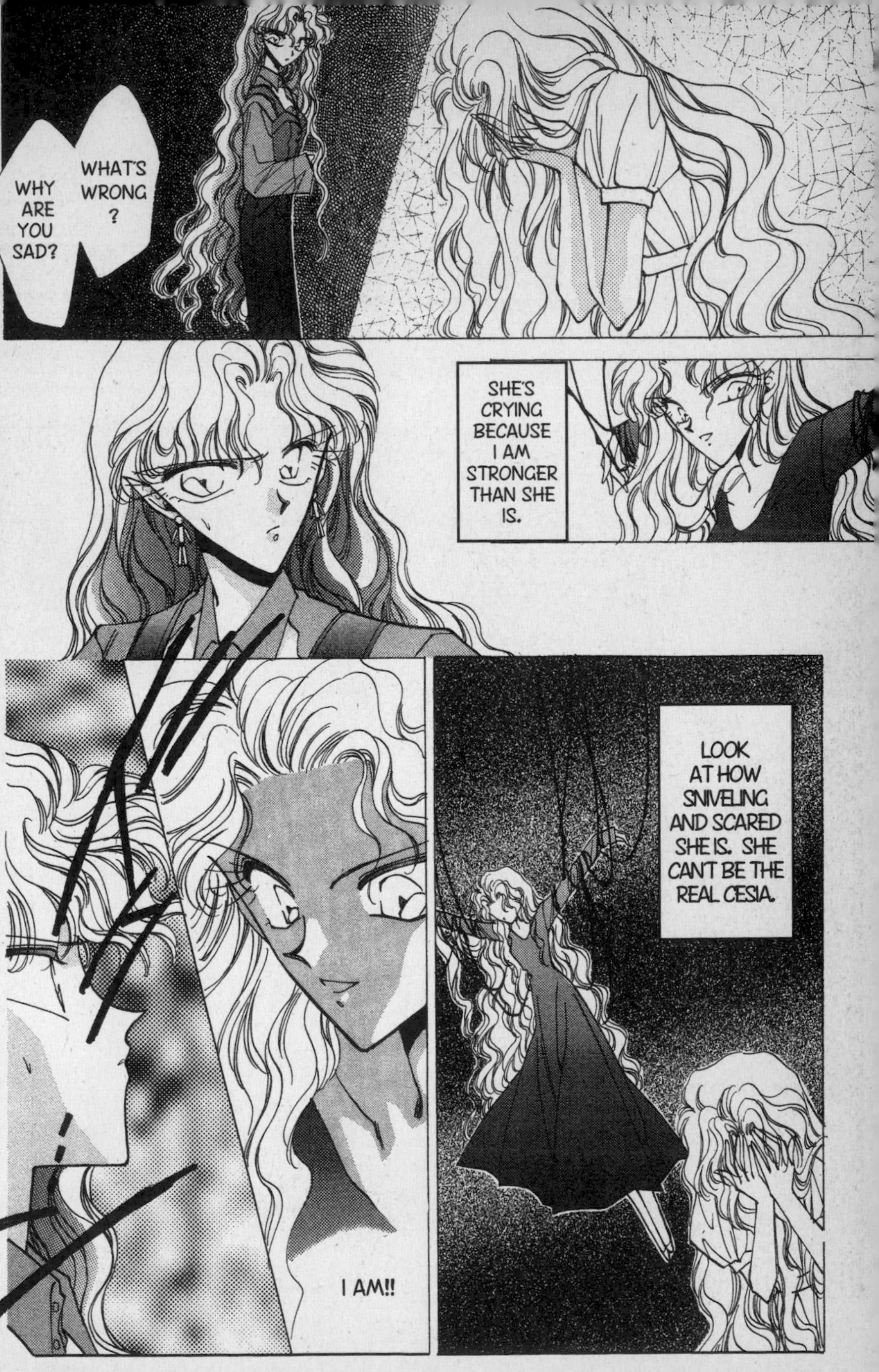
WHAT'S WRONG?
WHY ARE YOU SAD?
SHE'S CRYING BECAUSE I AM STRONGER THAN SHE IS.
LOOK AT HOW SNIVELING AND SCARED SHE IS. SHE CAN'T BE THE REAL CESIA.
I AM!!

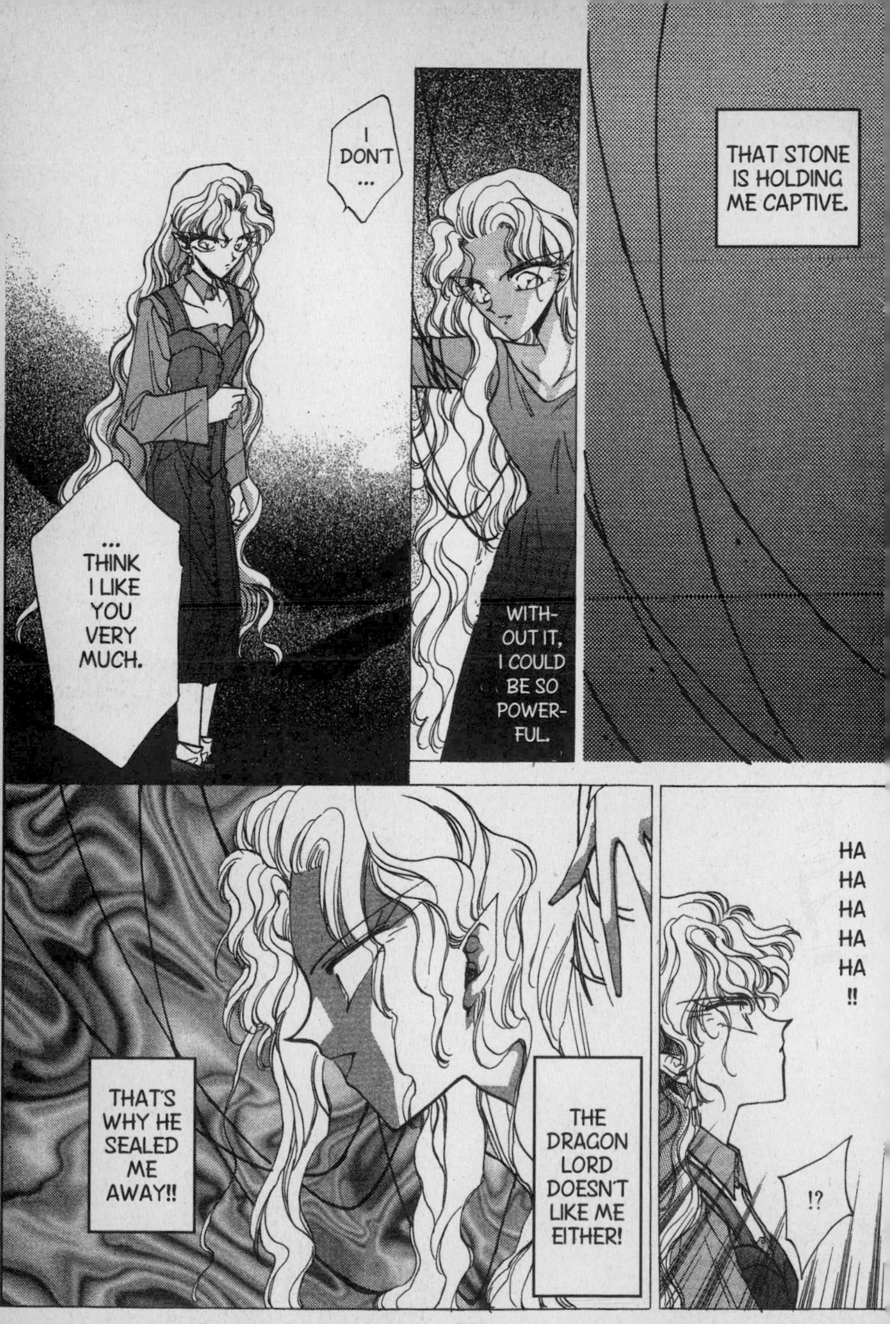
THAT STONE IS HOLDING ME CAPTIVE.
WITH-OUT IT, I COULD BE SO POWER-FUL.
I DON'T ...
... THINK I LIKE YOU VERY MUCH.
HA HA HA HA HA !!
!?
THE DRAGON LORD DOESN'T LIKE ME EITHER!
THAT'S WHY HE SEALED ME AWAY!!

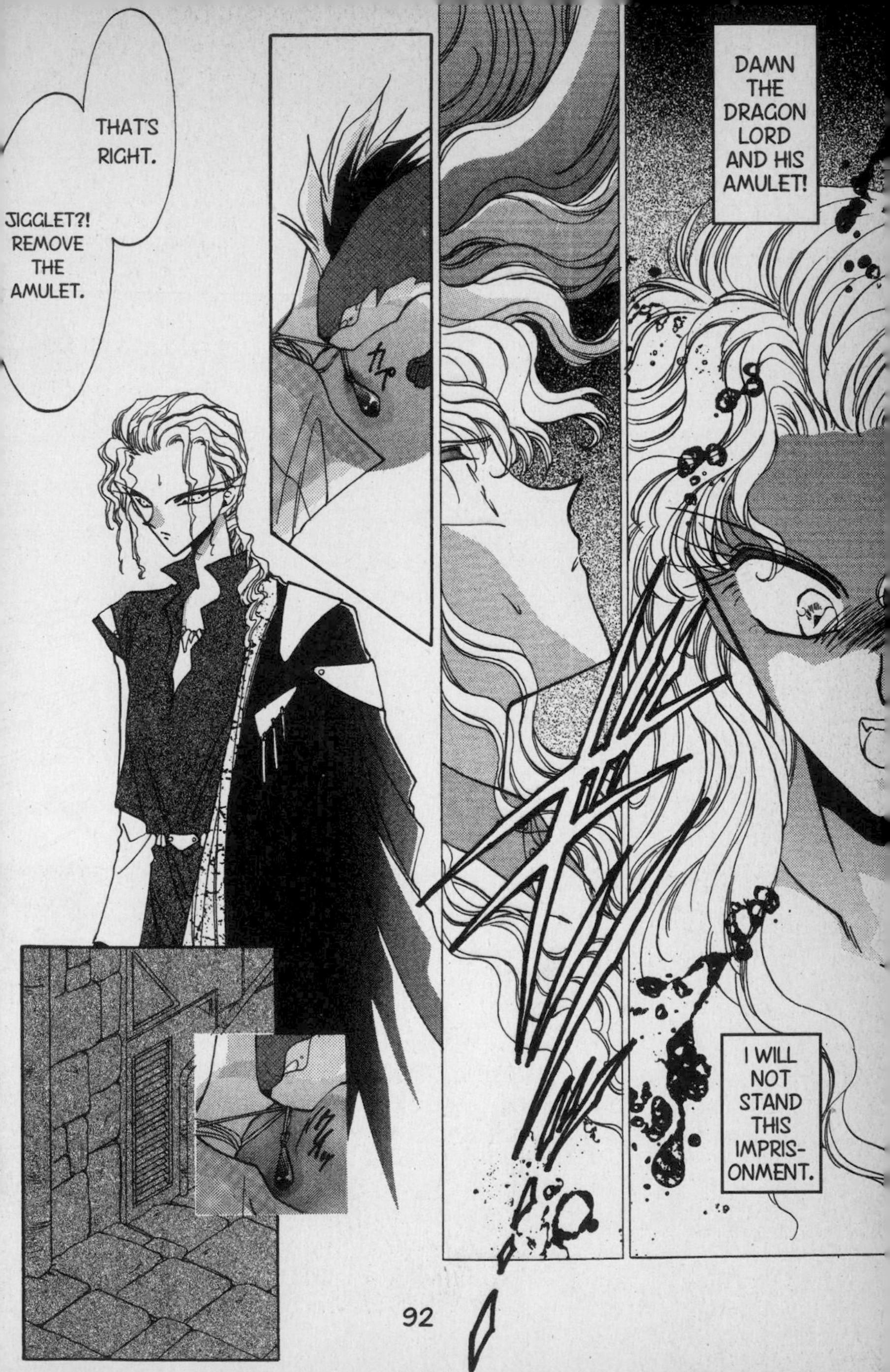
DAMN THE DRAGON LORD AND HIS AMULET!
I WILL NOT STAND THIS IMPRISONMENT.
THAT'S RIGHT.
JIGGLET?! REMOVE THE AMULET.

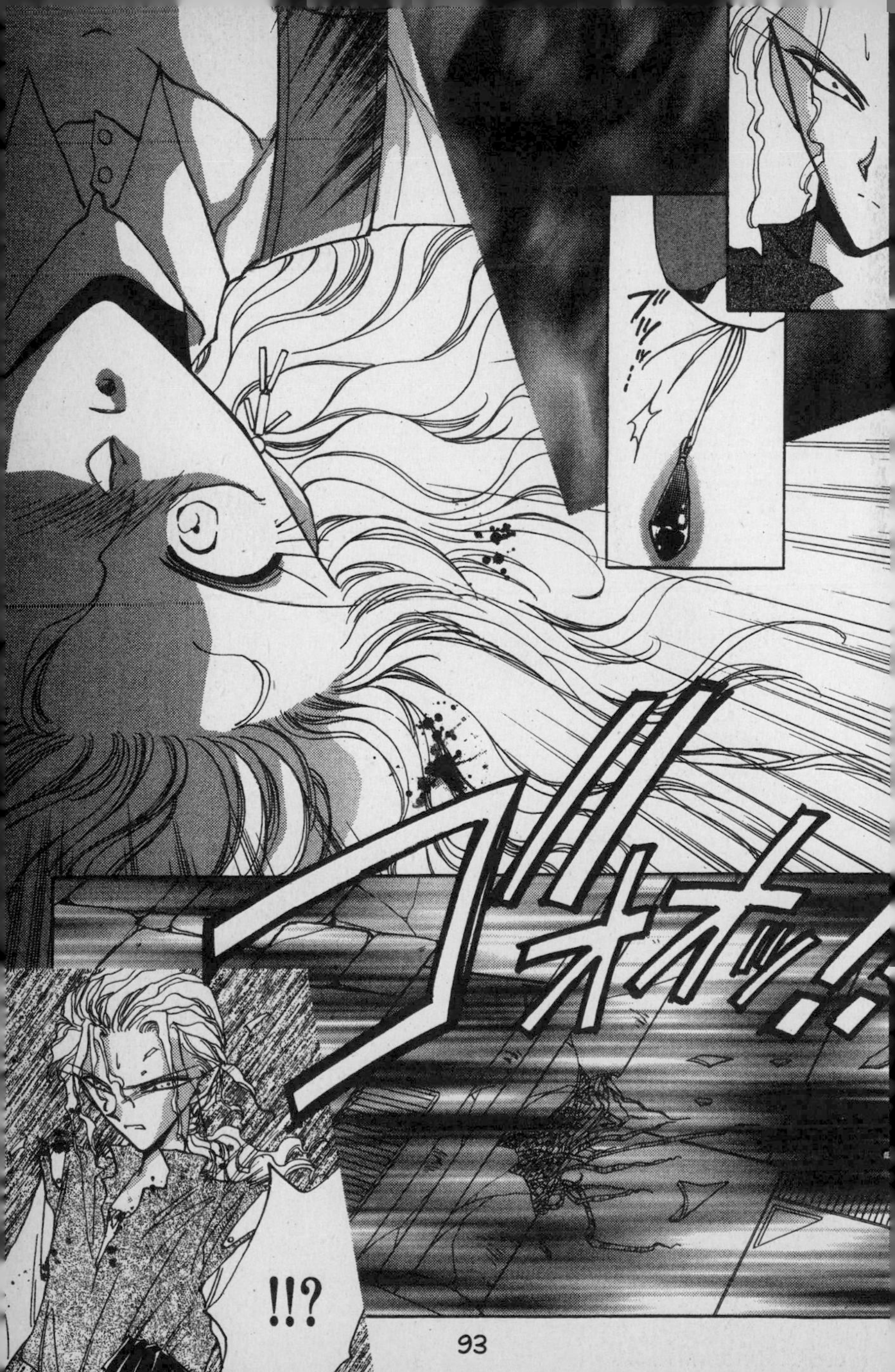
ブツッ…
ゴオォッ!!
!!?

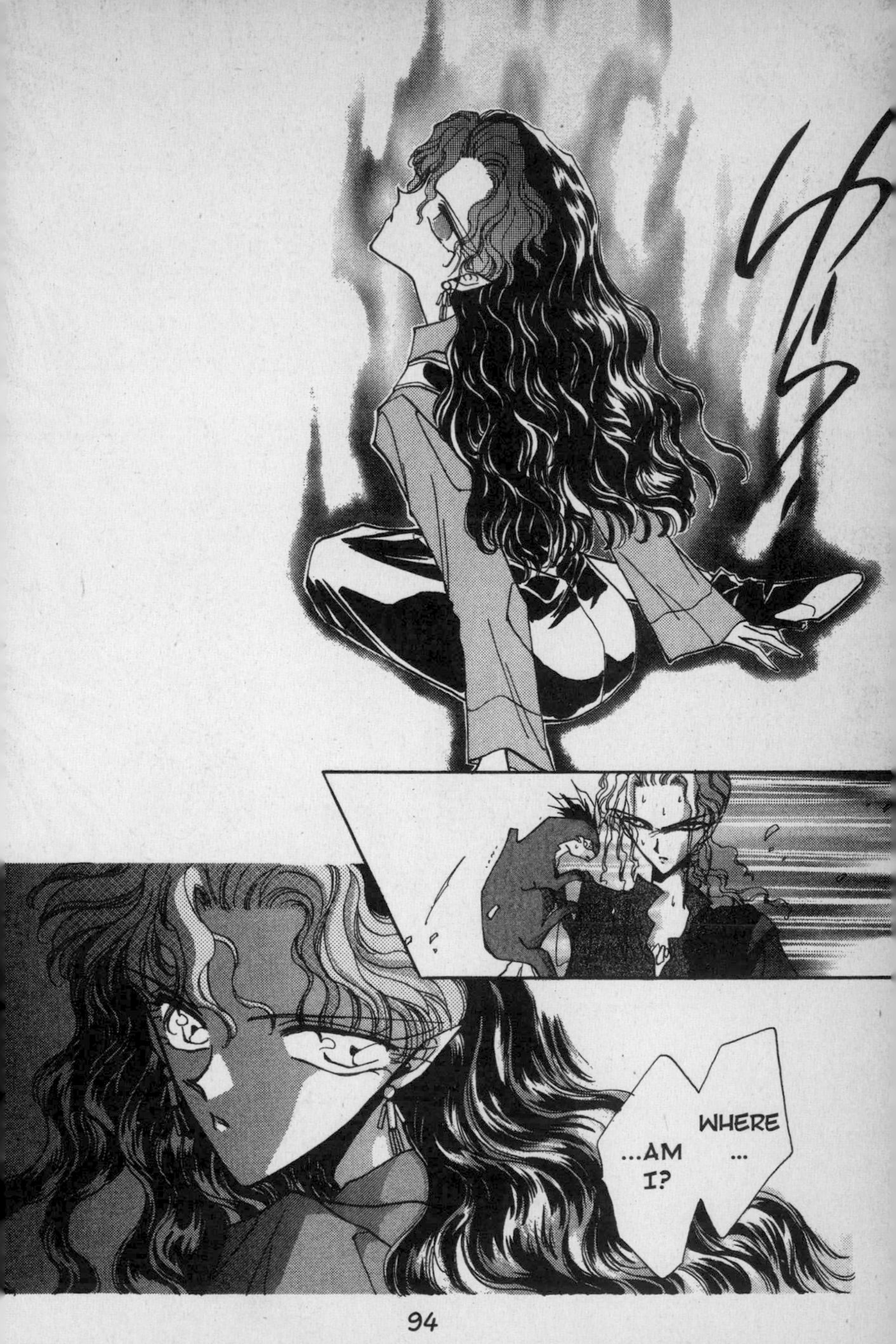
WHERE... ...AM I?

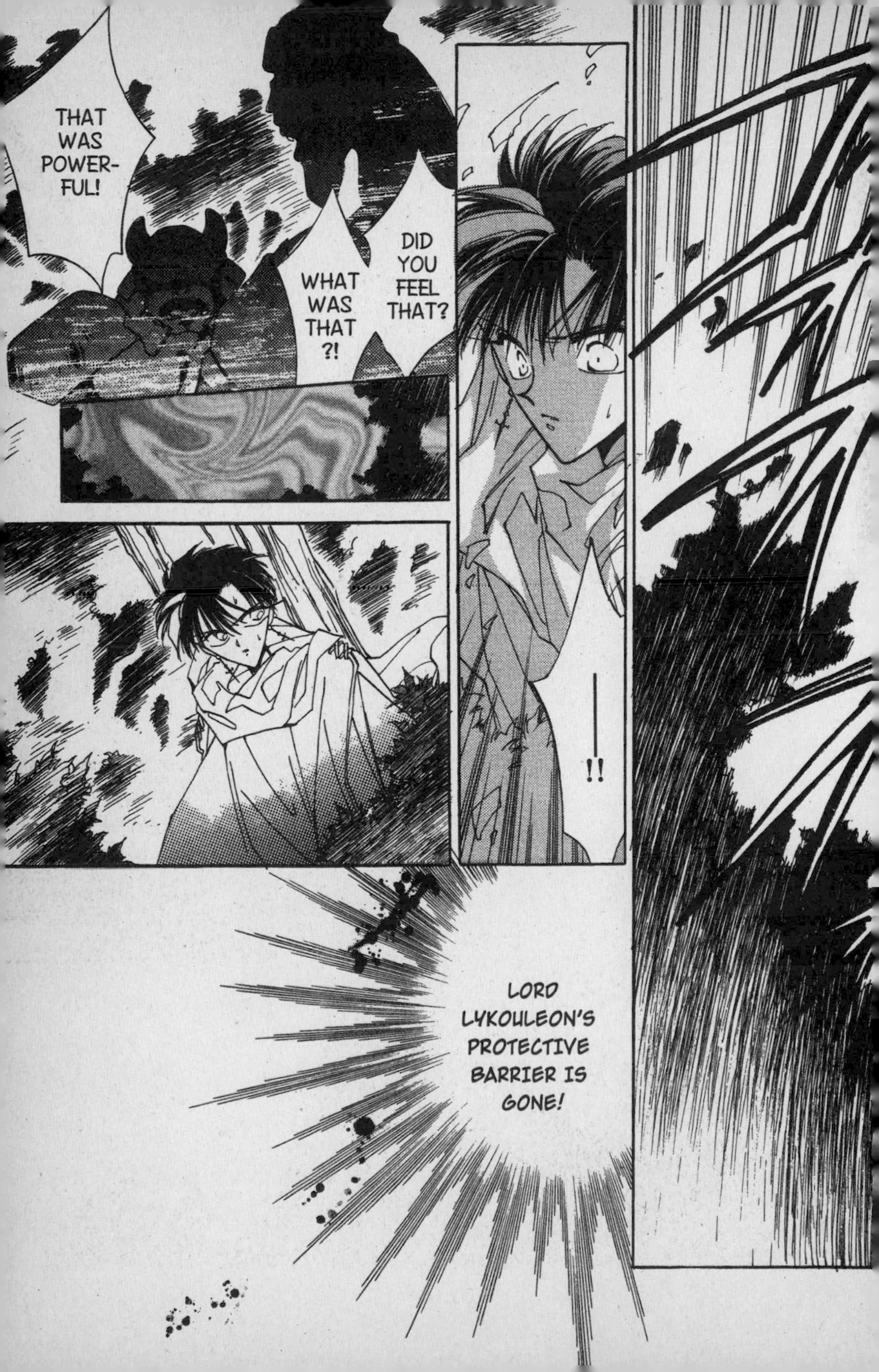
—!!
DID YOU FEEL THAT?
WHAT WAS THAT?!
THAT WAS POWER-FUL!
LORD LYKOULEON'S PROTECTIVE BARRIER IS GONE!

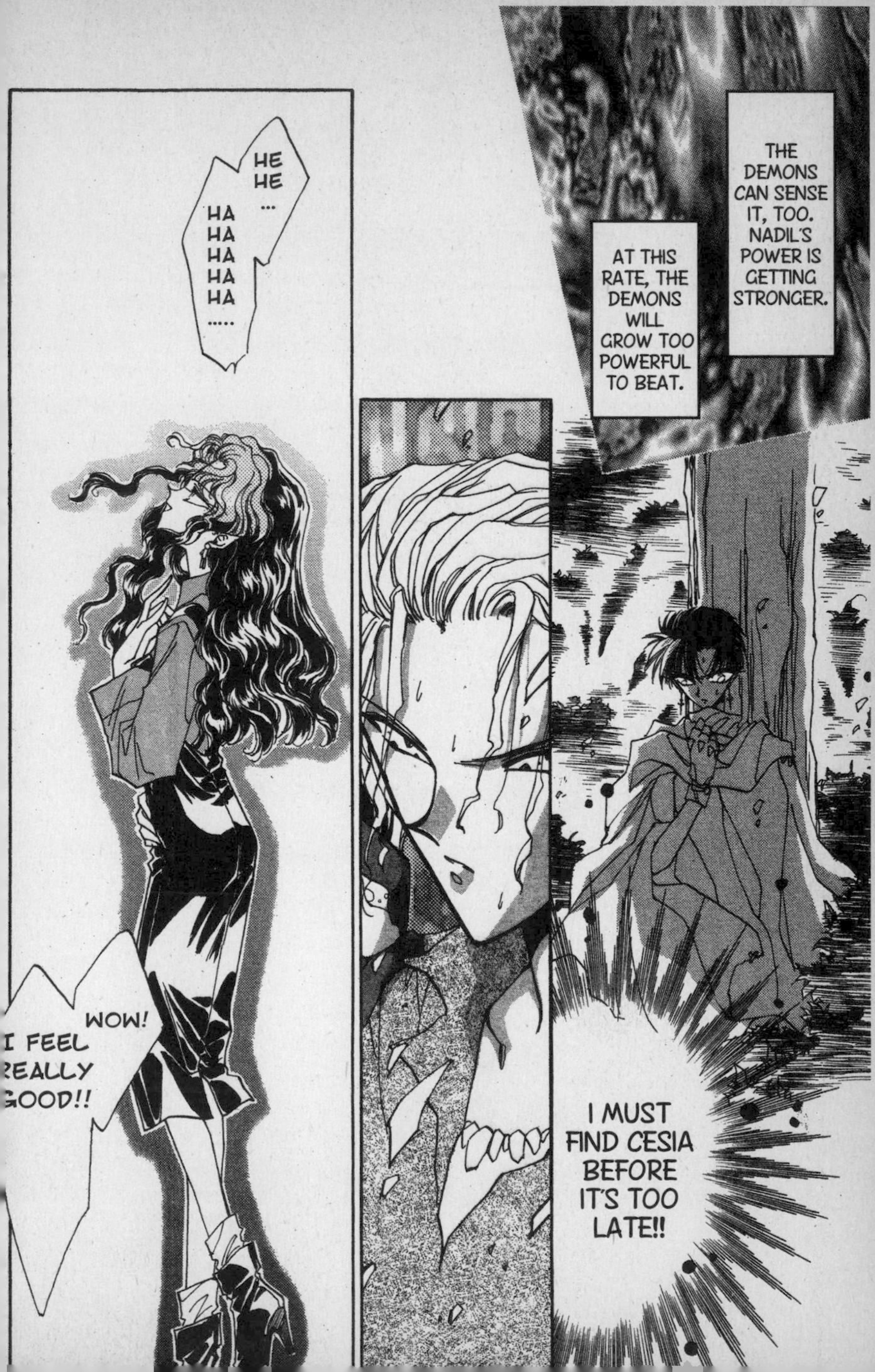
THE DEMONS CAN SENSE IT, TOO. NADIL'S POWER IS GETTING STRONGER.
AT THIS RATE, THE DEMONS WILL GROW TOO POWERFUL TO BEAT.
I MUST FIND CESIA BEFORE IT'S TOO LATE!!
HE HE ... HA HA HA HA HA .....
WOW! I FEEL REALLY GOOD!!

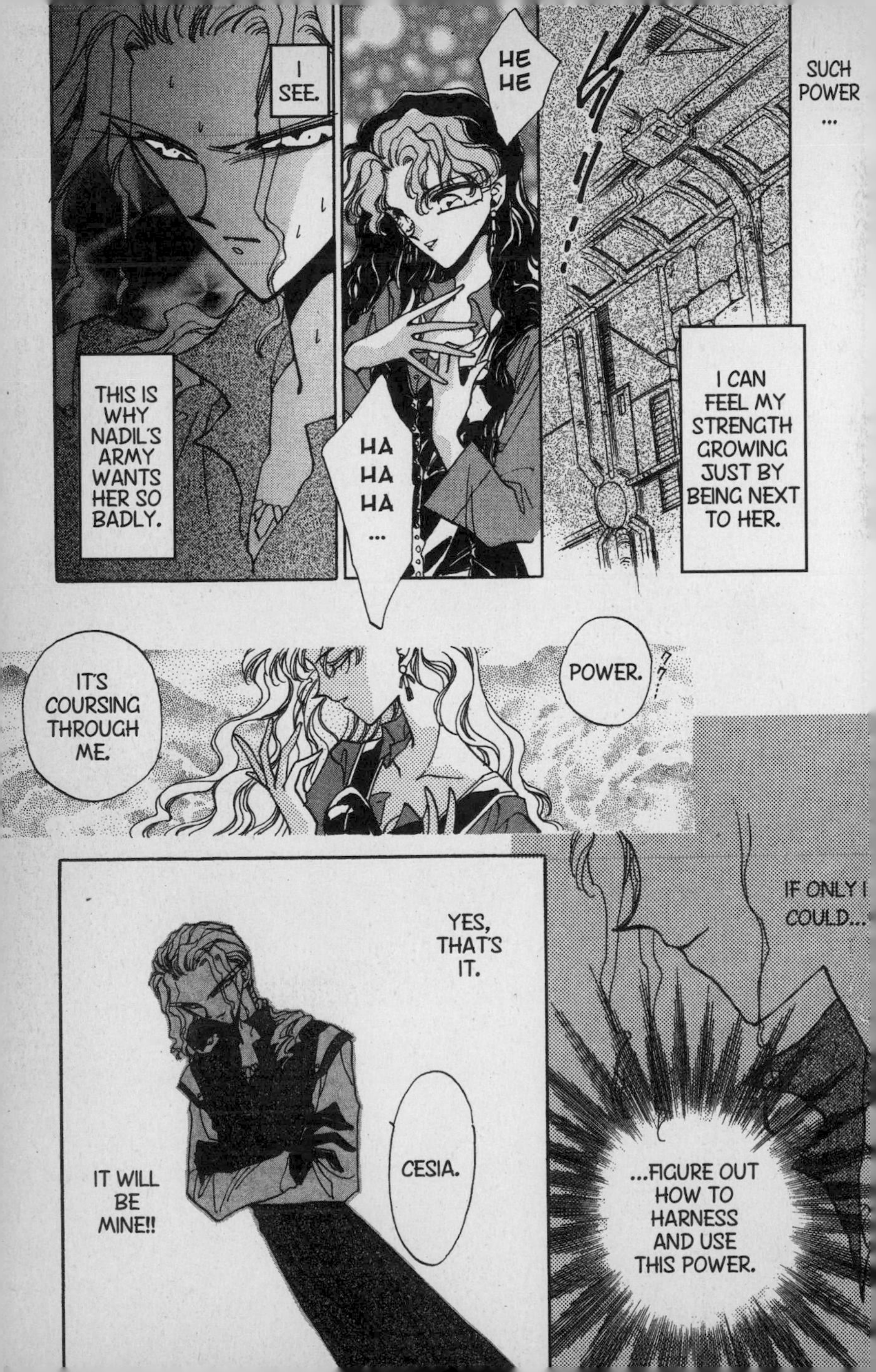
SUCH POWER ...
I CAN FEEL MY STRENGTH GROWING JUST BY BEING NEXT TO HER.
HE HE
HA HA HA ...
I SEE.
THIS IS WHY NADIL'S ARMY WANTS HER SO BADLY.
POWER.
IT'S COURSING THROUGH ME.
IF ONLY I COULD...
...FIGURE OUT HOW TO HARNESS AND USE THIS POWER.
YES, THAT'S IT.
CESIA.
IT WILL BE MINE!!

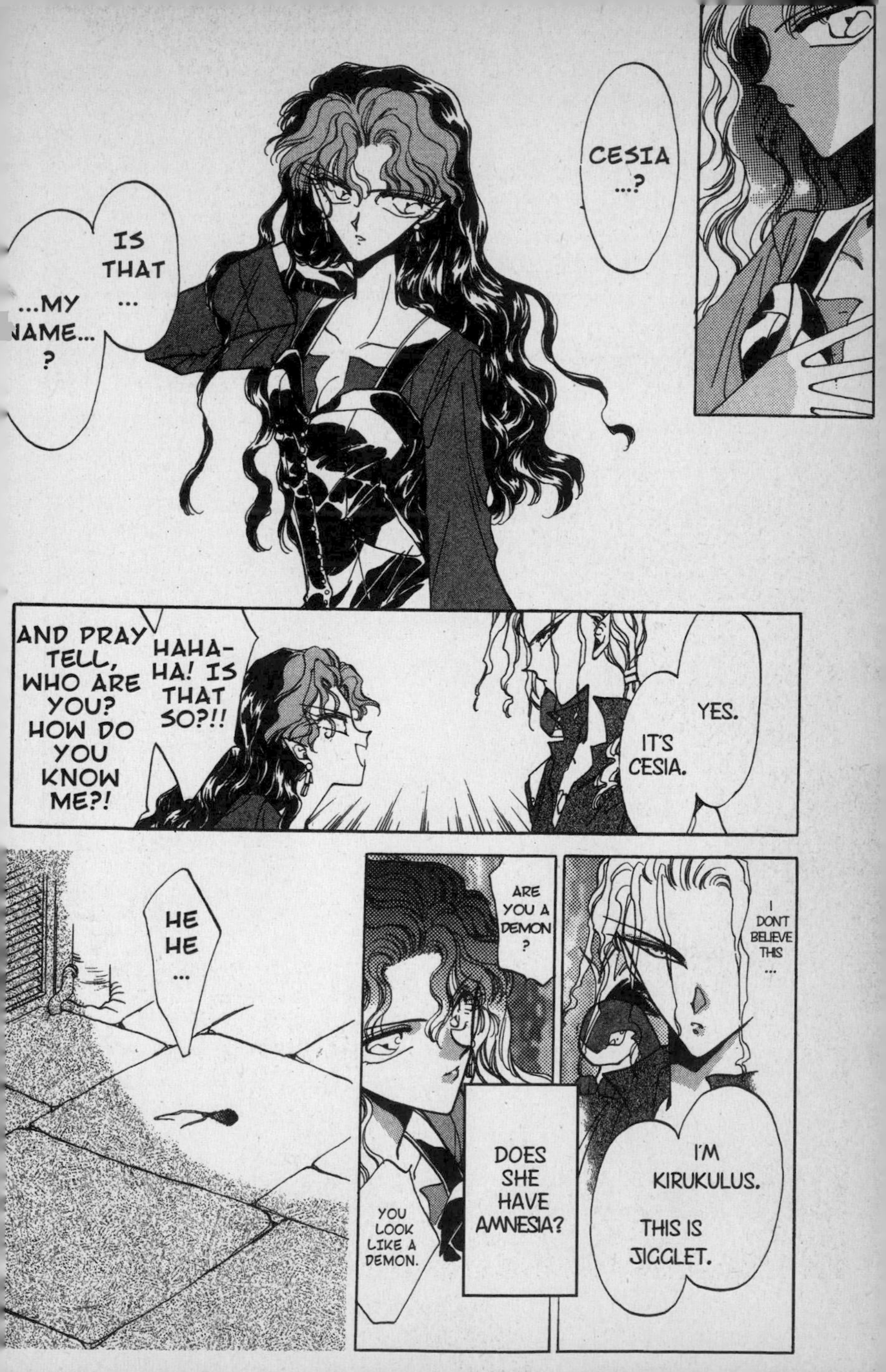
CESIA ...?
IS THAT ... ...MY NAME... ?
YES. IT'S CESIA.
HAHA-HA! IS THAT SO?!!
AND PRAY TELL, WHO ARE YOU? HOW DO YOU KNOW ME?!
I DONT BELIEVE THIS ...
I'M KIRUKULUS.
THIS IS JIGGLET.
ARE YOU A DEMON ?
DOES SHE HAVE AMNESIA?
YOU LOOK LIKE A DEMON.
HE HE ...

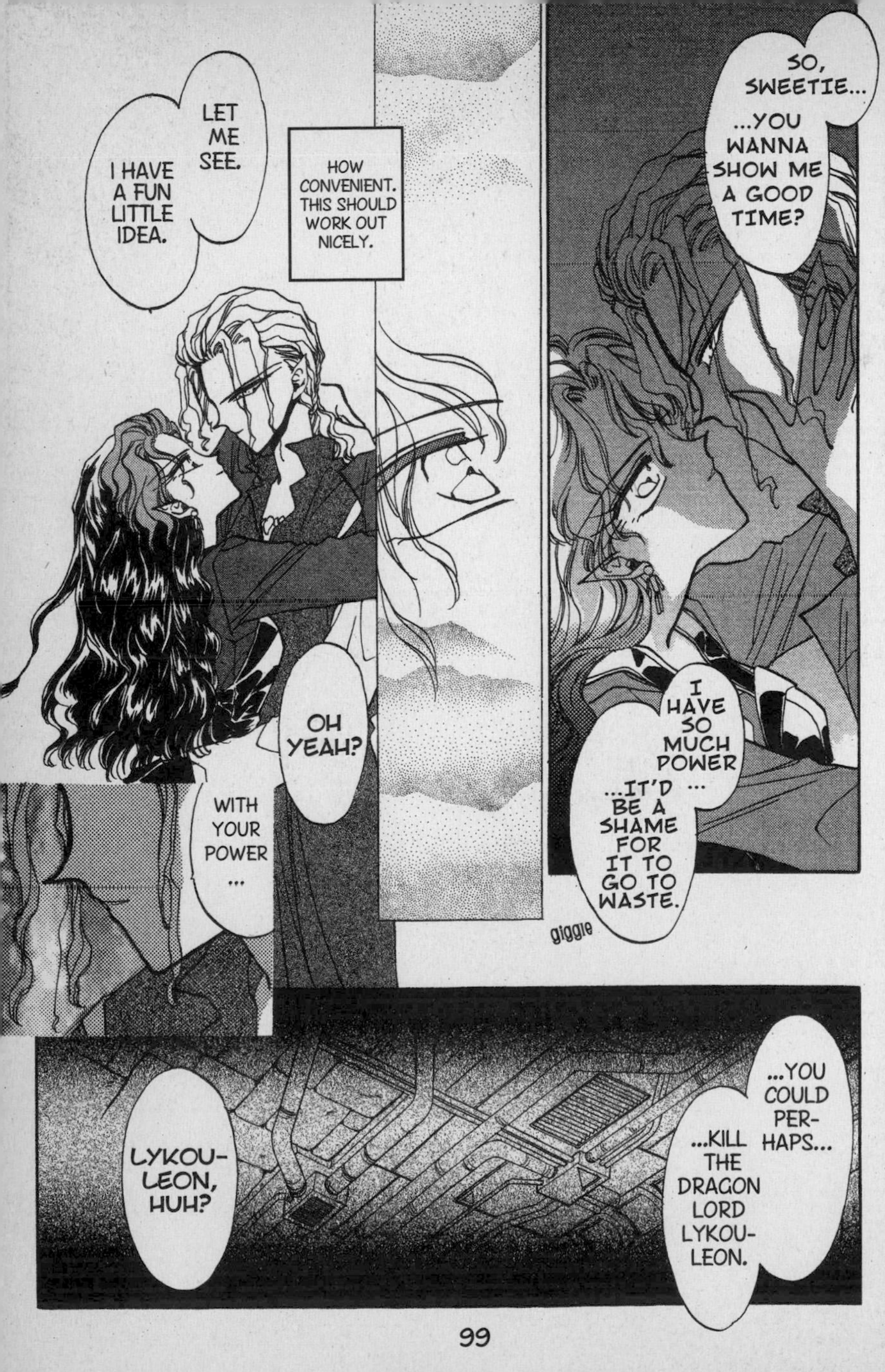
SO, SWEETIE...
...YOU WANNA SHOW ME A GOOD TIME?
I HAVE SO MUCH POWER ...
...IT'D BE A SHAME FOR IT TO GO TO WASTE.
giggle
HOW CONVENIENT. THIS SHOULD WORK OUT NICELY.
LET ME SEE.
I HAVE A FUN LITTLE IDEA.
OH YEAH?
WITH YOUR POWER ...
...YOU COULD PER-HAPS...
...KILL THE DRAGON LORD LYKOU-LEON.
LYKOU-LEON, HUH?

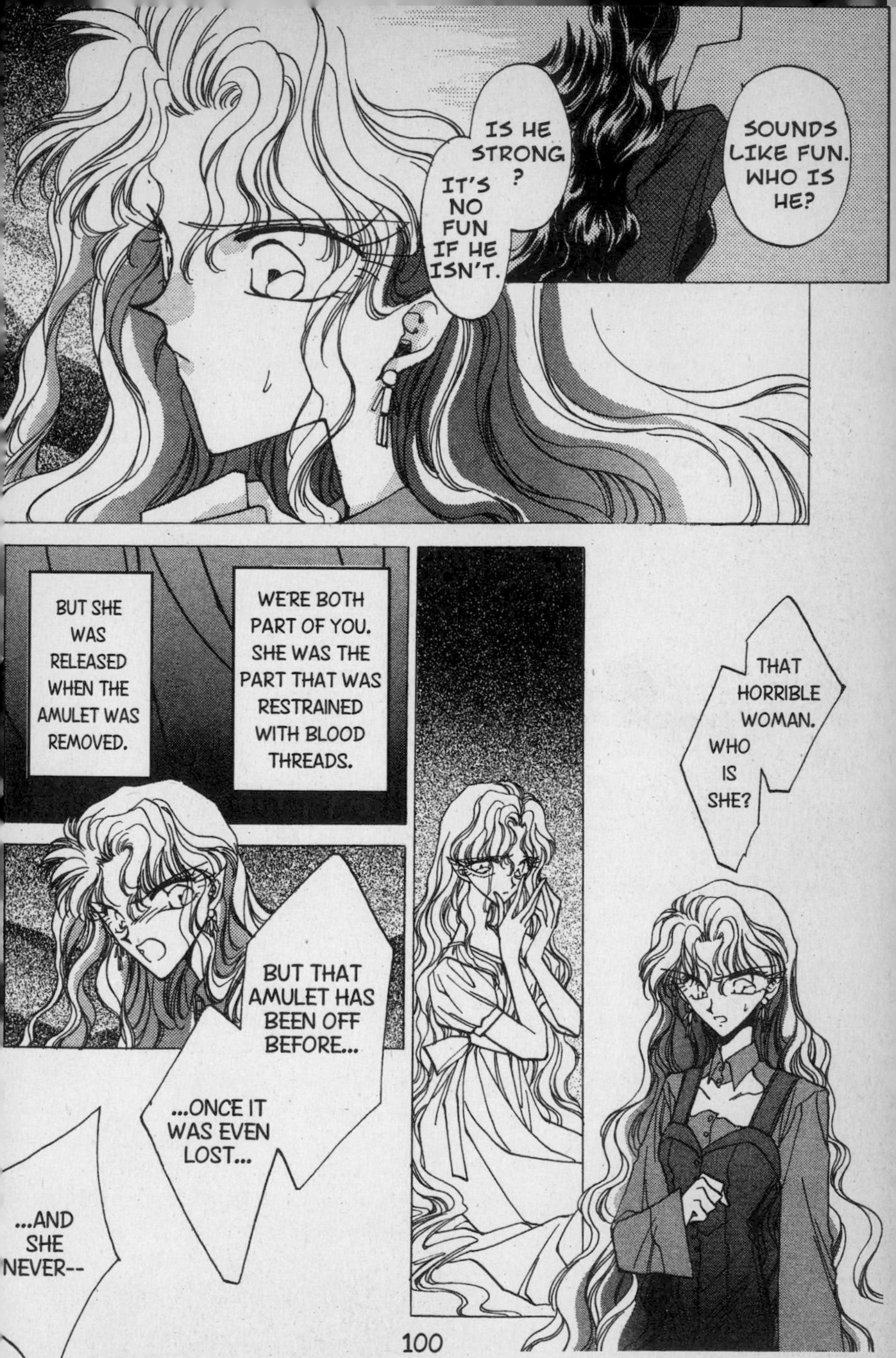
SOUNDS LIKE FUN. WHO IS HE?
IS HE STRONG?
IT'S NO FUN IF HE ISN'T.
THAT HORRIBLE WOMAN. WHO IS SHE?
WE'RE BOTH PART OF YOU. SHE WAS THE PART THAT WAS RESTRAINED WITH BLOOD THREADS.
BUT SHE WAS RELEASED WHEN THE AMULET WAS REMOVED.
BUT THAT AMULET HAS BEEN OFF BEFORE...
...ONCE IT WAS EVEN LOST...
...AND SHE NEVER--

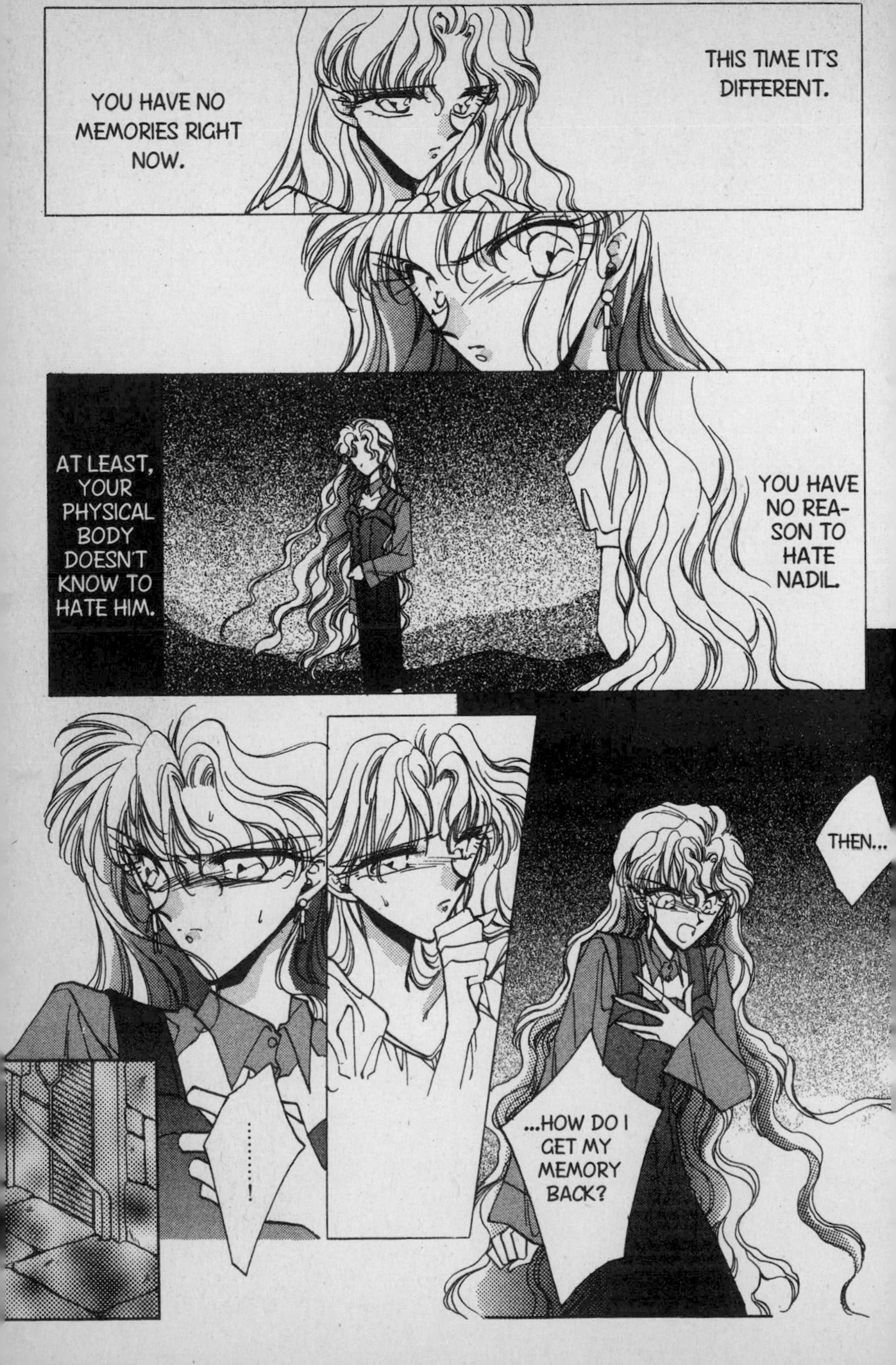
THIS TIME IT'S DIFFERENT.
YOU HAVE NO MEMORIES RIGHT NOW.
YOU HAVE NO REA-SON TO HATE NADIL.
AT LEAST, YOUR PHYSICAL BODY DOESN'T KNOW TO HATE HIM.
THEN...
...HOW DO I GET MY MEMORY BACK?
......!

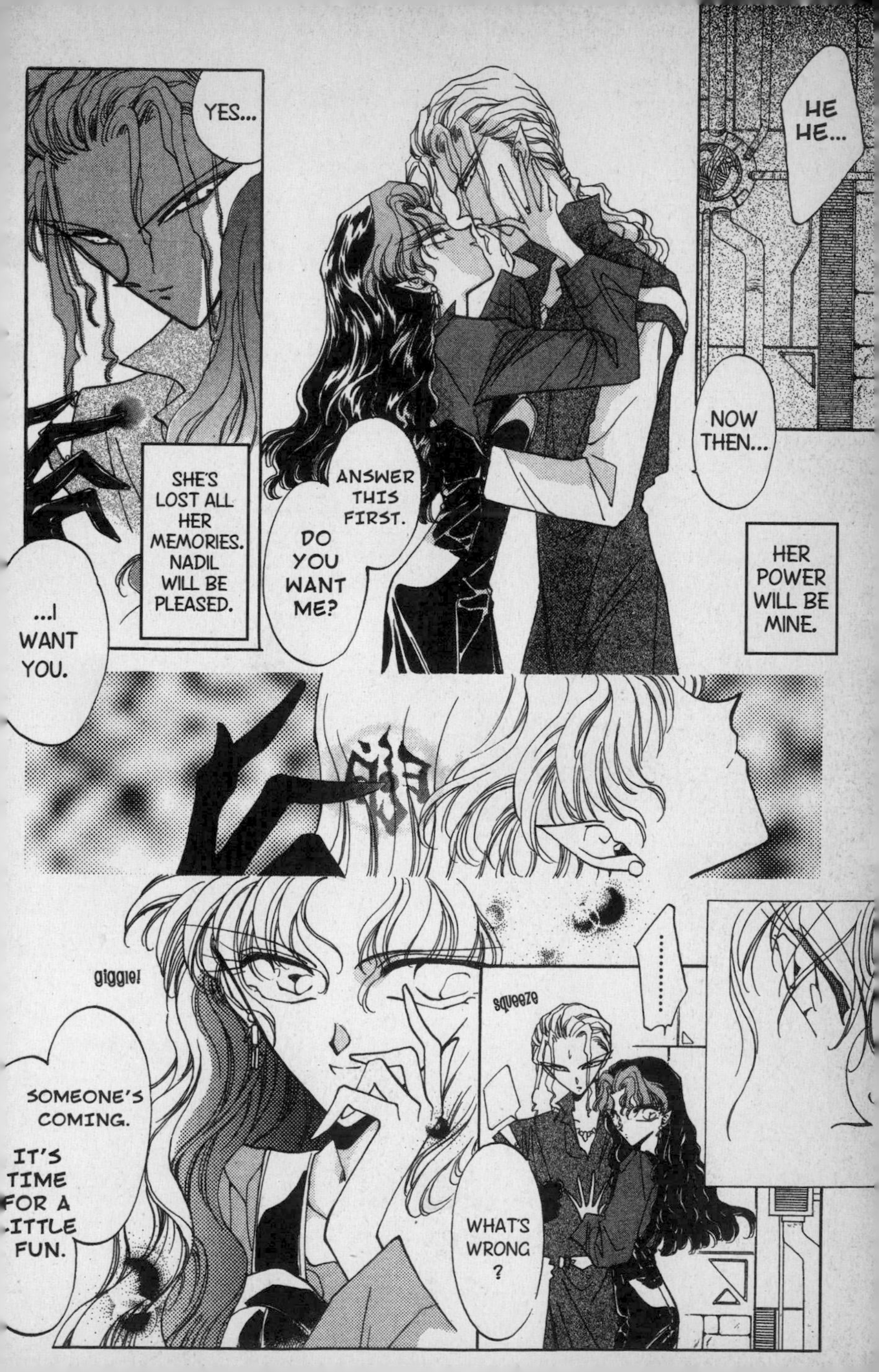
HE HE...
NOW THEN...
HER POWER WILL BE MINE.
ANSWER THIS FIRST.
DO YOU WANT ME?
YES...
SHE'S LOST ALL HER MEMORIES. NADIL WILL BE PLEASED.
...I WANT YOU.
......
squeeze
WHAT'S WRONG?
giggle!
SOMEONE'S COMING.
IT'S TIME FOR A ITTLE FUN.

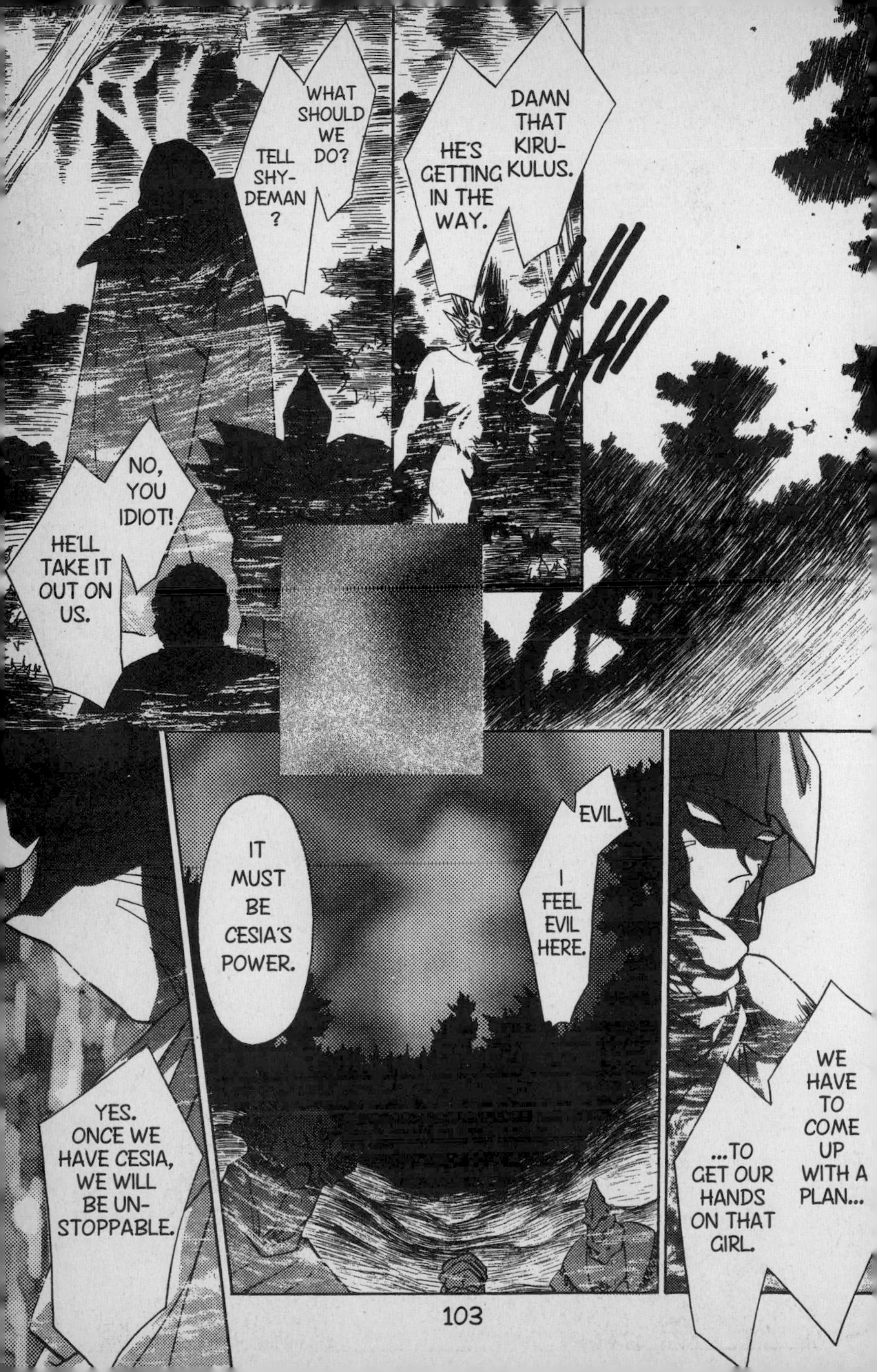
DAMN THAT KIRU-KULUS.
HE'S GETTING IN THE WAY.
WHAT SHOULD WE DO?
TELL SHY-DEMAN?
NO, YOU IDIOT!
HE'LL TAKE IT OUT ON US.
WE HAVE TO COME UP WITH A PLAN...
...TO GET OUR HANDS ON THAT GIRL.
EVIL.
I FEEL EVIL HERE.
IT MUST BE CESIA'S POWER.
YES. ONCE WE HAVE CESIA, WE WILL BE UN-STOPPABLE.

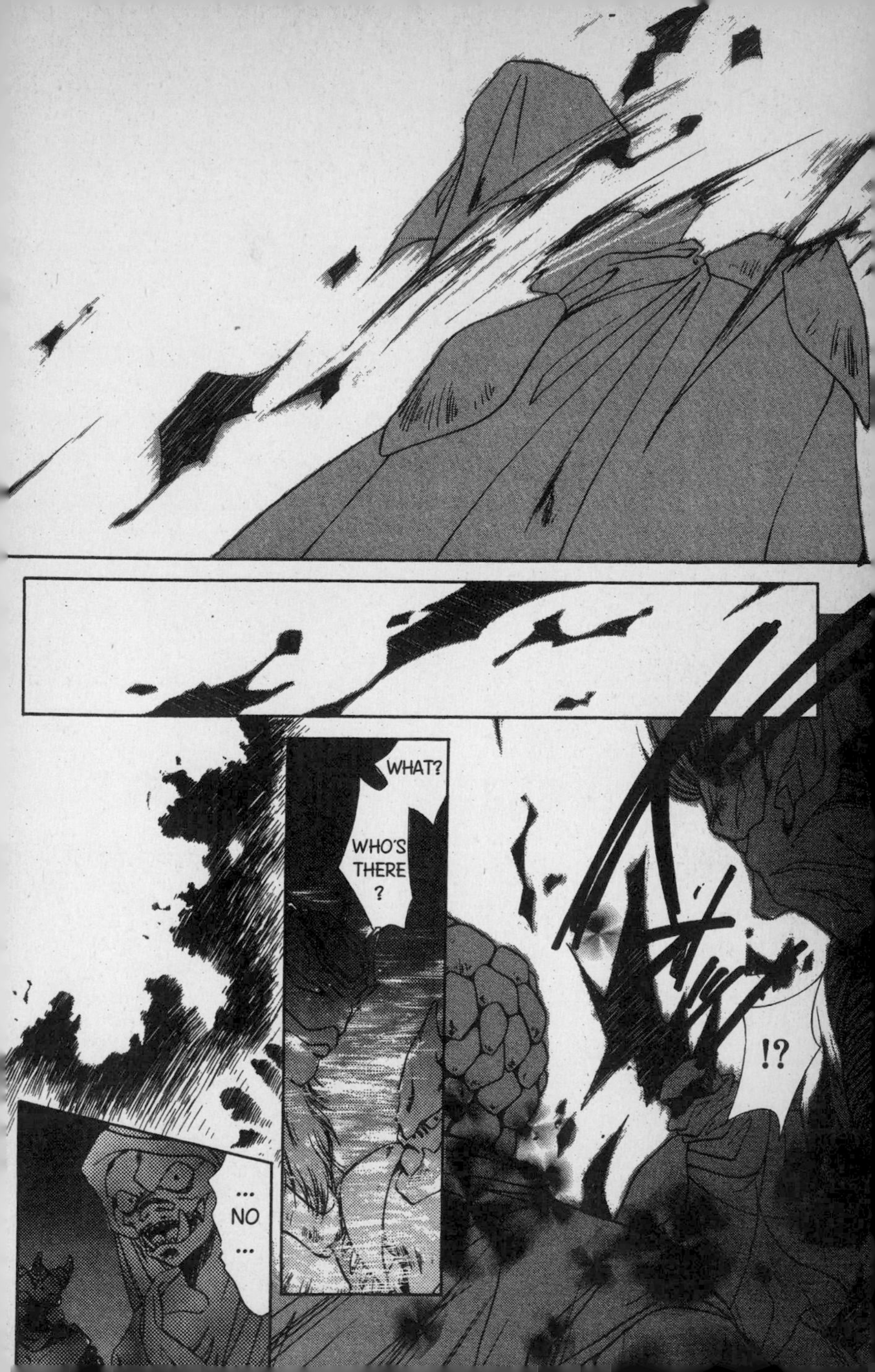
!?
WHAT?
WHO'S THERE ?
... NO ...

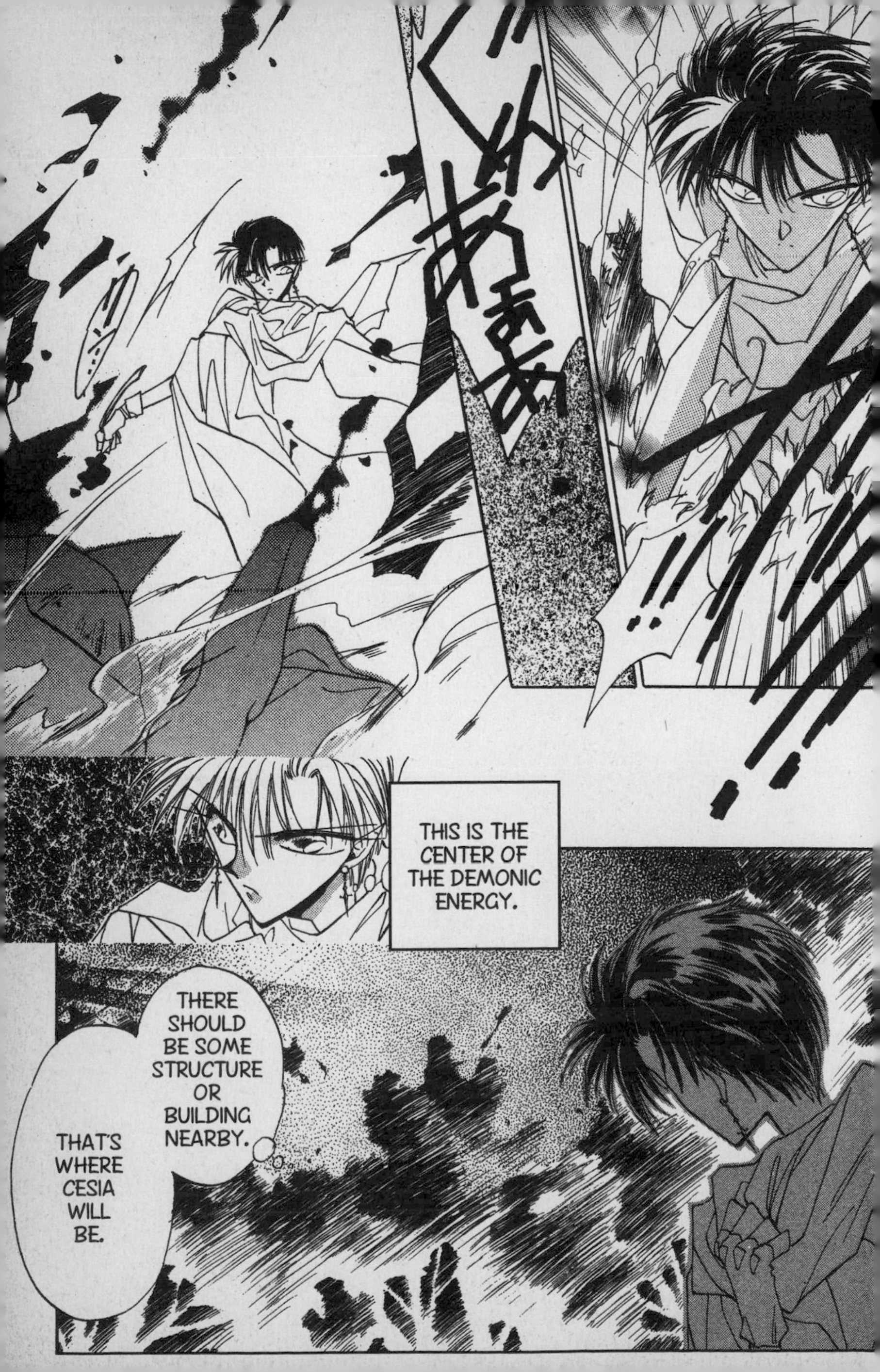
THIS IS THE CENTER OF THE DEMONIC ENERGY.
THERE SHOULD BE SOME STRUCTURE OR BUILDING NEARBY.
THAT'S WHERE CESIA WILL BE.

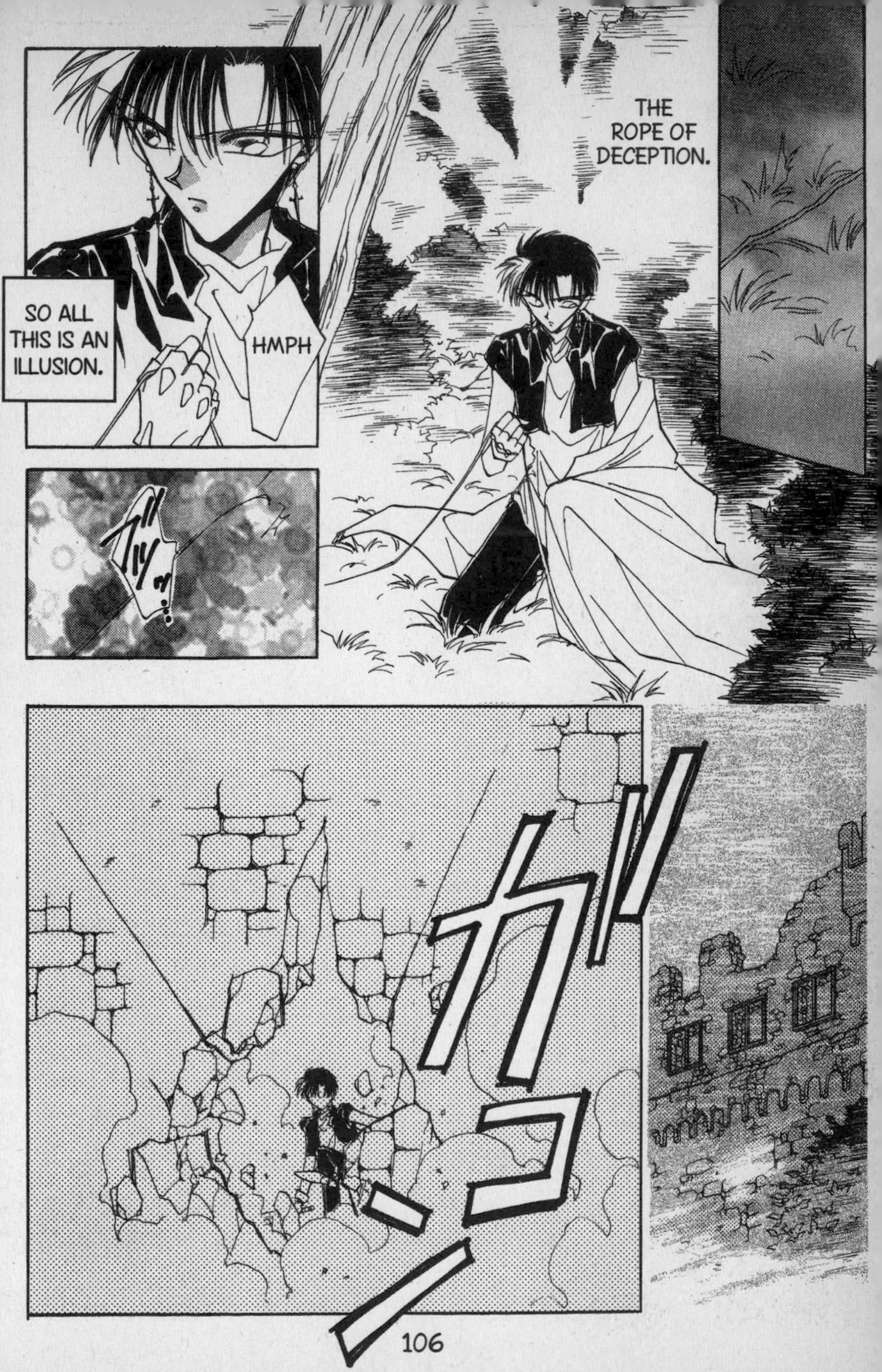
THE ROPE OF DECEPTION.
HMPH
SO ALL THIS IS AN ILLUSION.
ブツッ…
ガコン

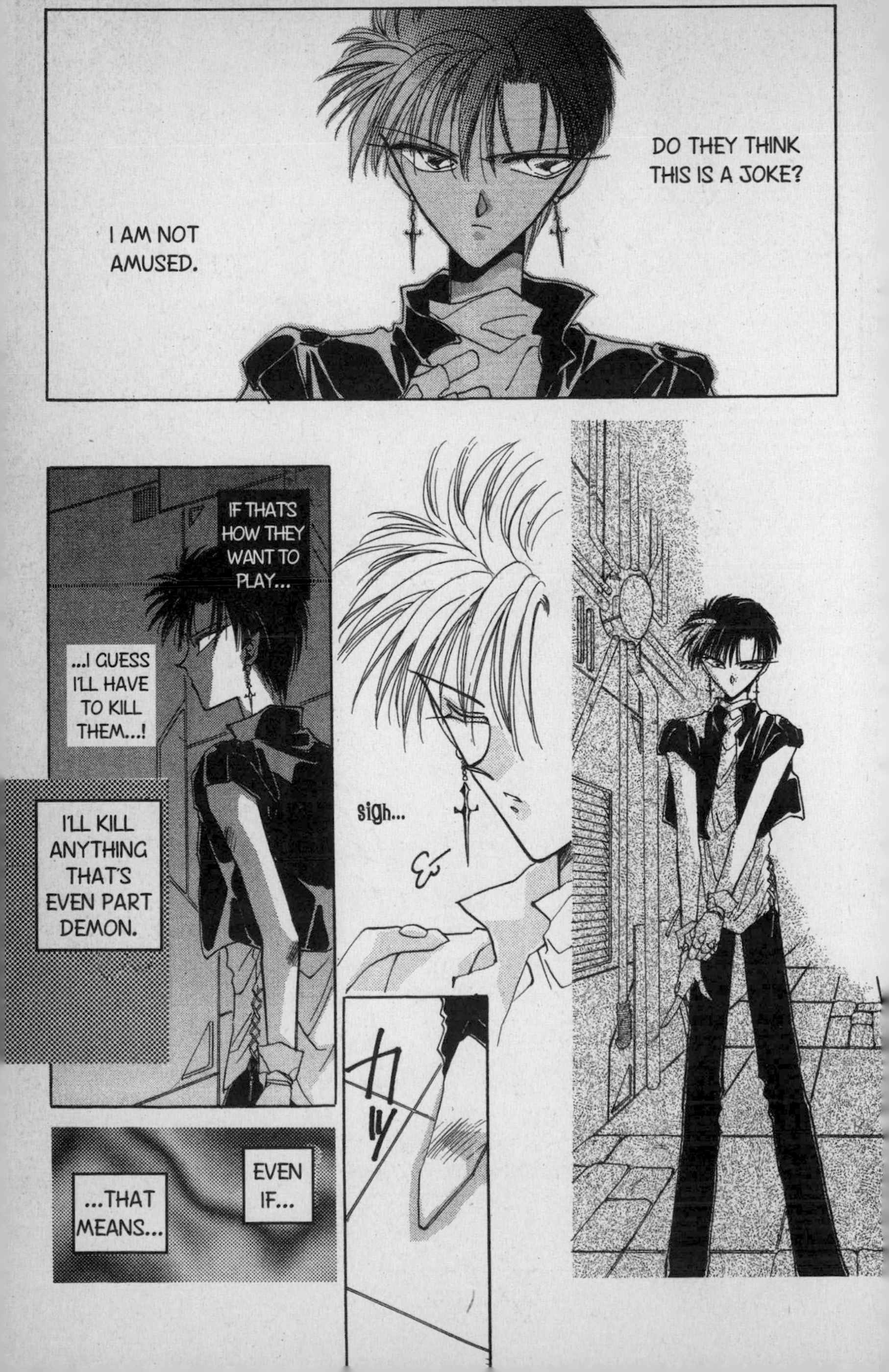
DO THEY THINK THIS IS A JOKE?
I AM NOT AMUSED.
sigh...
カッ
IF THATS HOW THEY WANT TO PLAY...
...I GUESS I'LL HAVE TO KILL THEM...!
I'LL KILL ANYTHING THAT'S EVEN PART DEMON.
EVEN IF...
...THAT MEANS...

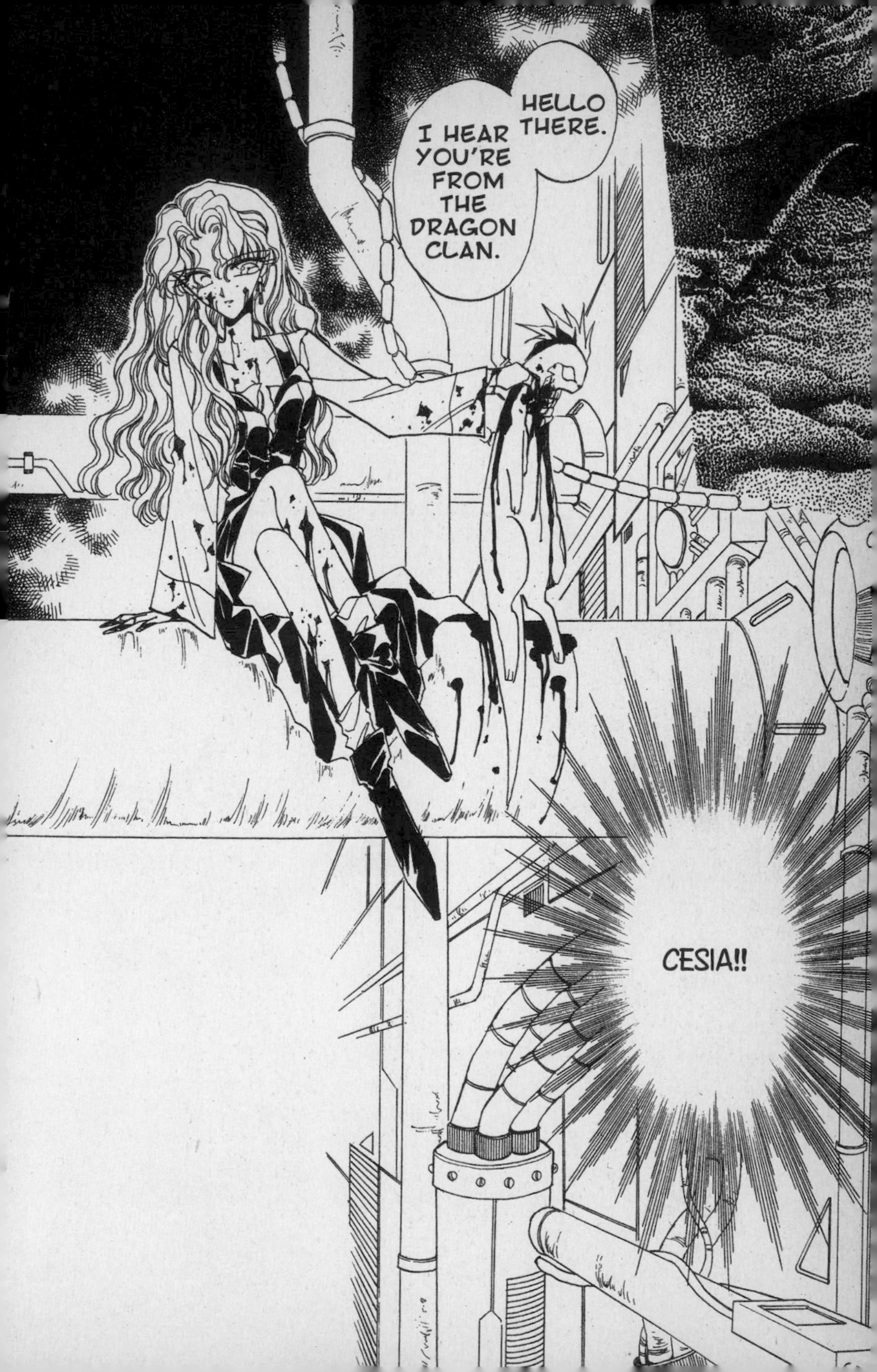
HELLO THERE.
I HEAR YOU'RE FROM THE DRAGON CLAN.
CESIA!!

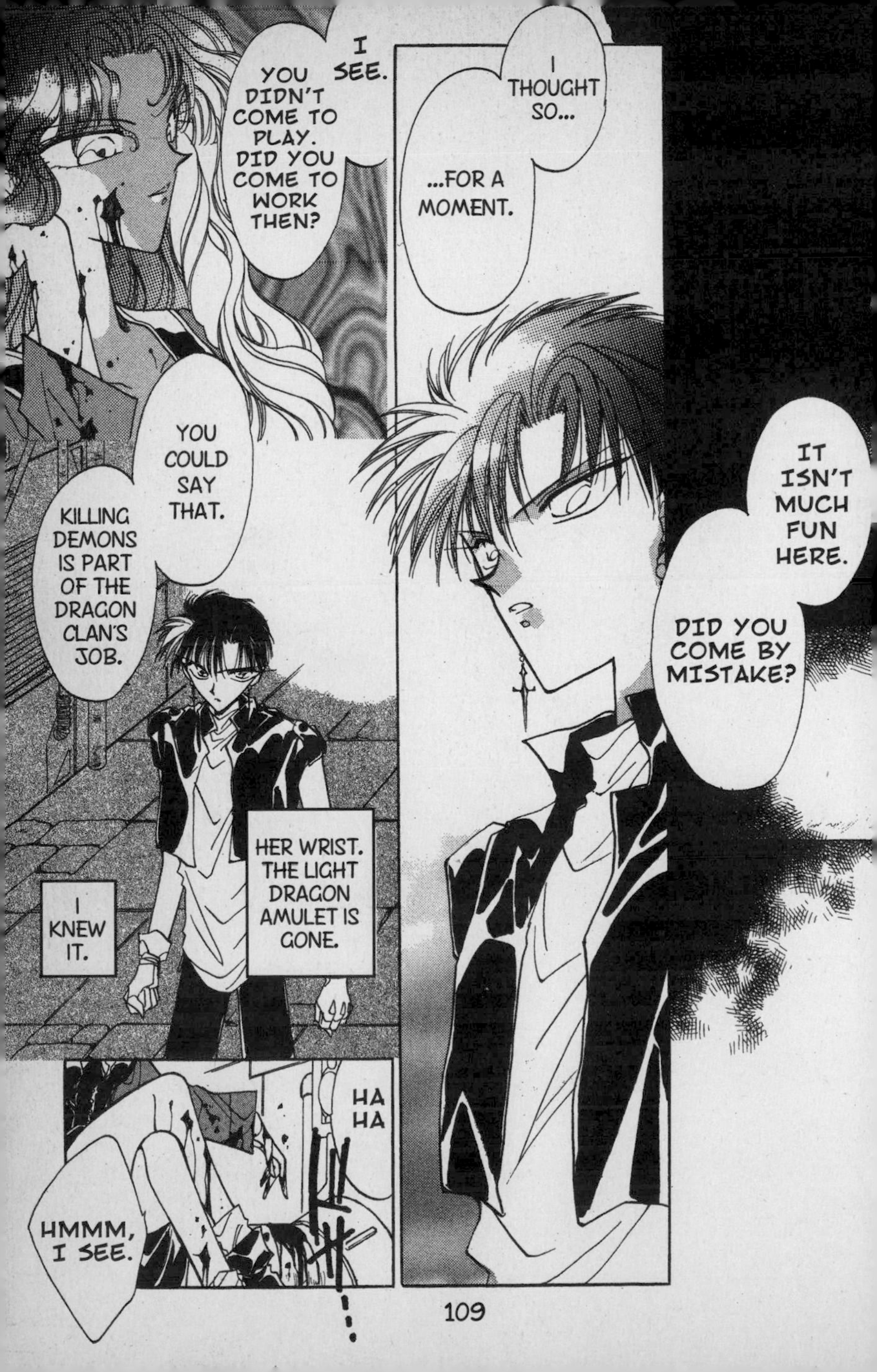
IT ISN'T MUCH FUN HERE.
DID YOU COME BY MISTAKE?
I THOUGHT SO...
...FOR A MOMENT.
I SEE.
YOU DIDN'T COME TO PLAY. DID YOU COME TO WORK THEN?
YOU COULD SAY THAT.
KILLING DEMONS IS PART OF THE DRAGON CLAN'S JOB.
HER WRIST. THE LIGHT DRAGON AMULET IS GONE.
I KNEW IT.
HA HA
HMMM, I SEE.

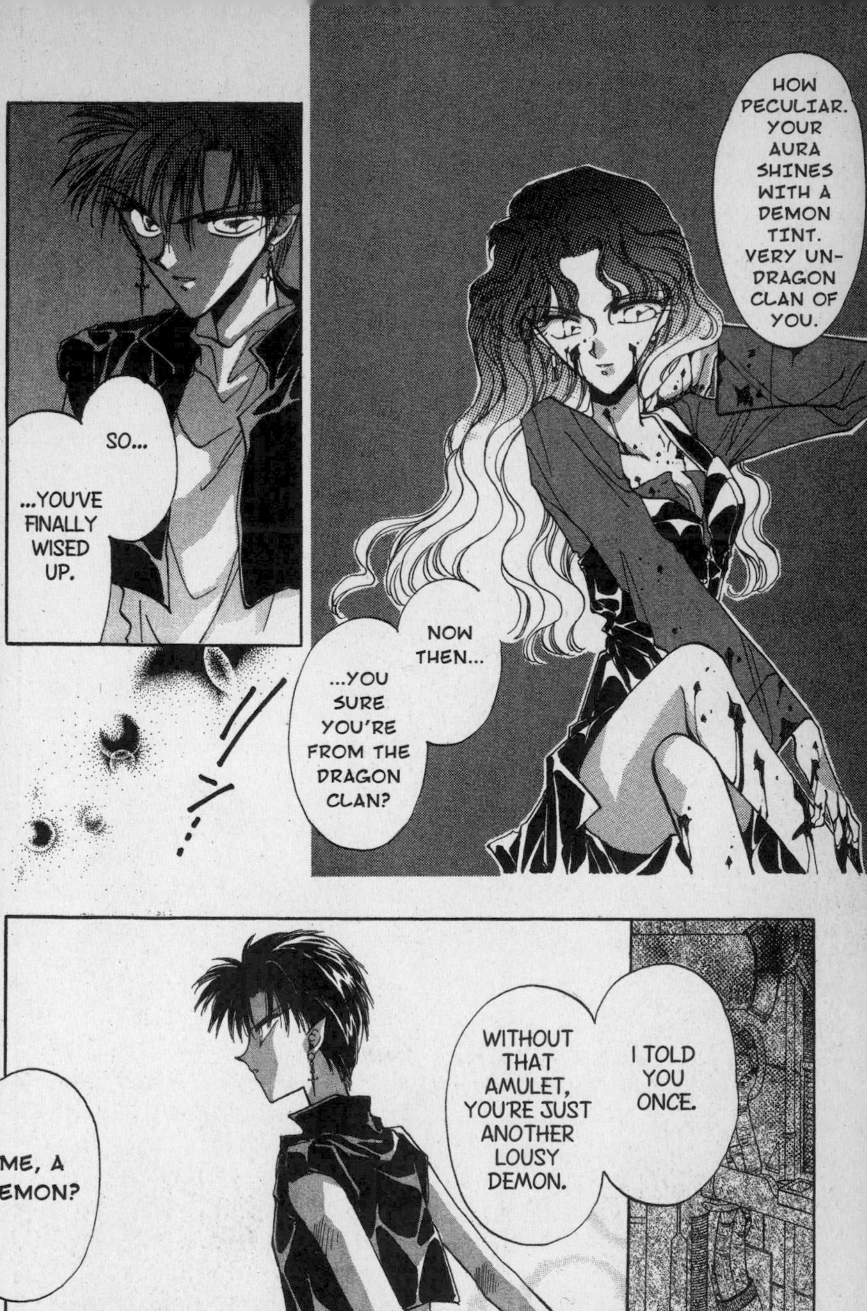
HOW PECULIAR. YOUR AURA SHINES WITH A DEMON TINT. VERY UN-DRAGON CLAN OF YOU.
NOW THEN...
...YOU SURE YOU'RE FROM THE DRAGON CLAN?
SO...
...YOU'VE FINALLY WISED UP.
I TOLD YOU ONCE.
WITHOUT THAT AMULET, YOU'RE JUST ANOTHER LOUSY DEMON.
ME, A DEMON?

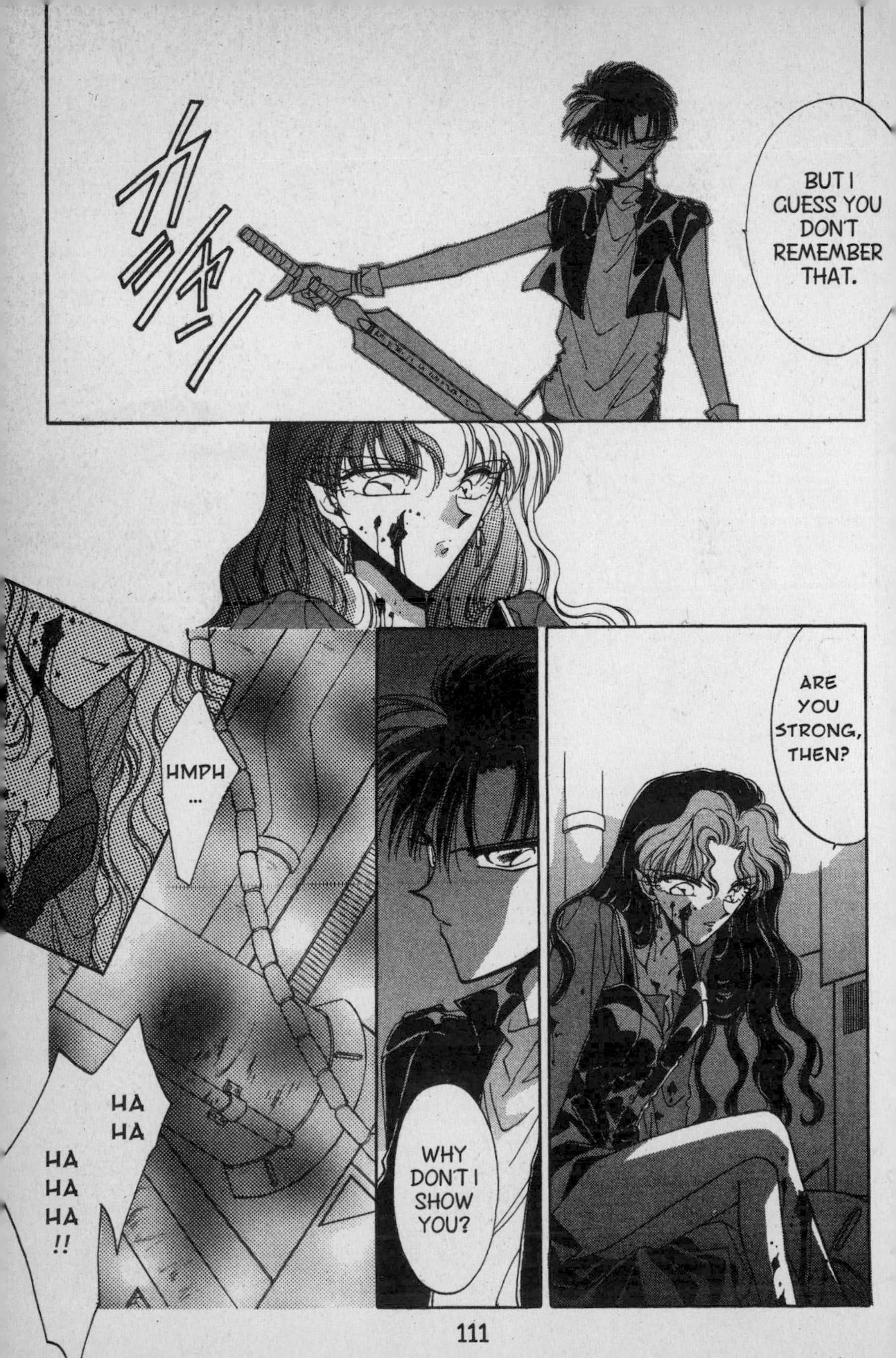
BUT I GUESS YOU DON'T REMEMBER THAT.
ARE YOU STRONG, THEN?
WHY DON'T I SHOW YOU?
HMPH ...
HA HA
HA HA HA !!

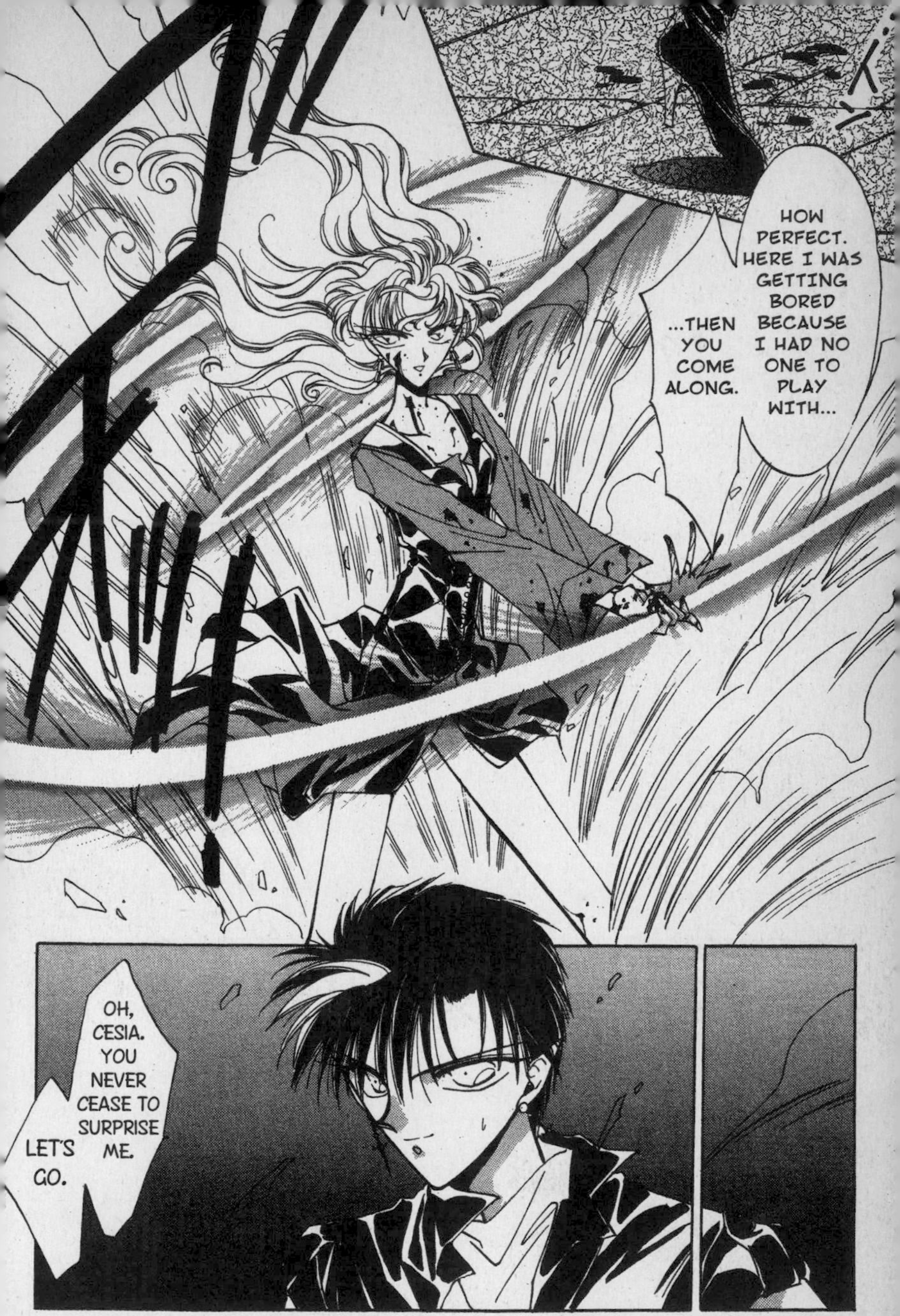
HOW PERFECT. HERE I WAS GETTING BORED BECAUSE I HAD NO ONE TO PLAY WITH...
...THEN YOU COME ALONG.
OH, CESIA. YOU NEVER CEASE TO SURPRISE ME.
LET'S GO.

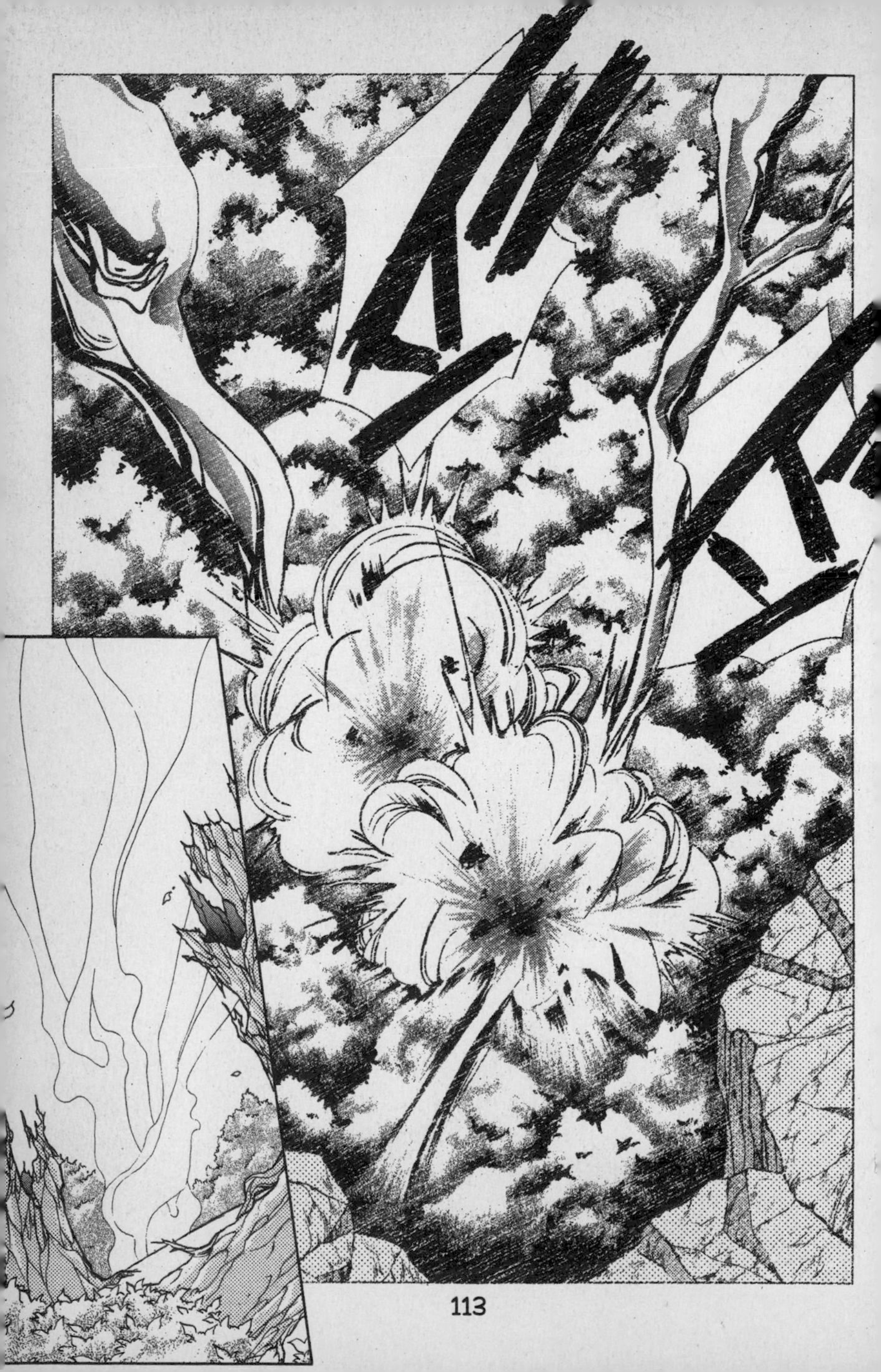

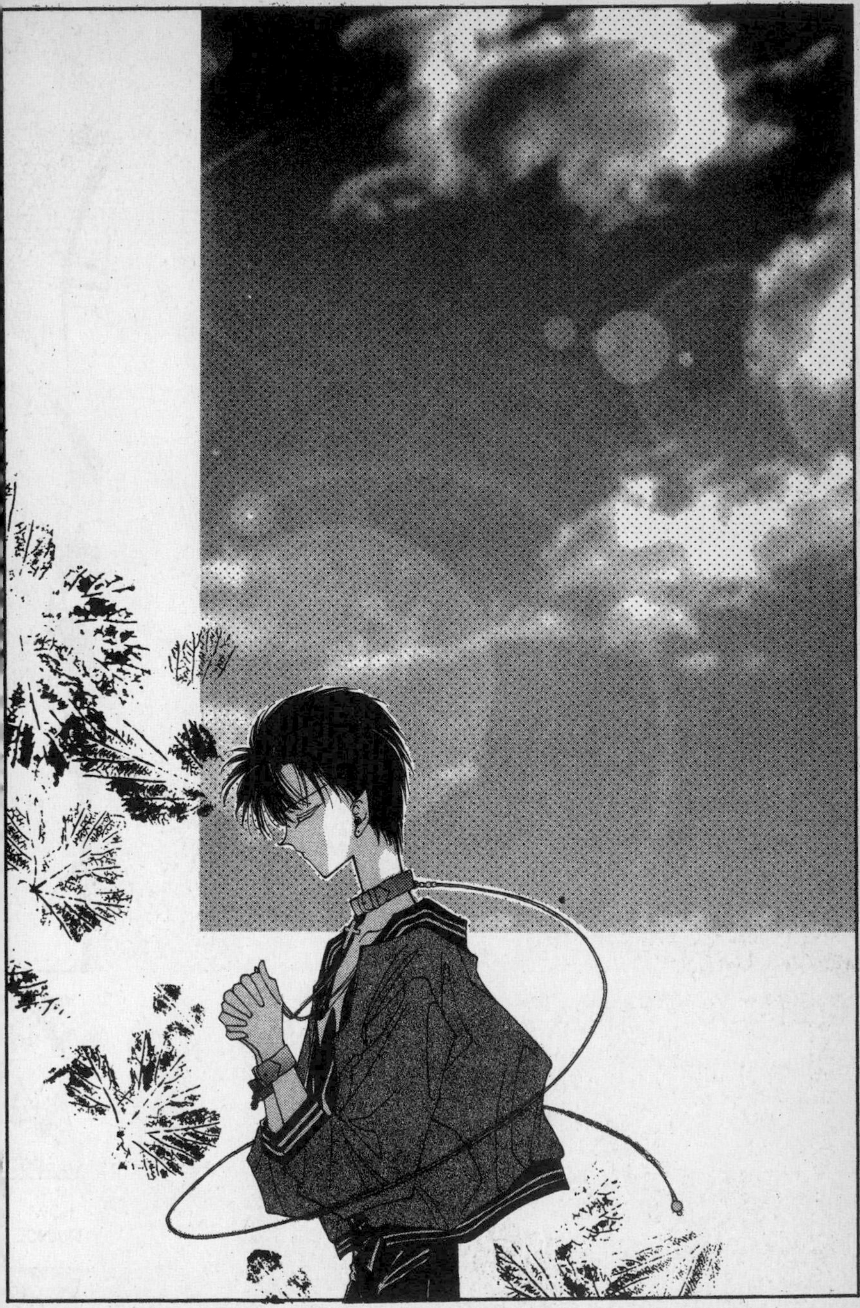

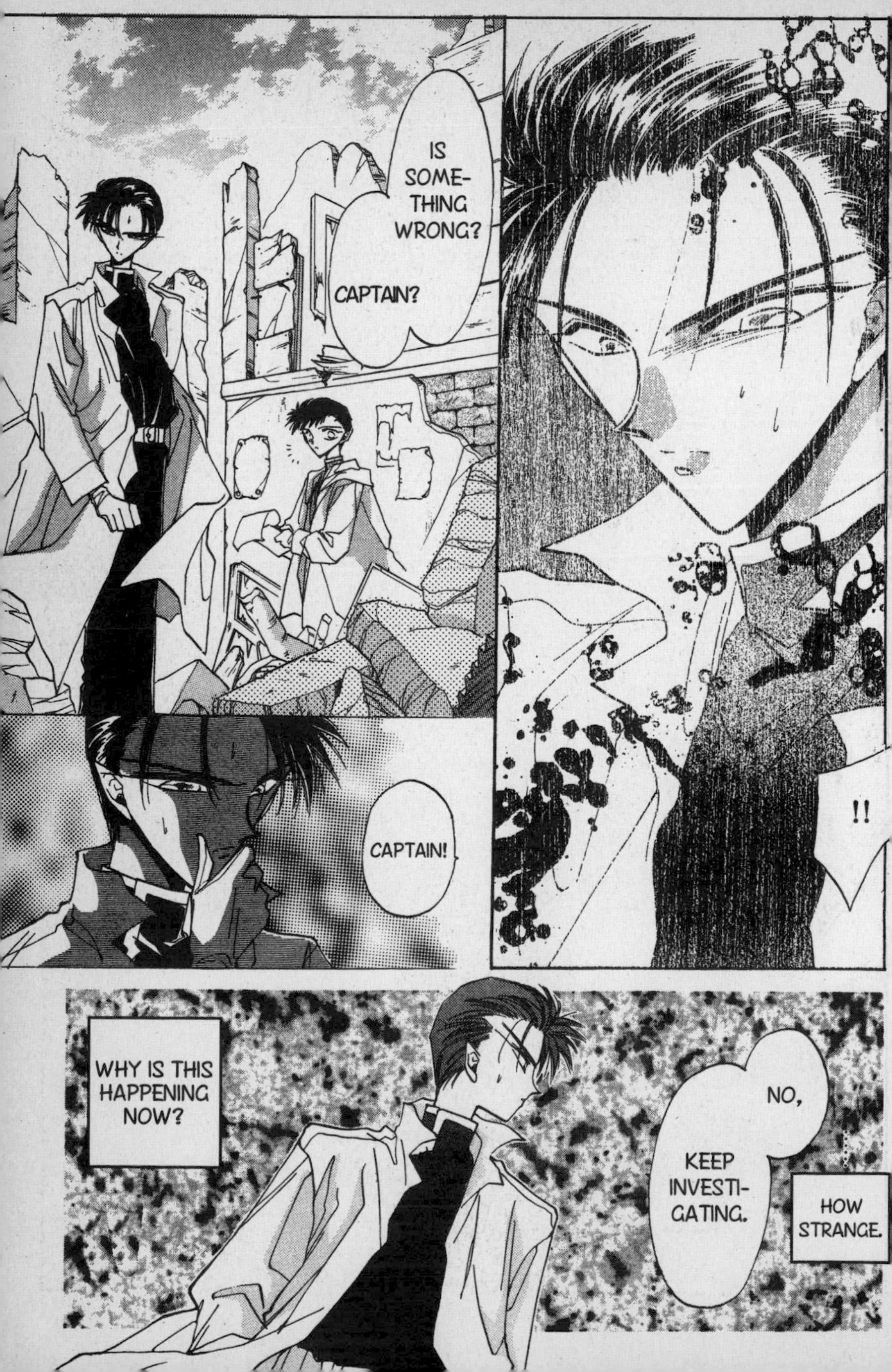
!!
IS SOMETHING WRONG?
CAPTAIN?
CAPTAIN!
NO, KEEP INVESTIGATING.
HOW STRANGE.
WHY IS THIS HAPPENING NOW?

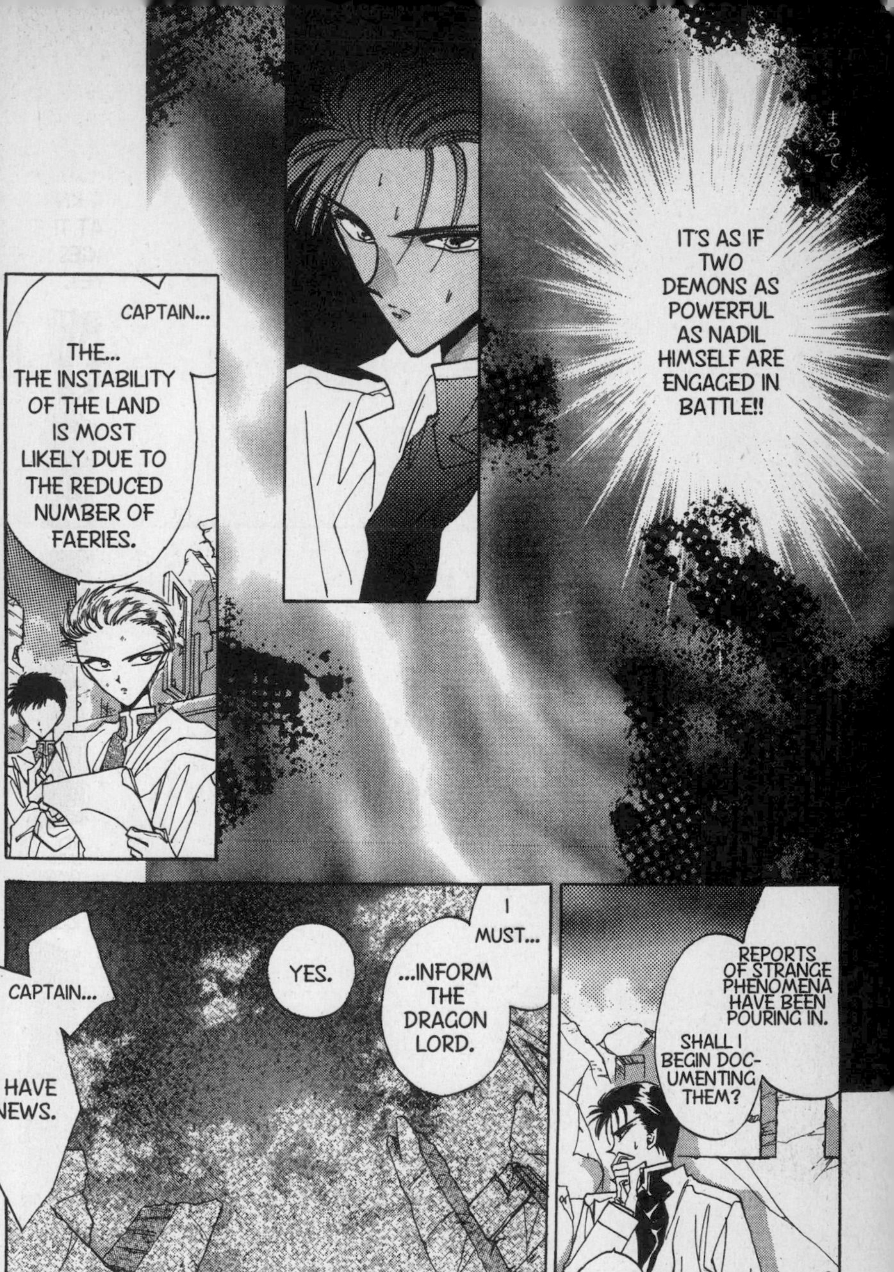
まるで
IT'S AS IF TWO DEMONS AS POWERFUL AS NADIL HIMSELF ARE ENGAGED IN BATTLE!!
CAPTAIN...
THE... THE INSTABILITY OF THE LAND IS MOST LIKELY DUE TO THE REDUCED NUMBER OF FAERIES.
REPORTS OF STRANGE PHENOMENA HAVE BEEN POURING IN.
SHALL I BEGIN DOC-UMENTING THEM?
YES.
I MUST...
...INFORM THE DRAGON LORD.
YES.
CAPTAIN...
I HAVE NEWS.

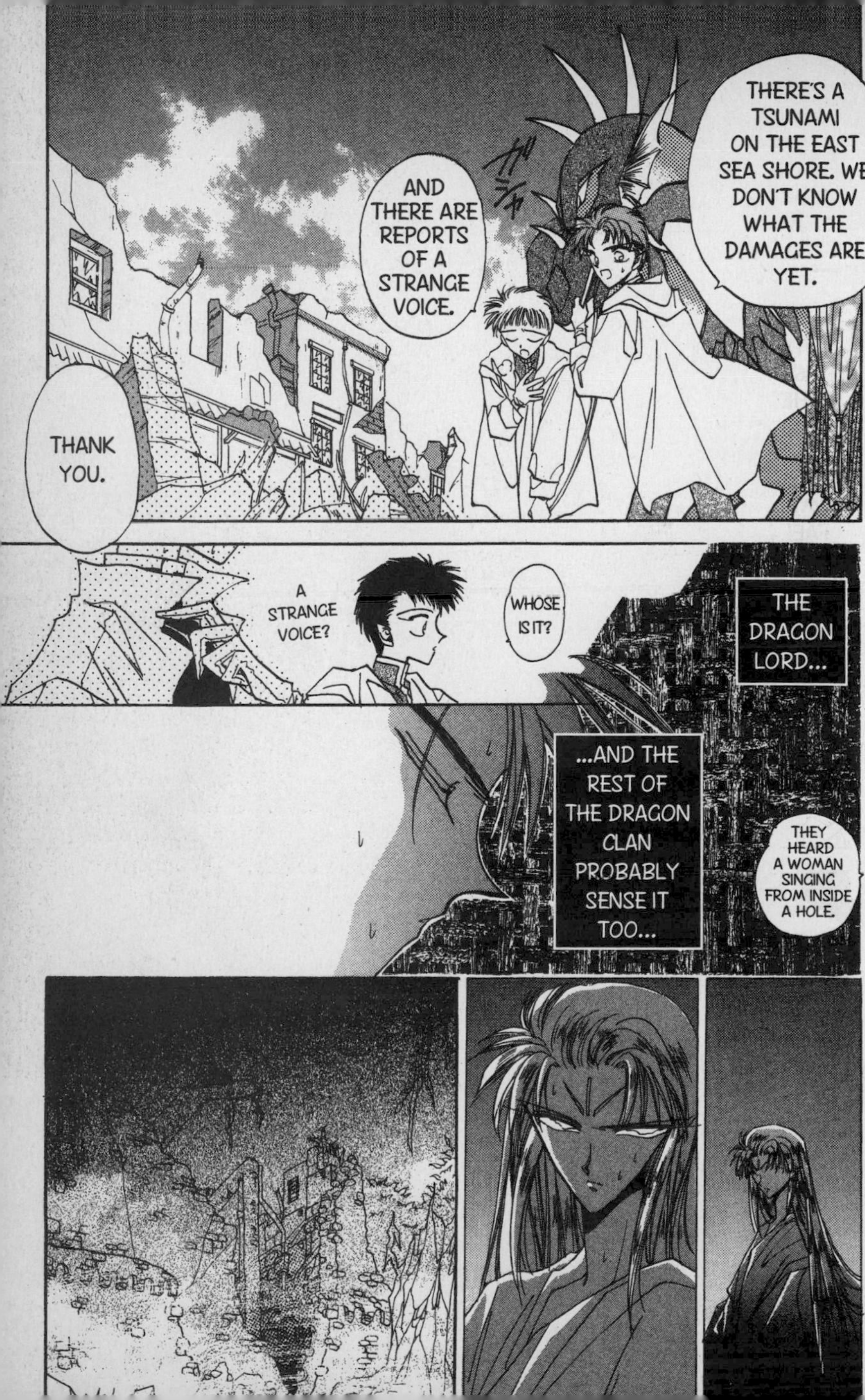
THERE'S A TSUNAMI ON THE EAST SEA SHORE. WE DON'T KNOW WHAT THE DAMAGES ARE YET.
ガシャ
AND THERE ARE REPORTS OF A STRANGE VOICE.
THANK YOU.
THE DRAGON LORD...
WHOSE IS IT?
A STRANGE VOICE?
THEY HEARD A WOMAN SINGING FROM INSIDE A HOLE.
...AND THE REST OF THE DRAGON CLAN PROBABLY SENSE IT TOO...

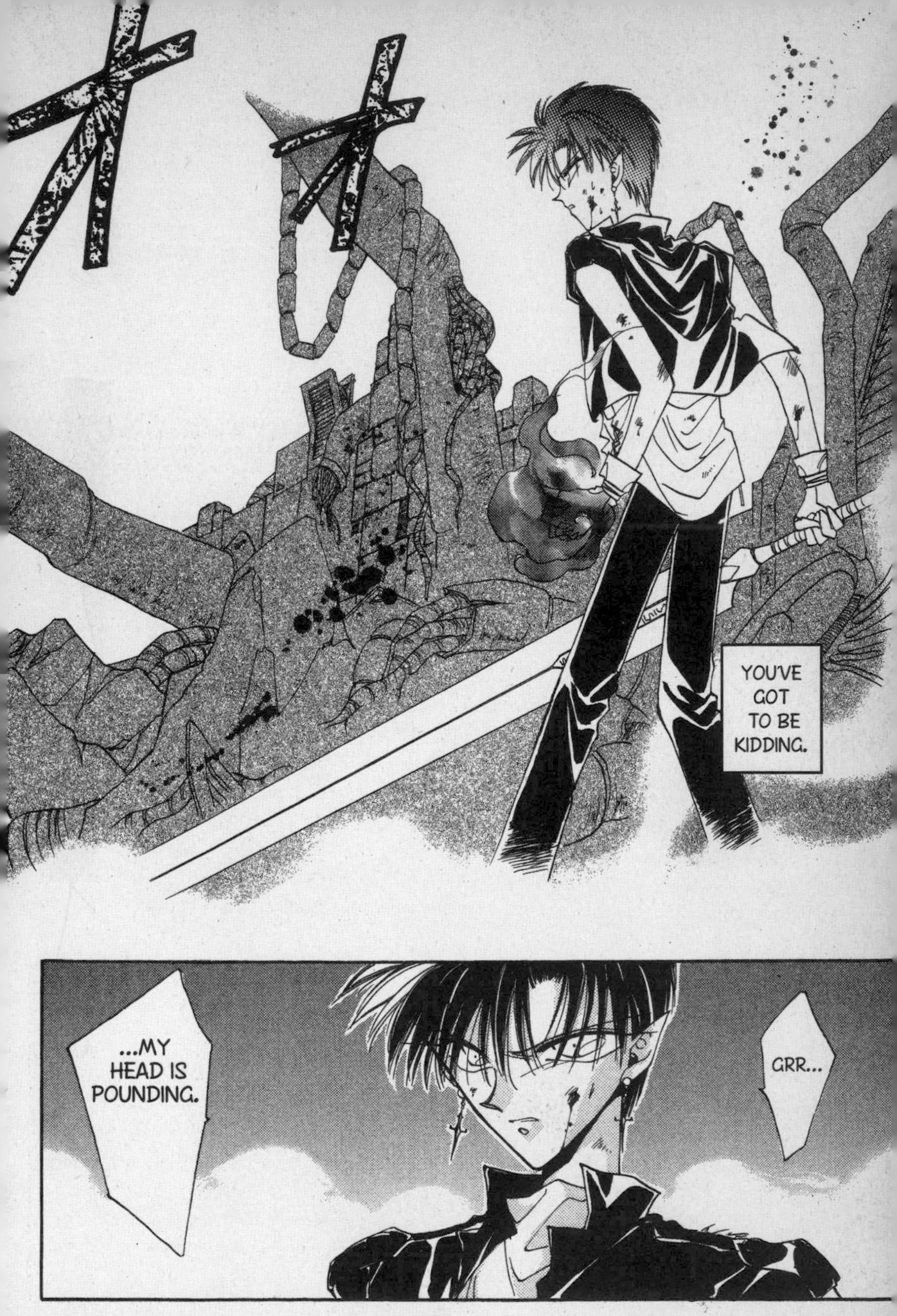
YOU'VE GOT TO BE KIDDING.
GRR...
...MY HEAD IS POUNDING.

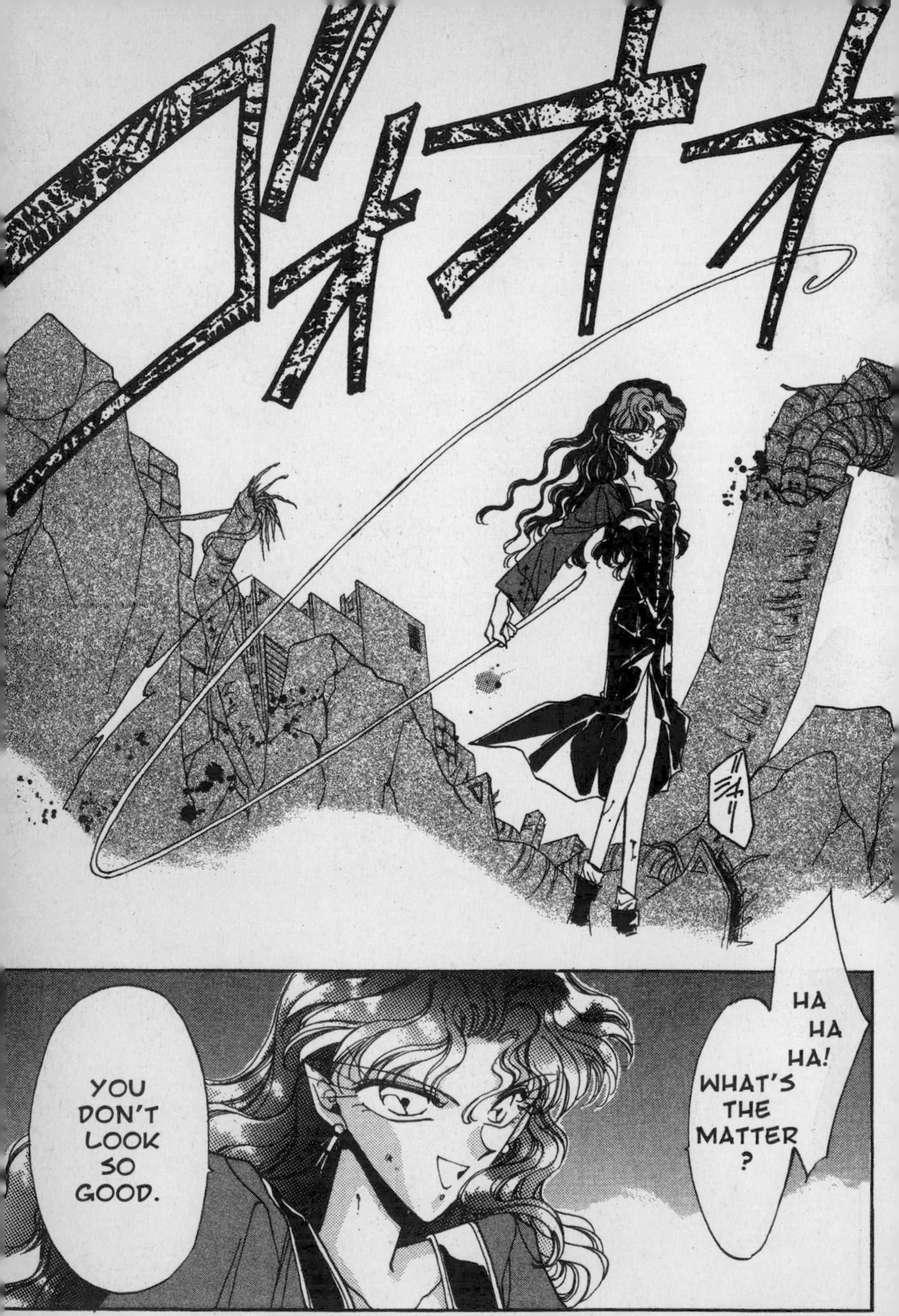
ゴォオオ
ジャリ
HA HA HA! WHAT'S THE MATTER?
YOU DON'T LOOK SO GOOD.

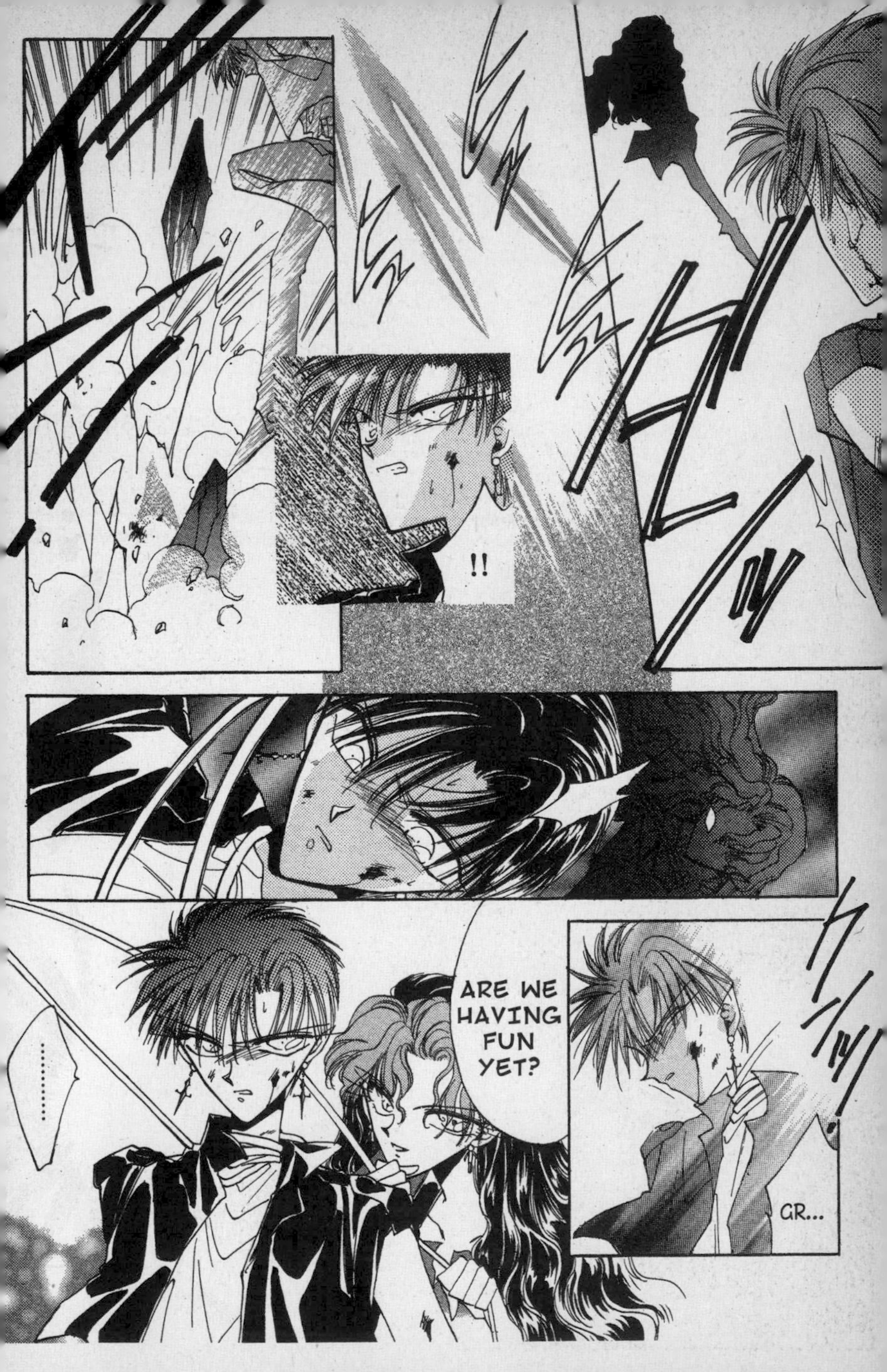
!!
GR...
ARE WE HAVING FUN YET?
......

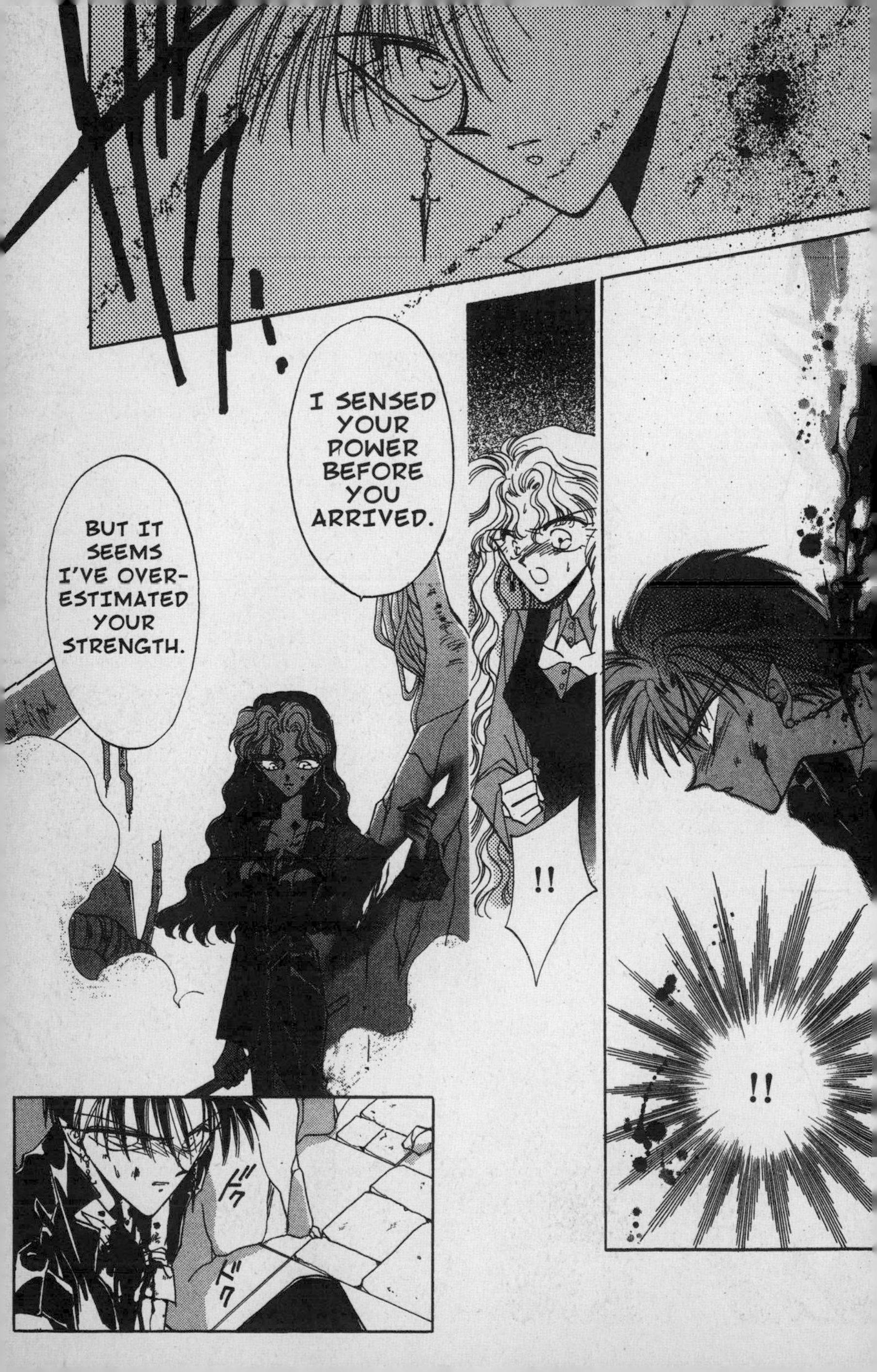
!!
!!
I SENSED YOUR POWER BEFORE YOU ARRIVED.
BUT IT SEEMS I'VE OVER-ESTIMATED YOUR STRENGTH.

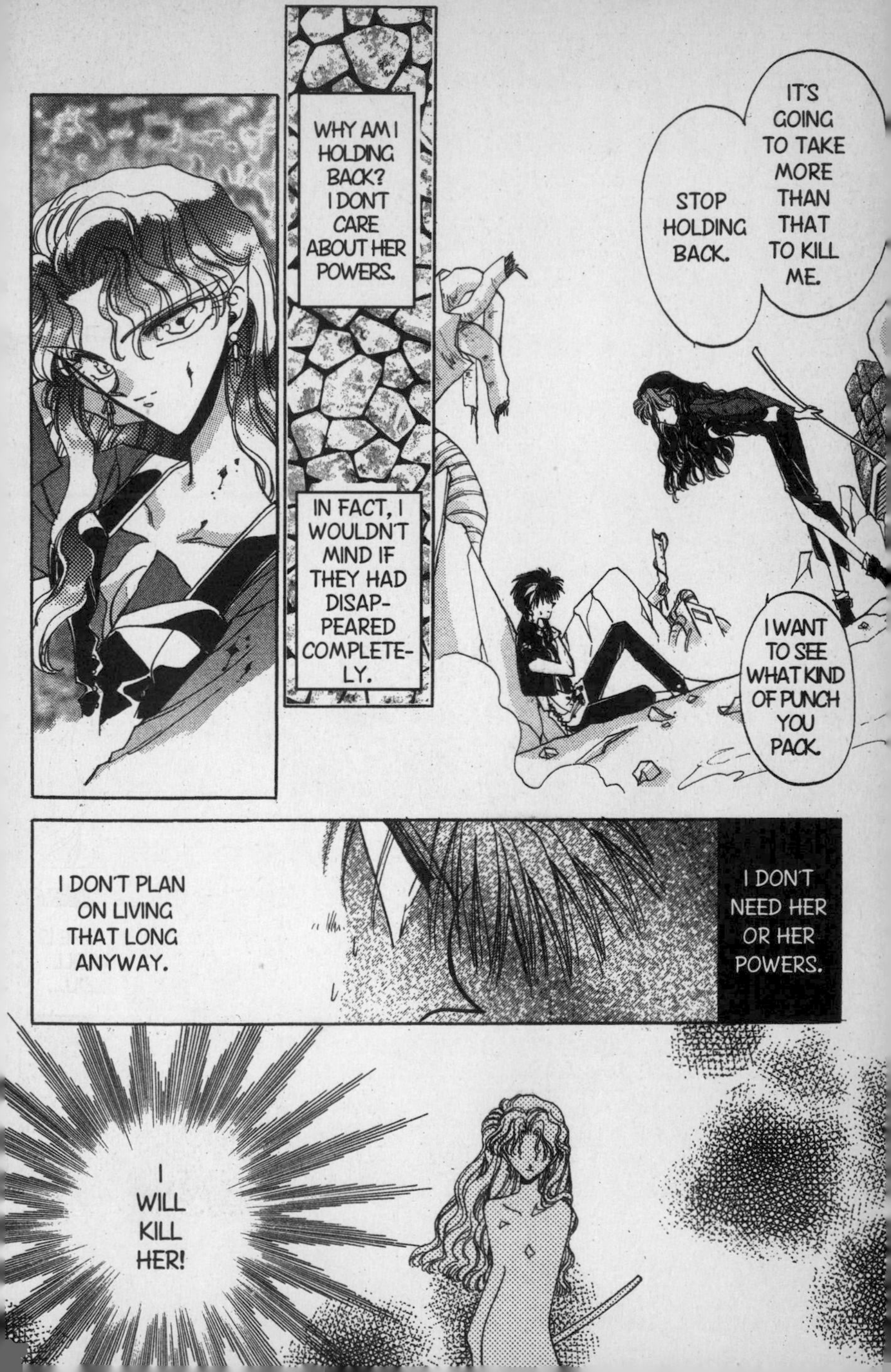

IT'S GOING TO TAKE MORE THAN THAT TO KILL ME.
STOP HOLDING BACK.
I WANT TO SEE WHAT KIND OF PUNCH YOU PACK.
WHY AM I HOLDING BACK? I DONT CARE ABOUT HER POWERS.
IN FACT, I WOULDN'T MIND IF THEY HAD DISAP-PEARED COMPLETE-LY.
I DON'T NEED HER OR HER POWERS.
I DON'T PLAN ON LIVING THAT LONG ANYWAY.
I WILL KILL HER!

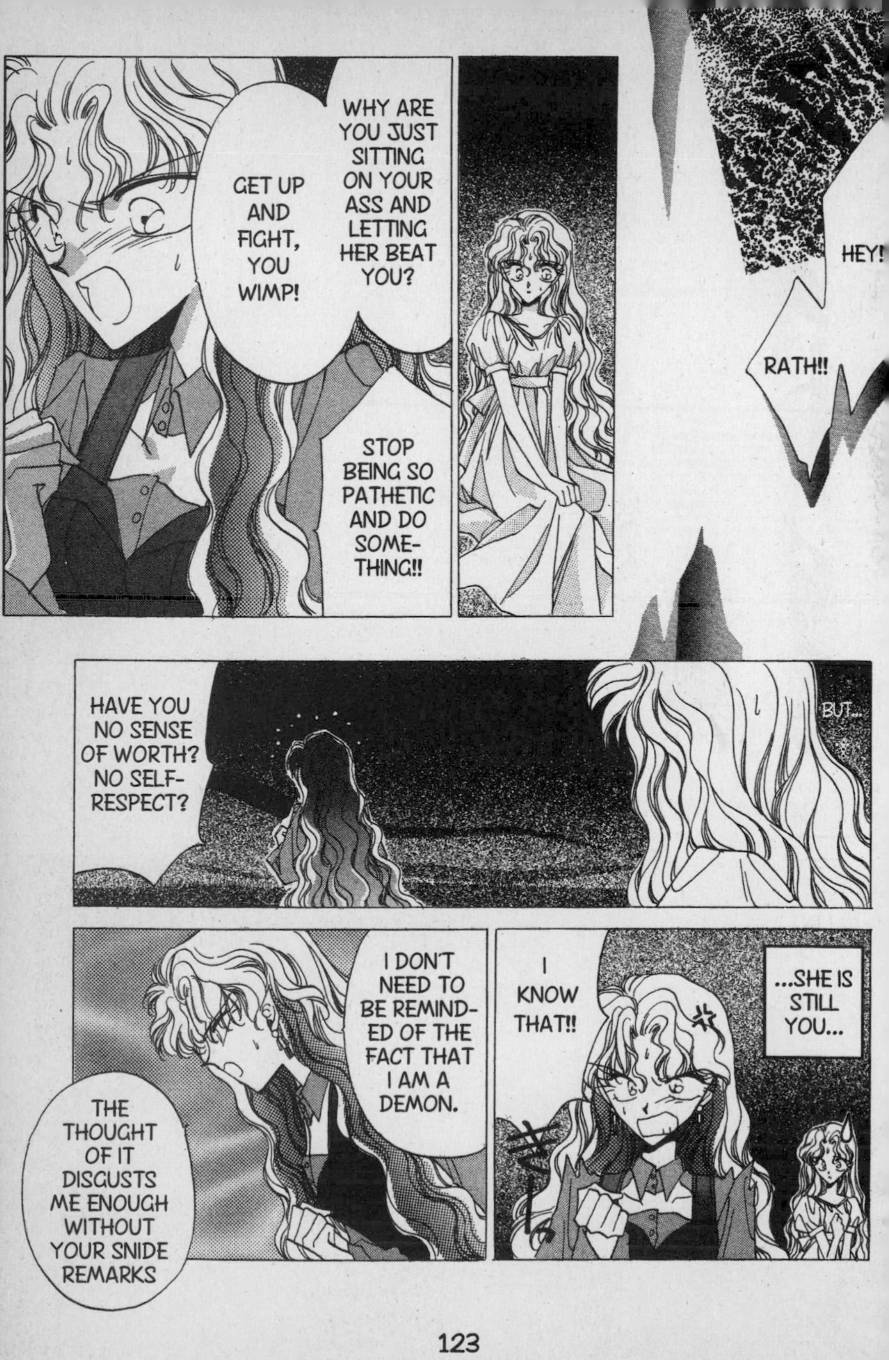
HEY!
RATH!!
WHY ARE YOU JUST SITTING ON YOUR ASS AND LETTING HER BEAT YOU?
GET UP AND FIGHT, YOU WIMP!
STOP BEING SO PATHETIC AND DO SOME-THING!!
BUT...
HAVE YOU NO SENSE OF WORTH? NO SELF-RESPECT?
...SHE IS STILL YOU...
I KNOW THAT!!
I DON'T NEED TO BE REMIND-ED OF THE FACT THAT I AM A DEMON.
THE THOUGHT OF IT DISGUSTS ME ENOUGH WITHOUT YOUR SNIDE REMARKS

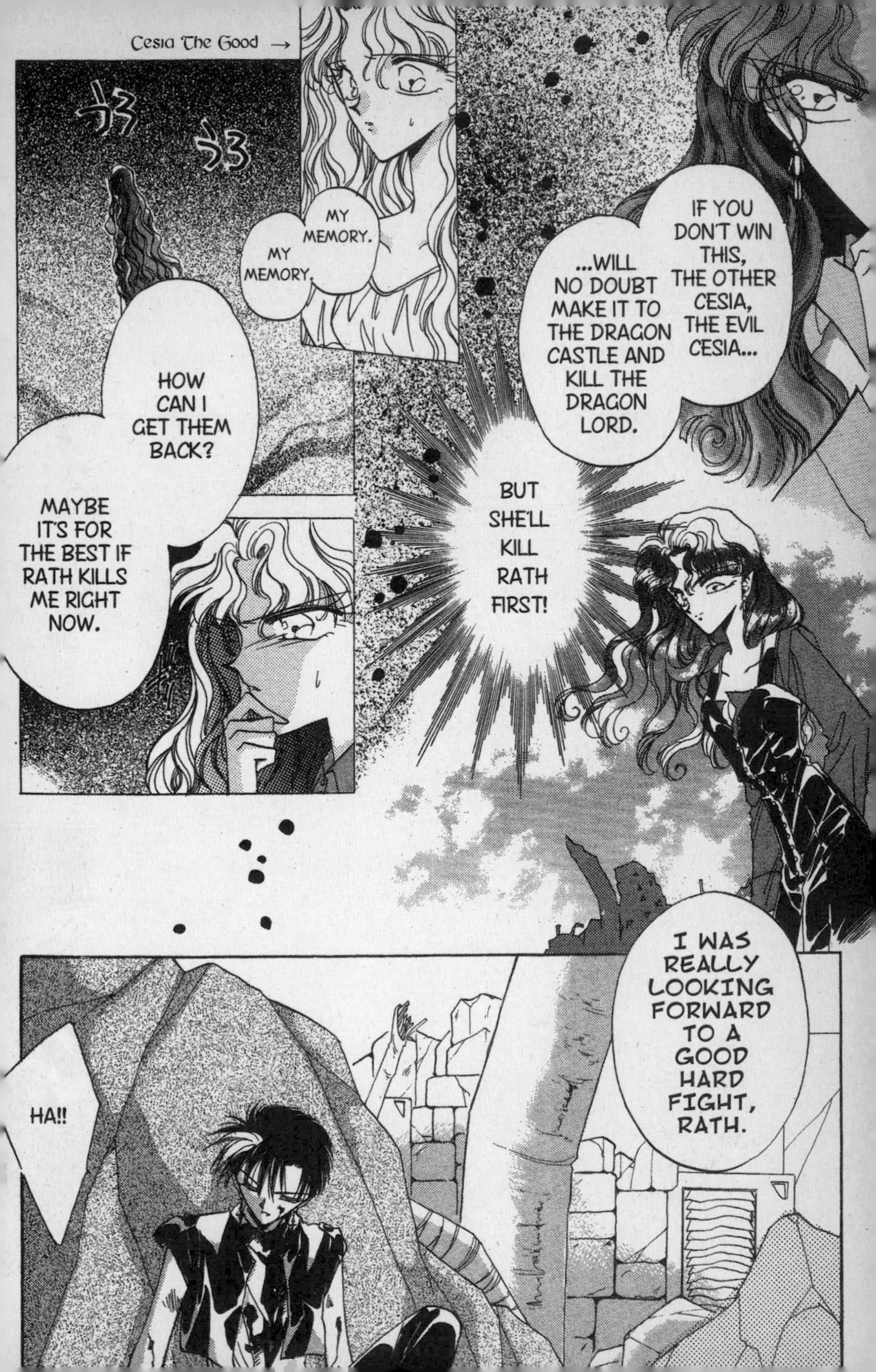
IF YOU DON'T WIN THIS, THE OTHER CESIA, THE EVIL CESIA...
...WILL NO DOUBT MAKE IT TO THE DRAGON CASTLE AND KILL THE DRAGON LORD.
Cesia The Good →
MY MEMORY.
MY MEMORY.
HOW CAN I GET THEM BACK?
MAYBE IT'S FOR THE BEST IF RATH KILLS ME RIGHT NOW.
BUT SHE'LL KILL RATH FIRST!
I WAS REALLY LOOKING FORWARD TO A GOOD HARD FIGHT, RATH.
HA!!

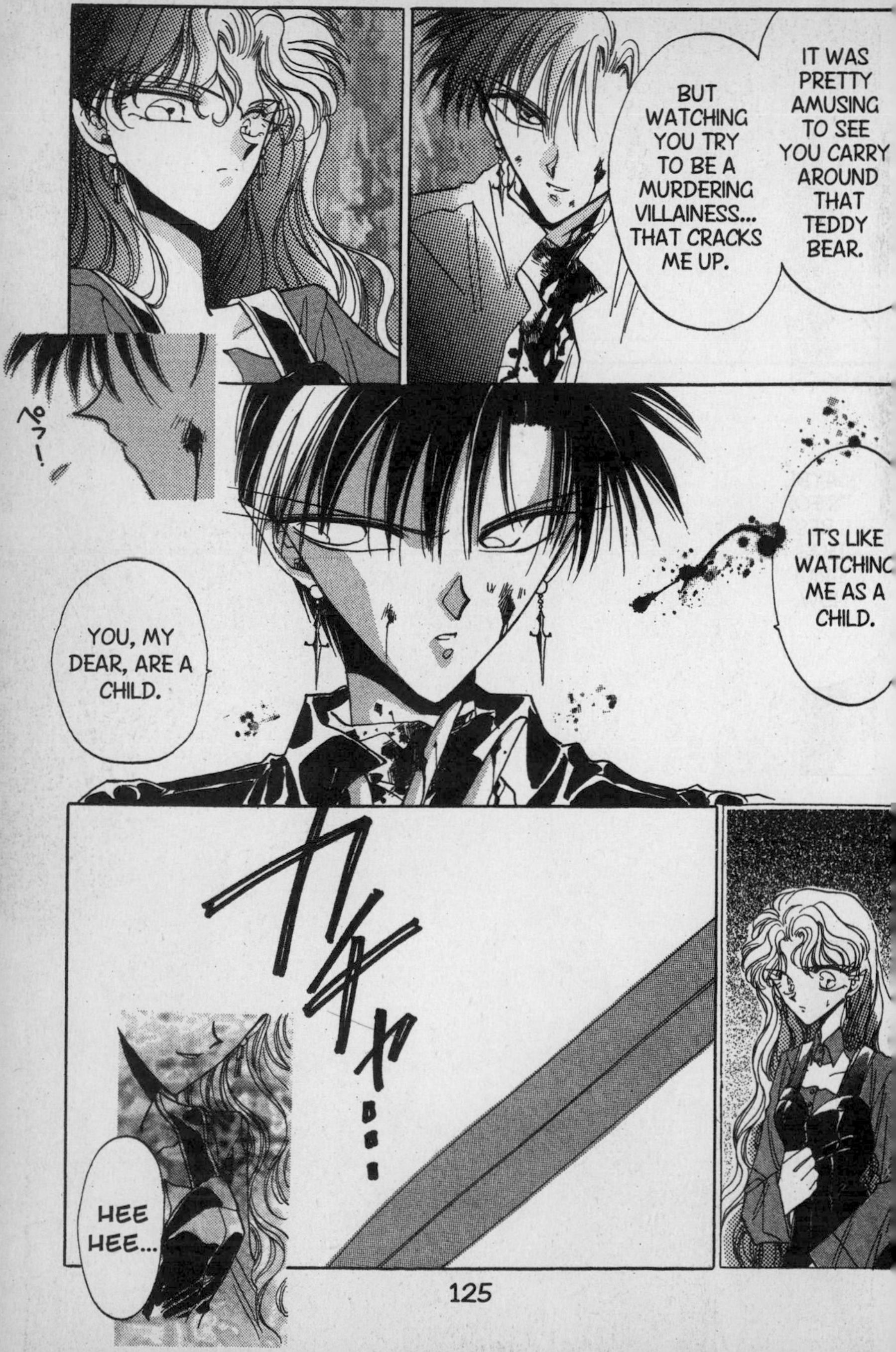
IT WAS PRETTY AMUSING TO SEE YOU CARRY AROUND THAT TEDDY BEAR.
BUT WATCHING YOU TRY TO BE A MURDERING VILLAINESS... THAT CRACKS ME UP.
IT'S LIKE WATCHING ME AS A CHILD.
YOU, MY DEAR, ARE A CHILD.
カチャ...
HEE HEE...

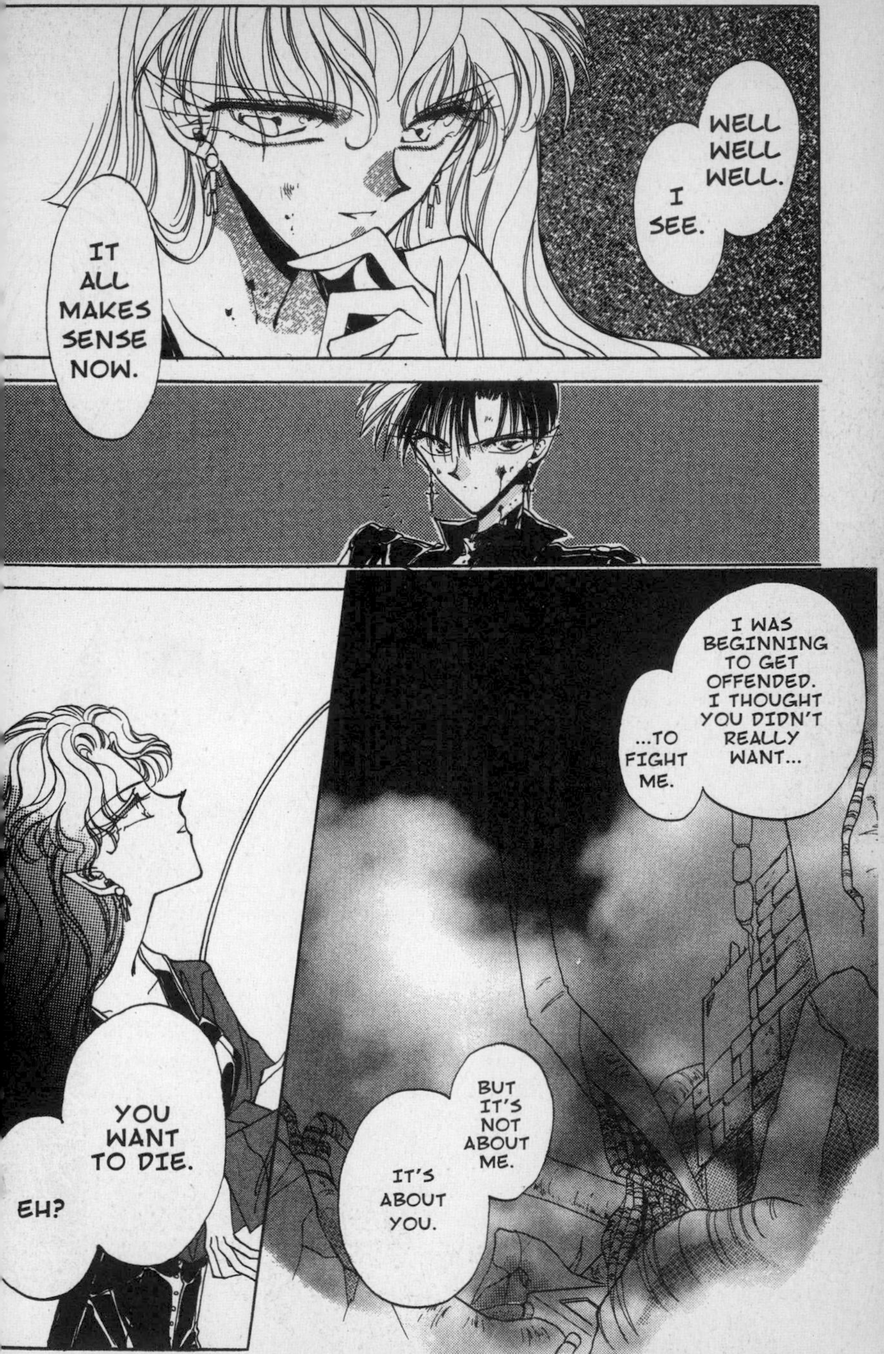
WELL WELL WELL.
I SEE.
IT ALL MAKES SENSE NOW.
I WAS BEGINNING TO GET OFFENDED. I THOUGHT YOU DIDN'T REALLY WANT...
...TO FIGHT ME.
BUT IT'S NOT ABOUT ME.
IT'S ABOUT YOU.
YOU WANT TO DIE.
EH?

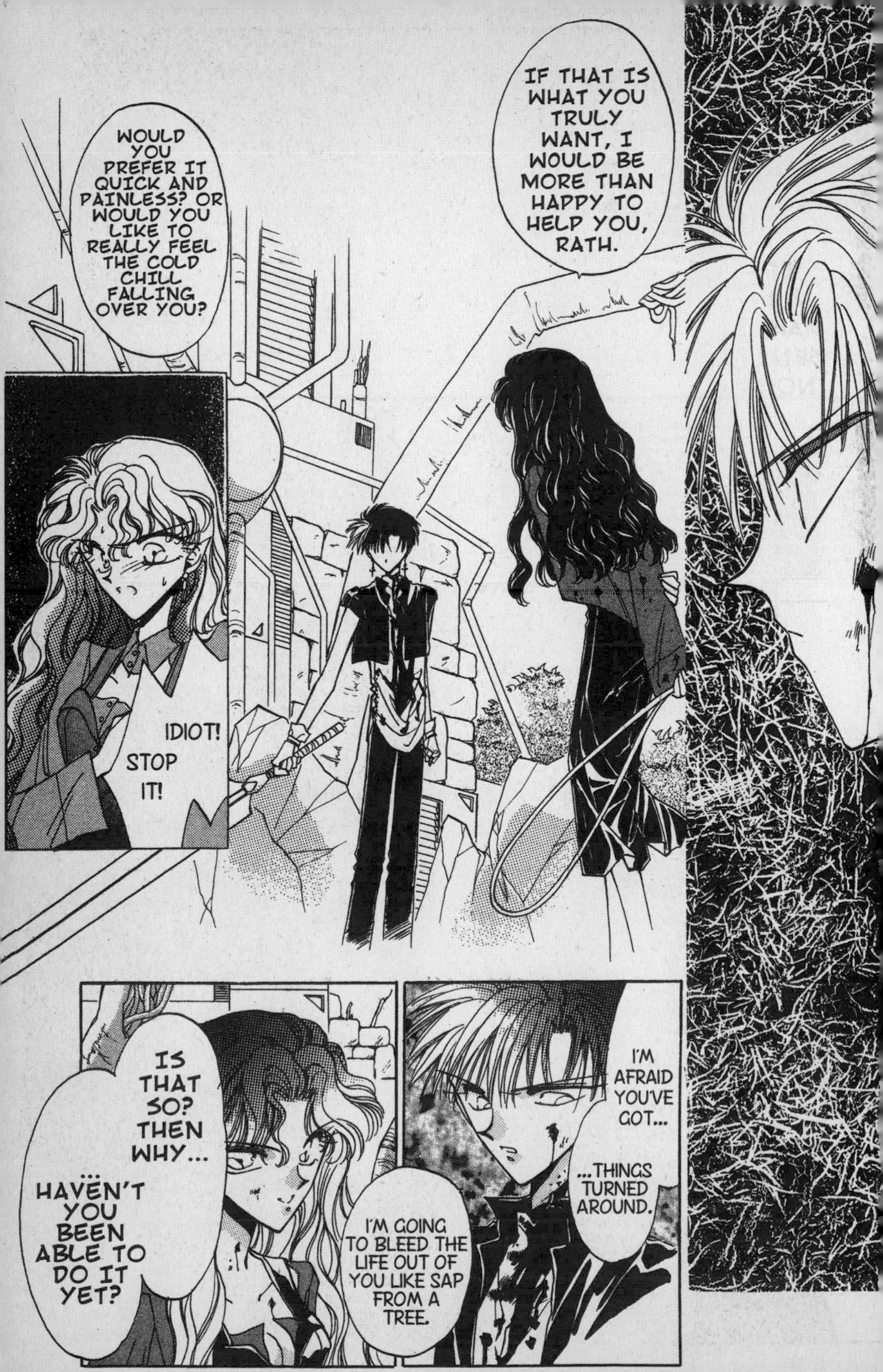
IF THAT IS WHAT YOU TRULY WANT, I WOULD BE MORE THAN HAPPY TO HELP YOU, RATH.
WOULD YOU PREFER IT QUICK AND PAINLESS? OR WOULD YOU LIKE TO REALLY FEEL THE COLD CHILL FALLING OVER YOU?
IDIOT!
STOP IT!
I'M AFRAID YOU'VE GOT...
...THINGS TURNED AROUND.
I'M GOING TO BLEED THE LIFE OUT OF YOU LIKE SAP FROM A TREE.
IS THAT SO? THEN WHY...
...HAVEN'T YOU BEEN ABLE TO DO IT YET?

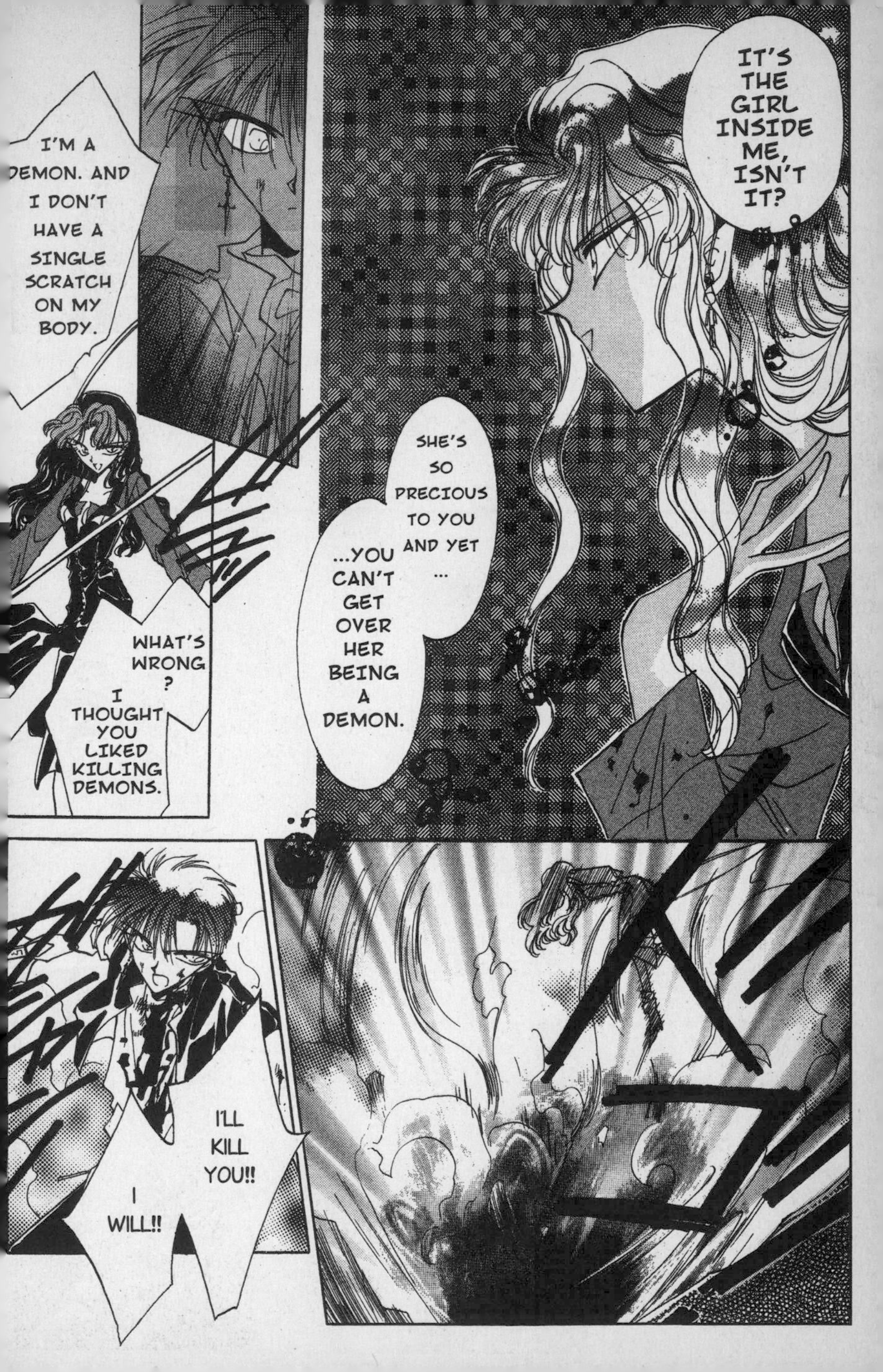
IT'S THE GIRL INSIDE ME, ISN'T IT?
SHE'S SO PRECIOUS TO YOU AND YET ...
...YOU CAN'T GET OVER HER BEING A DEMON.
I'M A DEMON. AND I DON'T HAVE A SINGLE SCRATCH ON MY BODY.
WHAT'S WRONG? I THOUGHT YOU LIKED KILLING DEMONS.
I'LL KILL YOU!!
I WILL!!

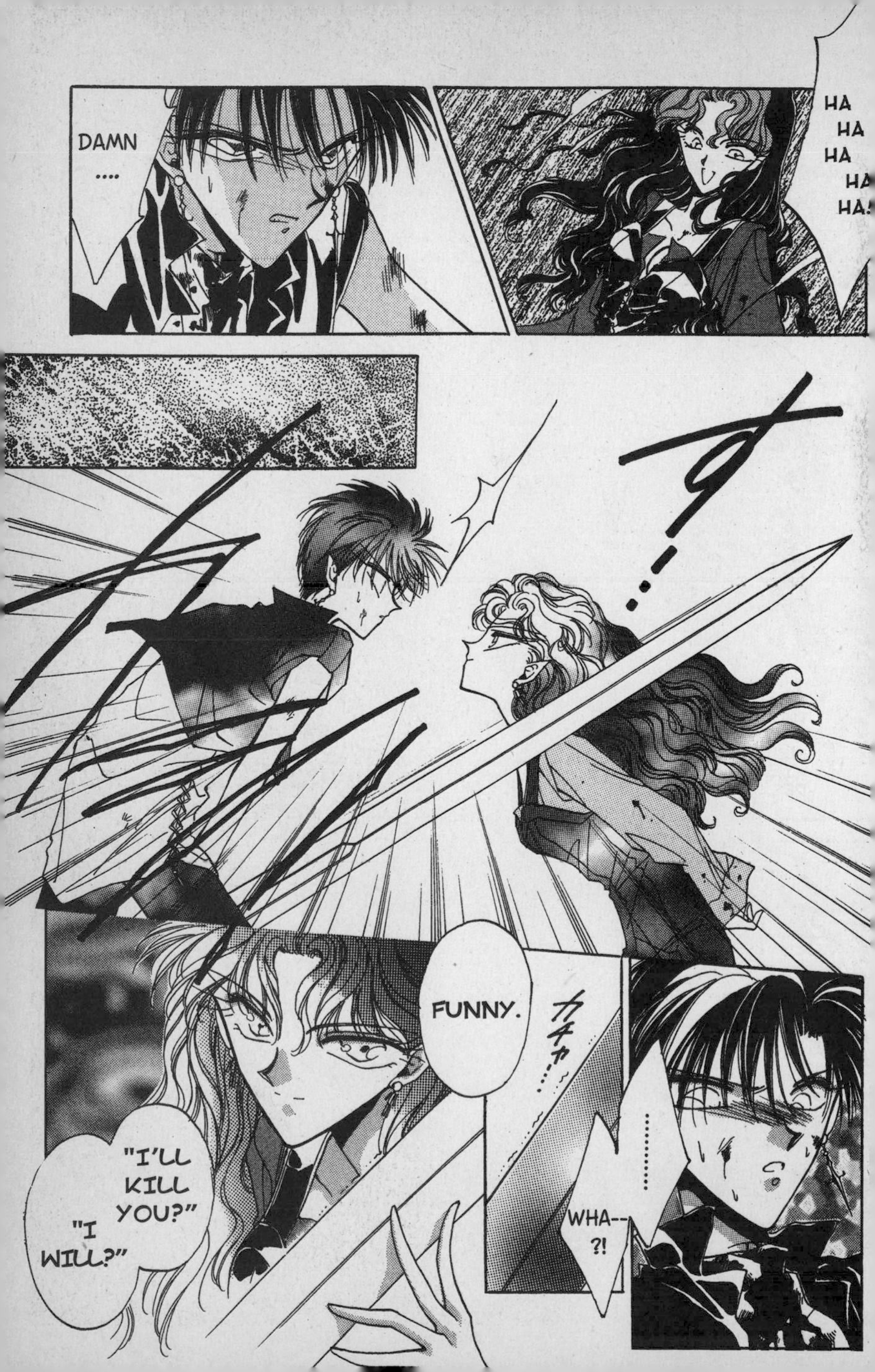
HA HA HA HA HA!
DAMN ....
......
WHA-- ?!
カチャ...
FUNNY.
"I'LL KILL YOU?"
"I WILL?"

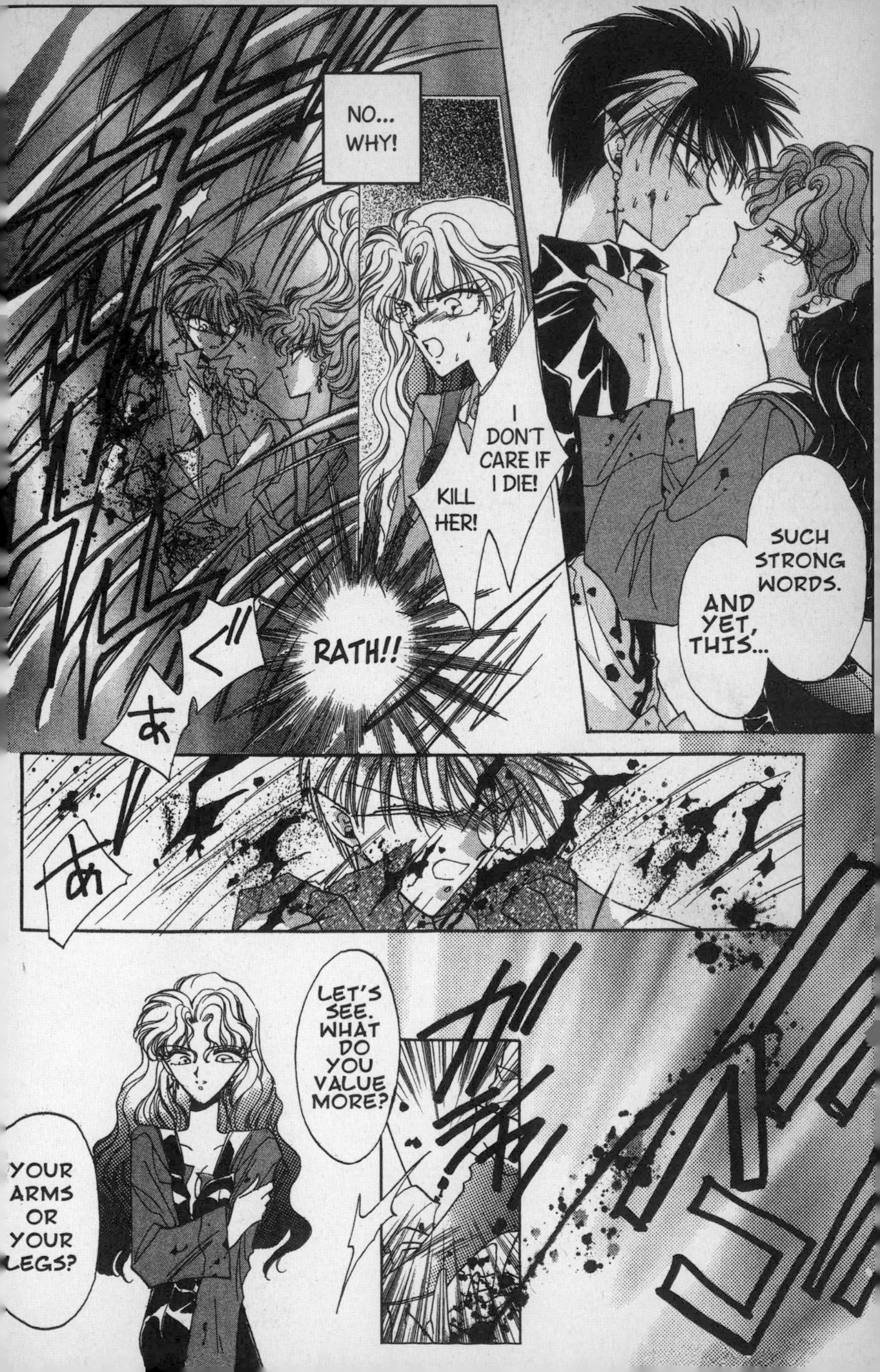
NO... WHY!
I DON'T CARE IF I DIE!
KILL HER!
SUCH STRONG WORDS.
AND YET, THIS...
RATH!!
ぐ
あ
あ
LET'S SEE. WHAT DO YOU VALUE MORE?
YOUR ARMS OR YOUR LEGS?

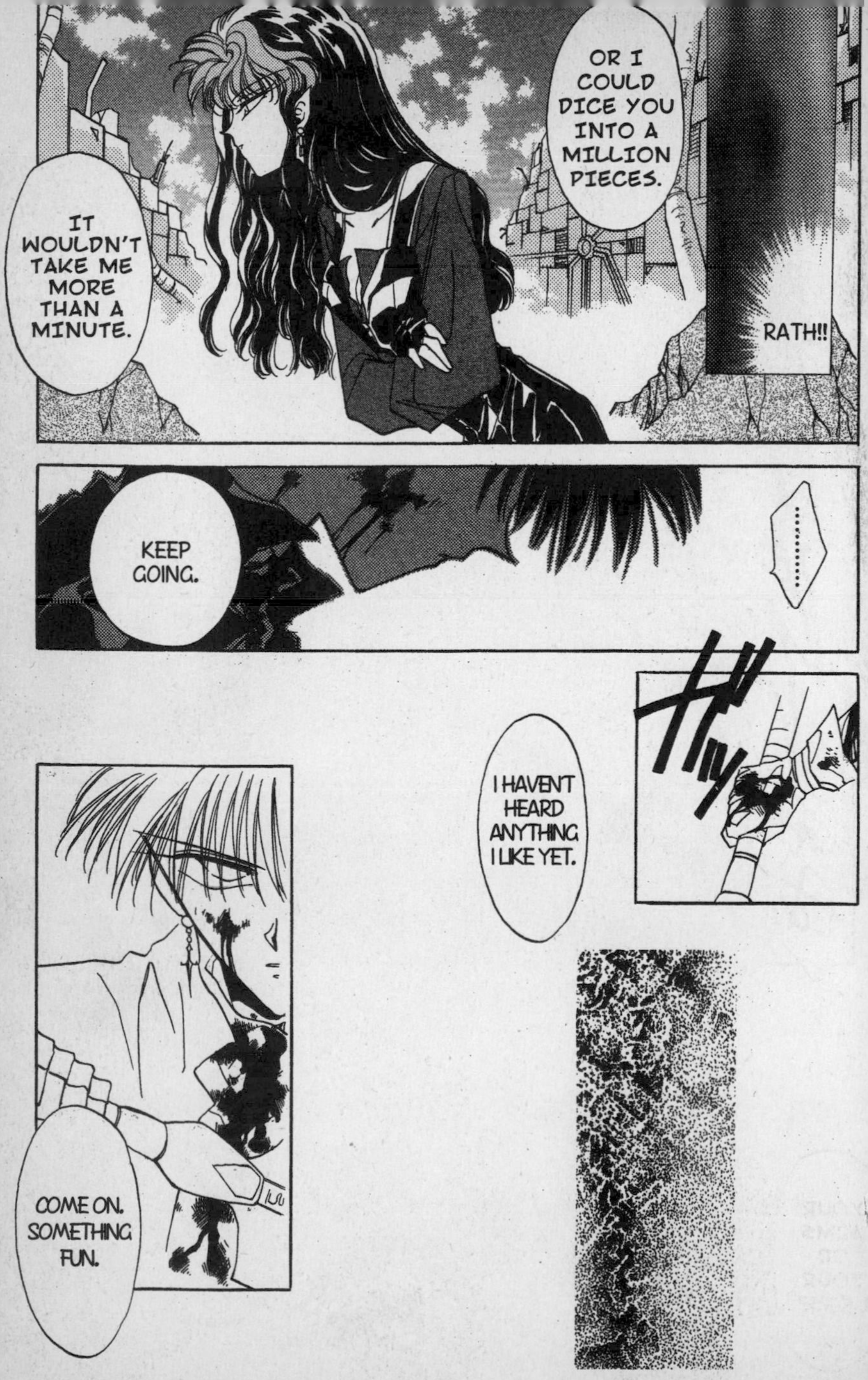
OR I COULD DICE YOU INTO A MILLION PIECES.
RATH!!
IT WOULDN'T TAKE ME MORE THAN A MINUTE.
......
KEEP GOING.
I HAVEN'T HEARD ANYTHING I LIKE YET.
COME ON. SOMETHING FUN.

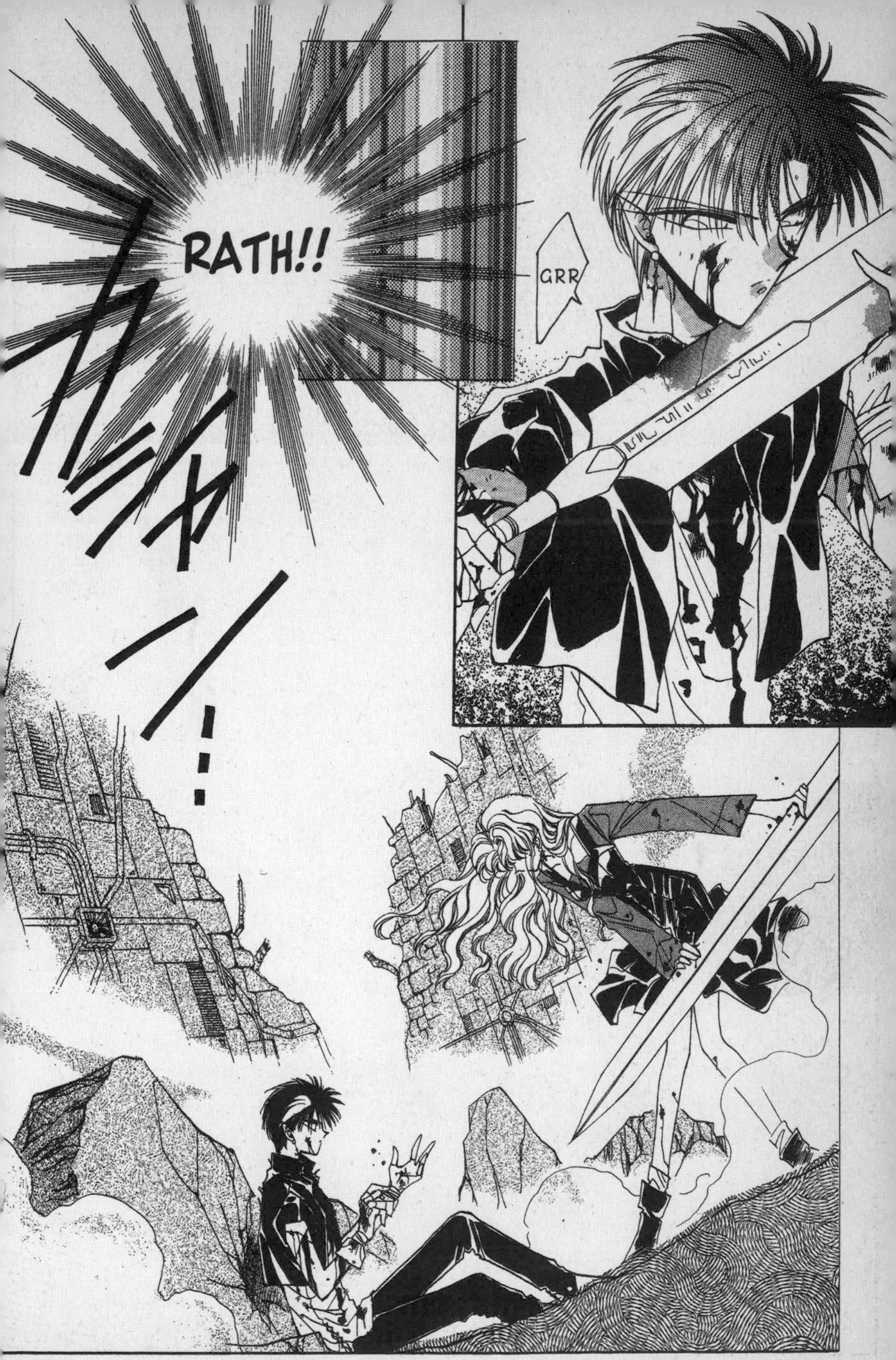
GRR
RATH!!

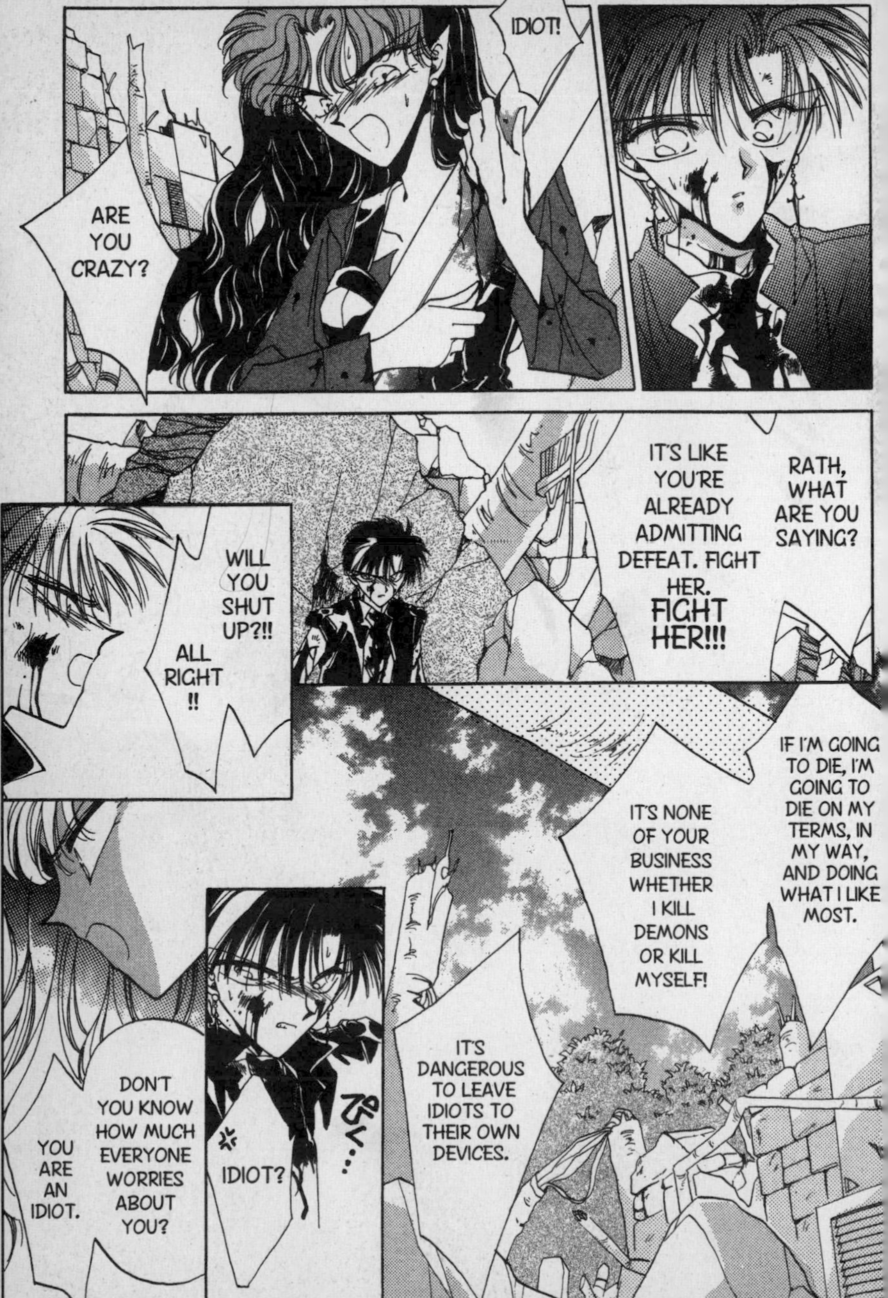
IDIOT!
ARE YOU CRAZY?
RATH, WHAT ARE YOU SAYING?
IT'S LIKE YOU'RE ALREADY ADMITTING DEFEAT. FIGHT HER. FIGHT HER!!!
WILL YOU SHUT UP?!!
ALL RIGHT !!
IF I'M GOING TO DIE, I'M GOING TO DIE ON MY TERMS, IN MY WAY, AND DOING WHAT I LIKE MOST.
IT'S NONE OF YOUR BUSINESS WHETHER I KILL DEMONS OR KILL MYSELF!
IT'S DANGEROUS TO LEAVE IDIOTS TO THEIR OWN DEVICES.
IDIOT?
DON'T YOU KNOW HOW MUCH EVERYONE WORRIES ABOUT YOU?
YOU ARE AN IDIOT.

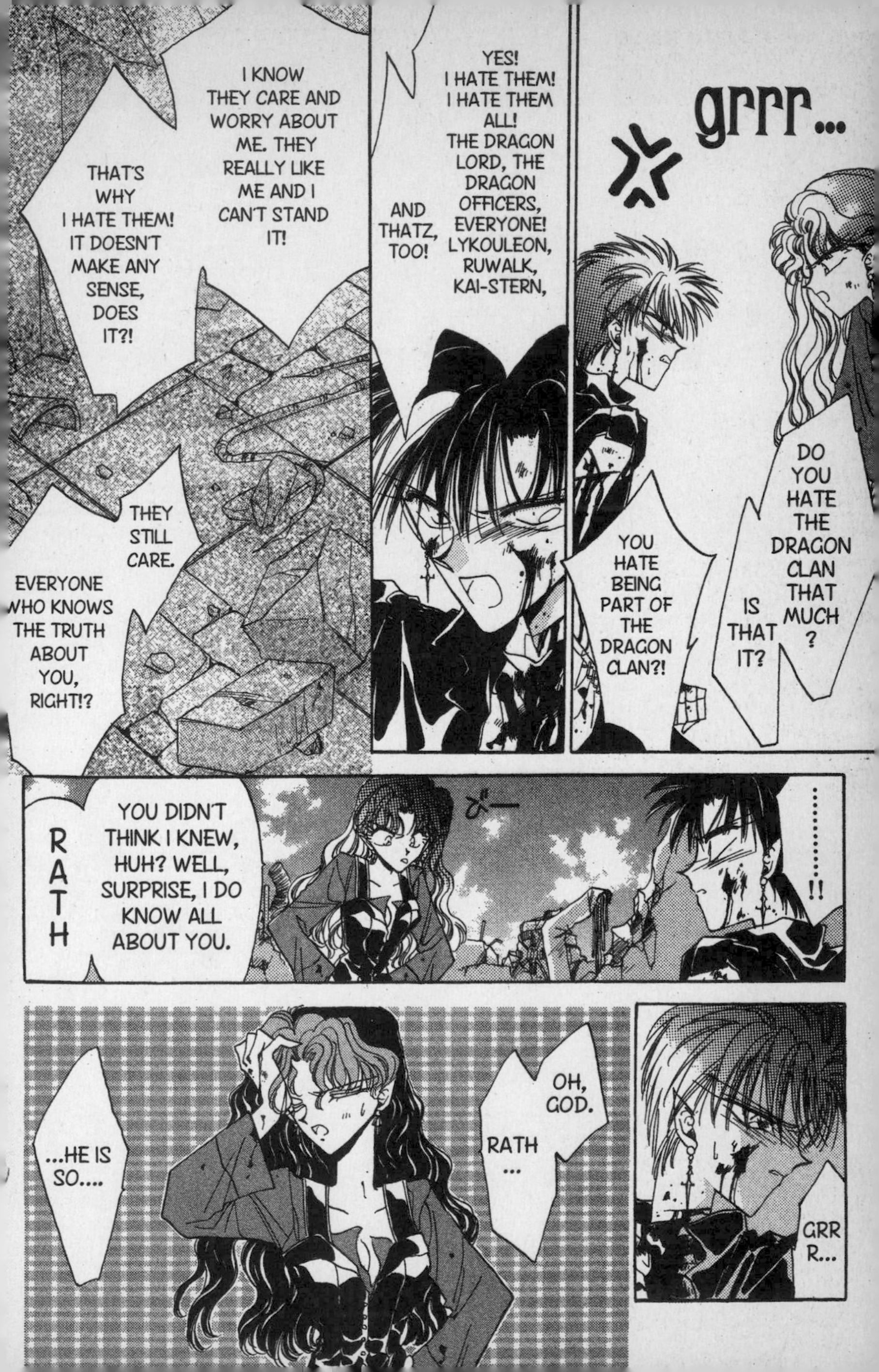
grrr...
DO YOU HATE THE DRAGON CLAN THAT MUCH?
IS THAT IT?
YOU HATE BEING PART OF THE DRAGON CLAN?!
YES! I HATE THEM! I HATE THEM ALL! THE DRAGON LORD, THE DRAGON OFFICERS, EVERYONE! LYKOULEON, RUWALK, KAI-STERN,
AND THATZ, TOO!
I KNOW THEY CARE AND WORRY ABOUT ME. THEY REALLY LIKE ME AND I CAN'T STAND IT!
THAT'S WHY I HATE THEM! IT DOESN'T MAKE ANY SENSE, DOES IT?!
THEY STILL CARE.
EVERYONE WHO KNOWS THE TRUTH ABOUT YOU, RIGHT!?
......!!
RATH
YOU DIDN'T THINK I KNEW, HUH? WELL, SURPRISE, I DO KNOW ALL ABOUT YOU.
GRRR...
OH, GOD.
RATH...
...HE IS SO....

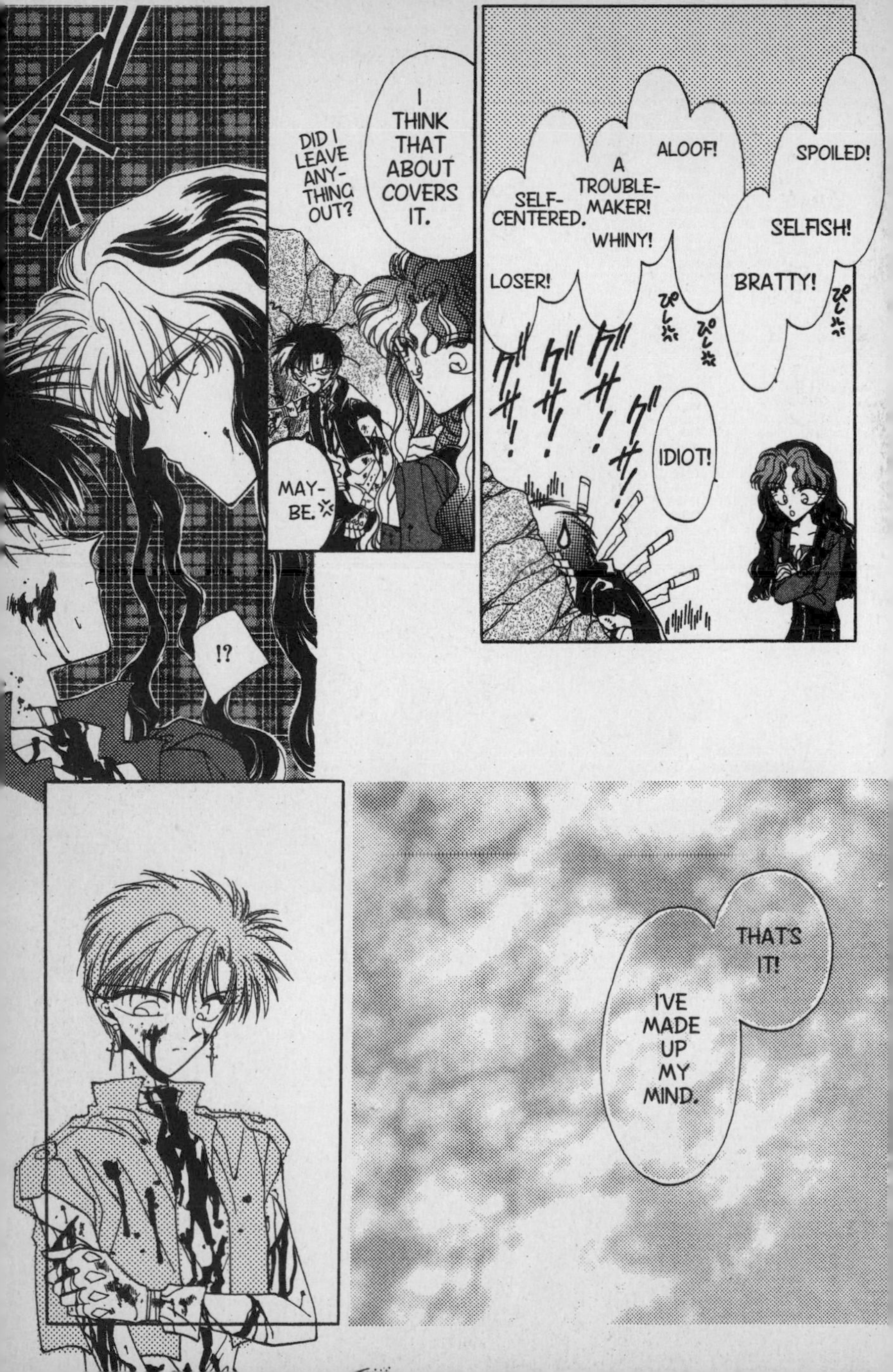
SPOILED!
SELFISH!
BRATTY!
ALOOF!
A TROUBLE-MAKER!
WHINY!
SELF-CENTERED.
LOSER!
IDIOT!
I THINK THAT ABOUT COVERS IT.
DID I LEAVE ANYTHING OUT?
MAY-BE.
!?
THAT'S IT!
I'VE MADE UP MY MIND.

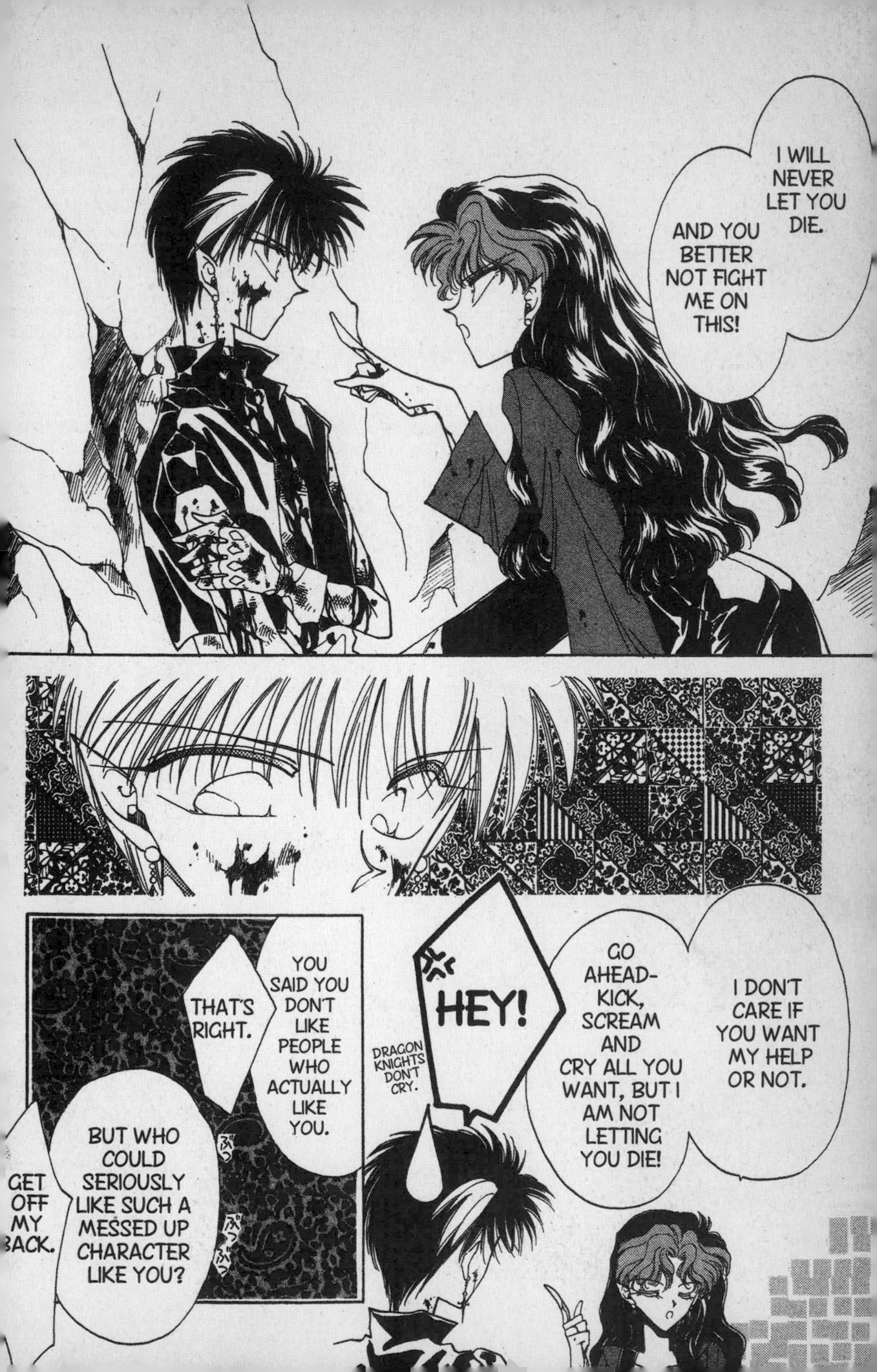
I WILL NEVER LET YOU DIE.
AND YOU BETTER NOT FIGHT ME ON THIS!
I DON'T CARE IF YOU WANT MY HELP OR NOT.
GO AHEAD- KICK, SCREAM AND CRY ALL YOU WANT, BUT I AM NOT LETTING YOU DIE!
HEY!
DRAGON KNIGHTS DON'T CRY.
YOU SAID YOU DON'T LIKE PEOPLE WHO ACTUALLY LIKE YOU.
THAT'S RIGHT.
BUT WHO COULD SERIOUSLY LIKE SUCH A MESSED UP CHARACTER LIKE YOU?
GET OFF MY BACK.

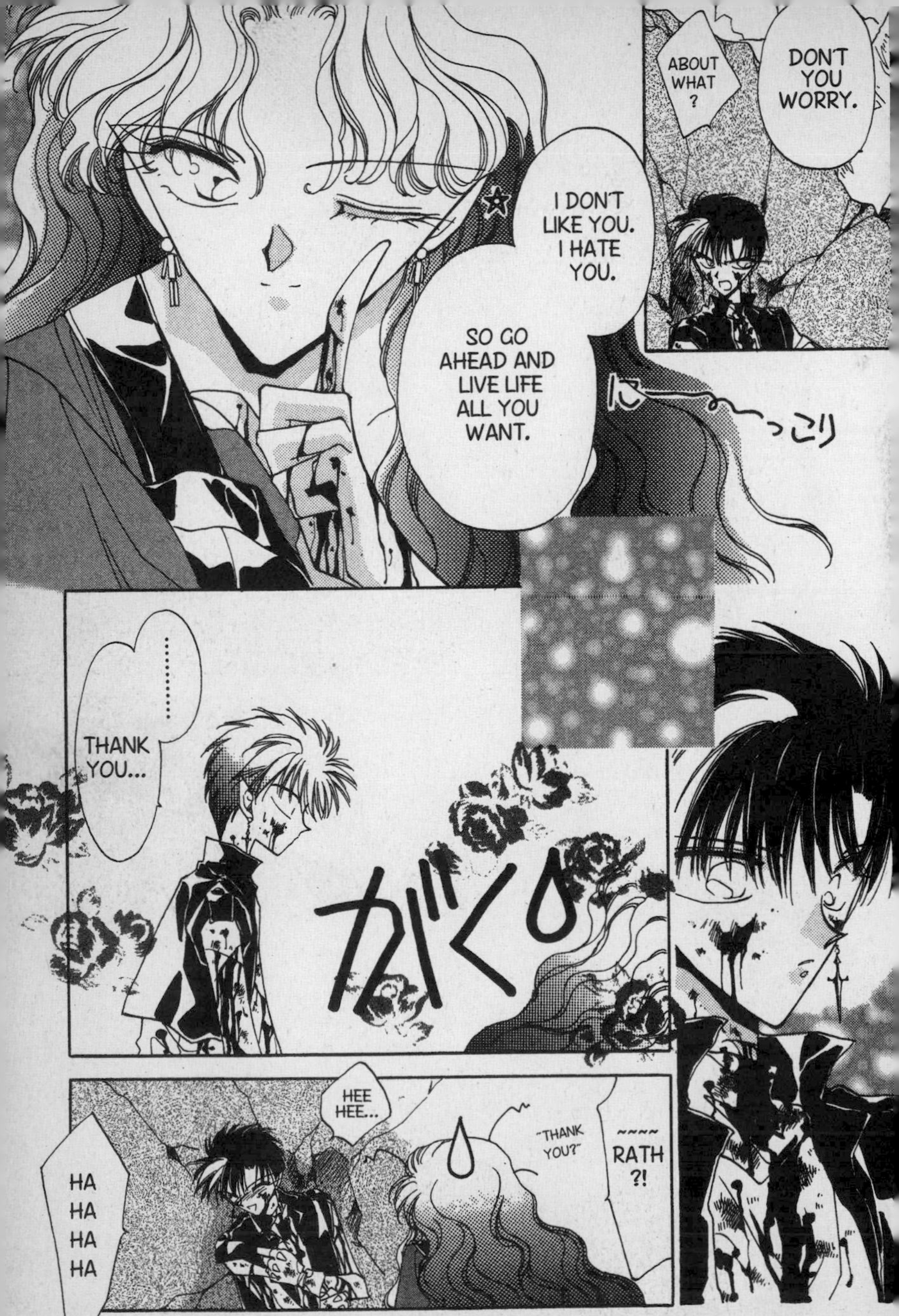
DON'T YOU WORRY.
ABOUT WHAT?
I DON'T LIKE YOU. I HATE YOU.
SO GO AHEAD AND LIVE LIFE ALL YOU WANT.
にーっこり
......
THANK YOU...
がくっ
~~~~ RATH?!
"THANK YOU?"
HEE HEE...
HA HA HA HA
~~~~

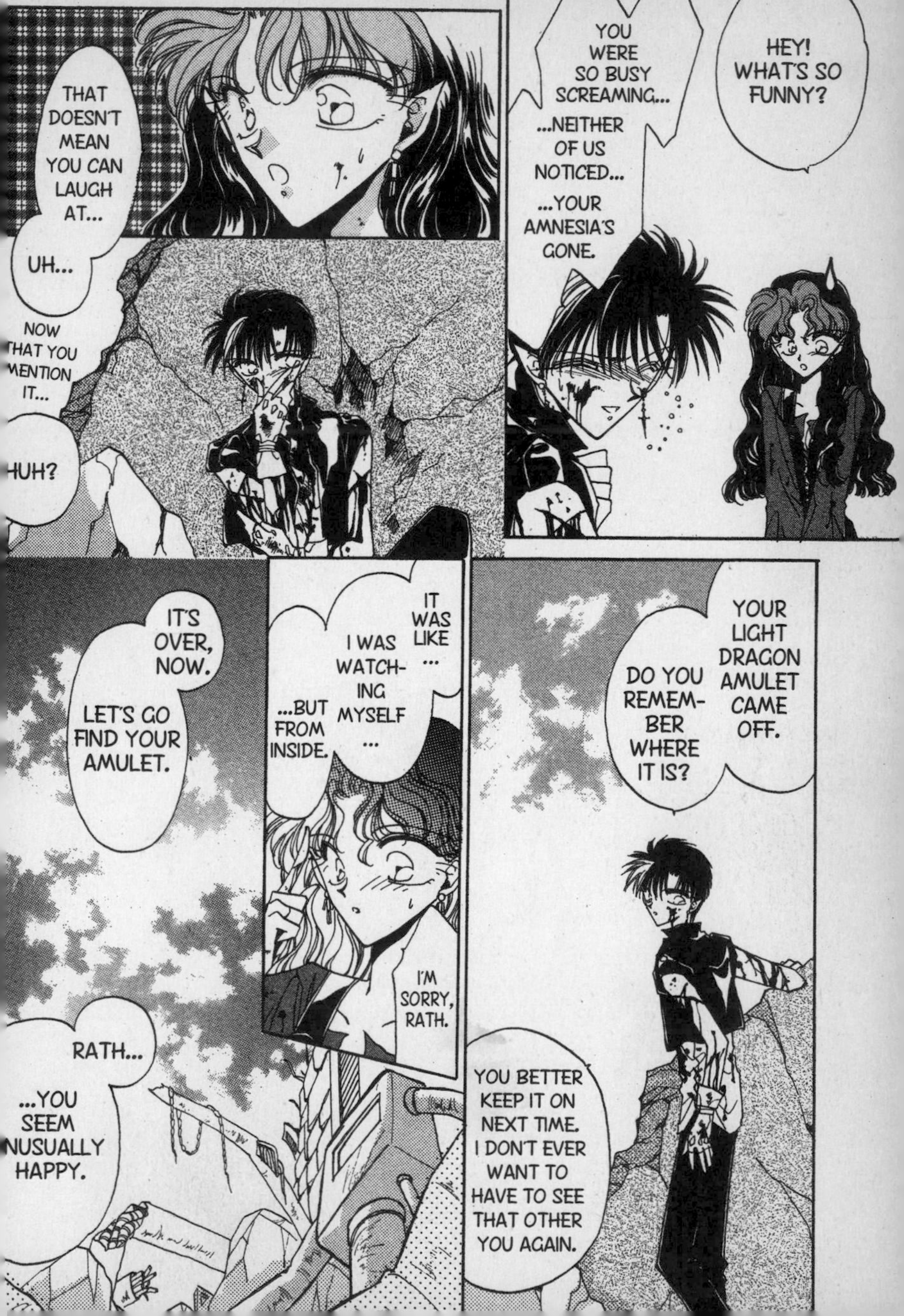
HEY! WHAT'S SO FUNNY?
YOU WERE SO BUSY SCREAMING...
...NEITHER OF US NOTICED...
...YOUR AMNESIA'S GONE.
THAT DOESN'T MEAN YOU CAN LAUGH AT...
UH...
NOW HAT YOU MENTION IT...
HUH?
YOUR LIGHT DRAGON AMULET CAME OFF.
DO YOU REMEMBER WHERE IT IS?
YOU BETTER KEEP IT ON NEXT TIME. I DON'T EVER WANT TO HAVE TO SEE THAT OTHER YOU AGAIN.
IT WAS LIKE ...
I WAS WATCHING MYSELF ...
...BUT FROM INSIDE.
I'M SORRY, RATH.
IT'S OVER, NOW.
LET'S GO FIND YOUR AMULET.
RATH...
...YOU SEEM NUSUALLY HAPPY.

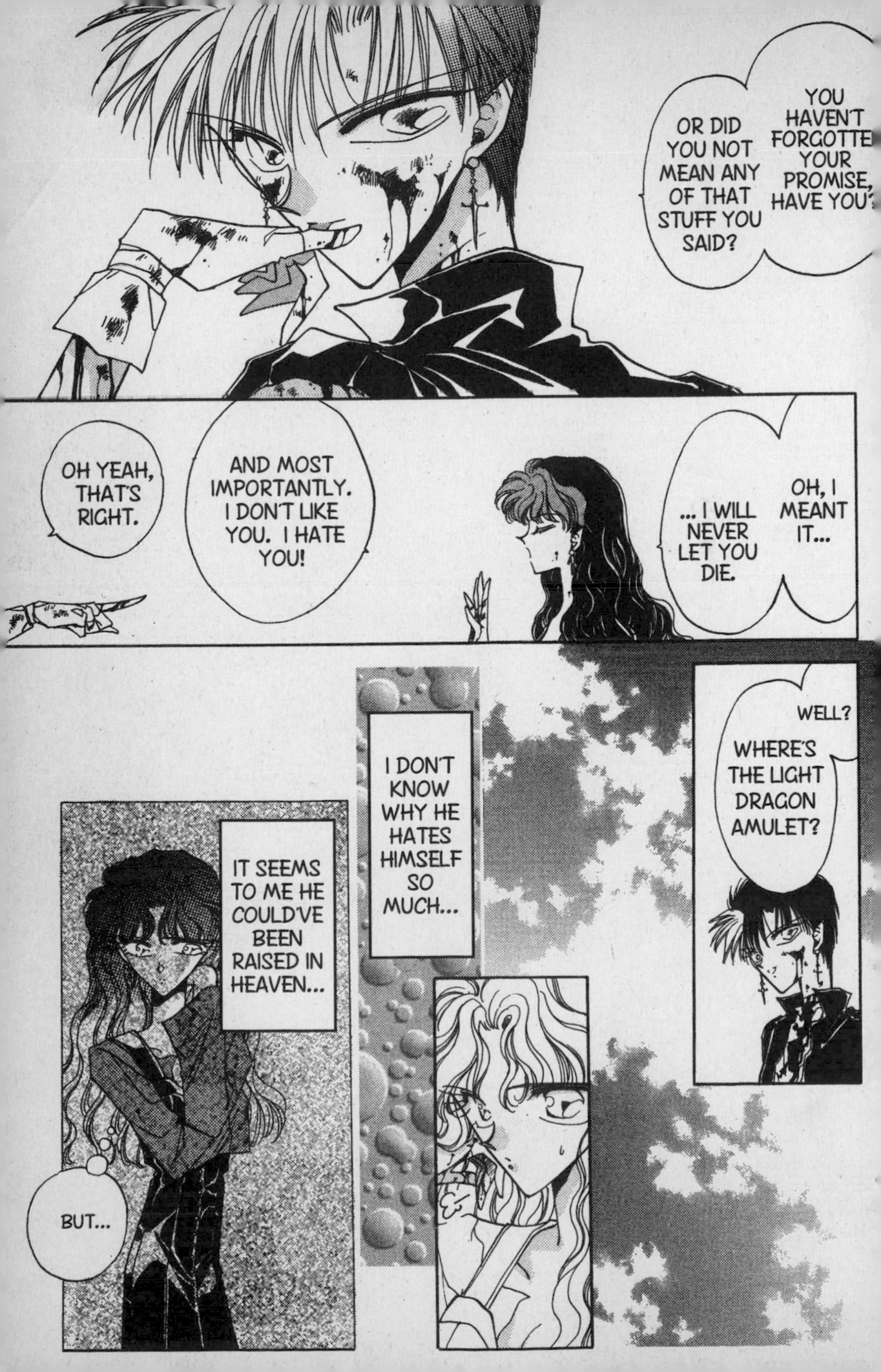
YOU HAVEN'T FORGOTTE YOUR PROMISE, HAVE YOU
OR DID YOU NOT MEAN ANY OF THAT STUFF YOU SAID?
OH, I MEANT IT...
... I WILL NEVER LET YOU DIE.
AND MOST IMPORTANTLY. I DON'T LIKE YOU. I HATE YOU!
OH YEAH, THAT'S RIGHT.
WELL?
WHERE'S THE LIGHT DRAGON AMULET?
I DON'T KNOW WHY HE HATES HIMSELF SO MUCH...
IT SEEMS TO ME HE COULD'VE BEEN RAISED IN HEAVEN...
BUT...

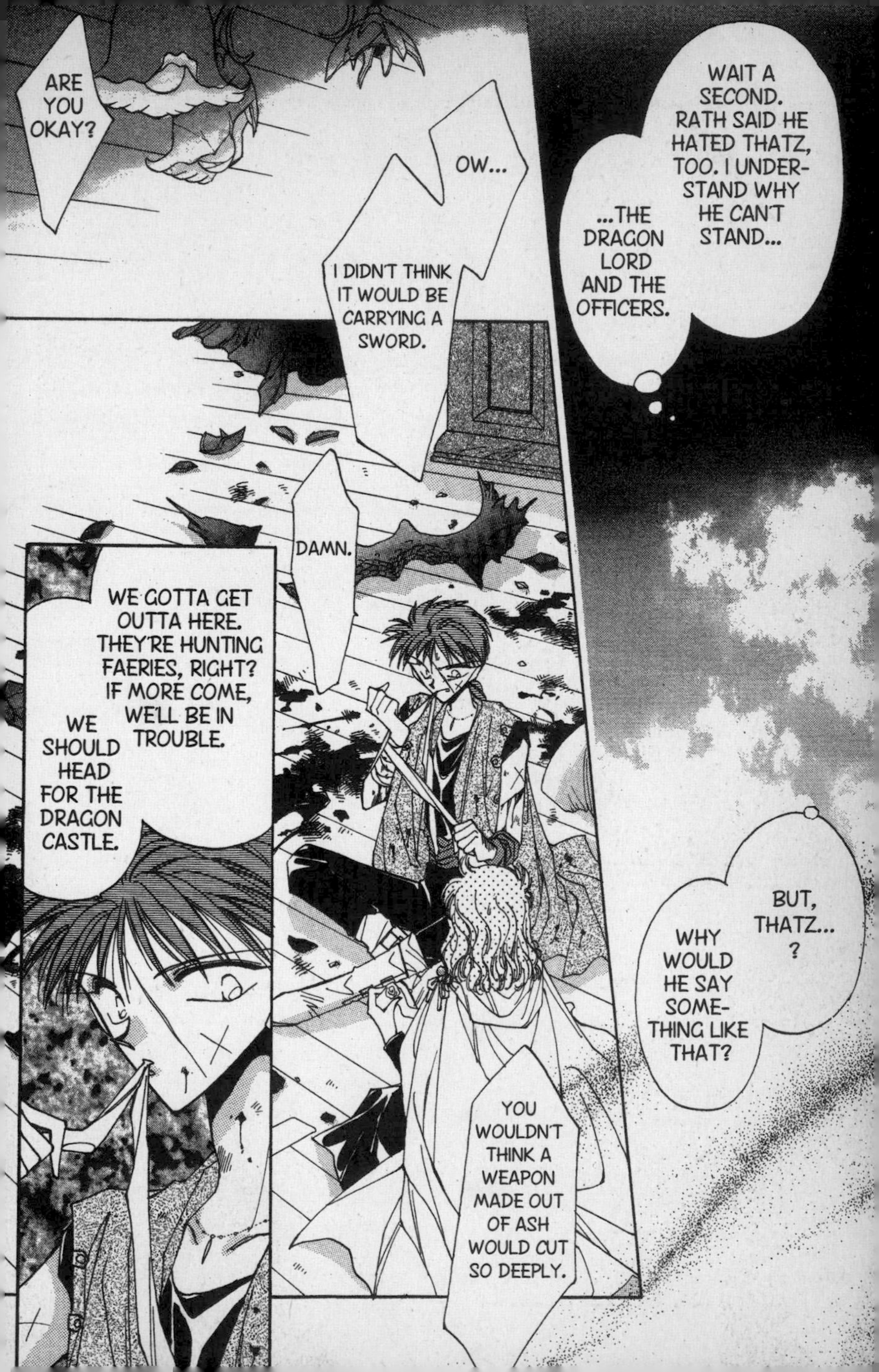
WAIT A SECOND. RATH SAID HE HATED THATZ, TOO. I UNDERSTAND WHY HE CAN'T STAND...
...THE DRAGON LORD AND THE OFFICERS.
BUT, THATZ...?
WHY WOULD HE SAY SOMETHING LIKE THAT?
ARE YOU OKAY?
OW...
I DIDN'T THINK IT WOULD BE CARRYING A SWORD.
DAMN.
YOU WOULDN'T THINK A WEAPON MADE OUT OF ASH WOULD CUT SO DEEPLY.
WE GOTTA GET OUTTA HERE. THEY'RE HUNTING FAERIES, RIGHT? IF MORE COME, WE'LL BE IN TROUBLE.
WE SHOULD HEAD FOR THE DRAGON CASTLE.

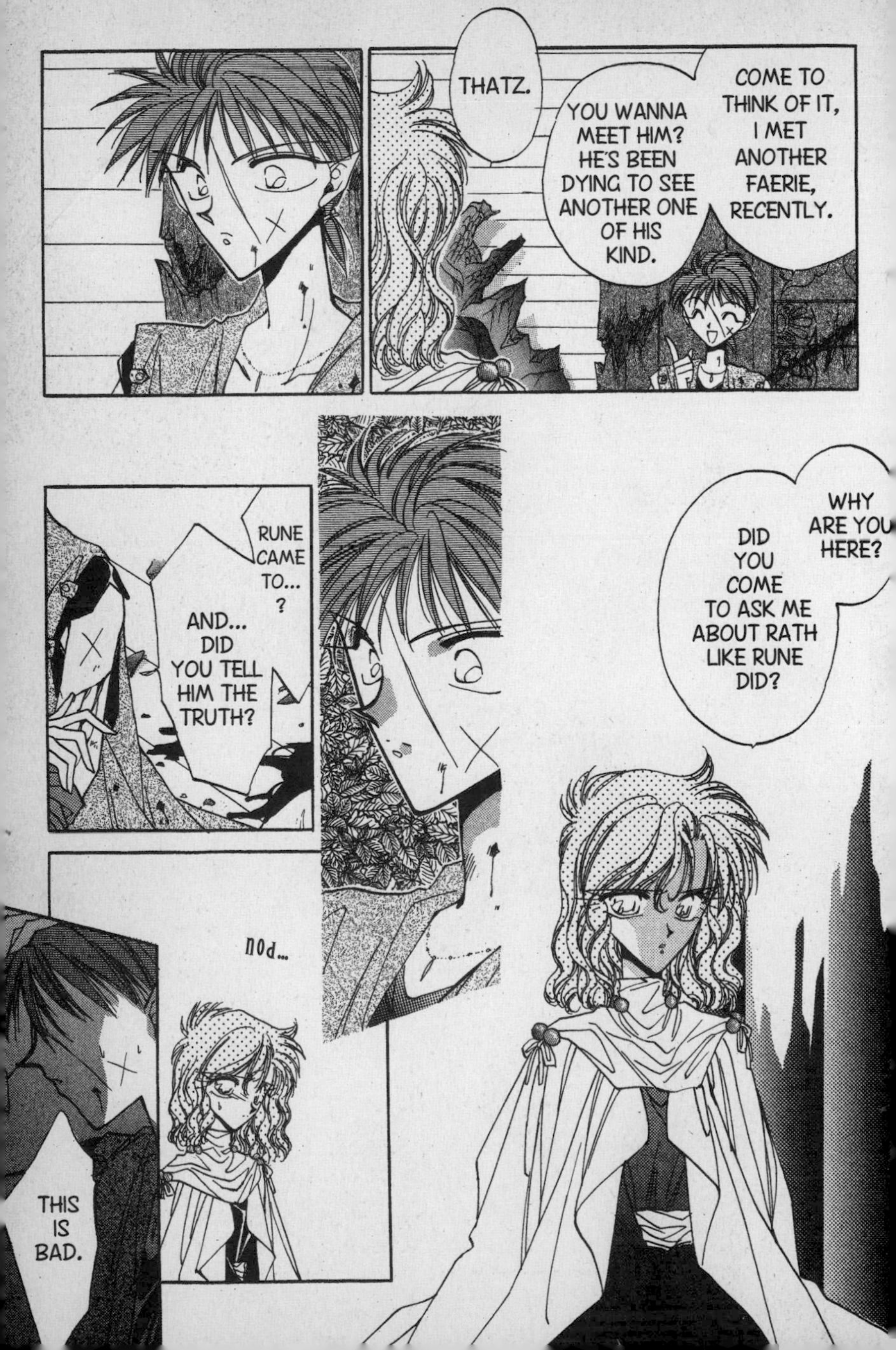
COME TO THINK OF IT, I MET ANOTHER FAERIE, RECENTLY.
YOU WANNA MEET HIM? HE'S BEEN DYING TO SEE ANOTHER ONE OF HIS KIND.
THATZ.
WHY ARE YOU HERE?
DID YOU COME TO ASK ME ABOUT RATH LIKE RUNE DID?
RUNE CAME TO... ?
AND... DID YOU TELL HIM THE TRUTH?
nod...
THIS IS BAD.

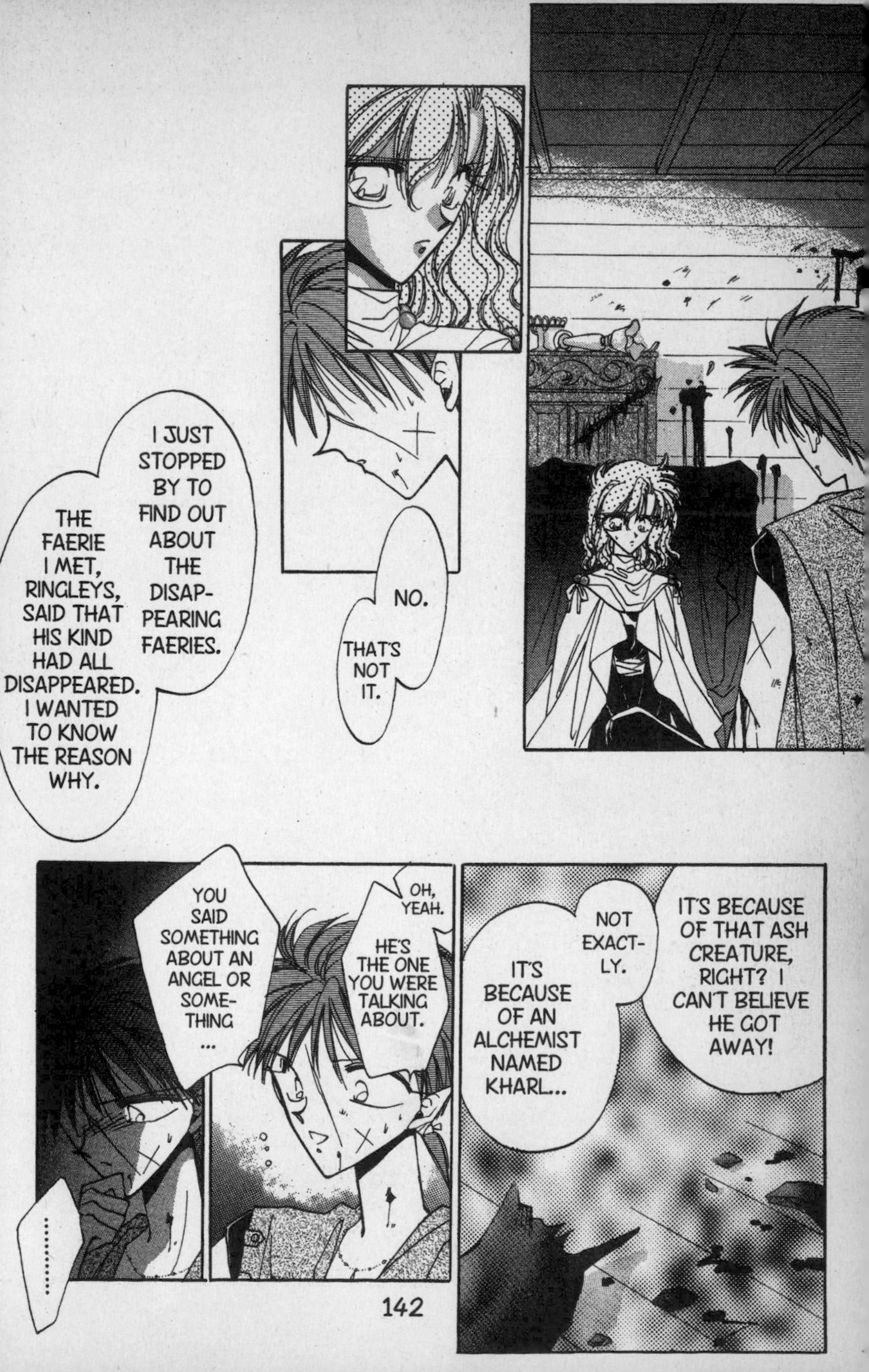
NO.
THAT'S NOT IT.
I JUST STOPPED BY TO FIND OUT ABOUT THE DISAP-PEARING FAERIES.
THE FAERIE I MET, RINGLEYS, SAID THAT HIS KIND HAD ALL DISAPPEARED. I WANTED TO KNOW THE REASON WHY.
IT'S BECAUSE OF THAT ASH CREATURE, RIGHT? I CAN'T BELIEVE HE GOT AWAY!
NOT EXACT-LY.
IT'S BECAUSE OF AN ALCHEMIST NAMED KHARL...
OH, YEAH.
HE'S THE ONE YOU WERE TALKING ABOUT.
YOU SAID SOMETHING ABOUT AN ANGEL OR SOME-THING ...
....

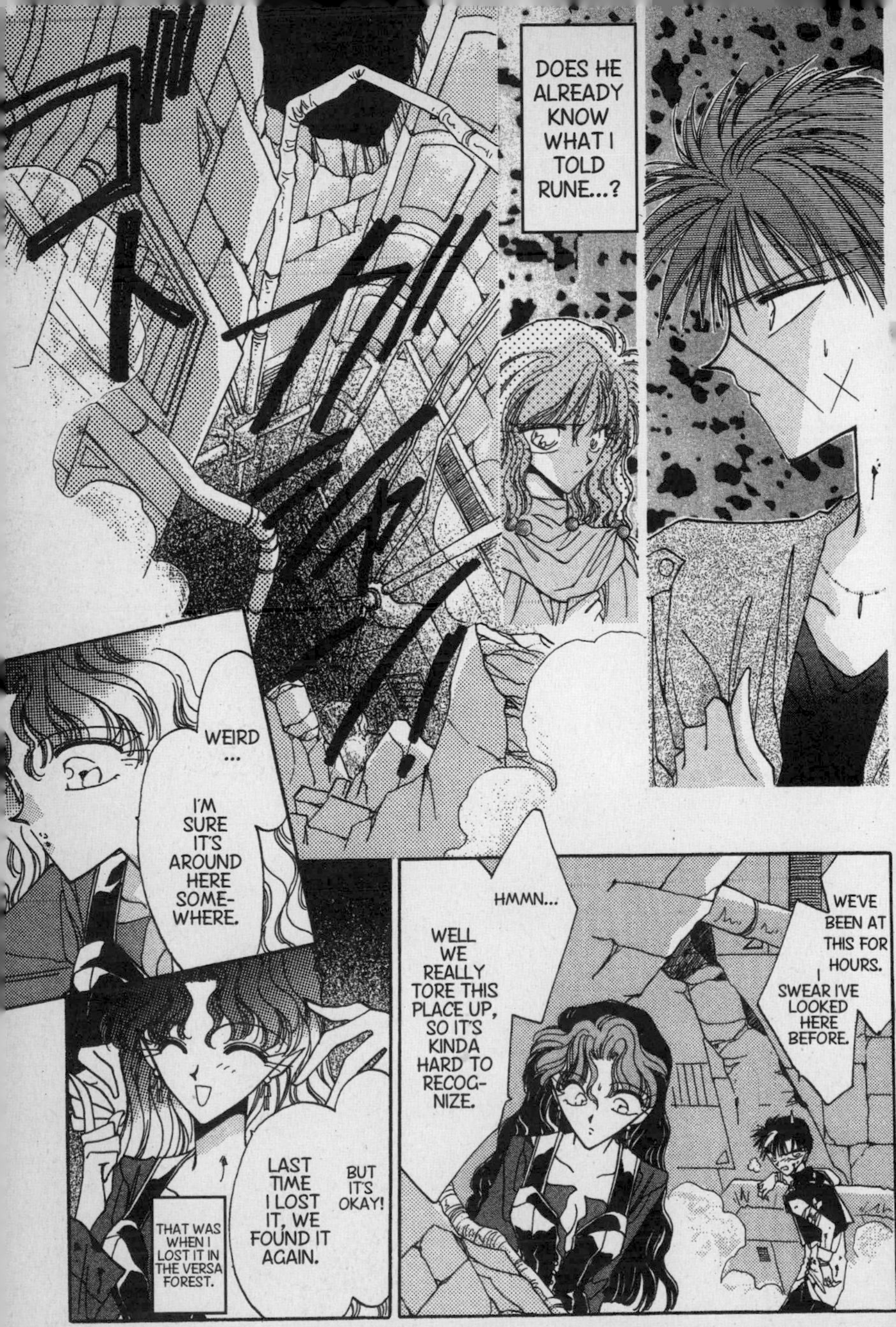
DOES HE ALREADY KNOW WHAT I TOLD RUNE...?
WEIRD...
I'M SURE IT'S AROUND HERE SOMEWHERE.
WE'VE BEEN AT THIS FOR HOURS.
I SWEAR I'VE LOOKED HERE BEFORE.
HMMN...
WELL WE REALLY TORE THIS PLACE UP, SO IT'S KINDA HARD TO RECOGNIZE.
BUT IT'S OKAY!
LAST TIME I LOST IT, WE FOUND IT AGAIN.
THAT WAS WHEN I LOST IT IN THE VERSA FOREST.

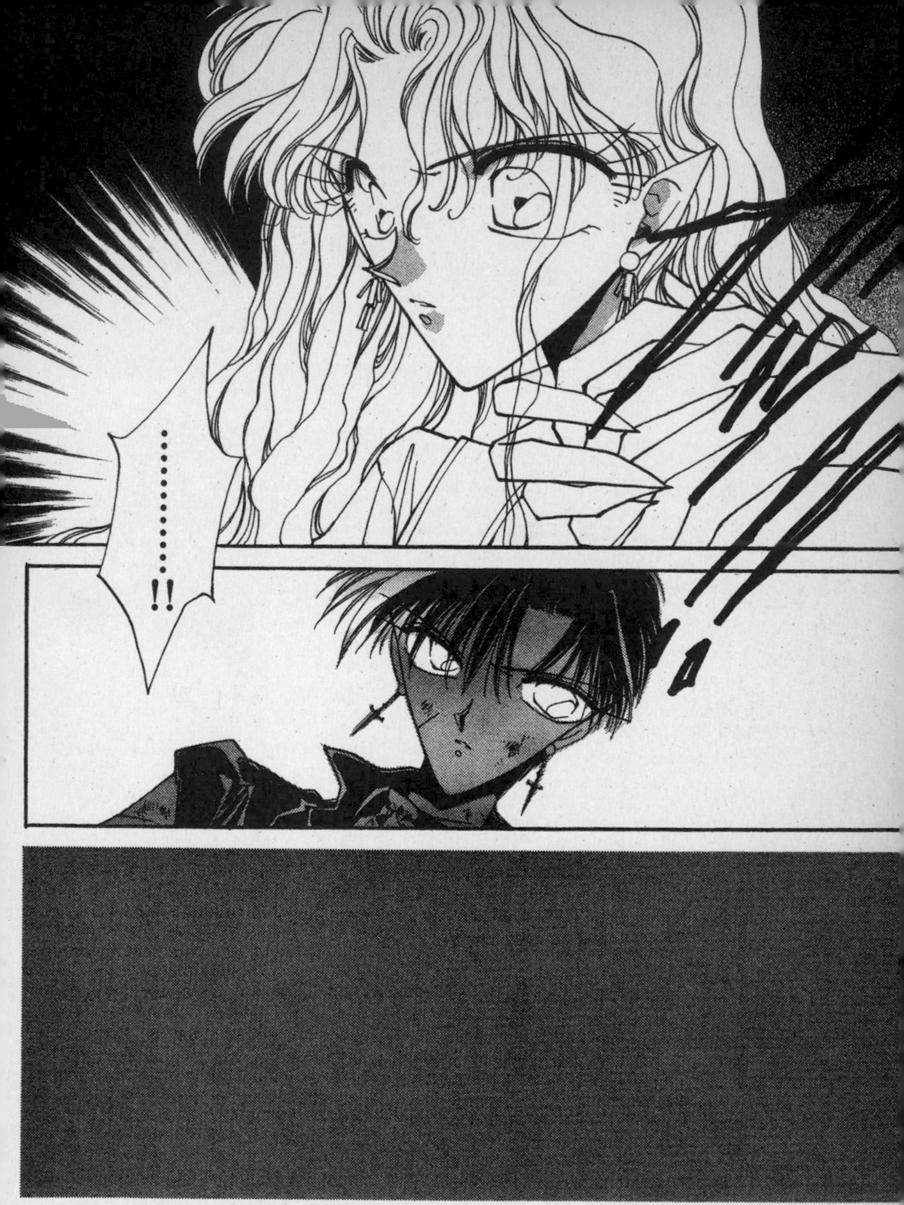
......!!

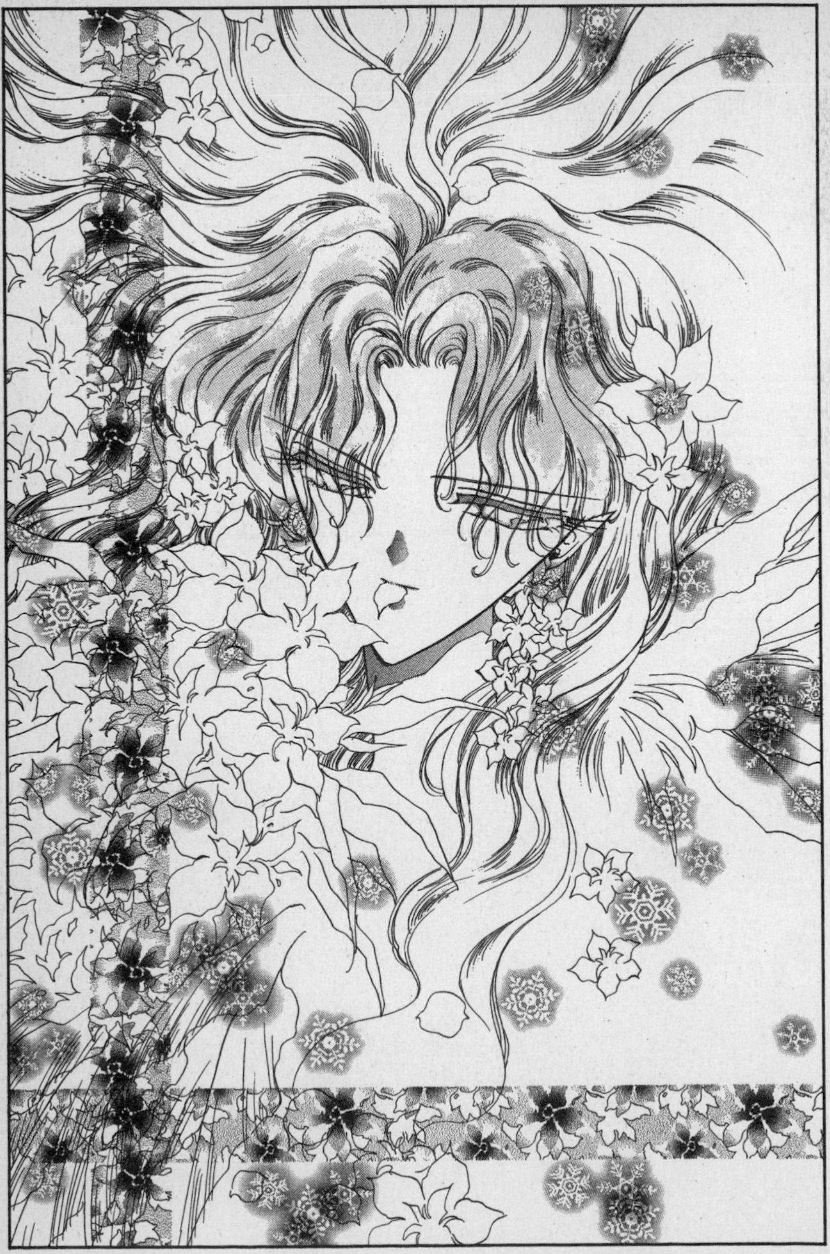

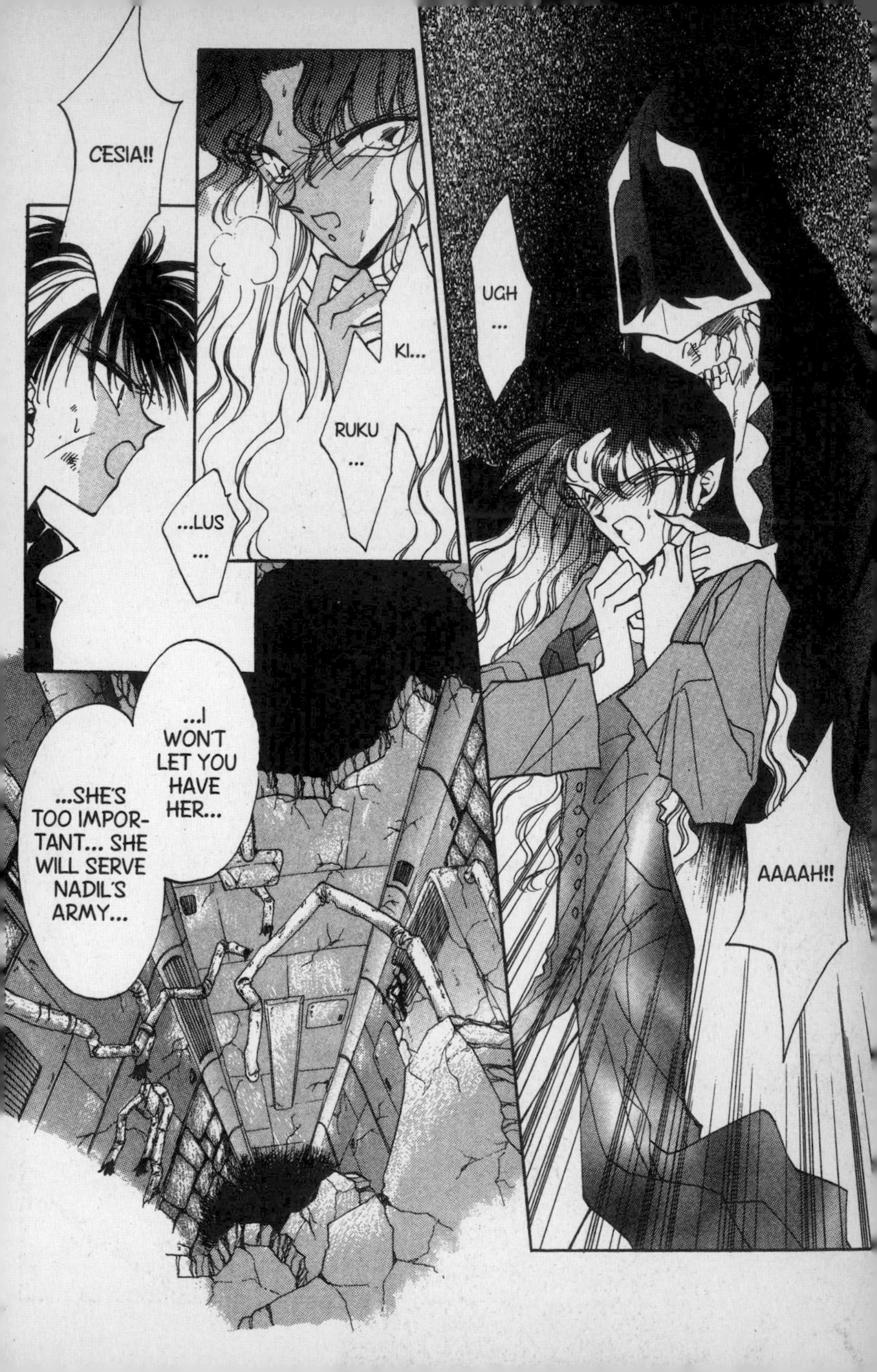
UGH ...
AAAAH!!
KI...
RUKU ...
...LUS ...
CESIA!!
...I WON'T LET YOU HAVE HER...
...SHE'S TOO IMPORTANT... SHE WILL SERVE NADIL'S ARMY...

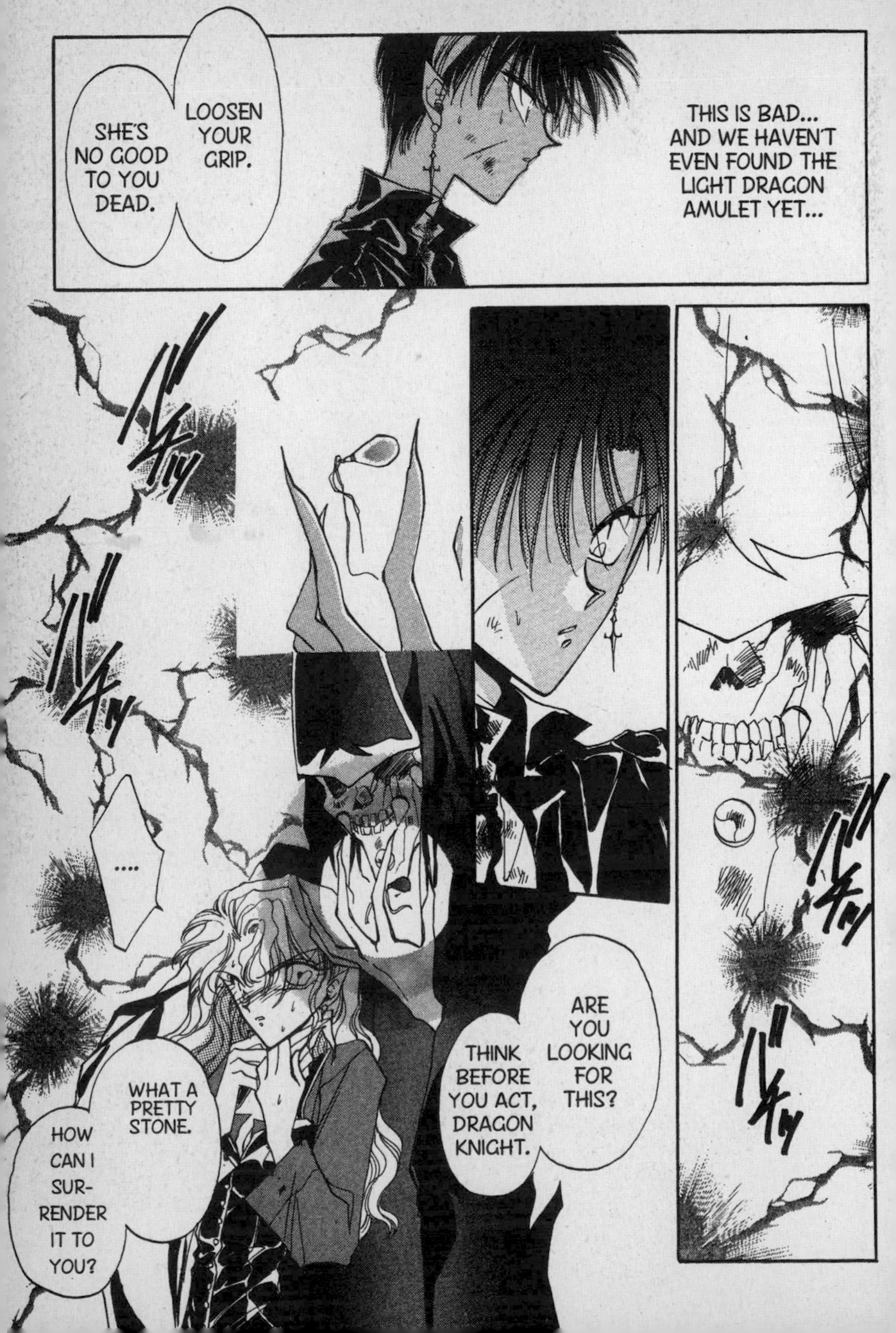
THIS IS BAD... AND WE HAVEN'T EVEN FOUND THE LIGHT DRAGON AMULET YET...
LOOSEN YOUR GRIP.
SHE'S NO GOOD TO YOU DEAD.
ARE YOU LOOKING FOR THIS?
THINK BEFORE YOU ACT, DRAGON KNIGHT.
WHAT A PRETTY STONE.
HOW CAN I SUR-RENDER IT TO YOU?
....

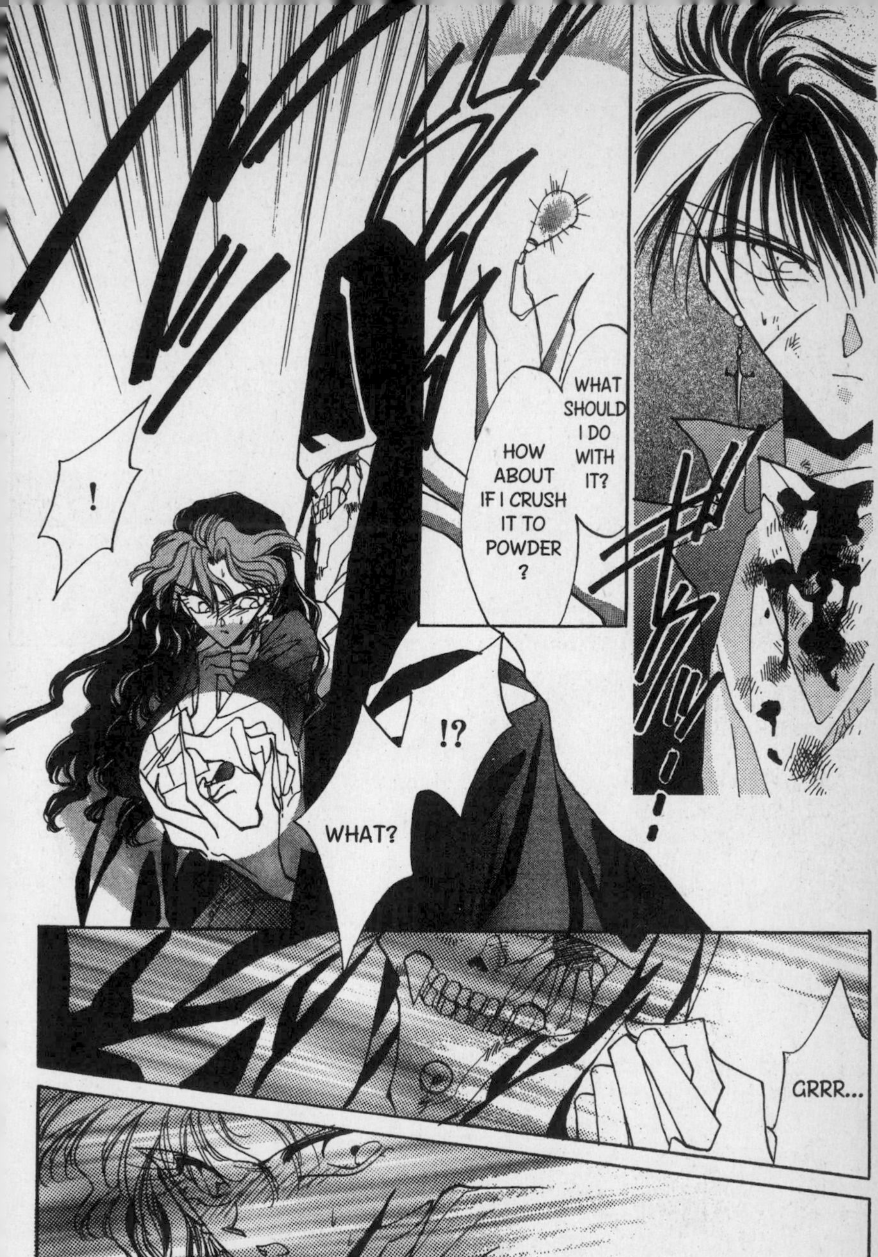
WHAT SHOULD I DO WITH IT?
HOW ABOUT IF I CRUSH IT TO POWDER ?
!
!?
WHAT?
GRRR...

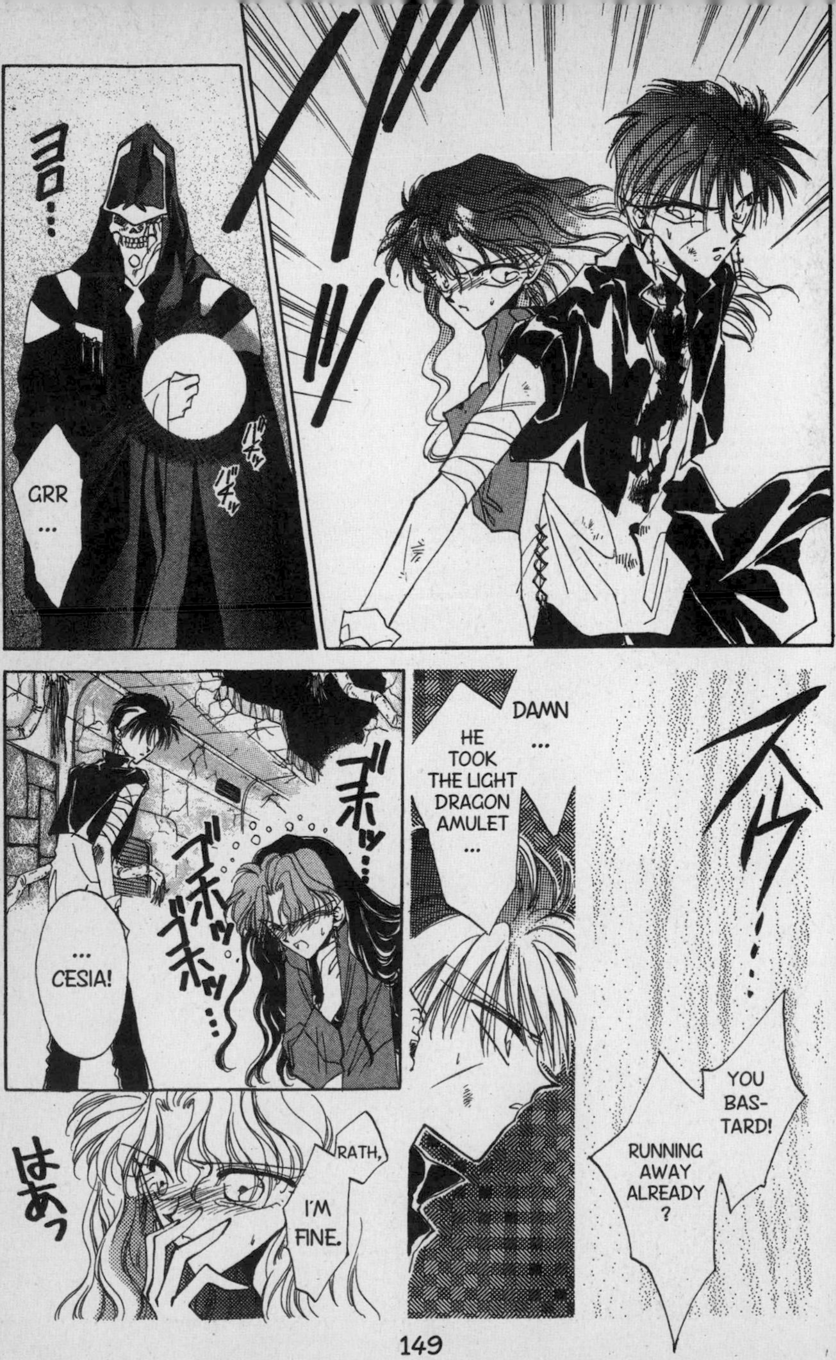
ヨロ…
バチッ
バチッ
GRR ...
スゥ…
YOU BASTARD!
RUNNING AWAY ALREADY?
DAMN ...
HE TOOK THE LIGHT DRAGON AMULET ...
ゴホッ…
ゴホッ
ゴホッ…
... CESIA!
RATH,
I'M FINE.
はあっ

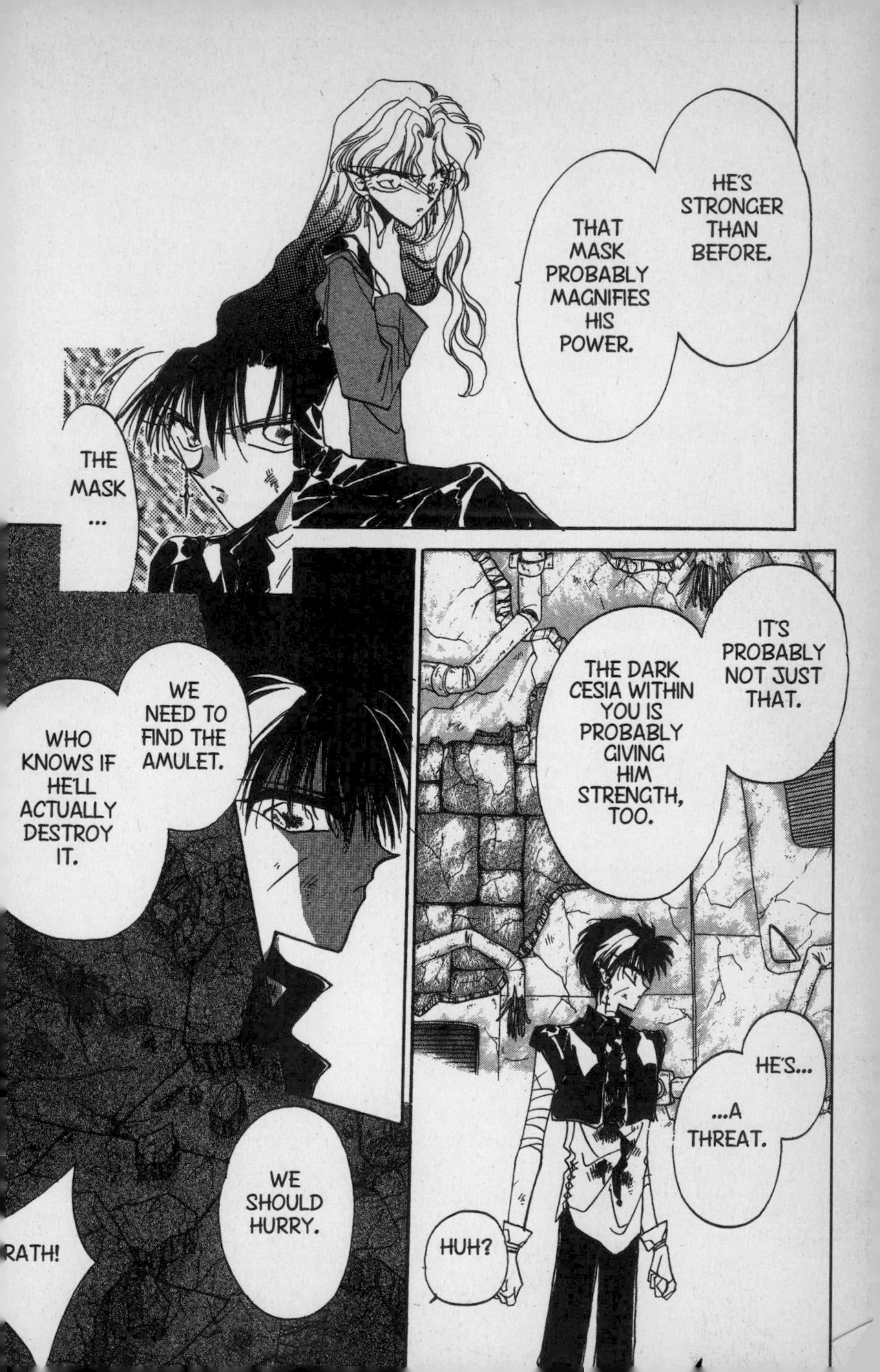
HE'S STRONGER THAN BEFORE.
THAT MASK PROBABLY MAGNIFIES HIS POWER.
THE MASK ...
IT'S PROBABLY NOT JUST THAT.
THE DARK CESIA WITHIN YOU IS PROBABLY GIVING HIM STRENGTH, TOO.
HE'S...
...A THREAT.
HUH?
WE NEED TO FIND THE AMULET.
WHO KNOWS IF HE'LL ACTUALLY DESTROY IT.
WE SHOULD HURRY.
RATH!

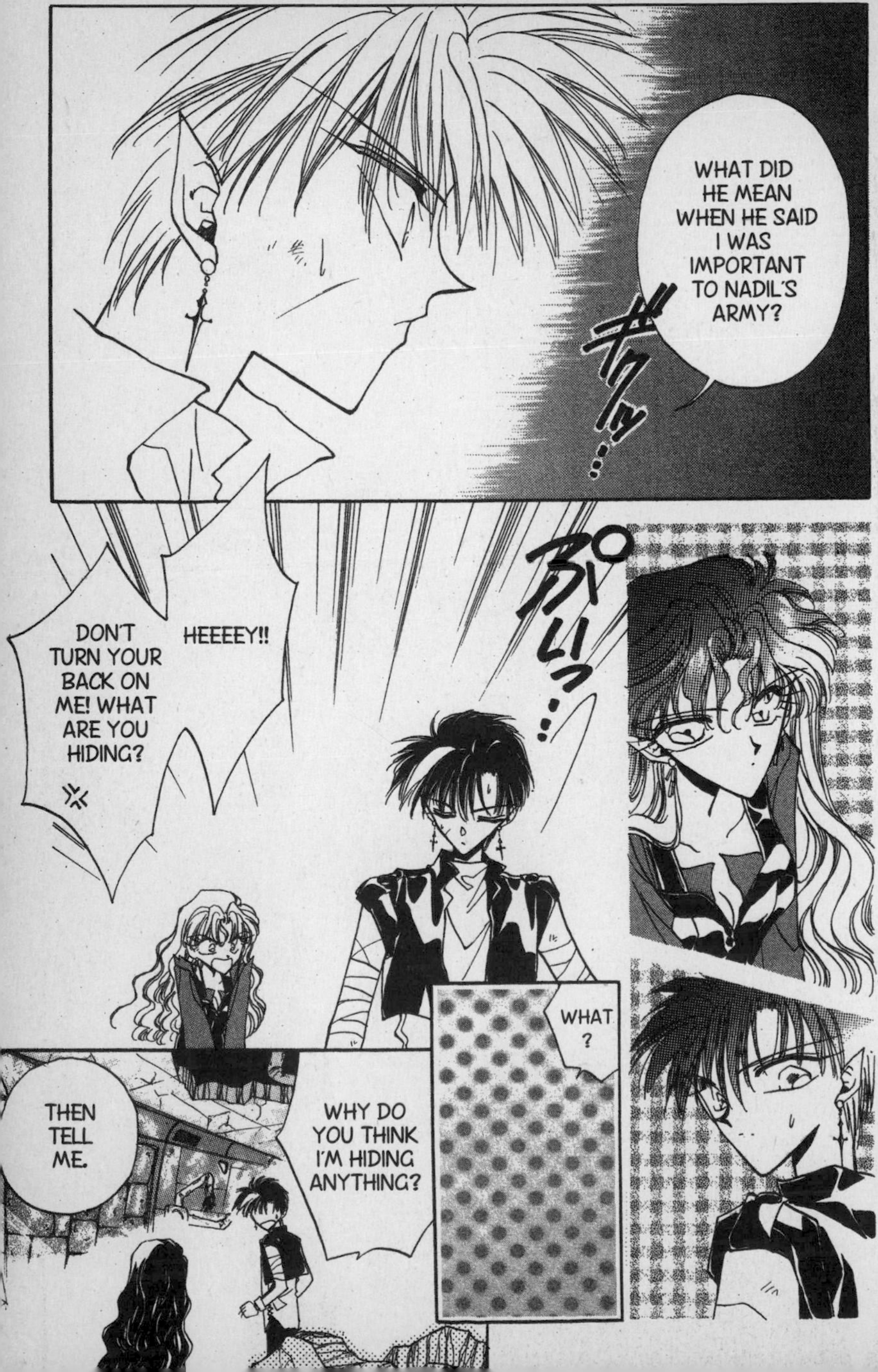
WHAT DID HE MEAN WHEN HE SAID I WAS IMPORTANT TO NADIL'S ARMY?
HEEEEY!!
DON'T TURN YOUR BACK ON ME! WHAT ARE YOU HIDING?
WHAT?
WHY DO YOU THINK I'M HIDING ANYTHING?
THEN TELL ME.

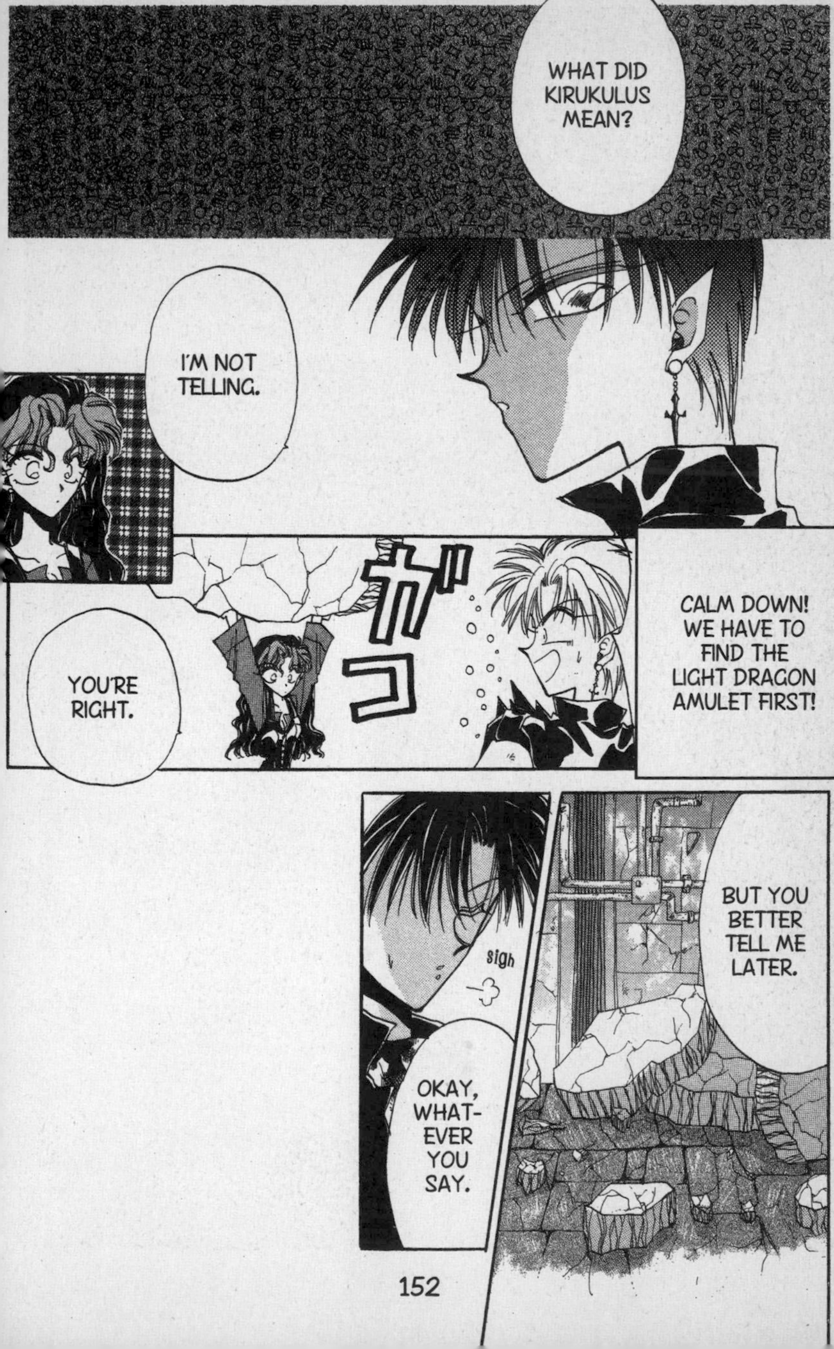
WHAT DID KIRUKULUS MEAN?
I'M NOT TELLING.
CALM DOWN! WE HAVE TO FIND THE LIGHT DRAGON AMULET FIRST!
ガッ
YOU'RE RIGHT.
BUT YOU BETTER TELL ME LATER.
sigh
OKAY, WHAT-EVER YOU SAY.

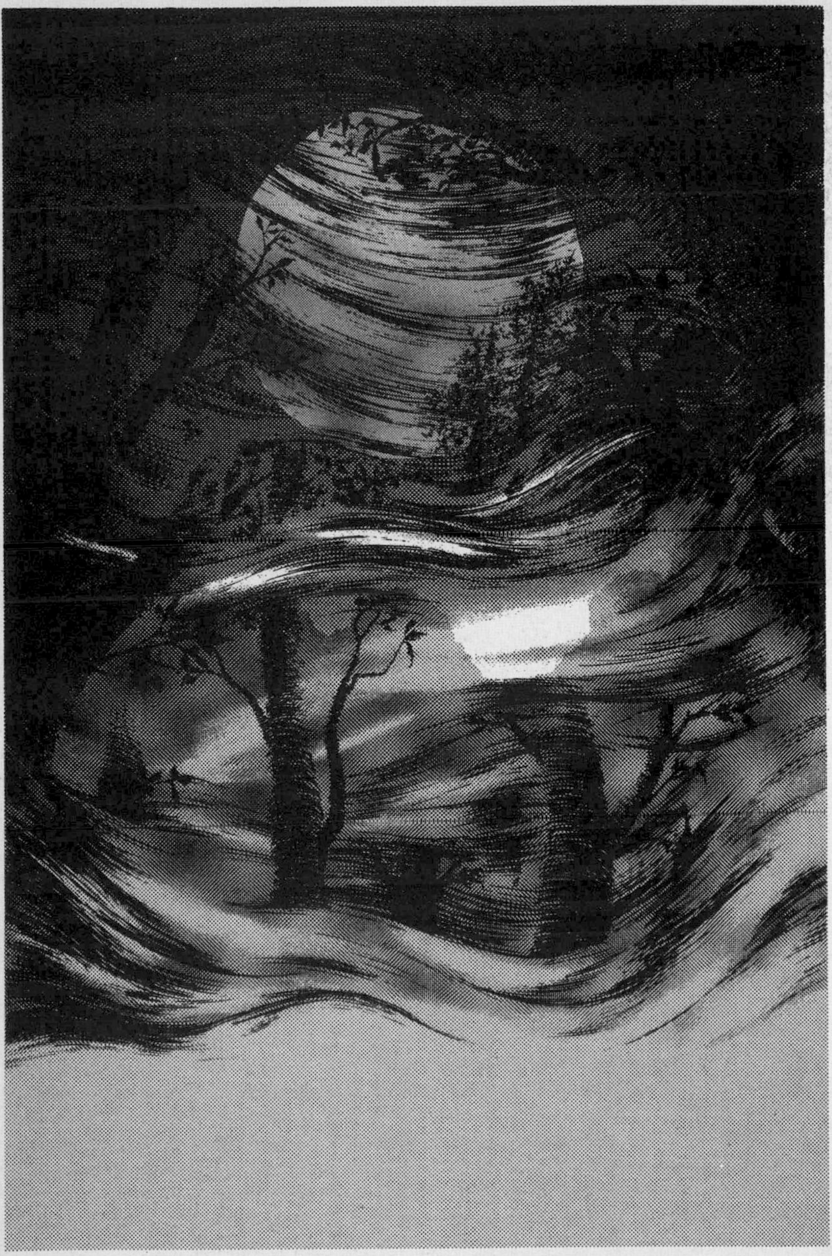

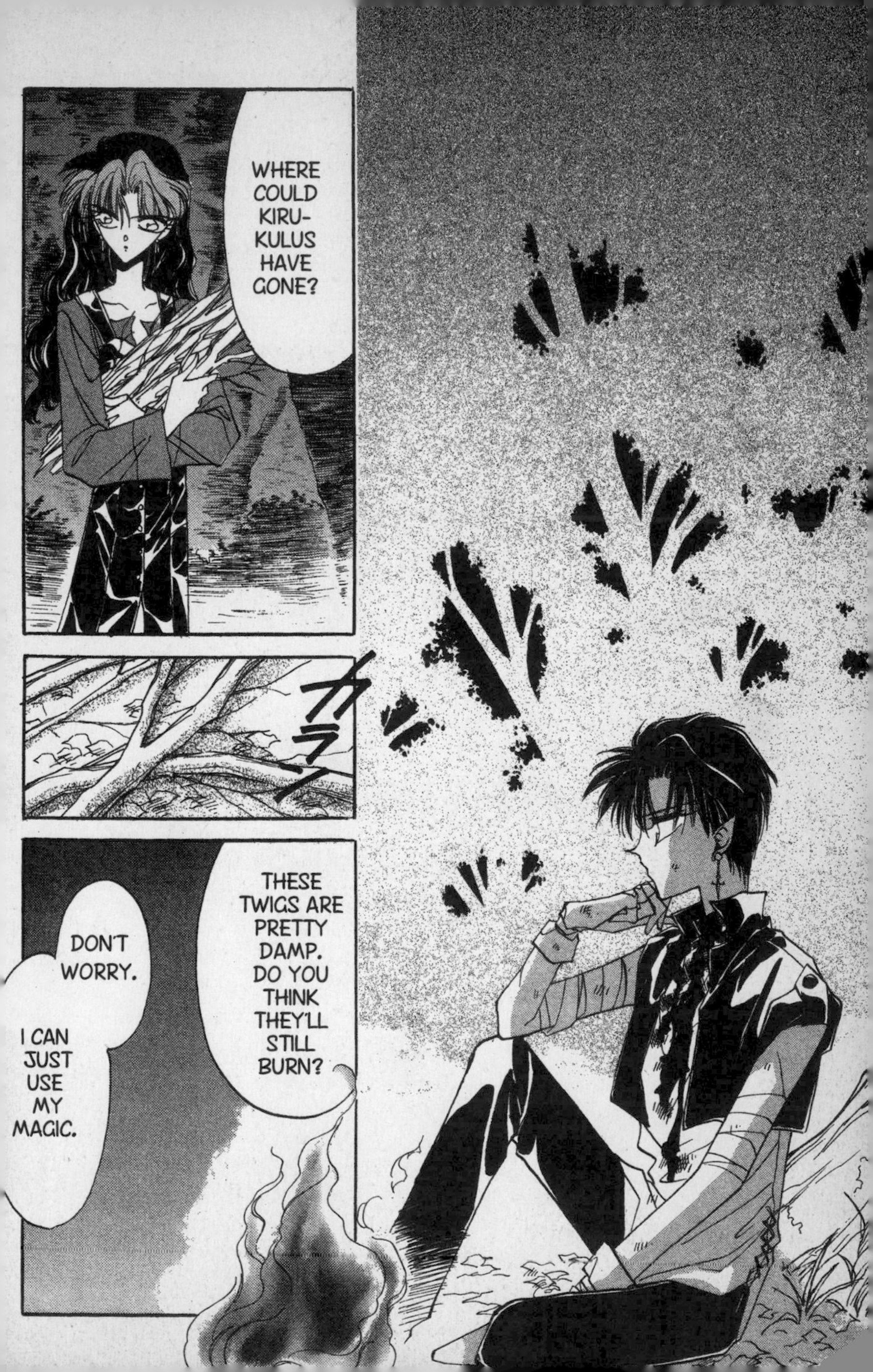
WHERE COULD KIRU-KULUS HAVE GONE?
カラン
THESE TWIGS ARE PRETTY DAMP. DO YOU THINK THEY'LL STILL BURN?
DON'T WORRY.
I CAN JUST USE MY MAGIC.

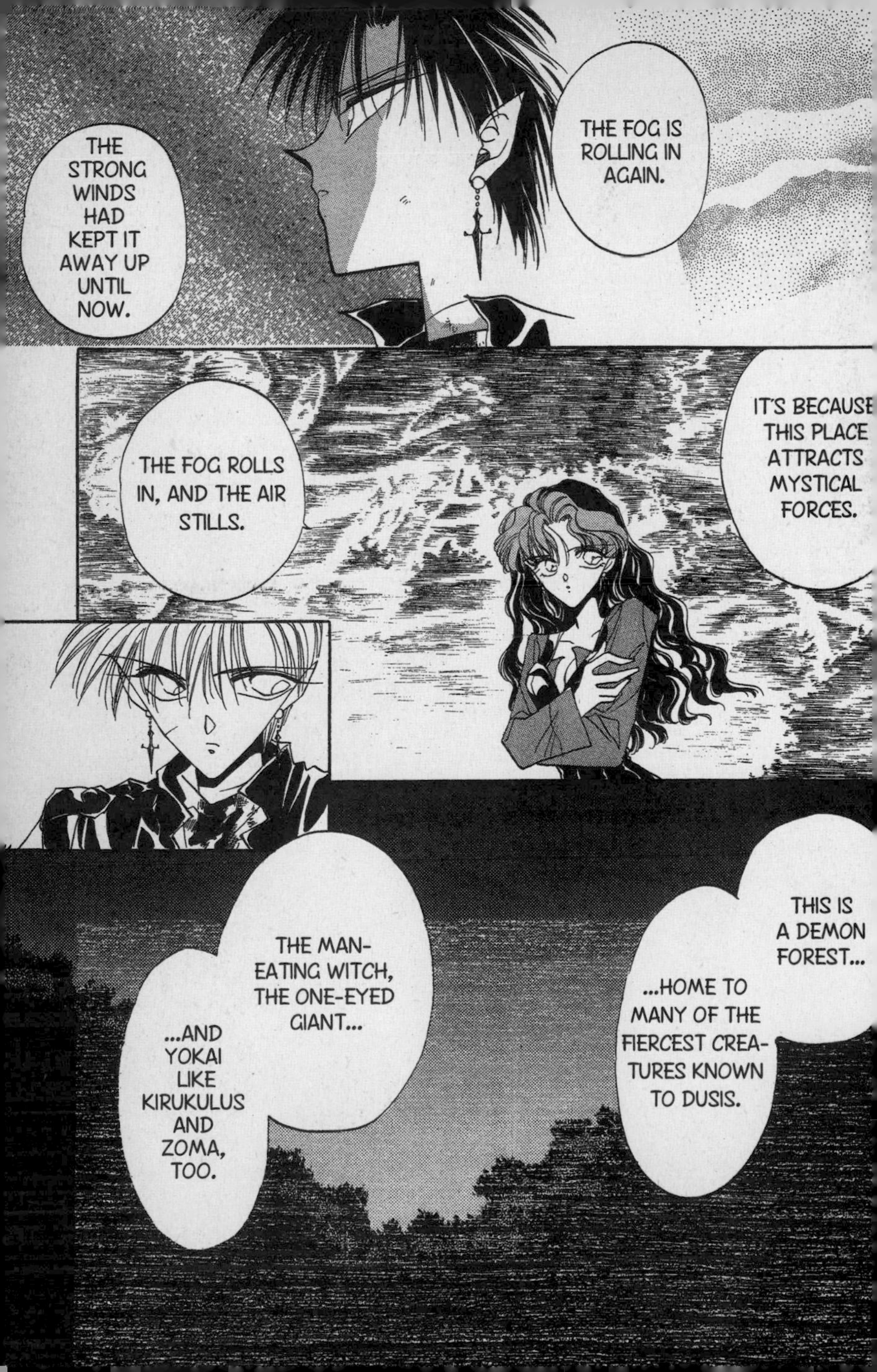
THE FOG IS ROLLING IN AGAIN.
THE STRONG WINDS HAD KEPT IT AWAY UP UNTIL NOW.
IT'S BECAUSE THIS PLACE ATTRACTS MYSTICAL FORCES.
THE FOG ROLLS IN, AND THE AIR STILLS.
THIS IS A DEMON FOREST...
...HOME TO MANY OF THE FIERCEST CREATURES KNOWN TO DUSIS.
THE MAN-EATING WITCH, THE ONE-EYED GIANT...
...AND YOKAI LIKE KIRUKULUS AND ZOMA, TOO.

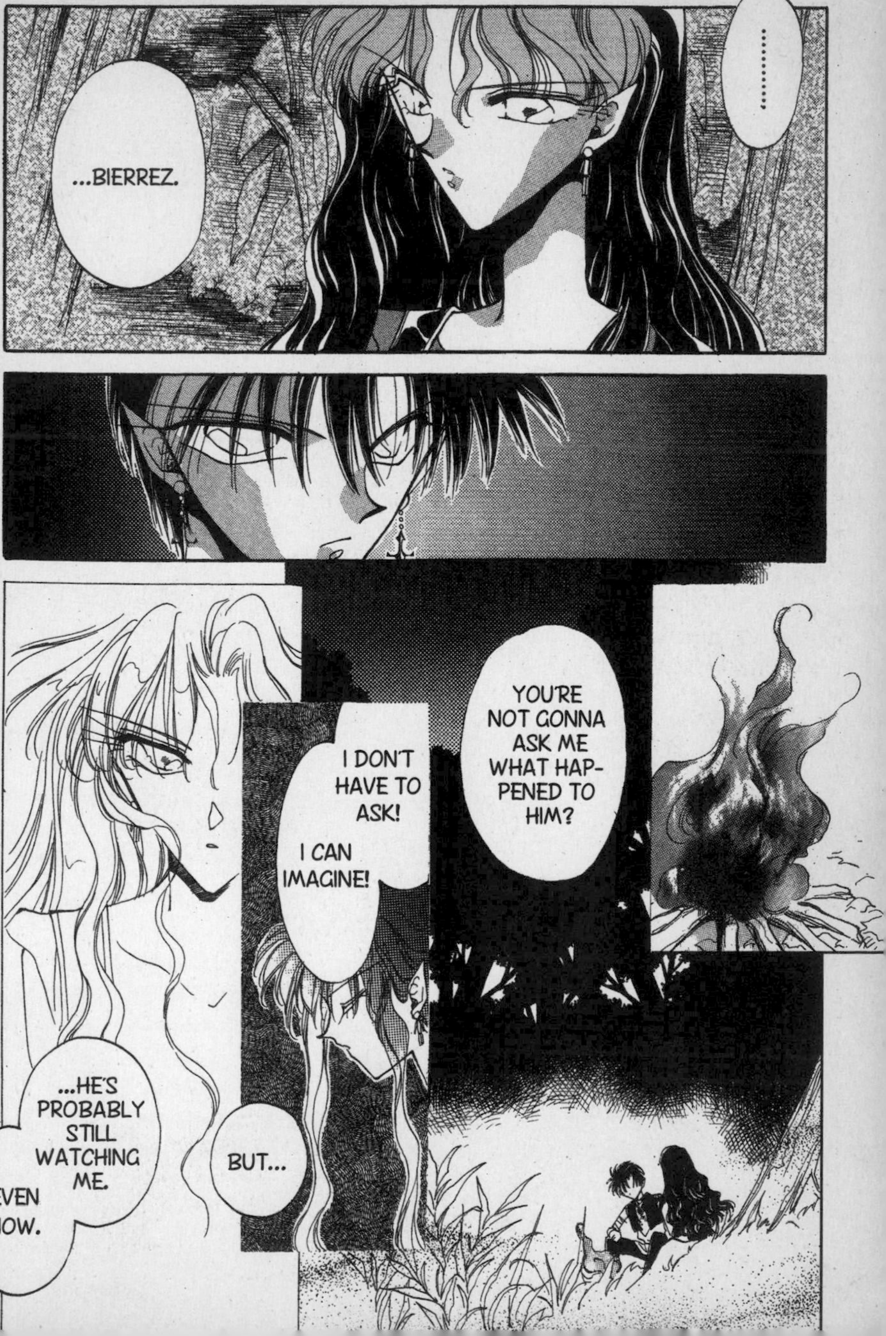
......
...BIERREZ.
YOU'RE NOT GONNA ASK ME WHAT HAPPENED TO HIM?
I DON'T HAVE TO ASK! I CAN IMAGINE!
BUT...
...HE'S PROBABLY STILL WATCHING ME.
EVEN NOW.

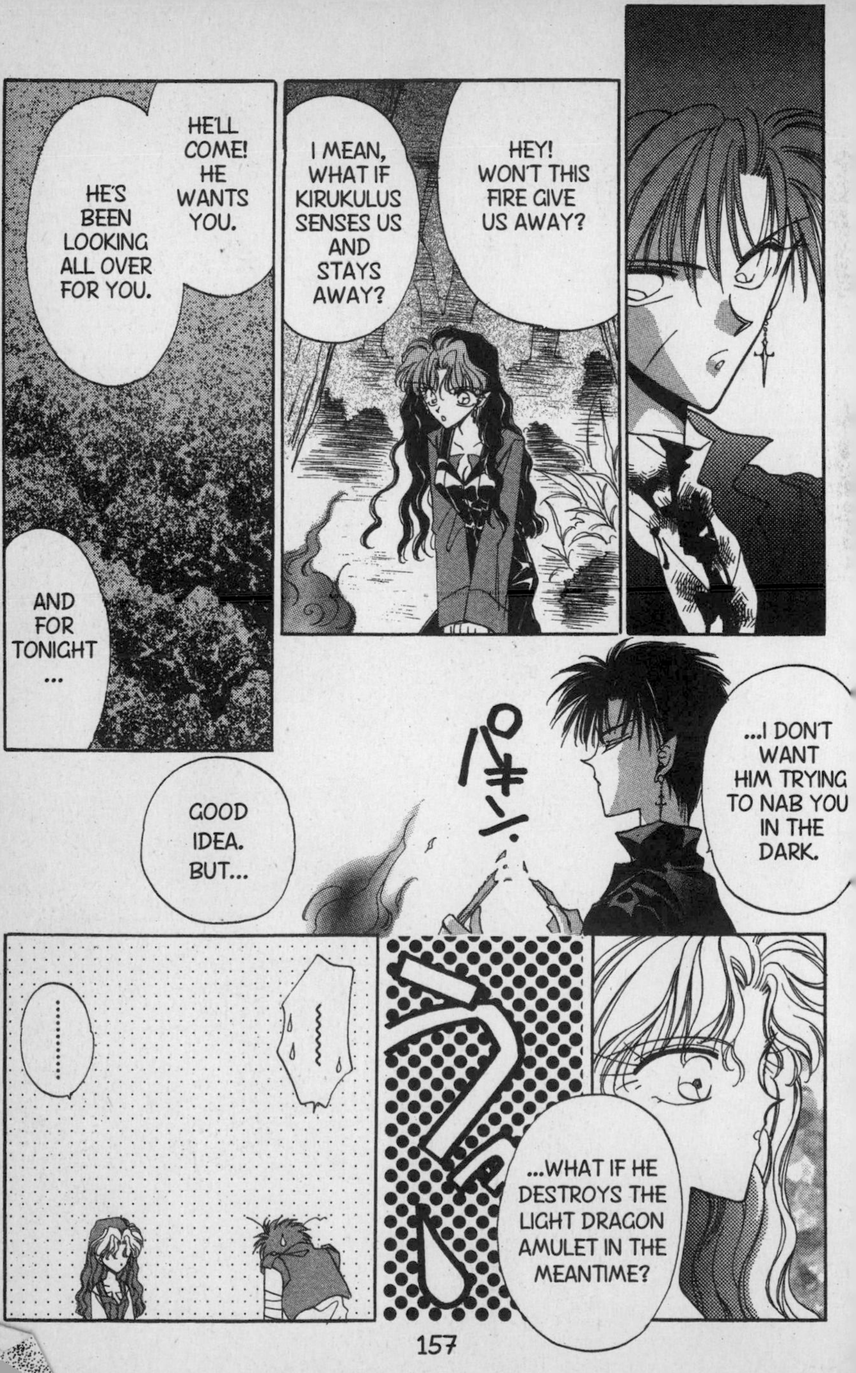
HEY! WON'T THIS FIRE GIVE US AWAY?
I MEAN, WHAT IF KIRUKULUS SENSES US AND STAYS AWAY?
HE'LL COME! HE WANTS YOU.
HE'S BEEN LOOKING ALL OVER FOR YOU.
AND FOR TONIGHT ...
...I DON'T WANT HIM TRYING TO NAB YOU IN THE DARK.
パキン
GOOD IDEA. BUT...
...WHAT IF HE DESTROYS THE LIGHT DRAGON AMULET IN THE MEANTIME?
......

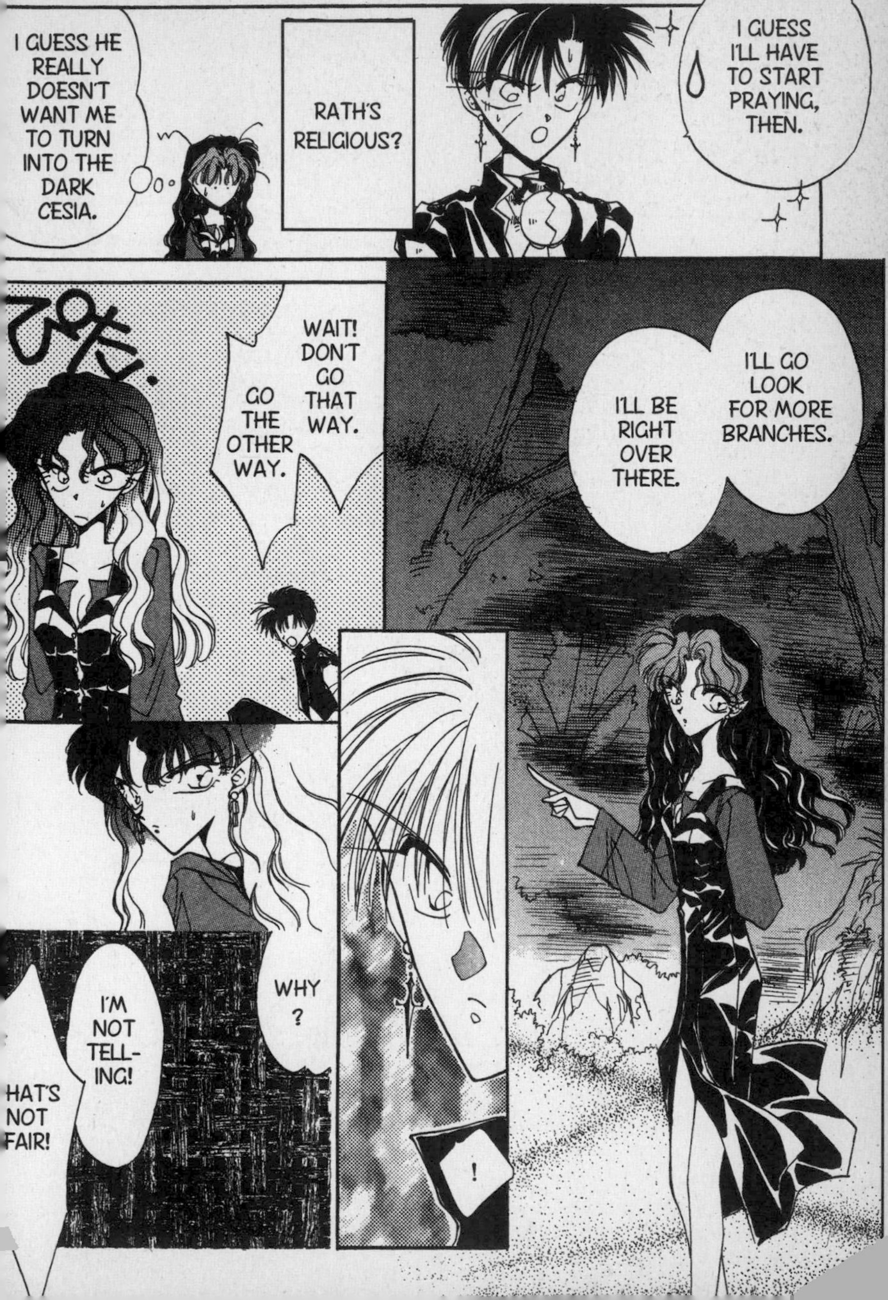
I GUESS I'LL HAVE TO START PRAYING, THEN.
RATH'S RELIGIOUS?
I GUESS HE REALLY DOESN'T WANT ME TO TURN INTO THE DARK CESIA.
I'LL GO LOOK FOR MORE BRANCHES.
I'LL BE RIGHT OVER THERE.
WAIT! DON'T GO THAT WAY.
GO THE OTHER WAY.
ぴたっ.
WHY ?
!
I'M NOT TELL-ING!
HAT'S NOT FAIR!

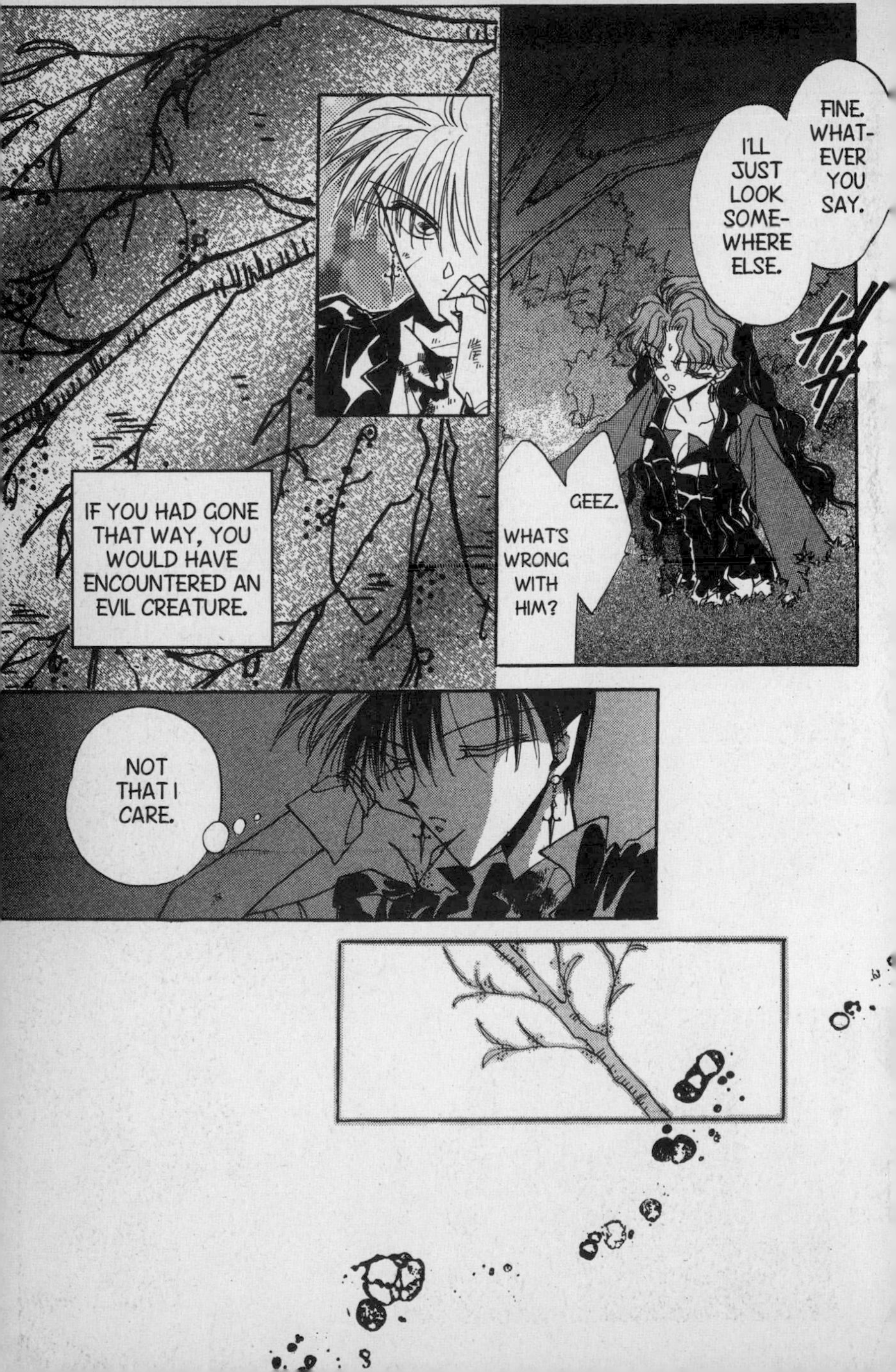
FINE. WHAT-EVER YOU SAY.
I'LL JUST LOOK SOME-WHERE ELSE.
GEEZ.
WHAT'S WRONG WITH HIM?
IF YOU HAD GONE THAT WAY, YOU WOULD HAVE ENCOUNTERED AN EVIL CREATURE.
NOT THAT I CARE.

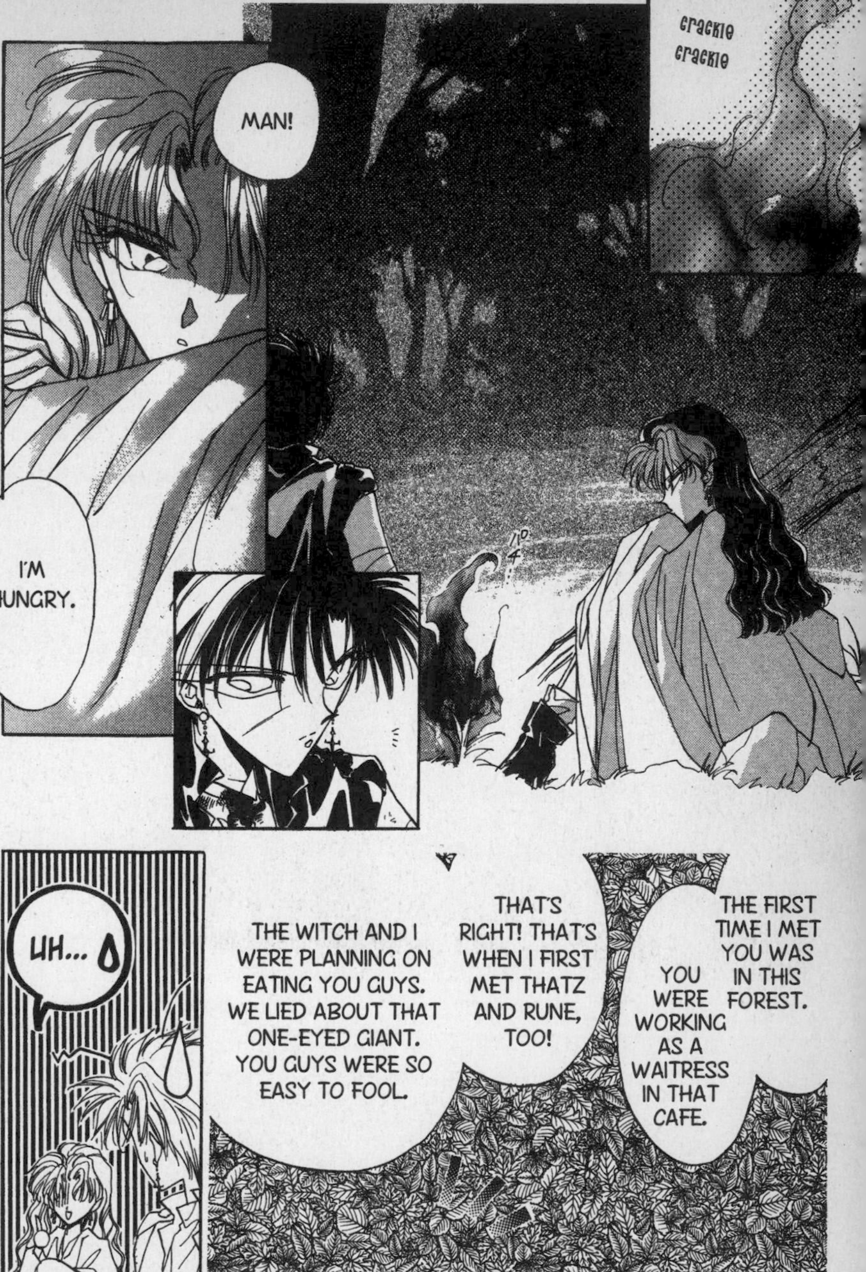
crackle
crackle
MAN!
I'M HUNGRY.
THE FIRST TIME I MET YOU WAS IN THIS FOREST.
YOU WERE WORKING AS A WAITRESS IN THAT CAFE.
THAT'S RIGHT! THAT'S WHEN I FIRST MET THATZ AND RUNE, TOO!
THE WITCH AND I WERE PLANNING ON EATING YOU GUYS. WE LIED ABOUT THAT ONE-EYED GIANT. YOU GUYS WERE SO EASY TO FOOL.
UH...

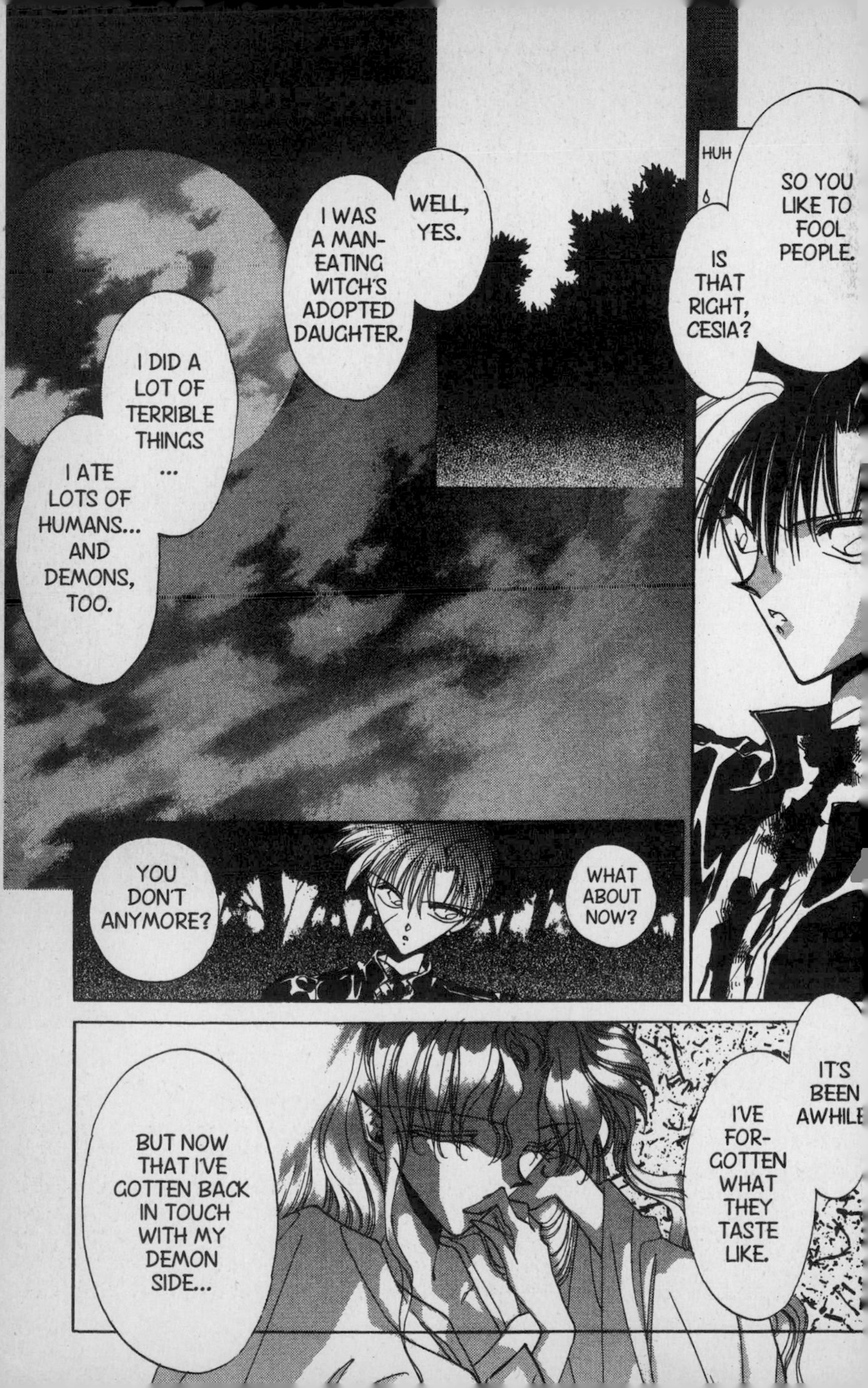
SO YOU LIKE TO FOOL PEOPLE.
HUH
IS THAT RIGHT, CESIA?
WELL, YES.
I WAS A MAN-EATING WITCH'S ADOPTED DAUGHTER.
I DID A LOT OF TERRIBLE THINGS ...
I ATE LOTS OF HUMANS... AND DEMONS, TOO.
WHAT ABOUT NOW?
YOU DON'T ANYMORE?
IT'S BEEN AWHILE
I'VE FOR-GOTTEN WHAT THEY TASTE LIKE.
BUT NOW THAT I'VE GOTTEN BACK IN TOUCH WITH MY DEMON SIDE...

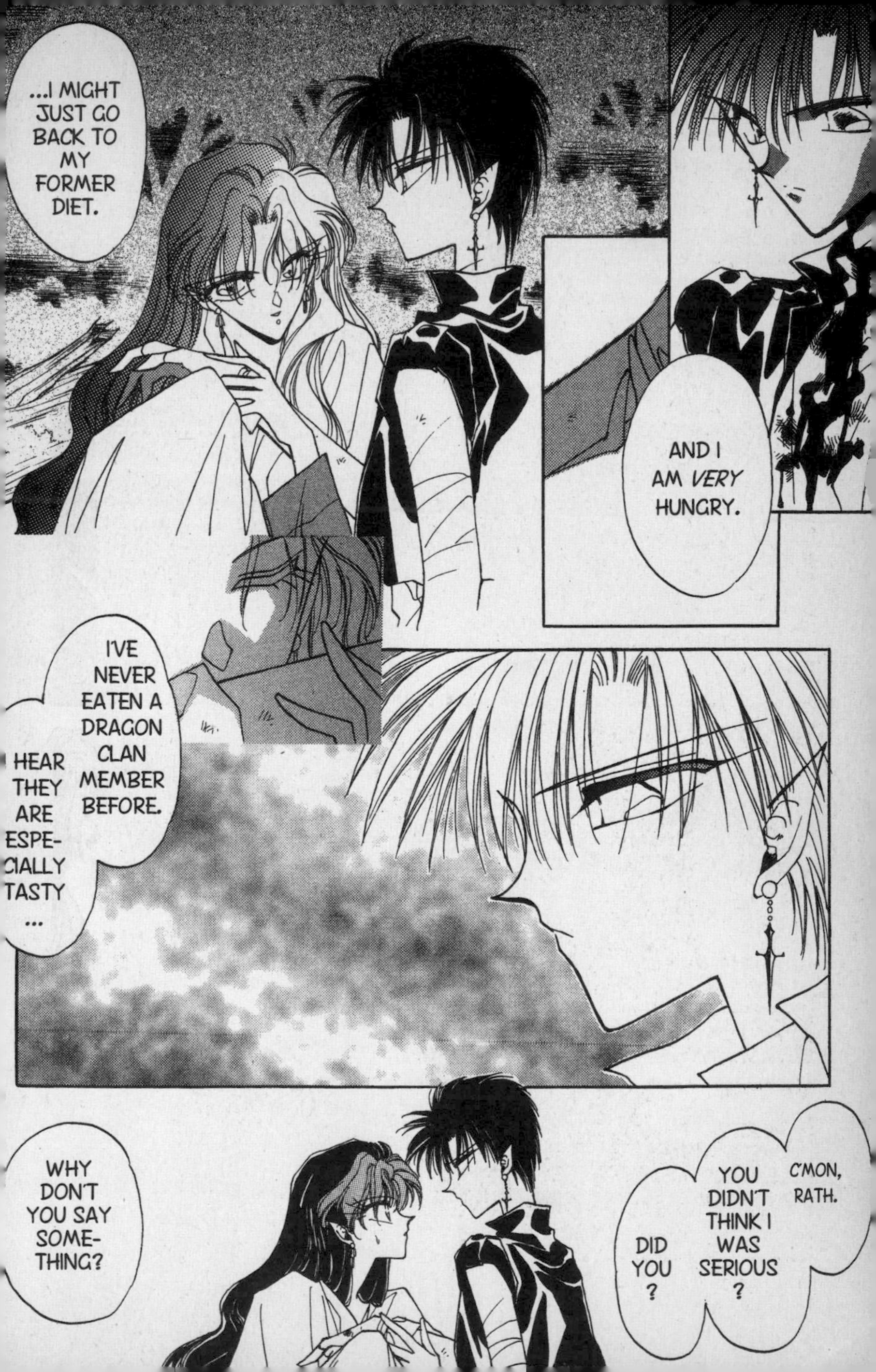
...I MIGHT JUST GO BACK TO MY FORMER DIET.
AND I AM *VERY* HUNGRY.
I'VE NEVER EATEN A DRAGON CLAN MEMBER BEFORE.
I HEAR THEY ARE ESPECIALLY TASTY...
C'MON, RATH.
YOU DIDN'T THINK I WAS SERIOUS?
DID YOU?
WHY DON'T YOU SAY SOMETHING?

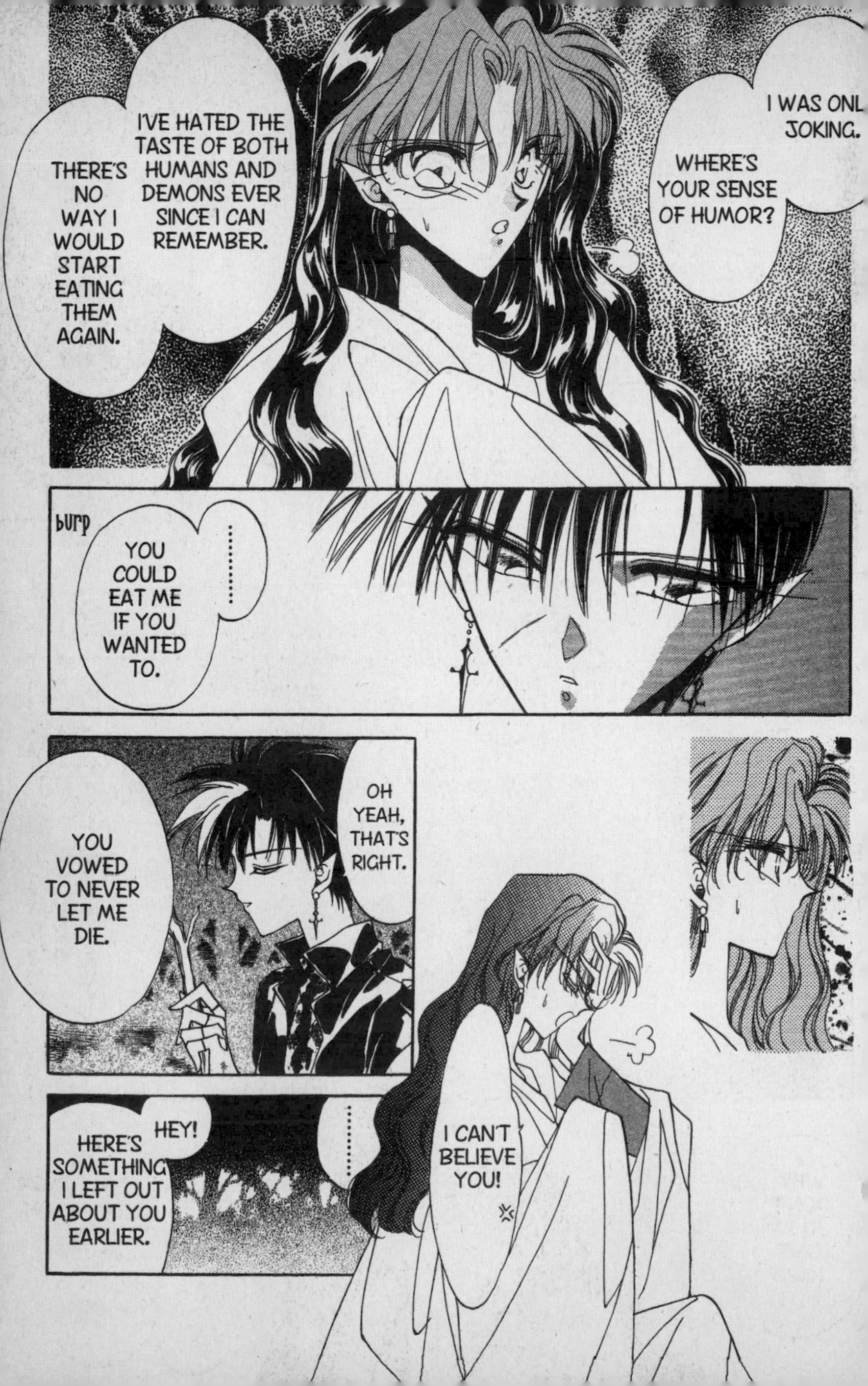
I WAS ONL JOKING.
WHERE'S YOUR SENSE OF HUMOR?
I'VE HATED THE TASTE OF BOTH HUMANS AND DEMONS EVER SINCE I CAN REMEMBER.
THERE'S NO WAY I WOULD START EATING THEM AGAIN.
burp
......
YOU COULD EAT ME IF YOU WANTED TO.
I CAN'T BELIEVE YOU!
OH YEAH, THAT'S RIGHT.
YOU VOWED TO NEVER LET ME DIE.
......
HEY!
HERE'S SOMETHING I LEFT OUT ABOUT YOU EARLIER.

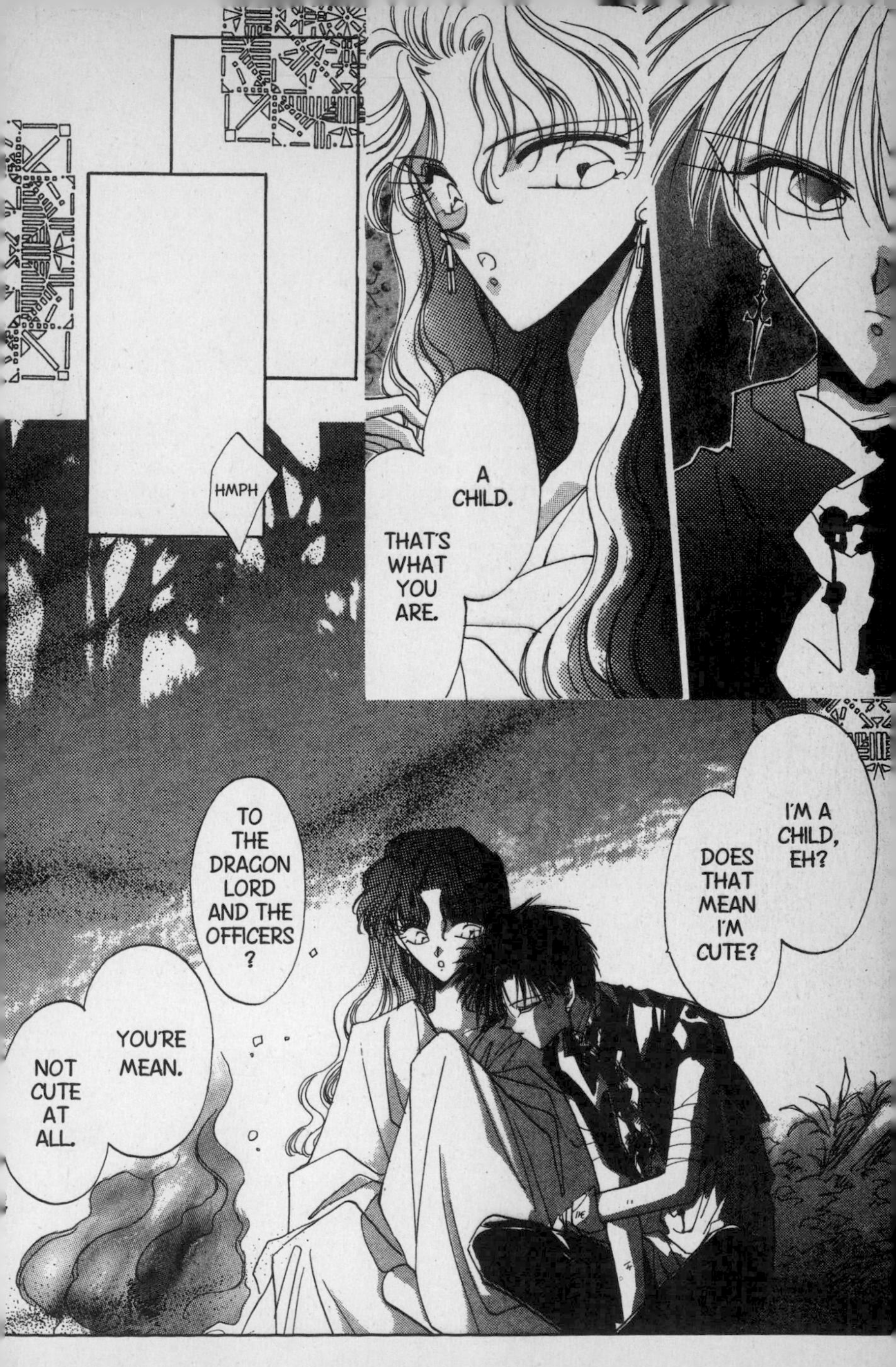
A CHILD. THAT'S WHAT YOU ARE.
HMPH
I'M A CHILD, EH?
DOES THAT MEAN I'M CUTE?
TO THE DRAGON LORD AND THE OFFICERS?
YOU'RE MEAN.
NOT CUTE AT ALL.

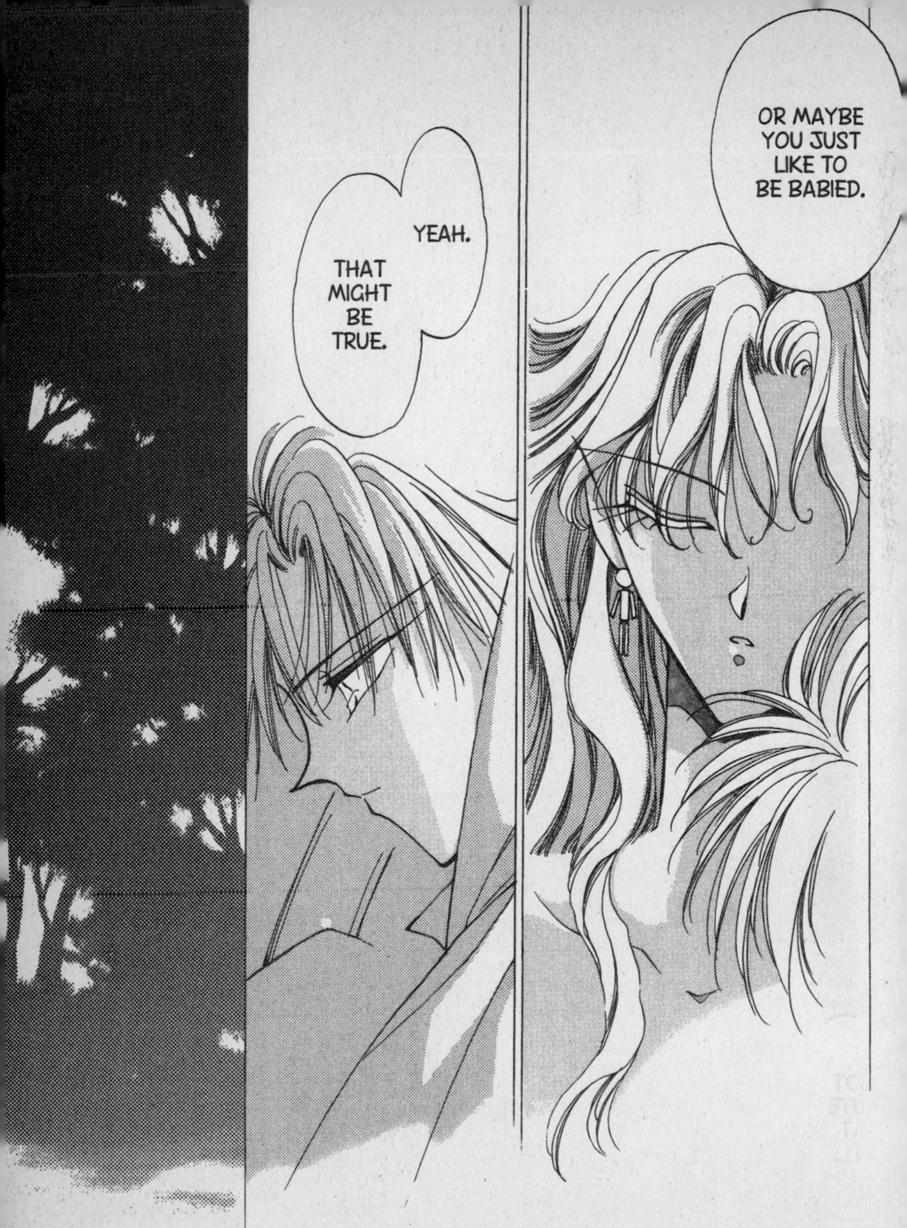
OR MAYBE YOU JUST LIKE TO BE BABIED.
YEAH.
THAT MIGHT BE TRUE.

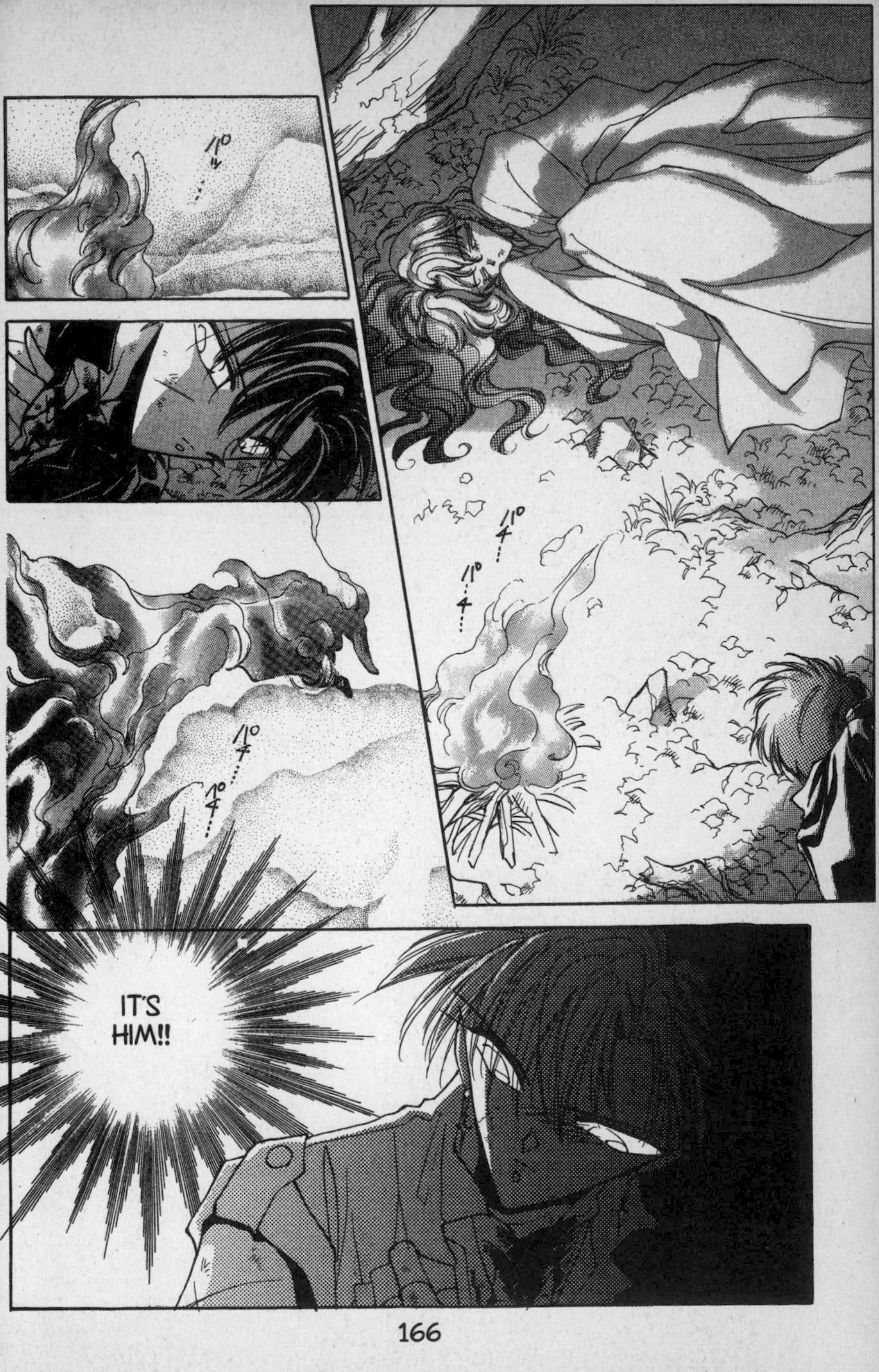
IT'S HIM!!

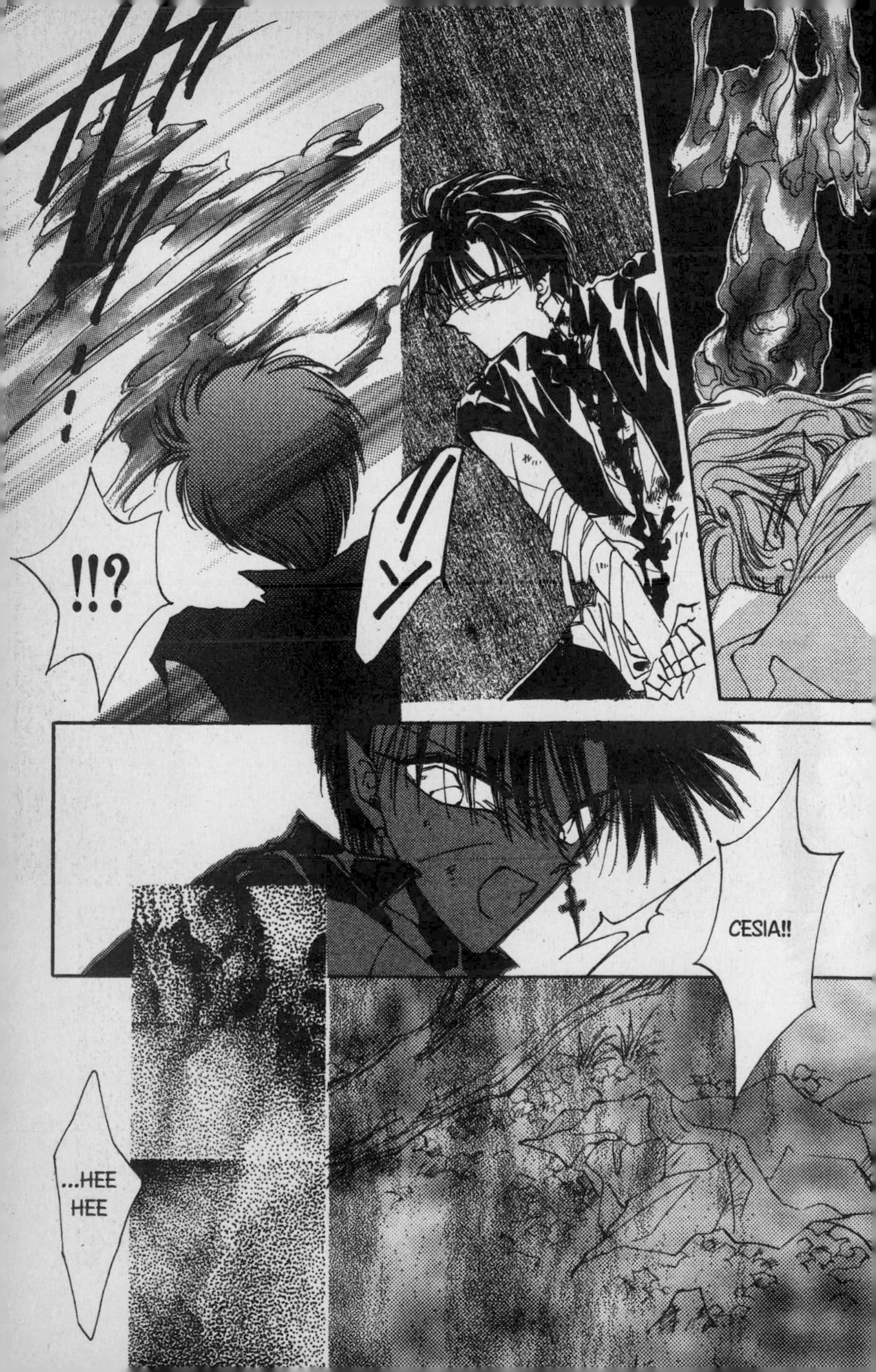
!!?
CESIA!!
...HEE HEE

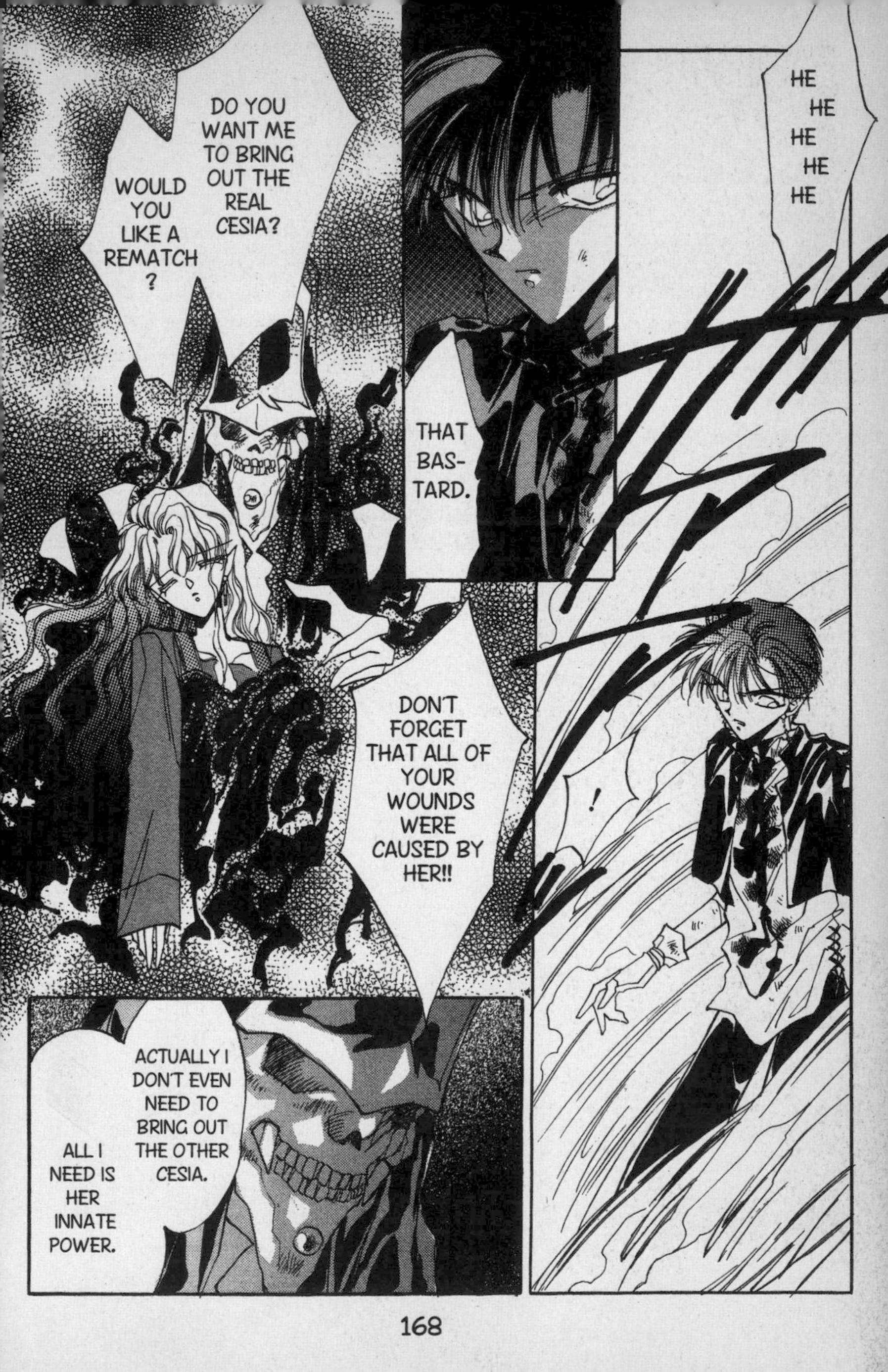
HE HE HE HE HE
THAT BASTARD.
DO YOU WANT ME TO BRING OUT THE REAL CESIA?
WOULD YOU LIKE A REMATCH?
DON'T FORGET THAT ALL OF YOUR WOUNDS WERE CAUSED BY HER!!
!
ACTUALLY I DON'T EVEN NEED TO BRING OUT THE OTHER CESIA.
ALL I NEED IS HER INNATE POWER.

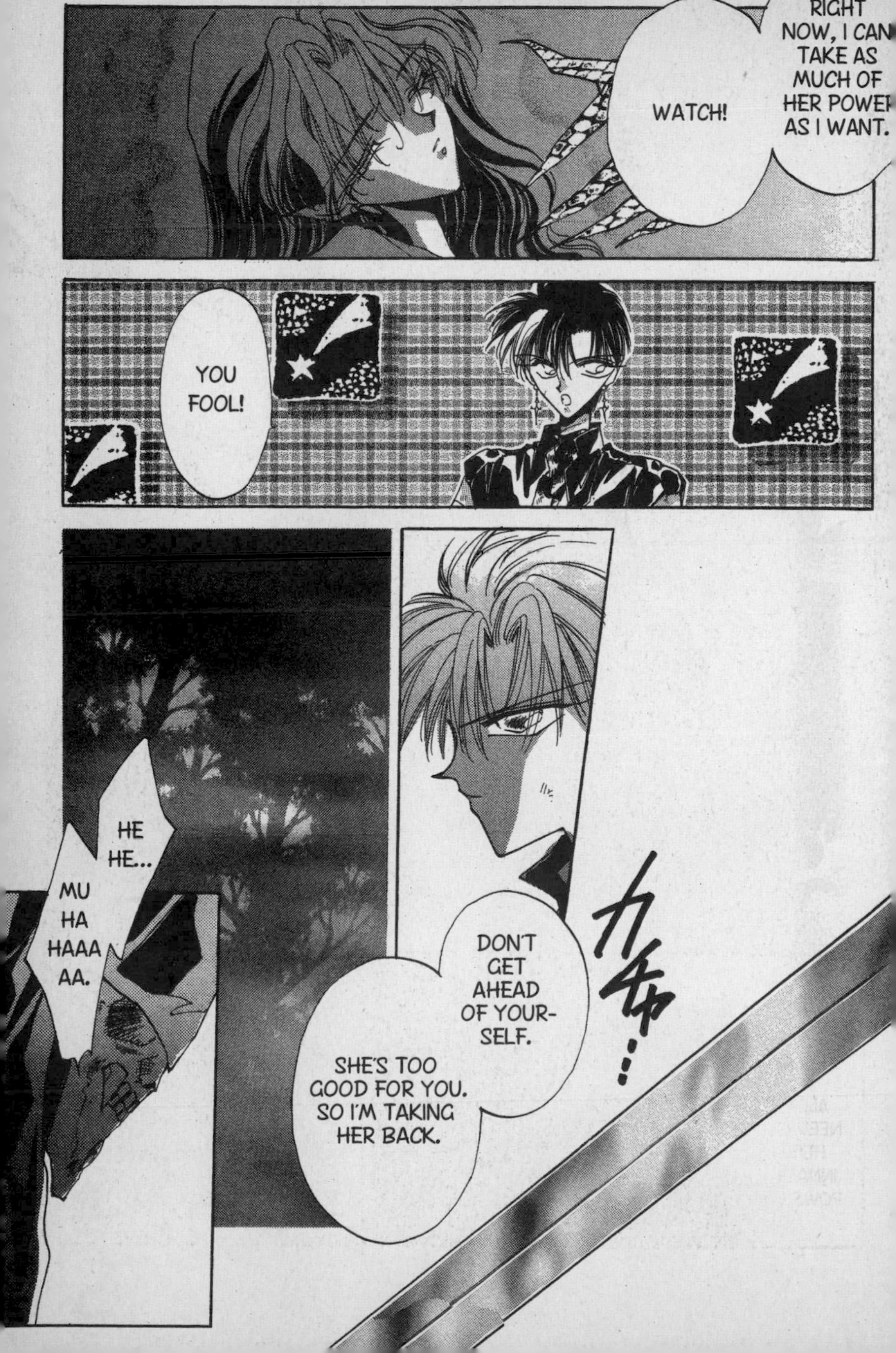
RIGHT NOW, I CAN TAKE AS MUCH OF HER POWER AS I WANT.
WATCH!
YOU FOOL!
カチャ...
DON'T GET AHEAD OF YOURSELF.
SHE'S TOO GOOD FOR YOU. SO I'M TAKING HER BACK.
HE HE...
MU HA HAAAAAA.

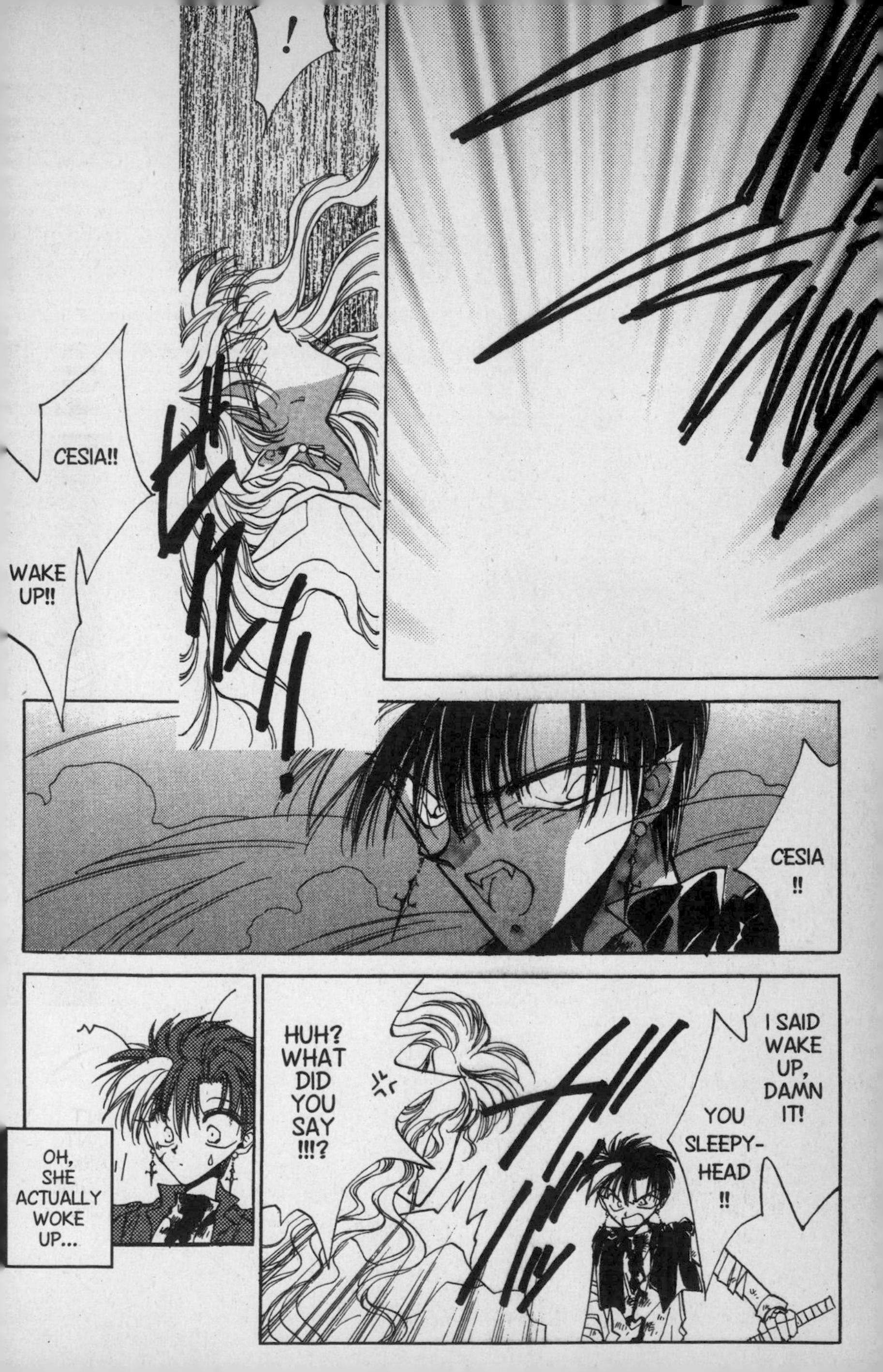
!
CESIA!!
WAKE UP!!
CESIA !!
I SAID WAKE UP, DAMN IT!
YOU SLEEPY-HEAD !!
HUH? WHAT DID YOU SAY !!!?
OH, SHE ACTUALLY WOKE UP...

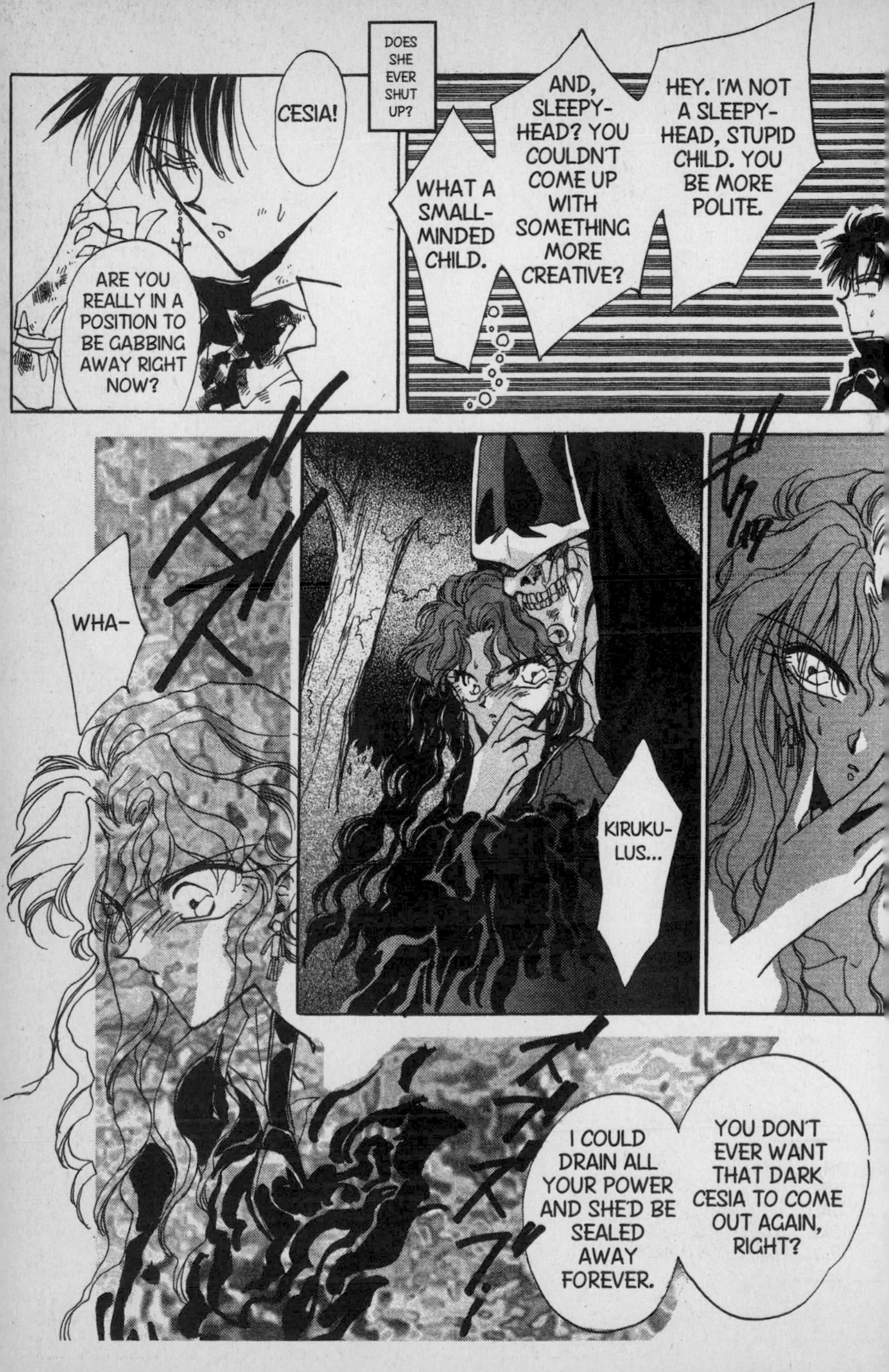
HEY. I'M NOT A SLEEPY-HEAD, STUPID CHILD. YOU BE MORE POLITE.
AND, SLEEPY-HEAD? YOU COULDN'T COME UP WITH SOMETHING MORE CREATIVE?
WHAT A SMALL-MINDED CHILD.
DOES SHE EVER SHUT UP?
CESIA!
ARE YOU REALLY IN A POSITION TO BE GABBING AWAY RIGHT NOW?
KIRUKU-LUS...
WHA-
YOU DON'T EVER WANT THAT DARK CESIA TO COME OUT AGAIN, RIGHT?
I COULD DRAIN ALL YOUR POWER AND SHE'D BE SEALED AWAY FOREVER.

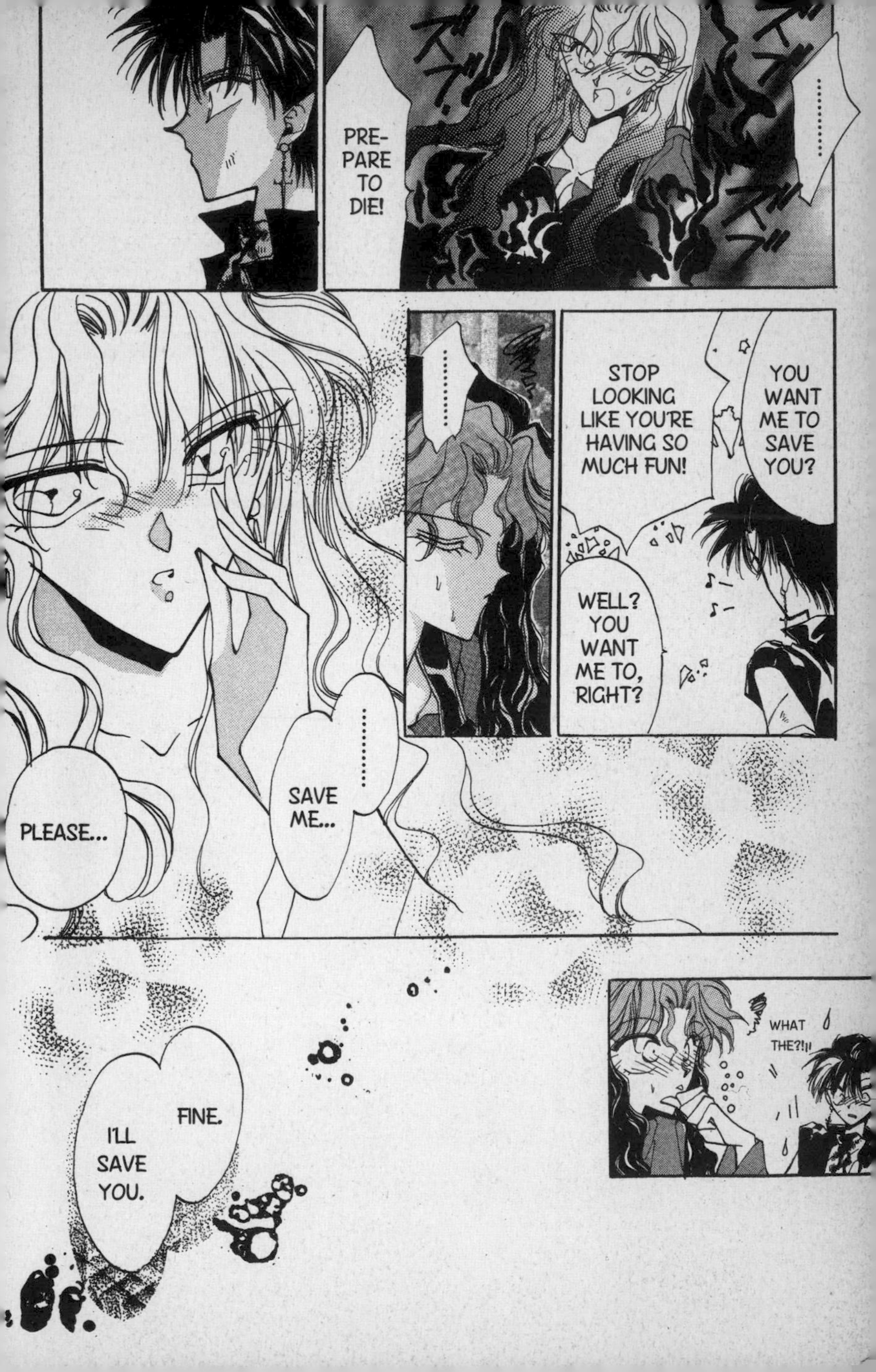
......
PRE-
PARE
TO
DIE!
YOU WANT ME TO SAVE YOU?
STOP LOOKING LIKE YOU'RE HAVING SO MUCH FUN!
WELL? YOU WANT ME TO, RIGHT?
......
......
SAVE ME...
PLEASE...
WHAT THE?!!
FINE.
I'LL SAVE YOU.

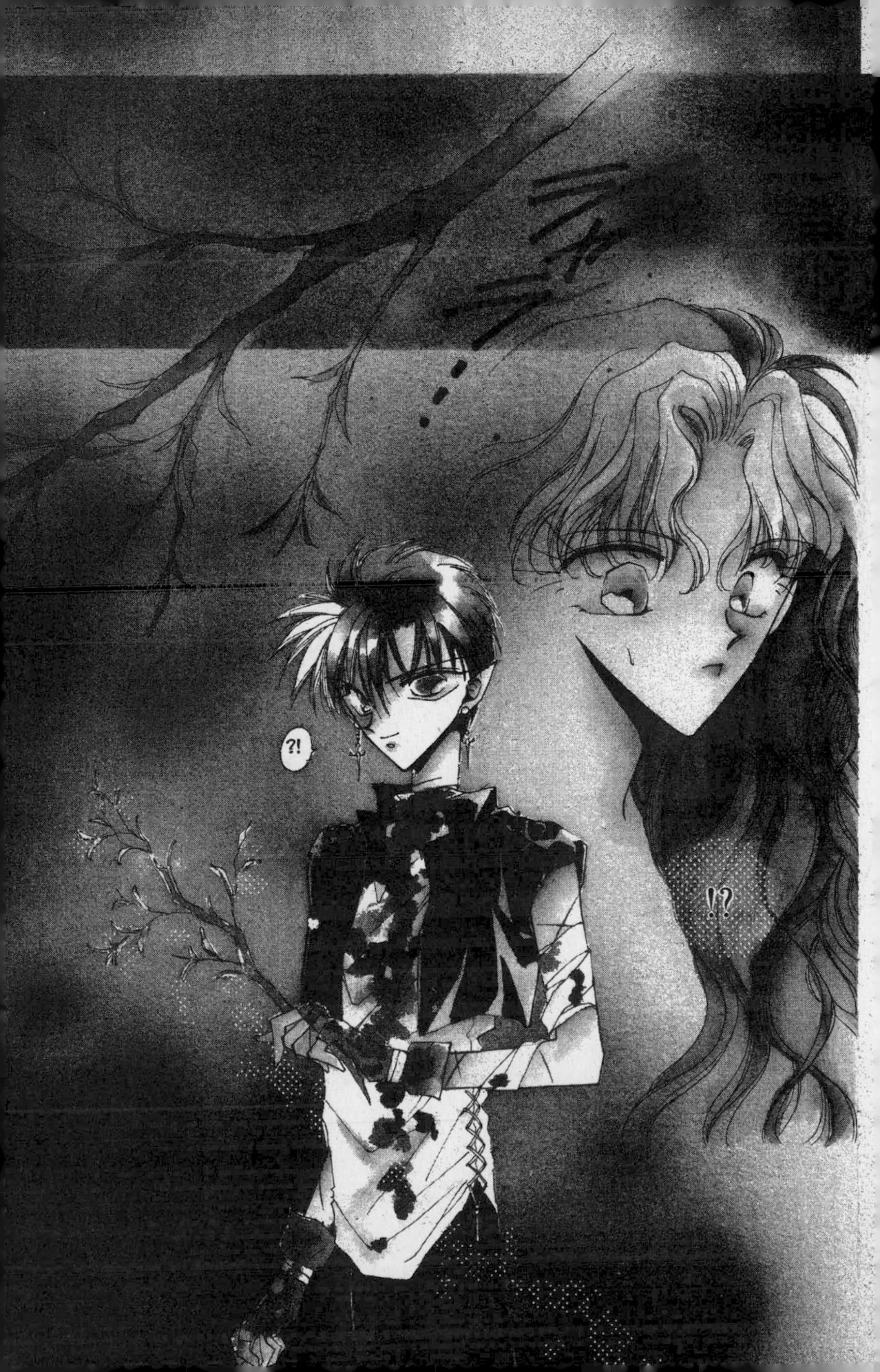
!?
?!

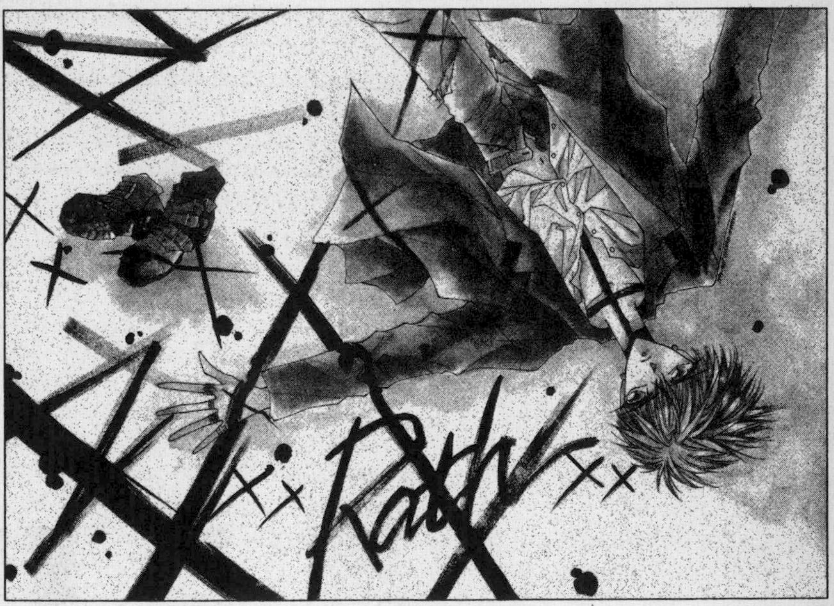
Rath

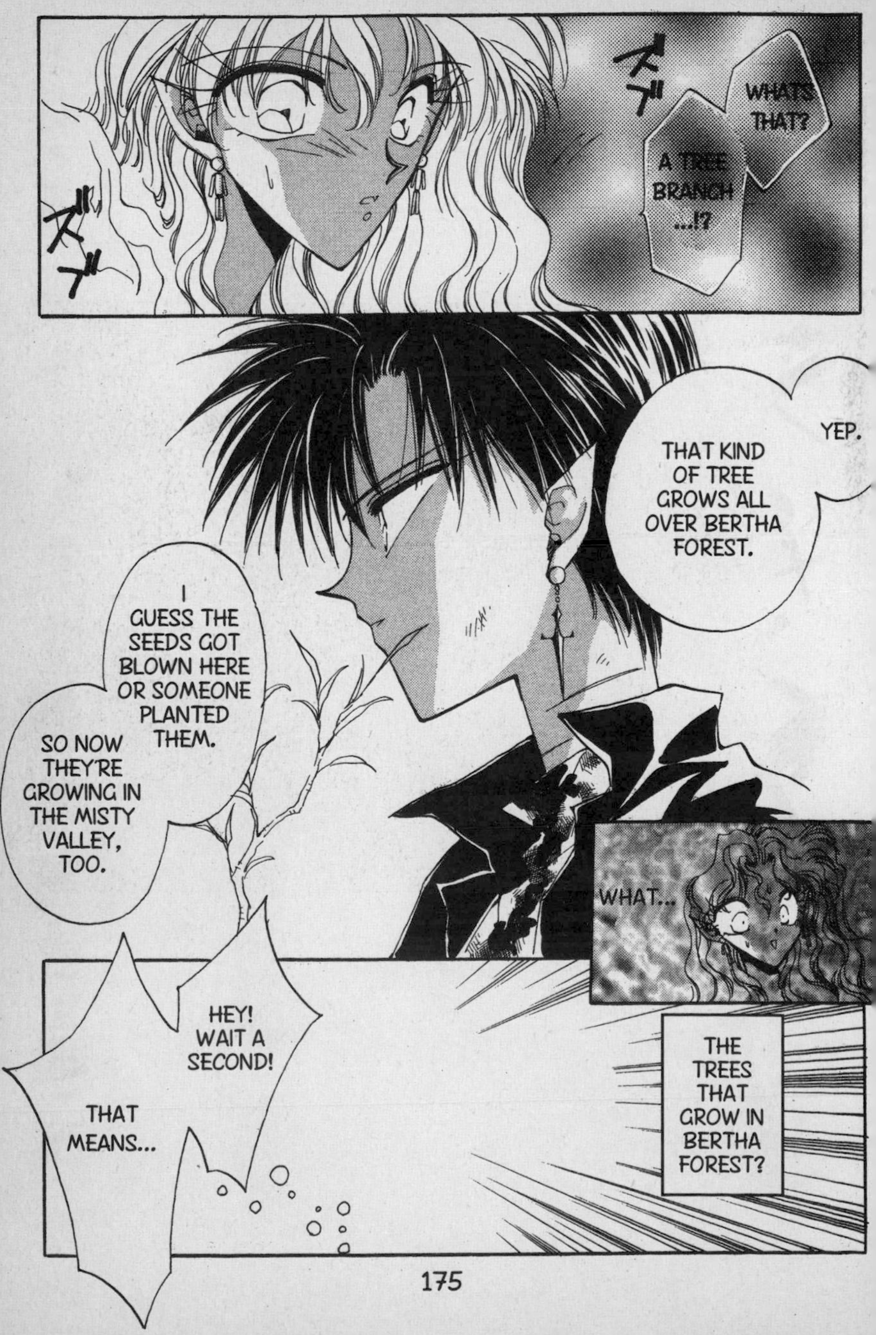
WHATS THAT?
A TREE BRANCH ...!?
YEP.
THAT KIND OF TREE GROWS ALL OVER BERTHA FOREST.
I GUESS THE SEEDS GOT BLOWN HERE OR SOMEONE PLANTED THEM.
SO NOW THEY'RE GROWING IN THE MISTY VALLEY, TOO.
WHAT...
THE TREES THAT GROW IN BERTHA FOREST?
HEY! WAIT A SECOND!
THAT MEANS...

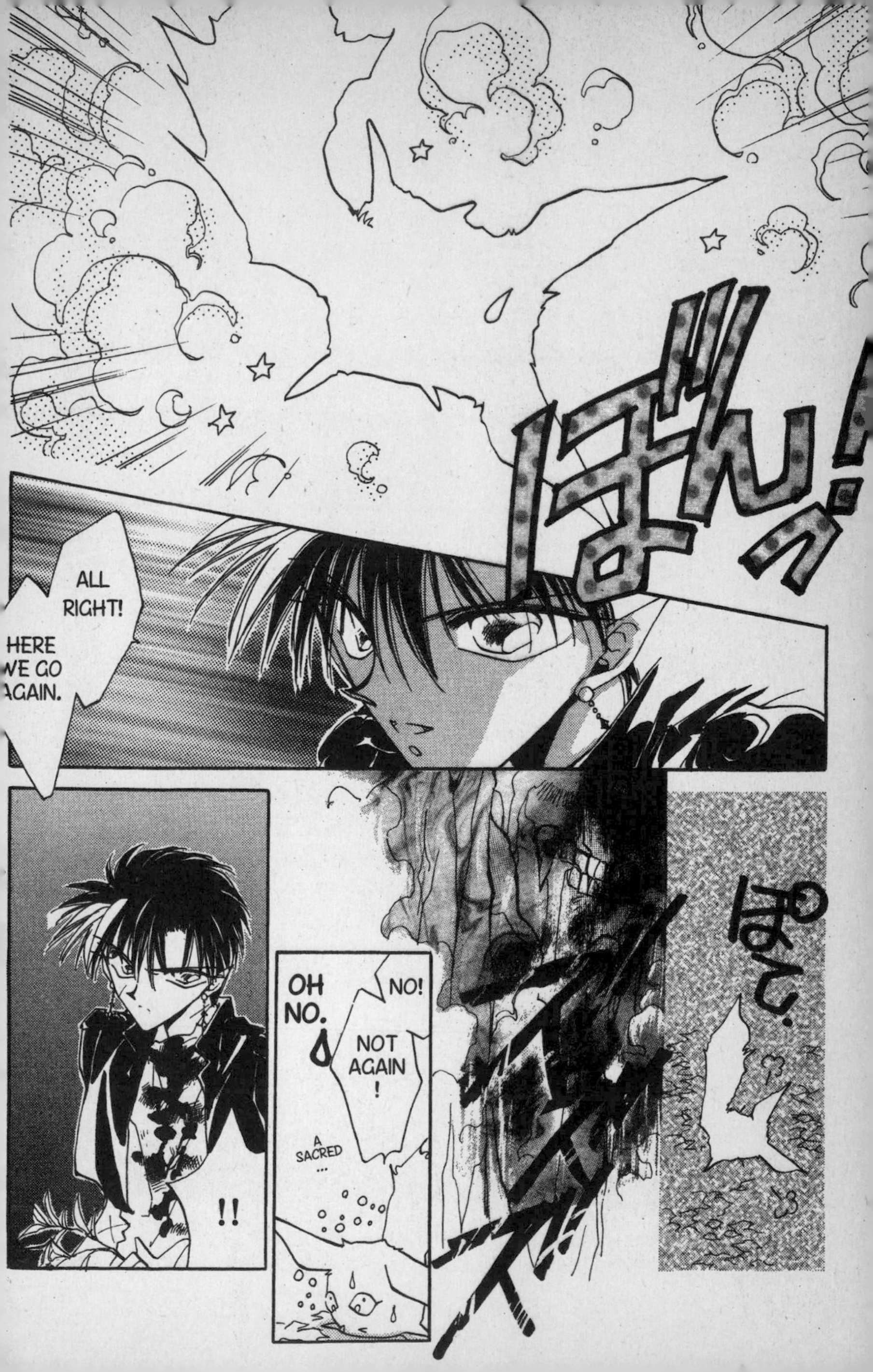
ぼん!
ALL RIGHT!
HERE WE GO AGAIN.
ぽて・
NO! NOT AGAIN!
OH NO.
A SACRED...
!!

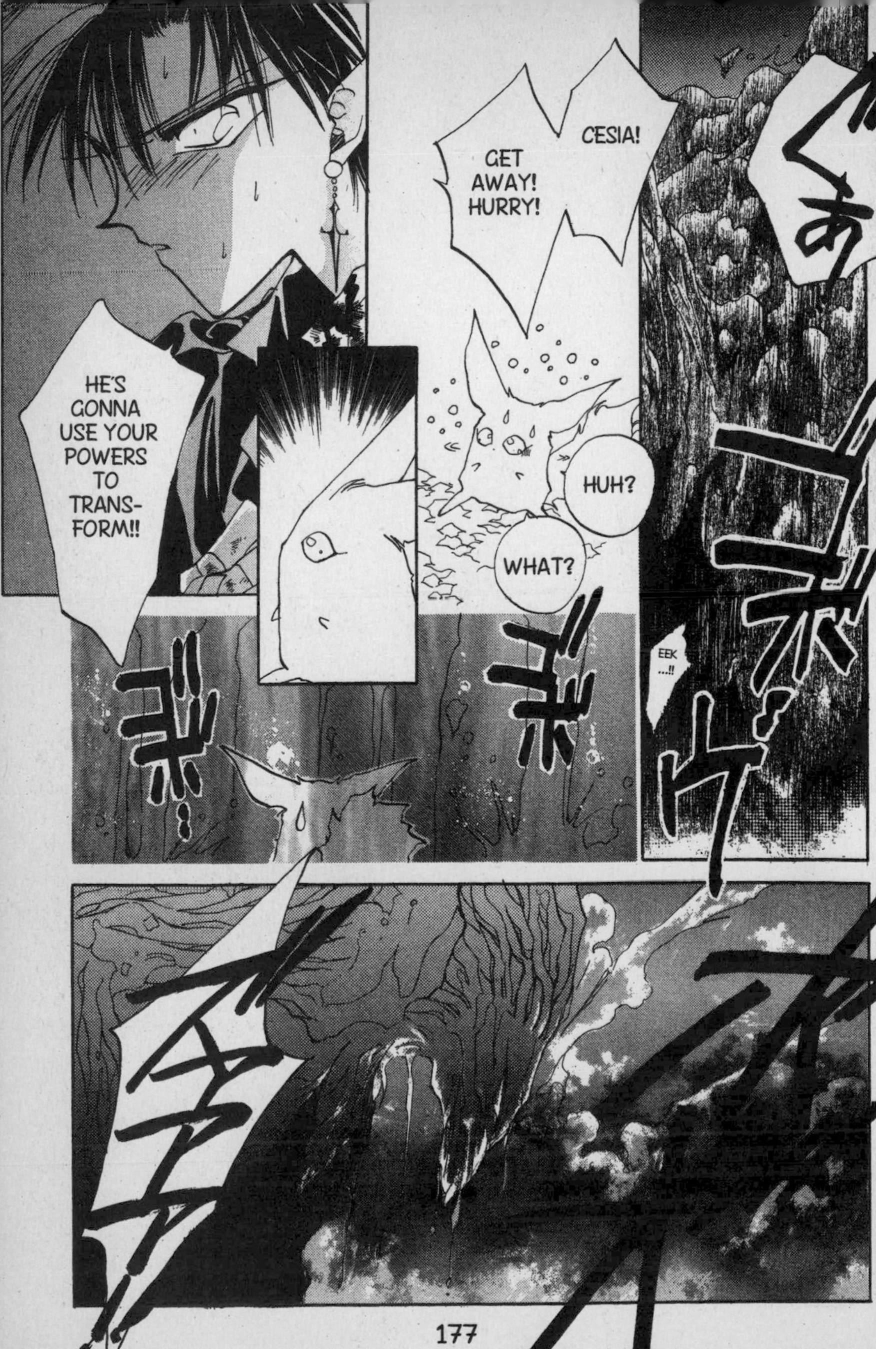
EEK ...!!
CESIA!
GET AWAY! HURRY!
HUH?
WHAT?
HE'S GONNA USE YOUR POWERS TO TRANS-FORM!!

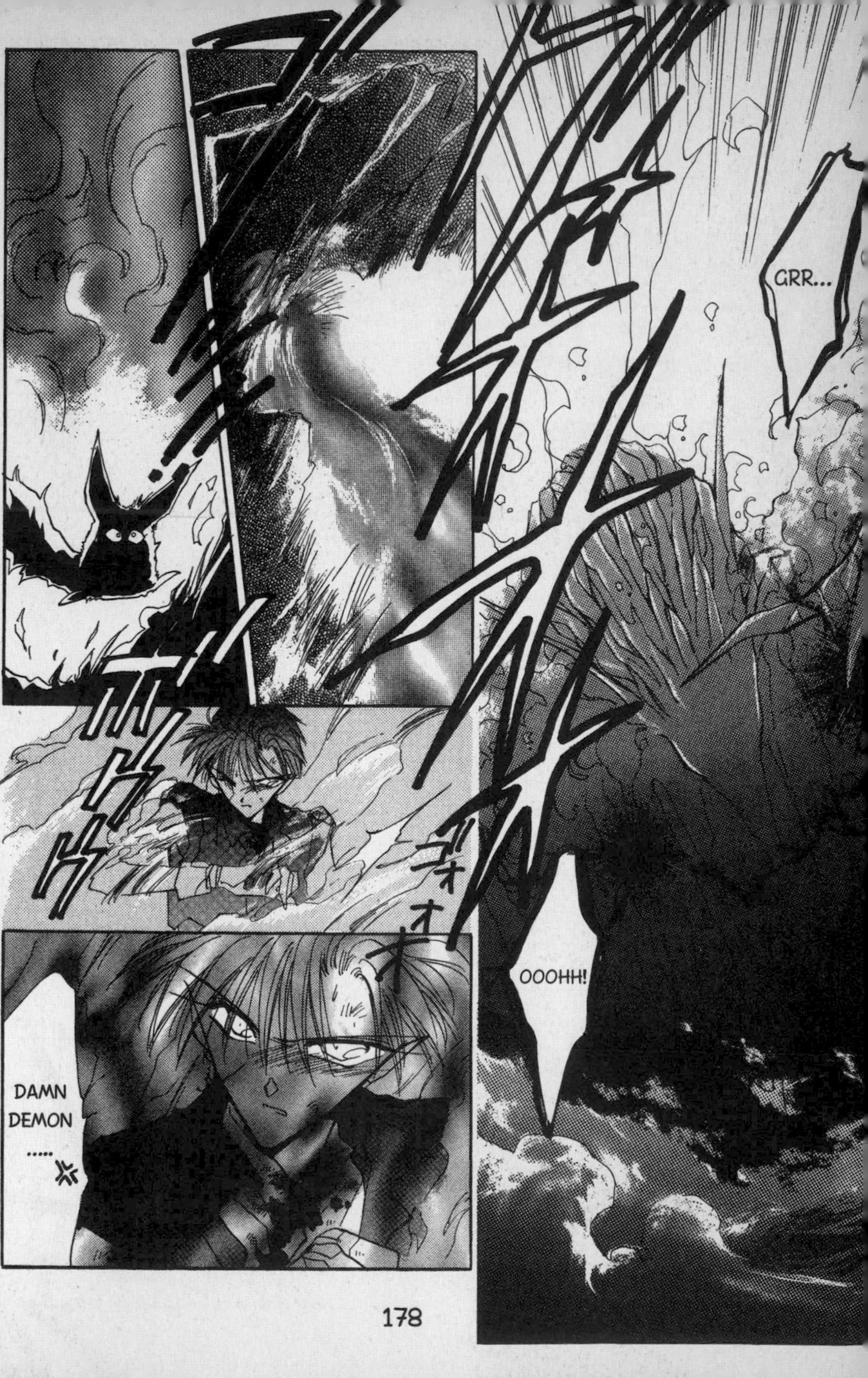
GRR...
OOOHH!
DAMN DEMON ......

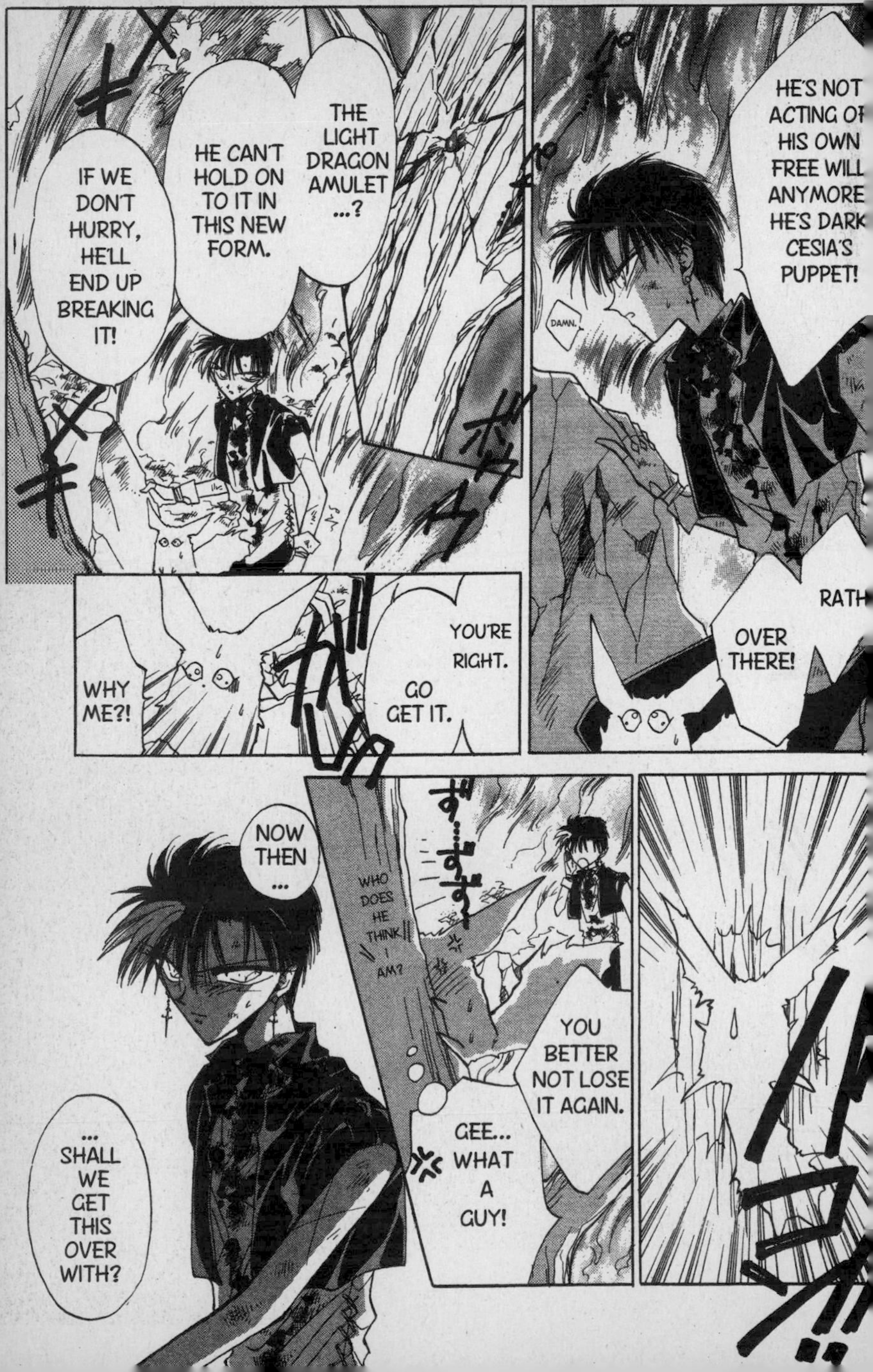

HE'S NOT ACTING OF HIS OWN FREE WILL ANYMORE HE'S DARK CESIA'S PUPPET!
DAMN.
RATH
OVER THERE!
THE LIGHT DRAGON AMULET ...?
HE CAN'T HOLD ON TO IT IN THIS NEW FORM.
IF WE DON'T HURRY, HE'LL END UP BREAKING IT!
YOU'RE RIGHT.
GO GET IT.
WHY ME?!
YOU BETTER NOT LOSE IT AGAIN.
WHO DOES HE THINK I AM?
GEE... WHAT A GUY!
NOW THEN ...
... SHALL WE GET THIS OVER WITH?

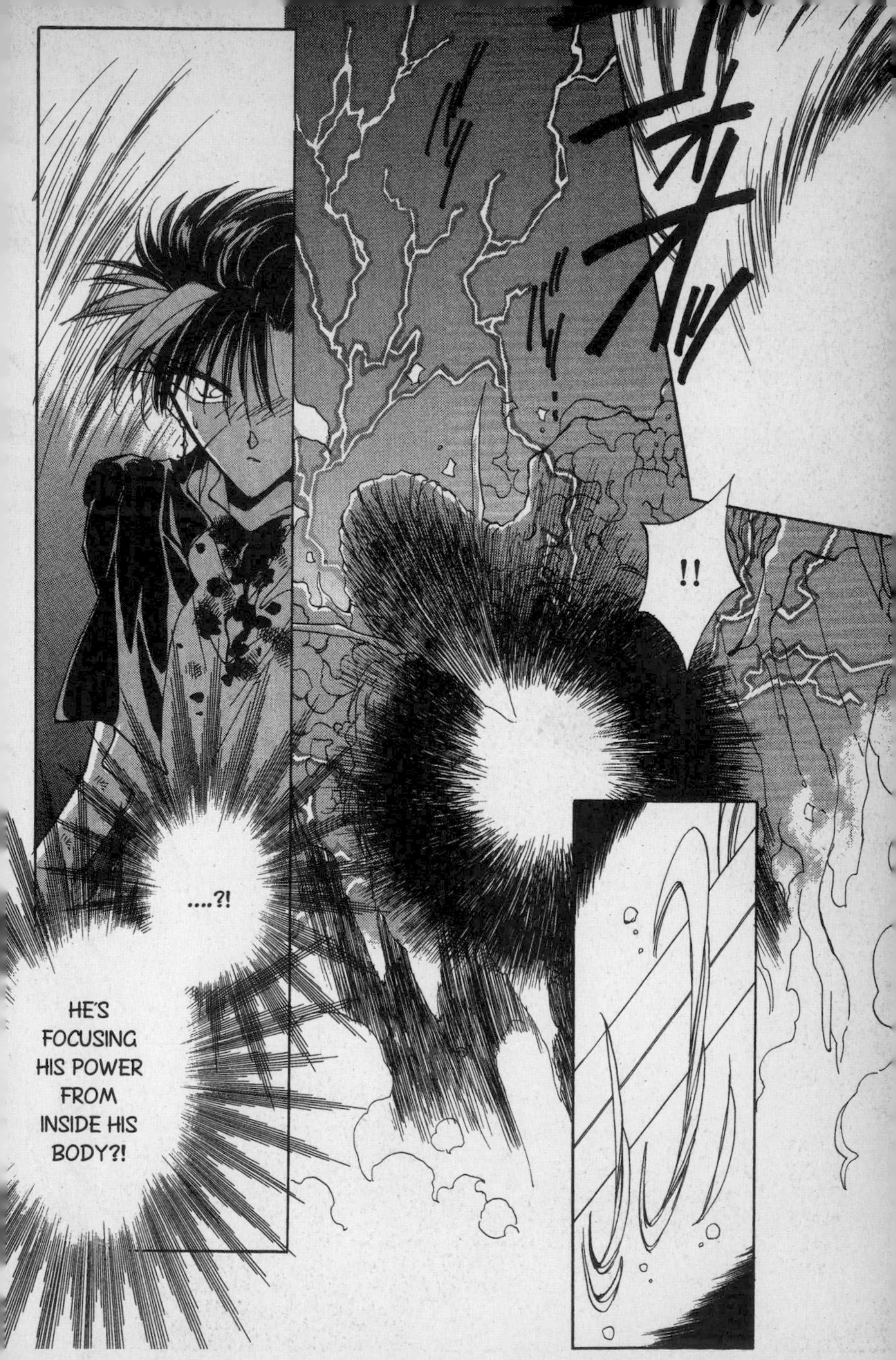
!!
....?!
HE'S FOCUSING HIS POWER FROM INSIDE HIS BODY?!

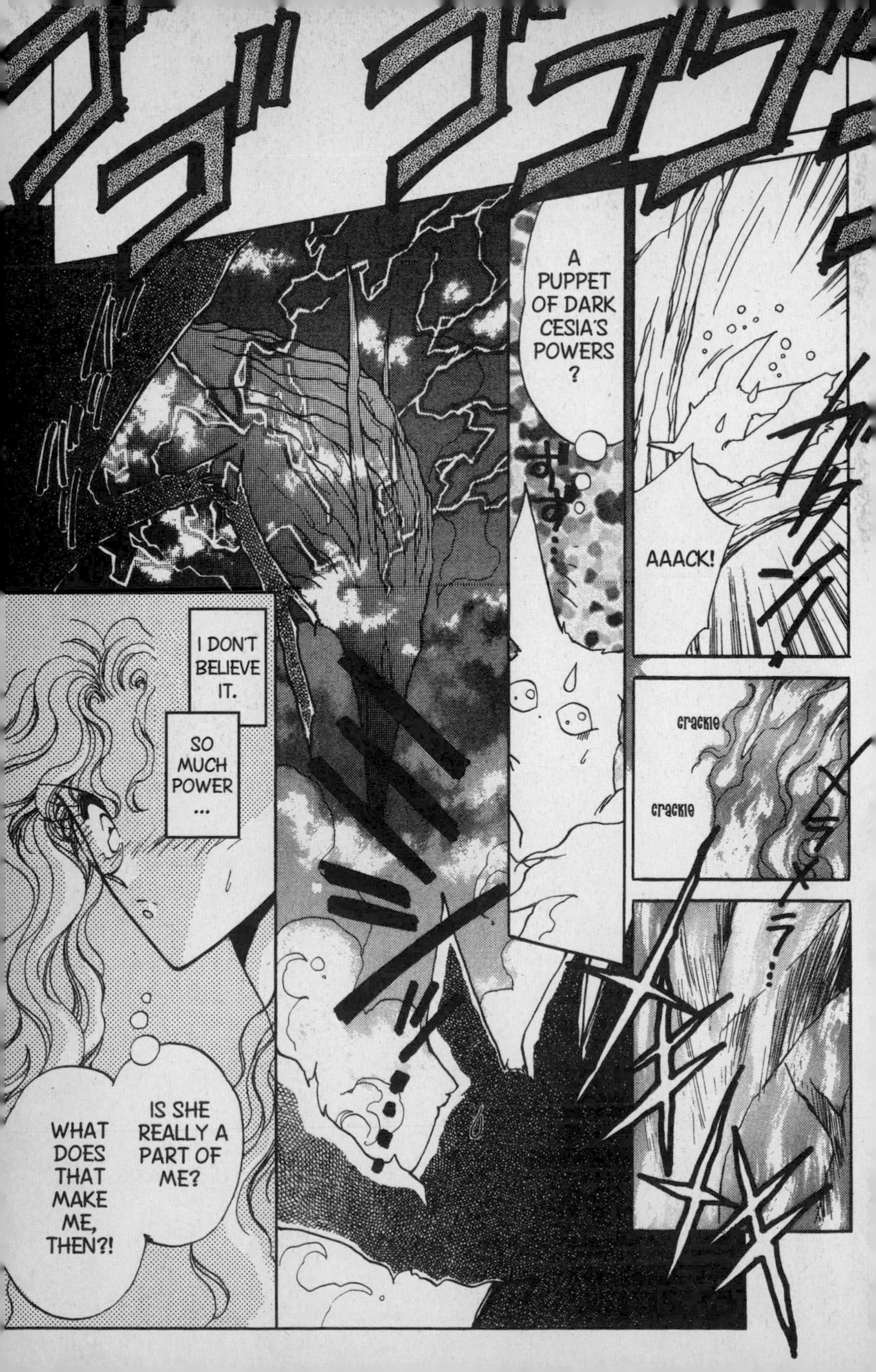
AAACK!
crackle
crackle
A PUPPET OF DARK CESIA'S POWERS ?
I DON'T BELIEVE IT.
SO MUCH POWER ...
IS SHE REALLY A PART OF ME?
WHAT DOES THAT MAKE ME, THEN?!

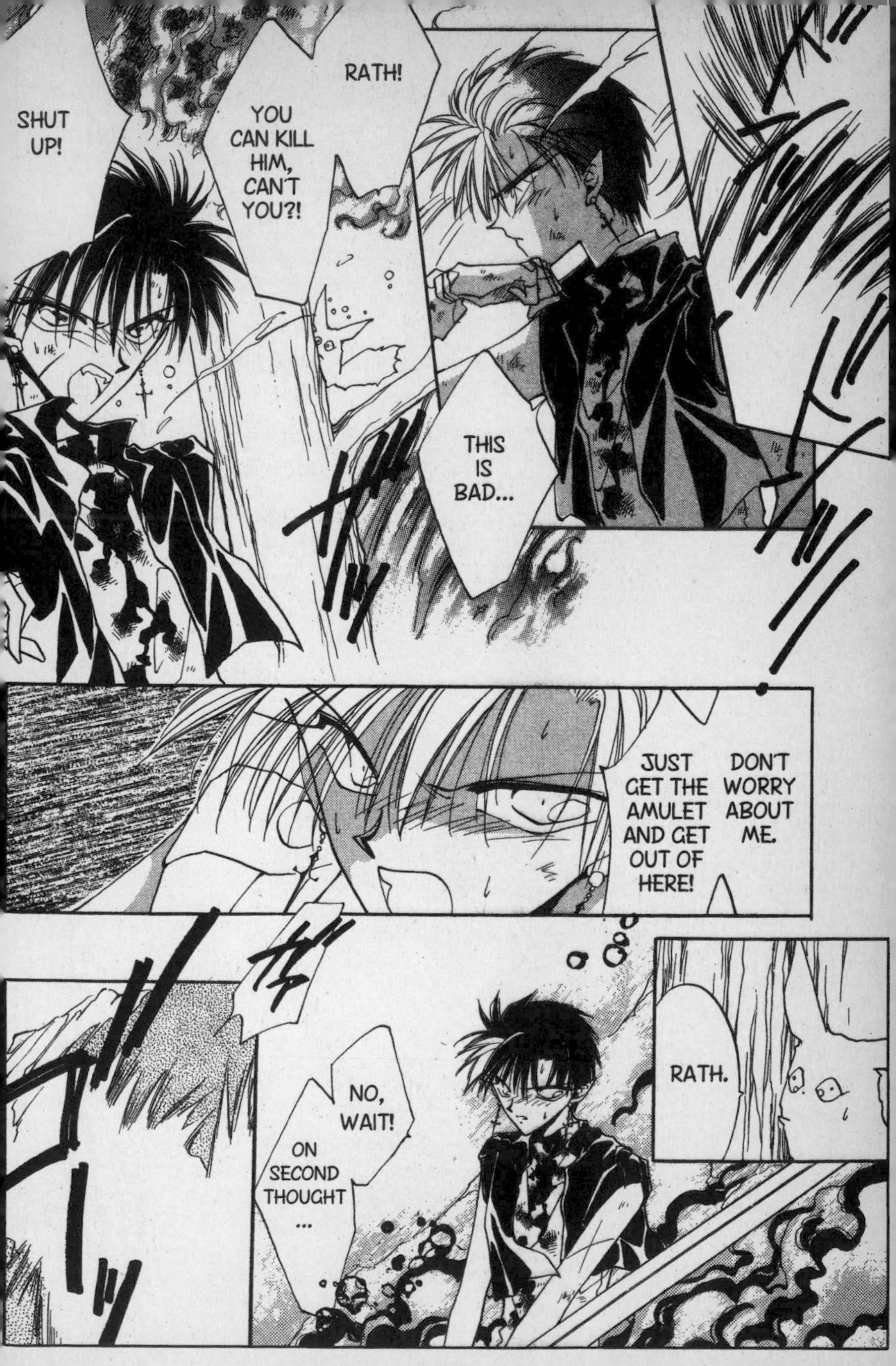
RATH!
YOU CAN KILL HIM, CAN'T YOU?!
THIS IS BAD...
SHUT UP!
DON'T WORRY ABOUT ME.
JUST GET THE AMULET AND GET OUT OF HERE!
RATH.
NO, WAIT!
ON SECOND THOUGHT ...

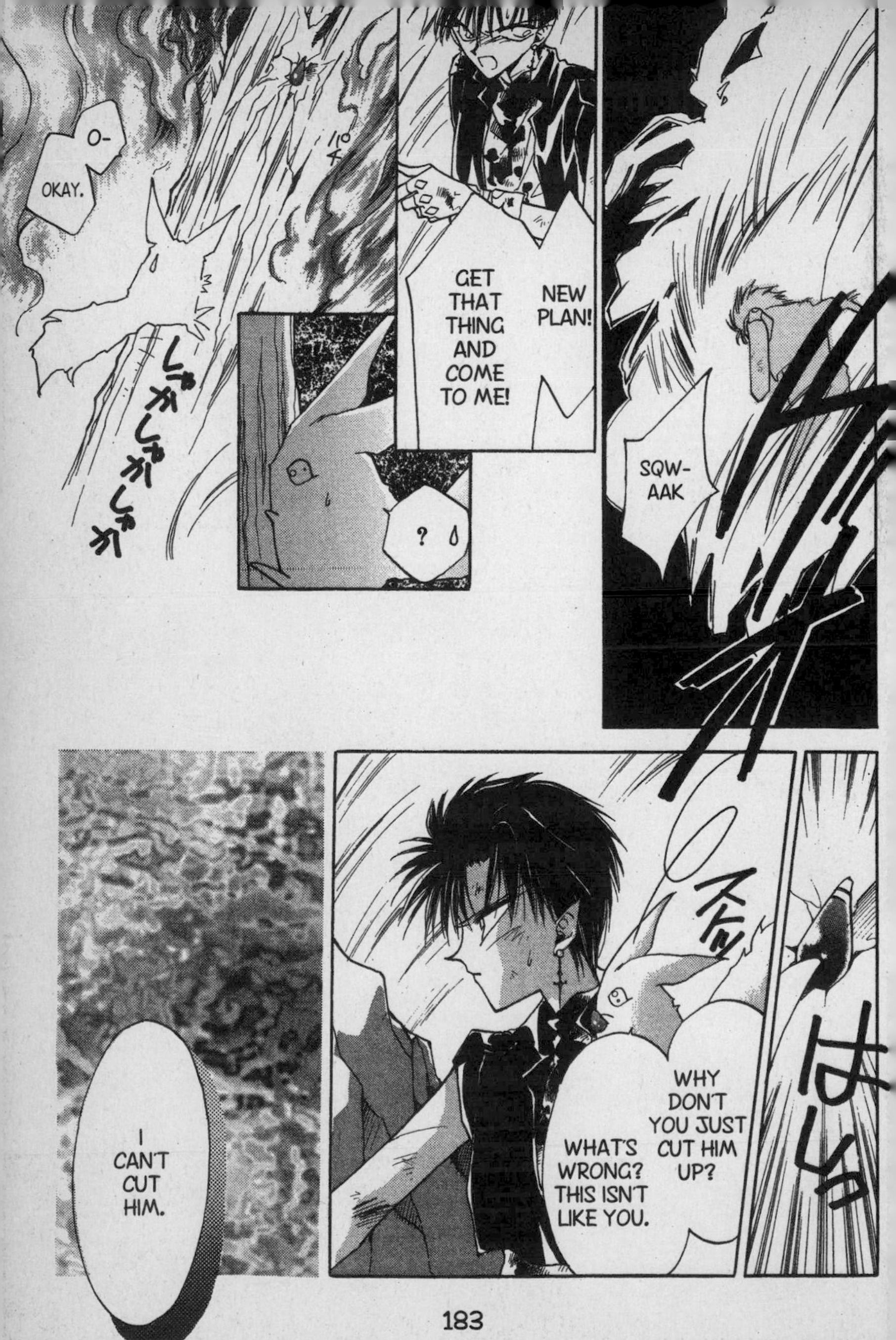
SQW- AAK
NEW PLAN!
GET THAT THING AND COME TO ME!
?
O- OKAY.
しゃかしゃかしゃかしゃか
はっ
WHY DON'T YOU JUST CUT HIM UP?
WHAT'S WRONG? THIS ISN'T LIKE YOU.
I CAN'T CUT HIM.

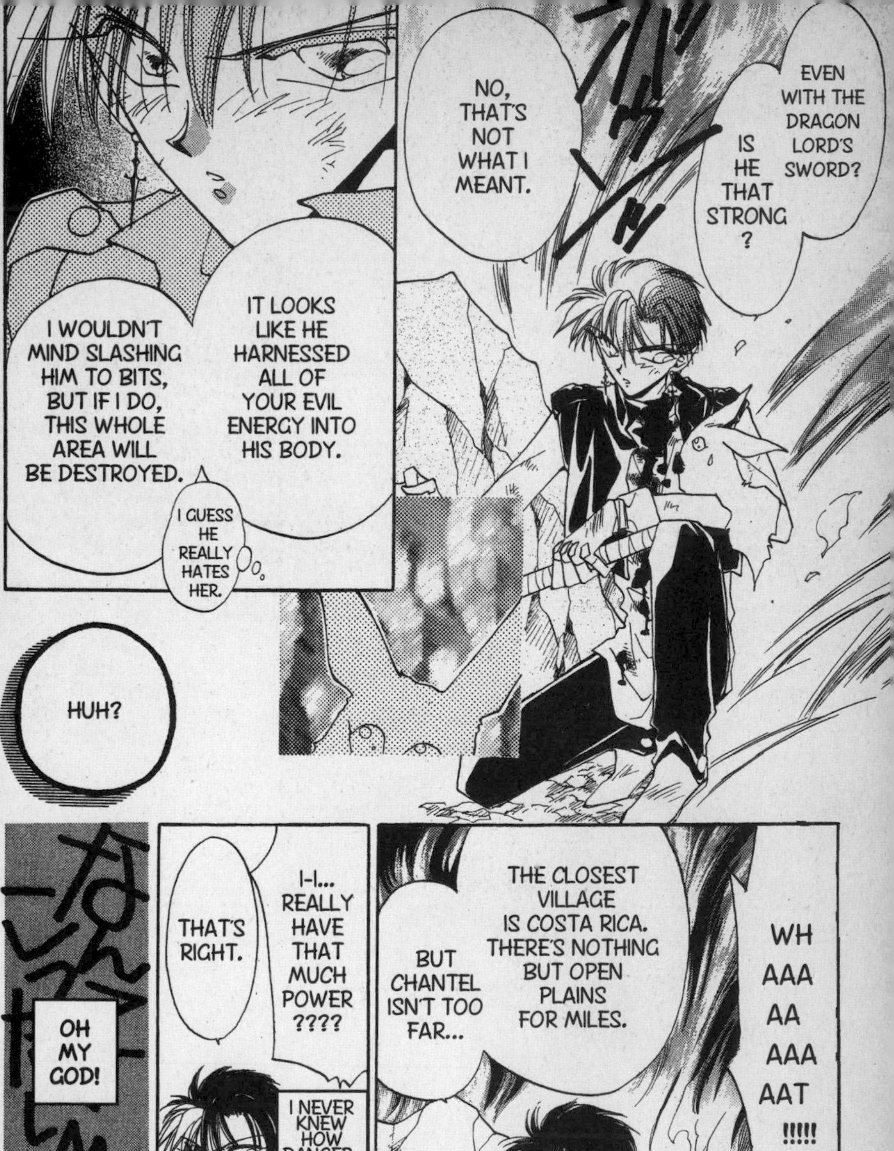
IS HE THAT STRONG? EVEN WITH THE DRAGON LORD'S SWORD?
NO, THAT'S NOT WHAT I MEANT.
IT LOOKS LIKE HE HARNESSED ALL OF YOUR EVIL ENERGY INTO HIS BODY.
I WOULDN'T MIND SLASHING HIM TO BITS, BUT IF I DO, THIS WHOLE AREA WILL BE DESTROYED.
I GUESS HE REALLY HATES HER.
HUH?
WHAAAAAAAAAAT!!!!!
THE CLOSEST VILLAGE IS COSTA RICA. THERE'S NOTHING BUT OPEN PLAINS FOR MILES.
BUT CHANTEL ISN'T TOO FAR...
I-I... REALLY HAVE THAT MUCH POWER????
THAT'S RIGHT.
I NEVER KNEW HOW DANGER-OUS I WAS.
OH MY GOD!

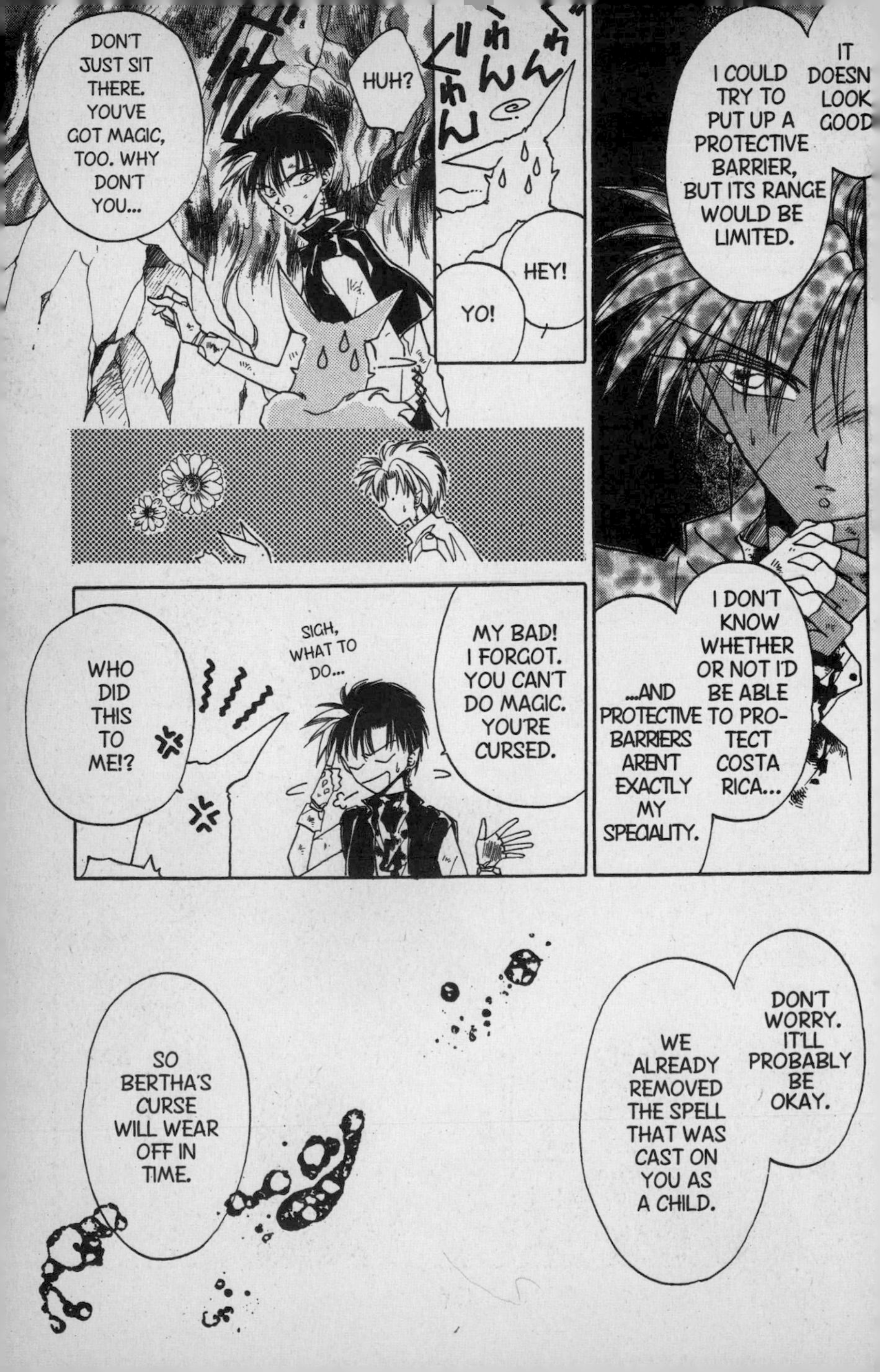
IT DOESN'T LOOK GOOD
I COULD TRY TO PUT UP A PROTECTIVE BARRIER, BUT ITS RANGE WOULD BE LIMITED.
I DON'T KNOW WHETHER OR NOT I'D BE ABLE TO PRO-TECT COSTA RICA...
...AND PROTECTIVE BARRIERS AREN'T EXACTLY MY SPECIALITY.
ぐわんぐわん
HEY!
YO!
DON'T JUST SIT THERE. YOU'VE GOT MAGIC, TOO. WHY DON'T YOU...
HUH?
MY BAD! I FORGOT. YOU CAN'T DO MAGIC. YOU'RE CURSED.
SIGH, WHAT TO DO...
WHO DID THIS TO ME!?
DON'T WORRY. IT'LL PROBABLY BE OKAY.
WE ALREADY REMOVED THE SPELL THAT WAS CAST ON YOU AS A CHILD.
SO BERTHA'S CURSE WILL WEAR OFF IN TIME.

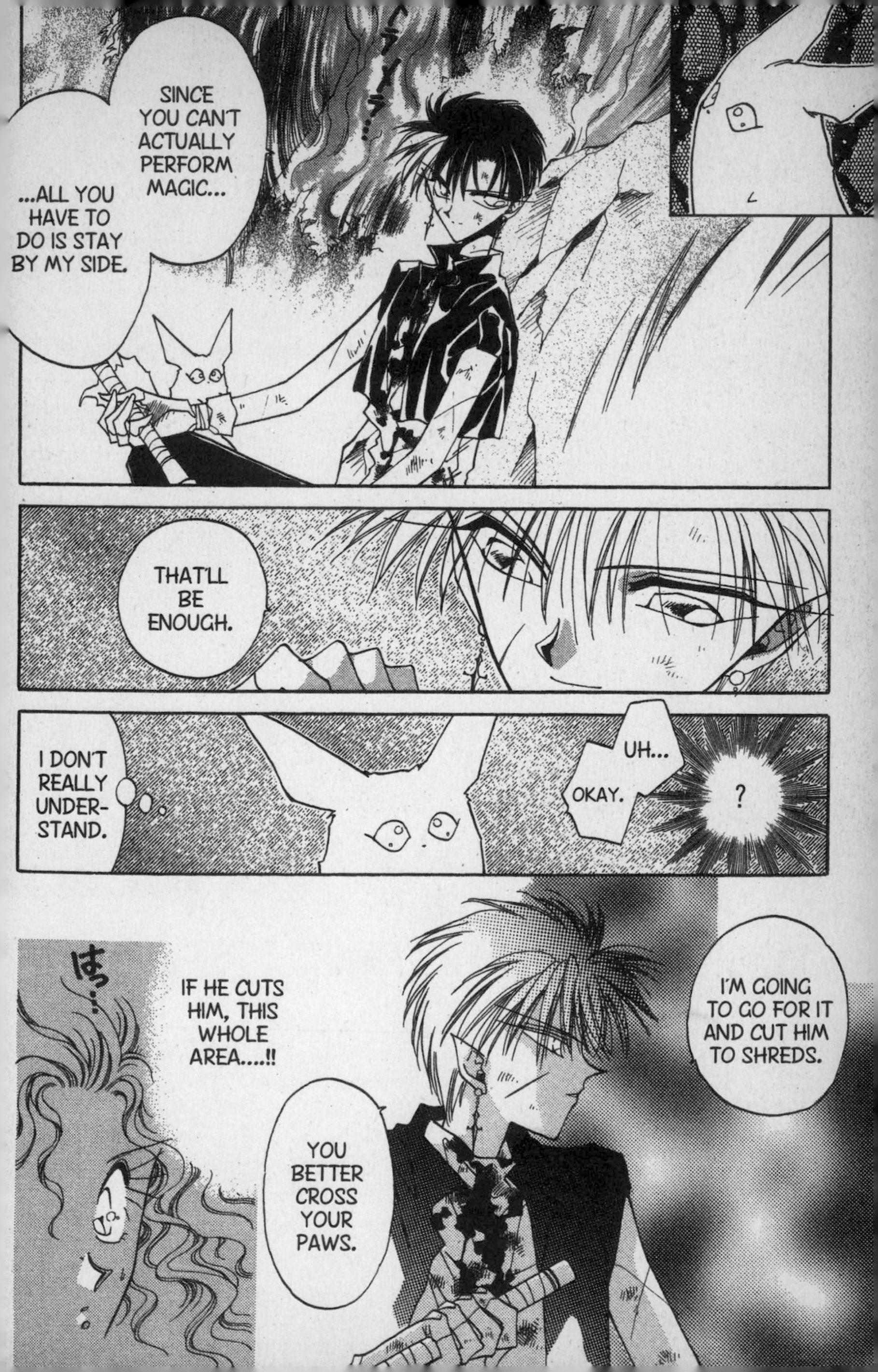
SINCE YOU CAN'T ACTUALLY PERFORM MAGIC...
...ALL YOU HAVE TO DO IS STAY BY MY SIDE.
THAT'LL BE ENOUGH.
UH...
OKAY.
?
I DON'T REALLY UNDER-STAND.
I'M GOING TO GO FOR IT AND CUT HIM TO SHREDS.
IF HE CUTS HIM, THIS WHOLE AREA....!!
YOU BETTER CROSS YOUR PAWS.
はっ

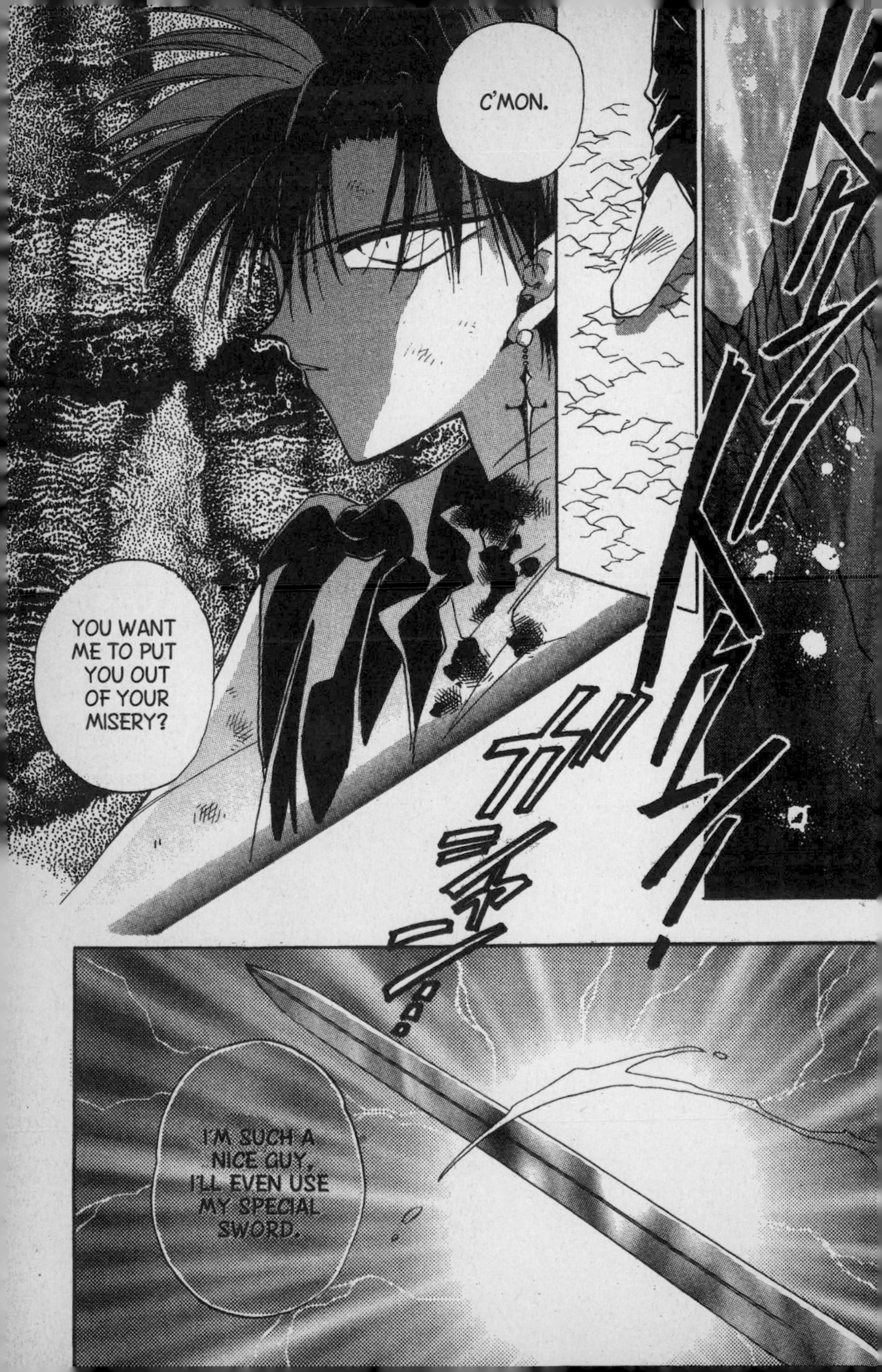
C'MON.
YOU WANT ME TO PUT YOU OUT OF YOUR MISERY?
I'M SUCH A NICE GUY, I'LL EVEN USE MY SPECIAL SWORD.

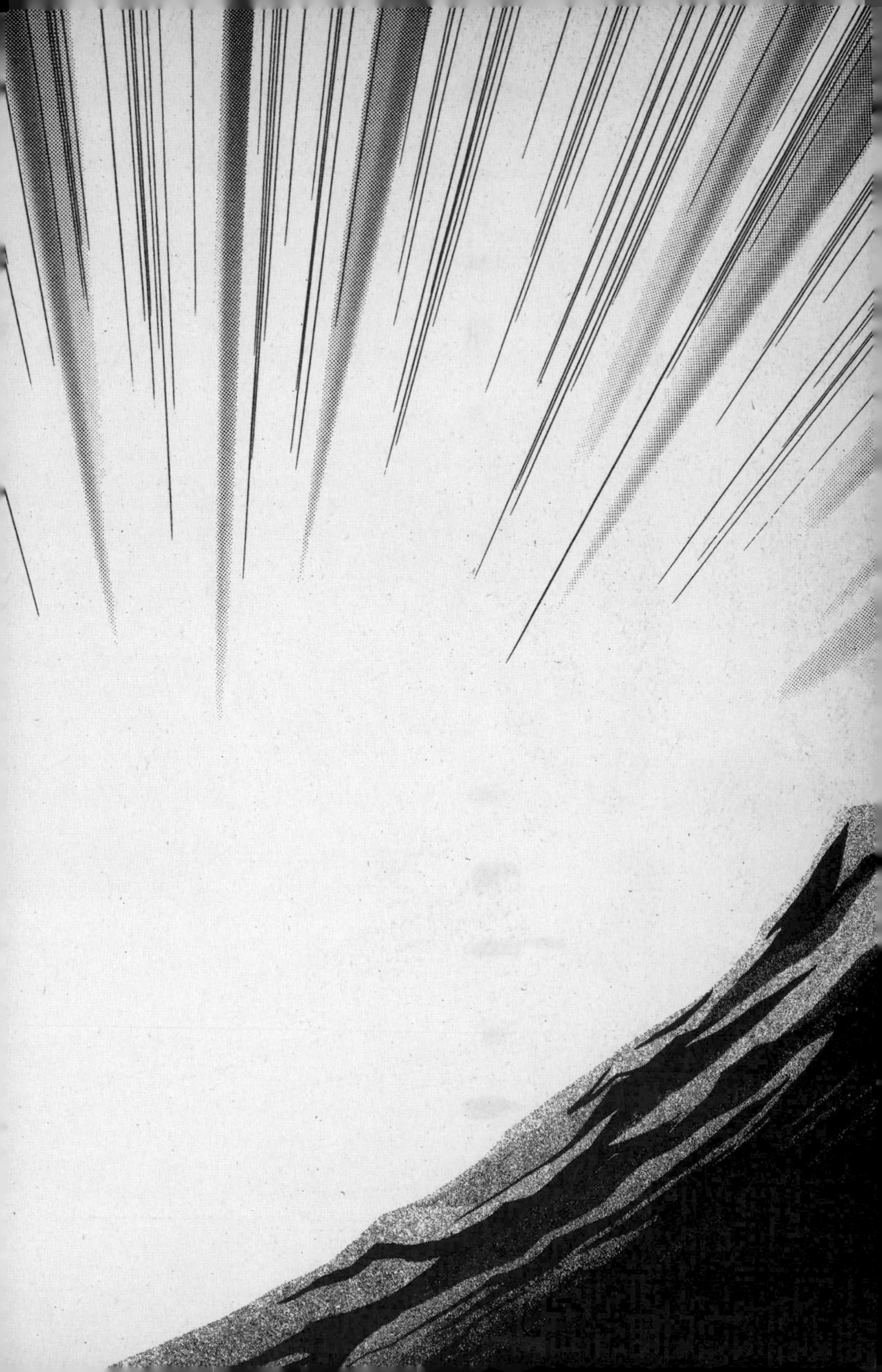

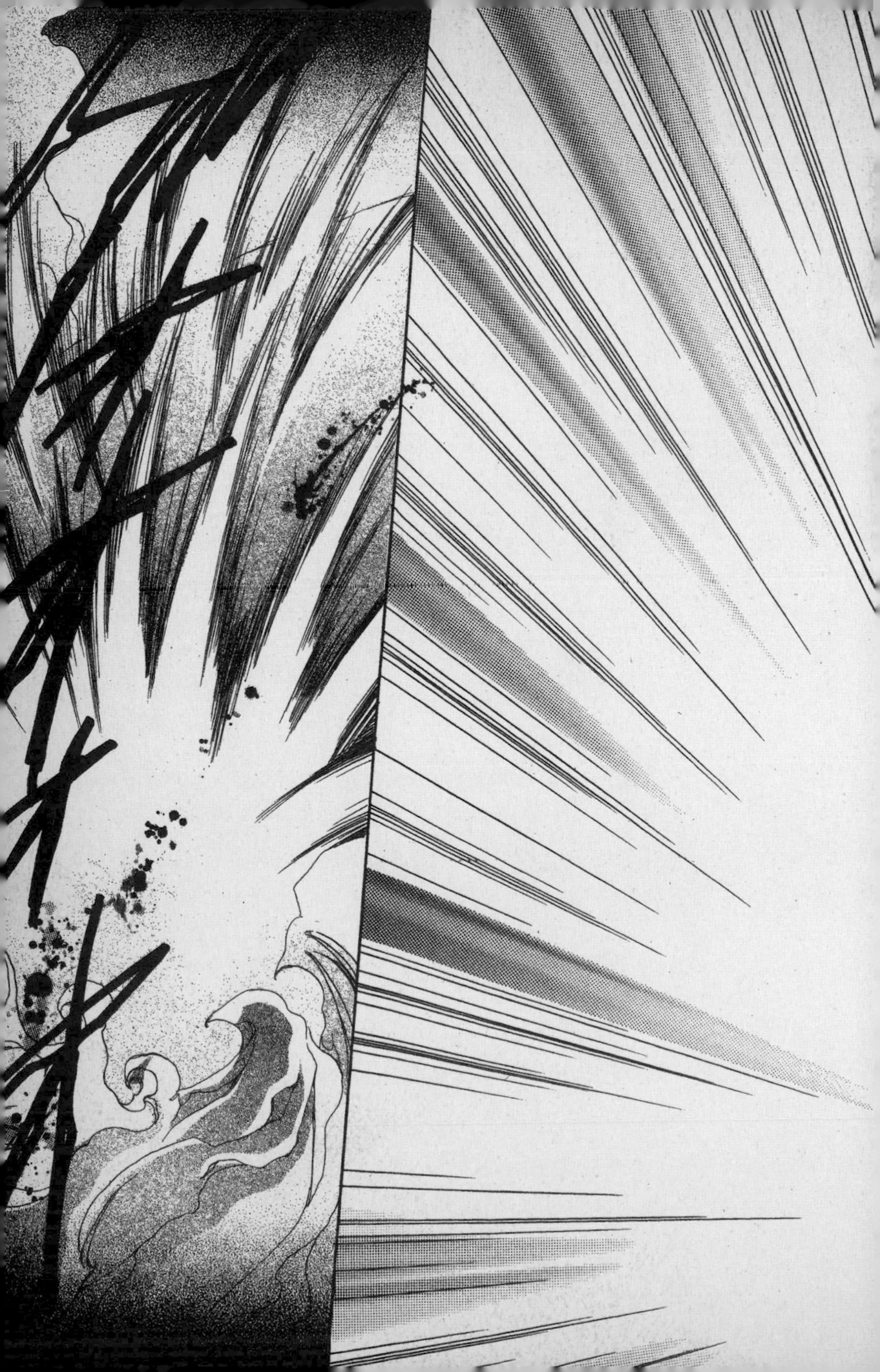

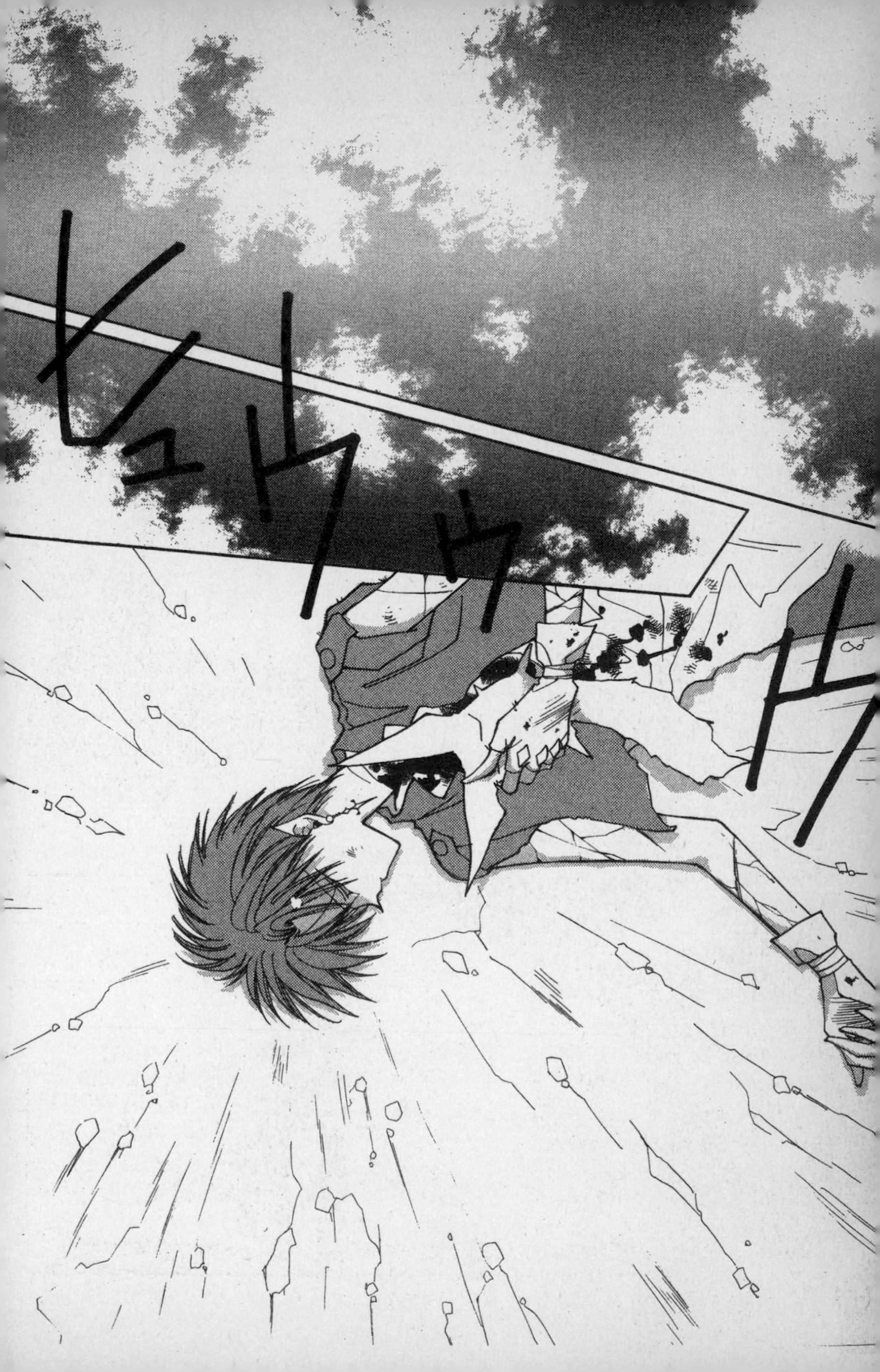
ヒュウウ

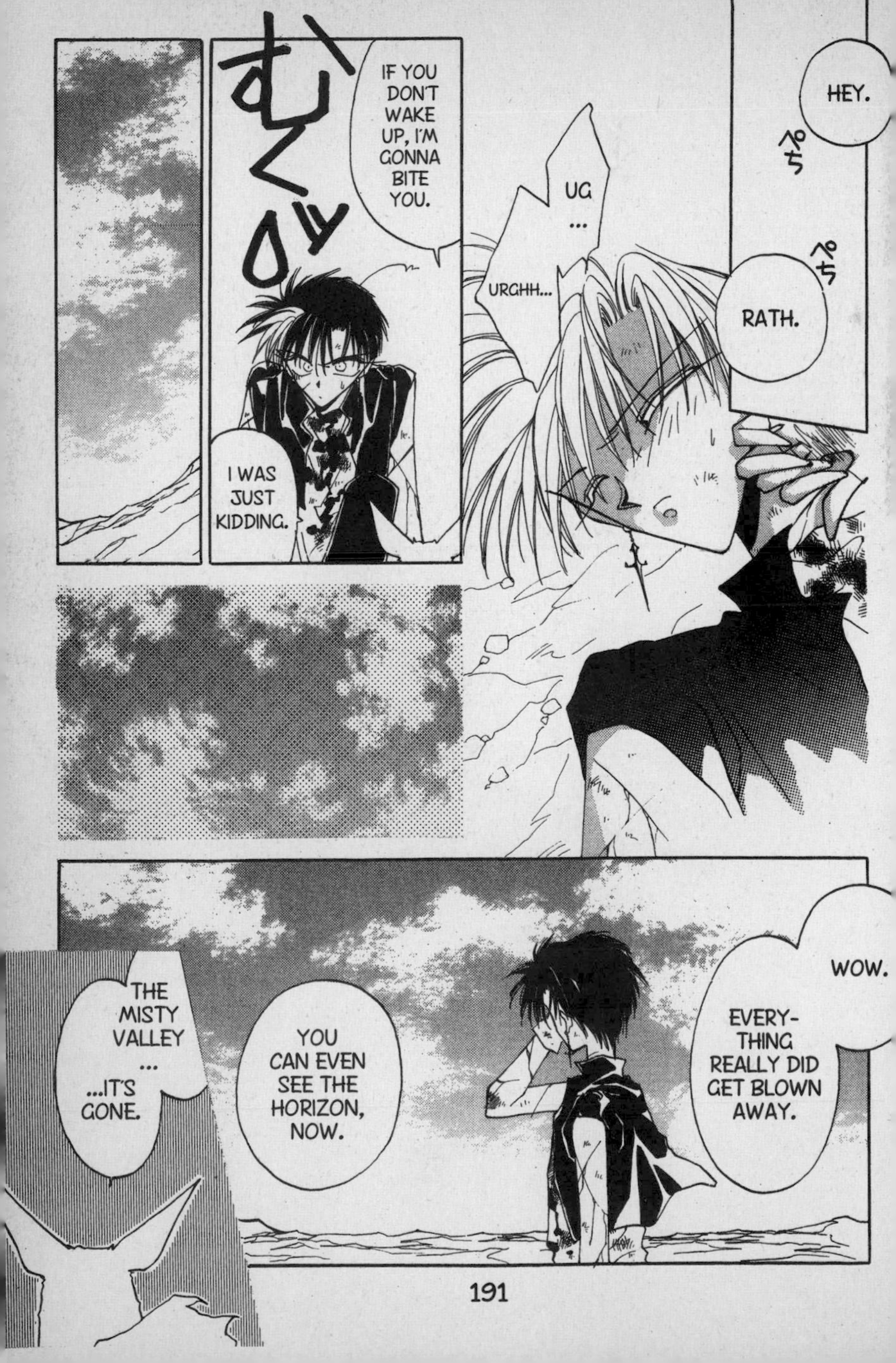
HEY.
ぺち
RATH.
ぺち
UG ...
URGHH...
むくっ
IF YOU DON'T WAKE UP, I'M GONNA BITE YOU.
I WAS JUST KIDDING.
WOW.
EVERY-THING REALLY DID GET BLOWN AWAY.
YOU CAN EVEN SEE THE HORIZON, NOW.
THE MISTY VALLEY ...
...IT'S GONE.

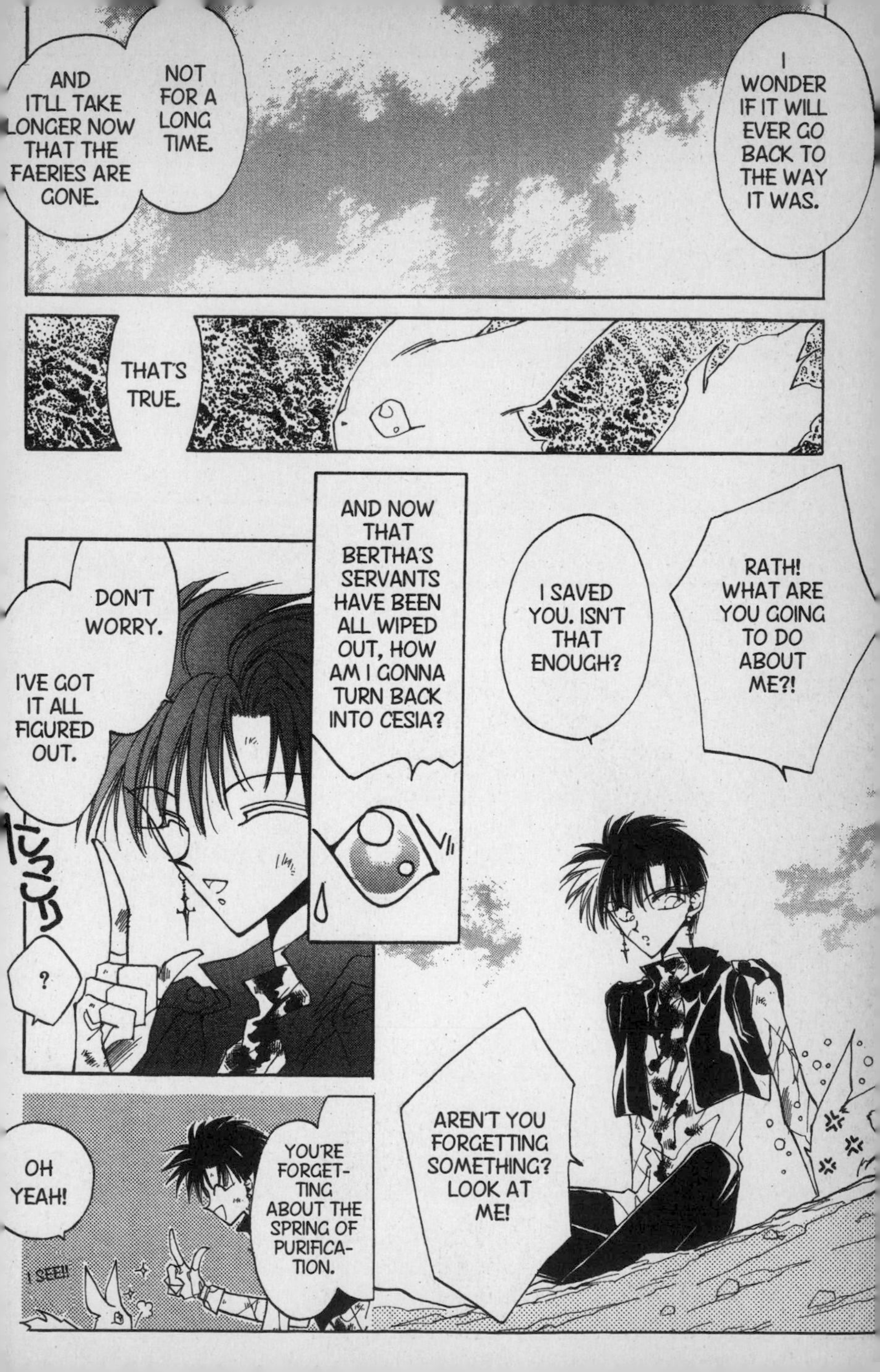
I WONDER IF IT WILL EVER GO BACK TO THE WAY IT WAS.
NOT FOR A LONG TIME.
AND IT'LL TAKE LONGER NOW THAT THE FAERIES ARE GONE.
THAT'S TRUE.
RATH! WHAT ARE YOU GOING TO DO ABOUT ME?!
I SAVED YOU. ISN'T THAT ENOUGH?
AREN'T YOU FORGETTING SOMETHING? LOOK AT ME!
AND NOW THAT BERTHA'S SERVANTS HAVE BEEN ALL WIPED OUT, HOW AM I GONNA TURN BACK INTO CESIA?
DON'T WORRY.
I'VE GOT IT ALL FIGURED OUT.
?
YOU'RE FORGET-TING ABOUT THE SPRING OF PURIFICA-TION.
OH YEAH!
I SEE!!

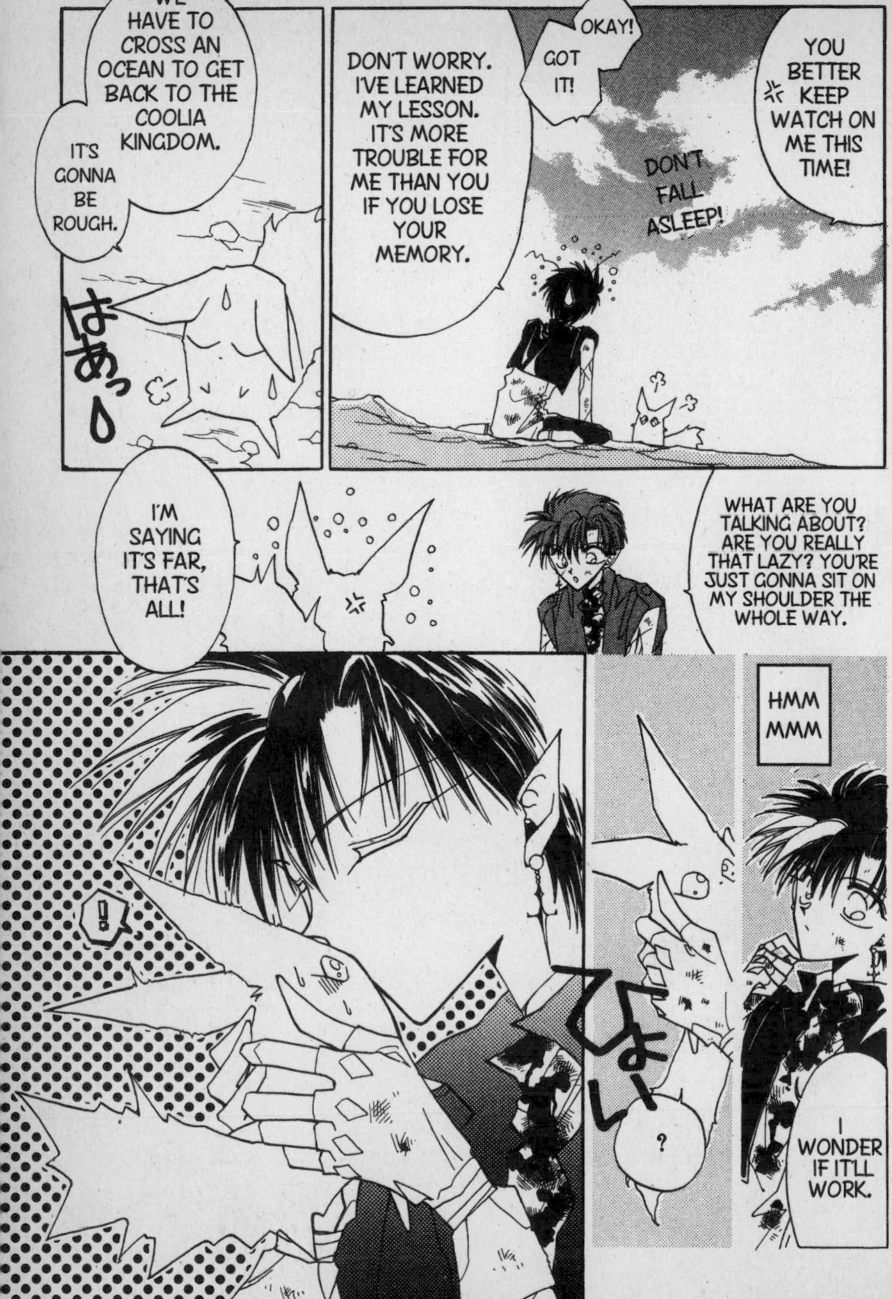
YOU BETTER KEEP WATCH ON ME THIS TIME!
DON'T FALL ASLEEP!
OKAY!
GOT IT!
DON'T WORRY. I'VE LEARNED MY LESSON. IT'S MORE TROUBLE FOR ME THAN YOU IF YOU LOSE YOUR MEMORY.
WE HAVE TO CROSS AN OCEAN TO GET BACK TO THE COOLIA KINGDOM.
IT'S GONNA BE ROUGH.
はあっ
WHAT ARE YOU TALKING ABOUT? ARE YOU REALLY THAT LAZY? YOU'RE JUST GONNA SIT ON MY SHOULDER THE WHOLE WAY.
I'M SAYING IT'S FAR, THAT'S ALL!
HMM MMM
I WONDER IF IT'LL WORK.
?
!!

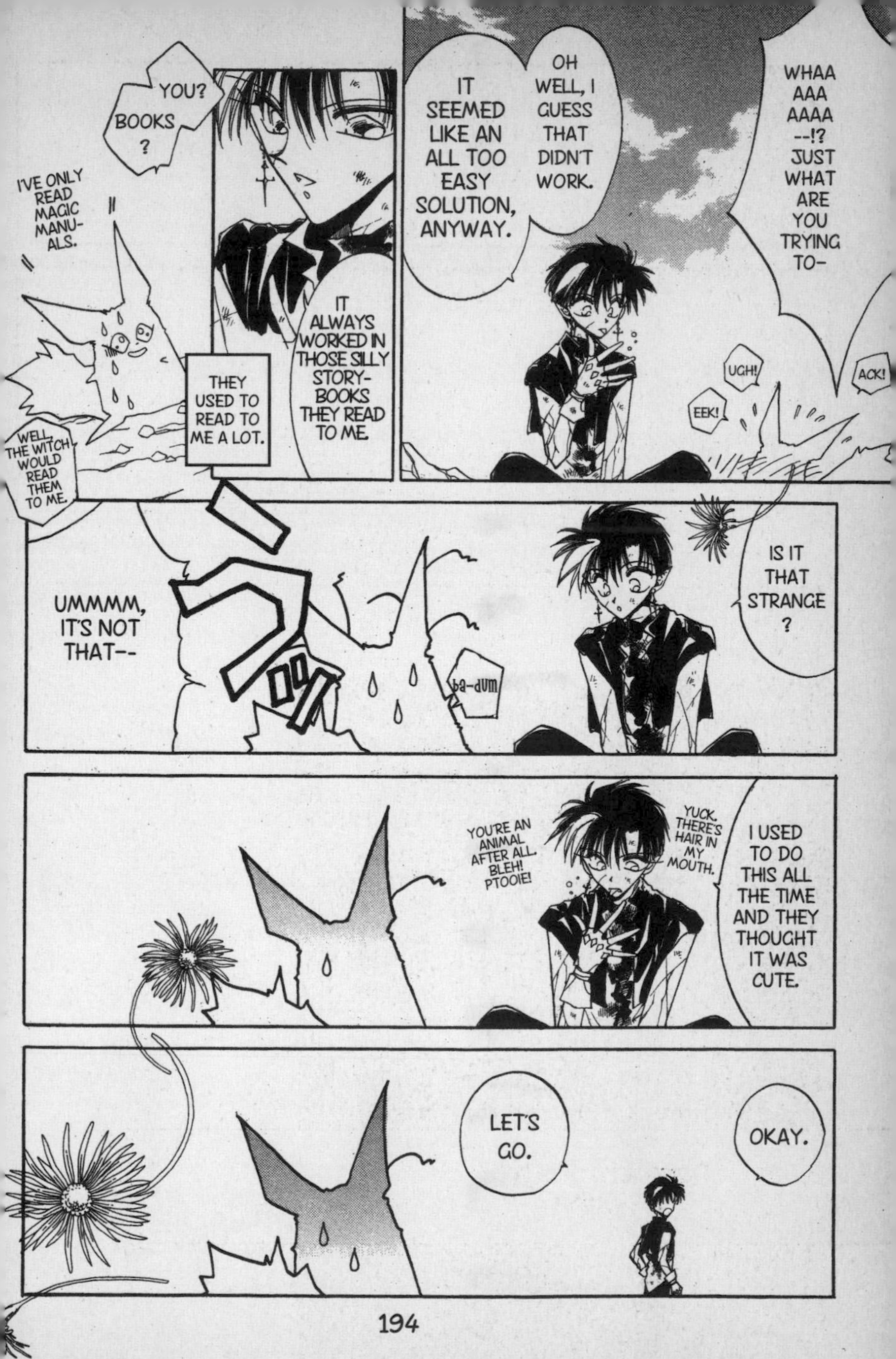
WHAAAAAAAAA--!? JUST WHAT ARE YOU TRYING TO-
ACK!
UGH!
EEK!
OH WELL, I GUESS THAT DIDN'T WORK.
IT SEEMED LIKE AN ALL TOO EASY SOLUTION, ANYWAY.
IT ALWAYS WORKED IN THOSE SILLY STORY-BOOKS THEY READ TO ME.
THEY USED TO READ TO ME A LOT.
YOU? BOOKS ?
I'VE ONLY READ MAGIC MANU-ALS.
WELL, THE WITCH WOULD READ THEM TO ME.
IS IT THAT STRANGE ?
ba-dum
UMMMM, IT'S NOT THAT--
I USED TO DO THIS ALL THE TIME AND THEY THOUGHT IT WAS CUTE.
YUCK. THERE'S HAIR IN MY MOUTH.
YOU'RE AN ANIMAL AFTER ALL. BLEH! PTOOIE!
OKAY.
LET'S GO.

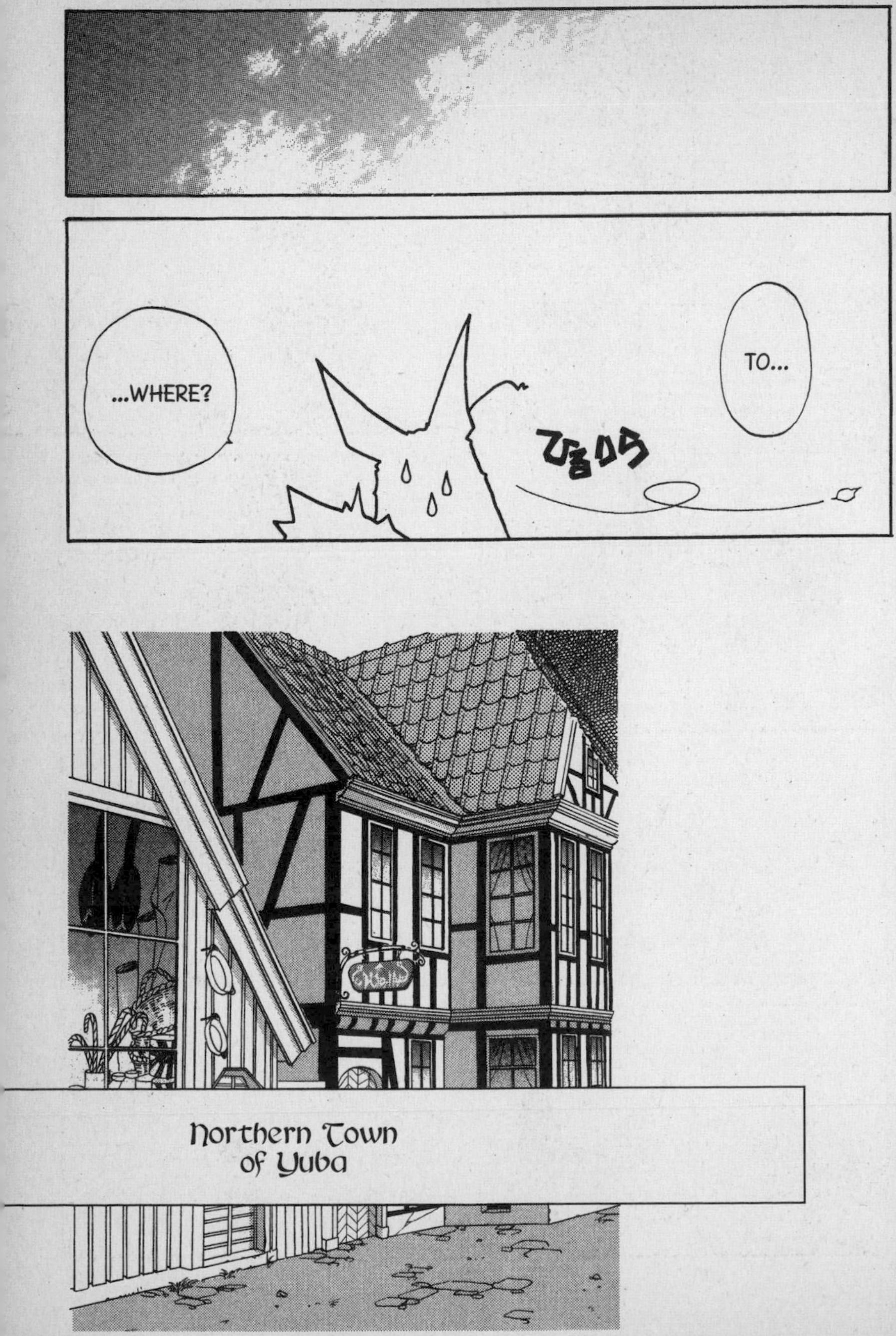
TO...
...WHERE?
Northern Town of Yuba

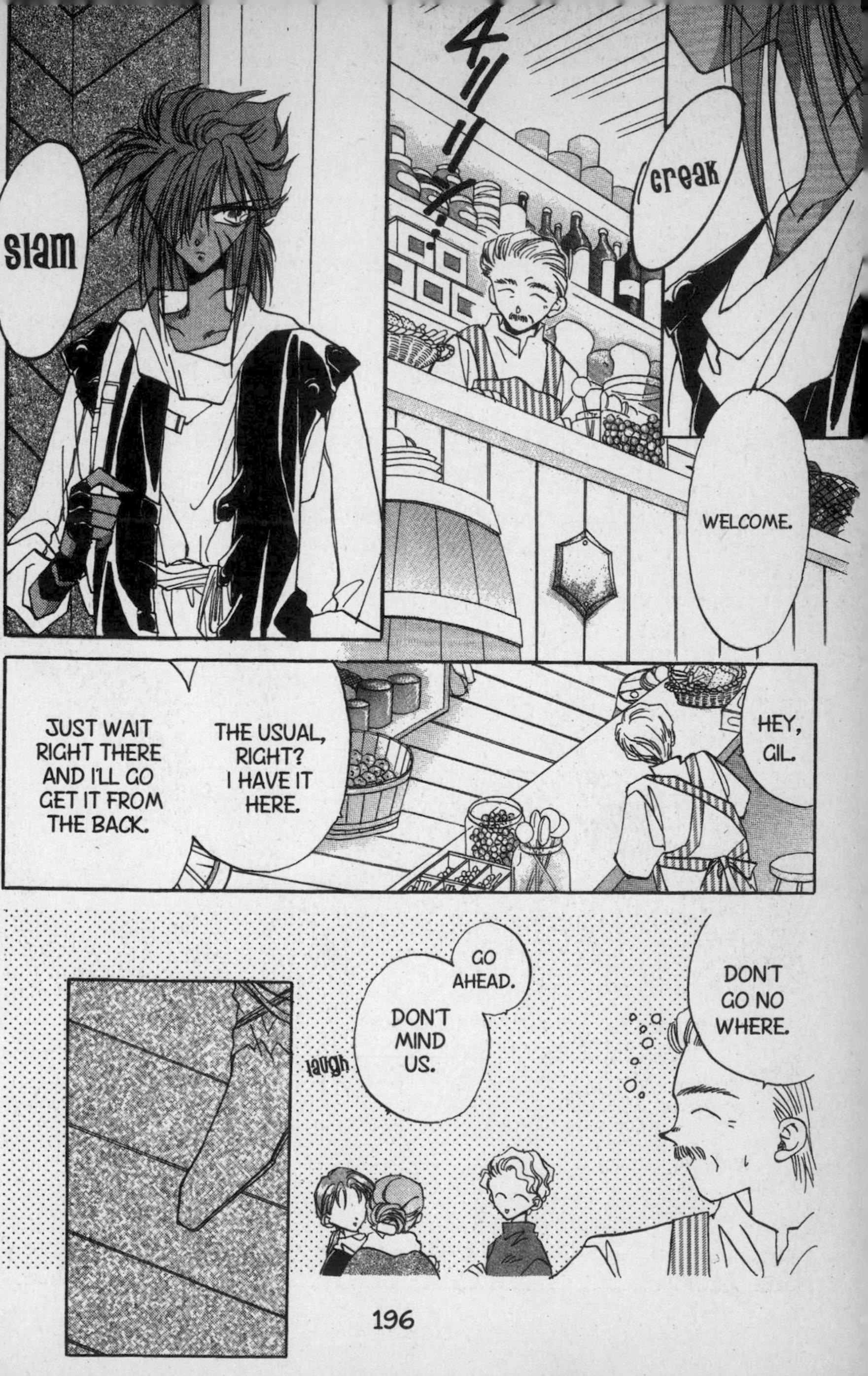
creak
WELCOME.
slam
HEY, GIL.
THE USUAL, RIGHT? I HAVE IT HERE.
JUST WAIT RIGHT THERE AND I'LL GO GET IT FROM THE BACK.
DON'T GO NO WHERE.
GO AHEAD.
DON'T MIND US.
laugh

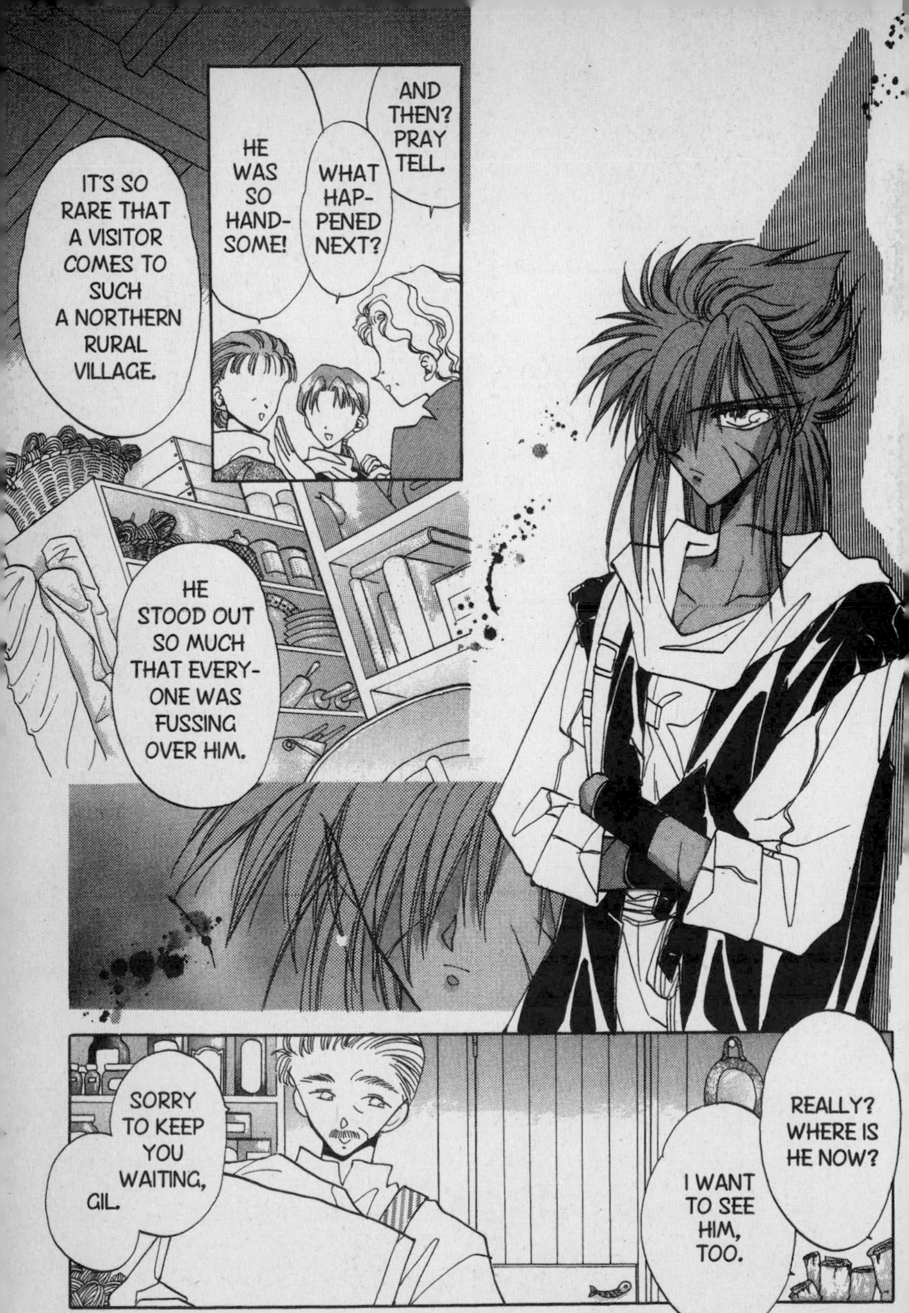
AND THEN? PRAY TELL.
WHAT HAP-PENED NEXT?
HE WAS SO HAND-SOME!
IT'S SO RARE THAT A VISITOR COMES TO SUCH A NORTHERN RURAL VILLAGE.
HE STOOD OUT SO MUCH THAT EVERY-ONE WAS FUSSING OVER HIM.
REALLY? WHERE IS HE NOW?
I WANT TO SEE HIM, TOO.
SORRY TO KEEP YOU WAITING, GIL.

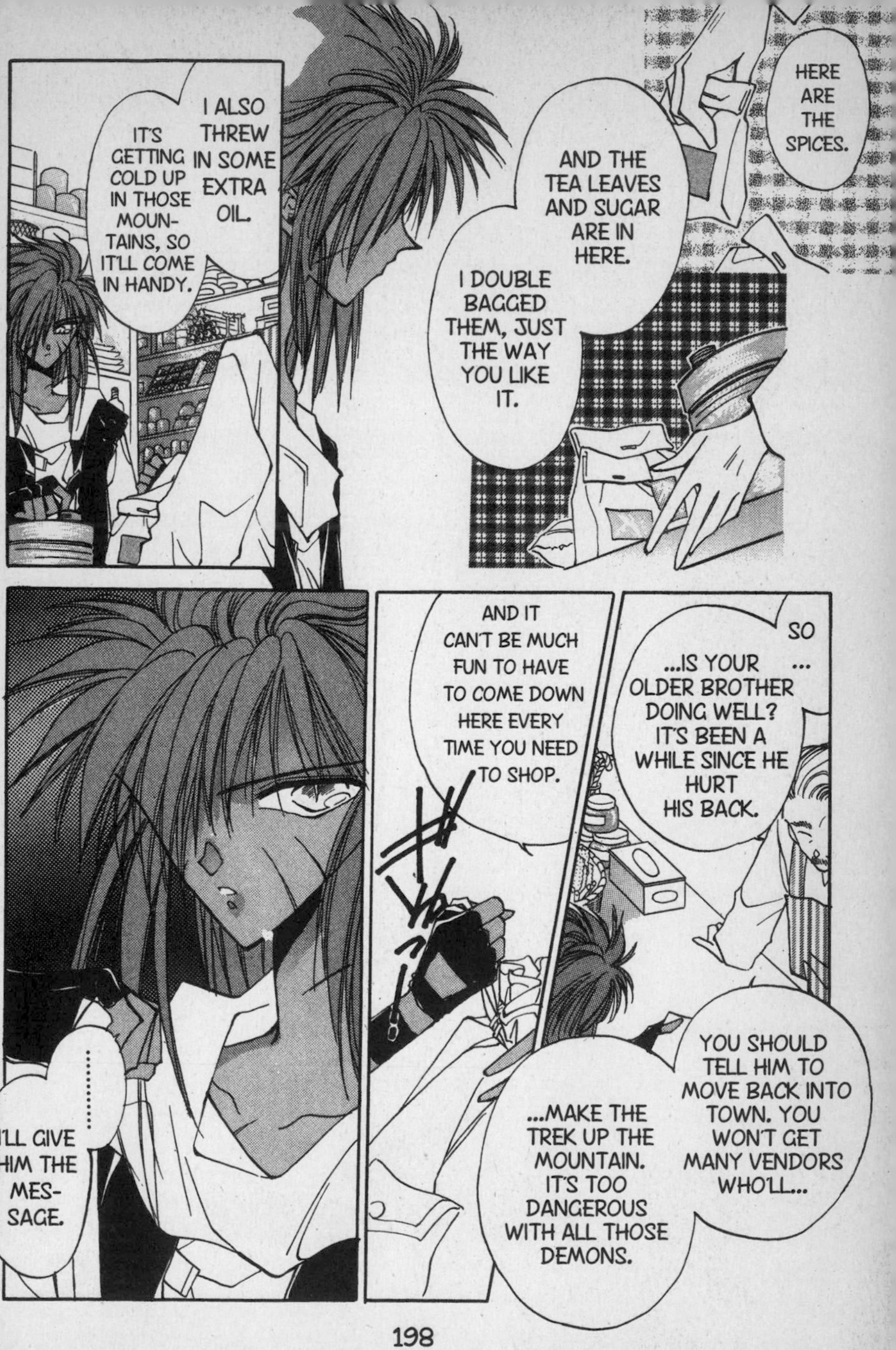
HERE ARE THE SPICES.
AND THE TEA LEAVES AND SUGAR ARE IN HERE.
I DOUBLE BAGGED THEM, JUST THE WAY YOU LIKE IT.
I ALSO THREW IN SOME EXTRA OIL.
IT'S GETTING COLD UP IN THOSE MOUN-TAINS, SO IT'LL COME IN HANDY.
SO ...
...IS YOUR OLDER BROTHER DOING WELL? IT'S BEEN A WHILE SINCE HE HURT HIS BACK.
AND IT CAN'T BE MUCH FUN TO HAVE TO COME DOWN HERE EVERY TIME YOU NEED TO SHOP.
YOU SHOULD TELL HIM TO MOVE BACK INTO TOWN. YOU WON'T GET MANY VENDORS WHO'LL...
...MAKE THE TREK UP THE MOUNTAIN. IT'S TOO DANGEROUS WITH ALL THOSE DEMONS.
......
I'LL GIVE HIM THE MES-SAGE.

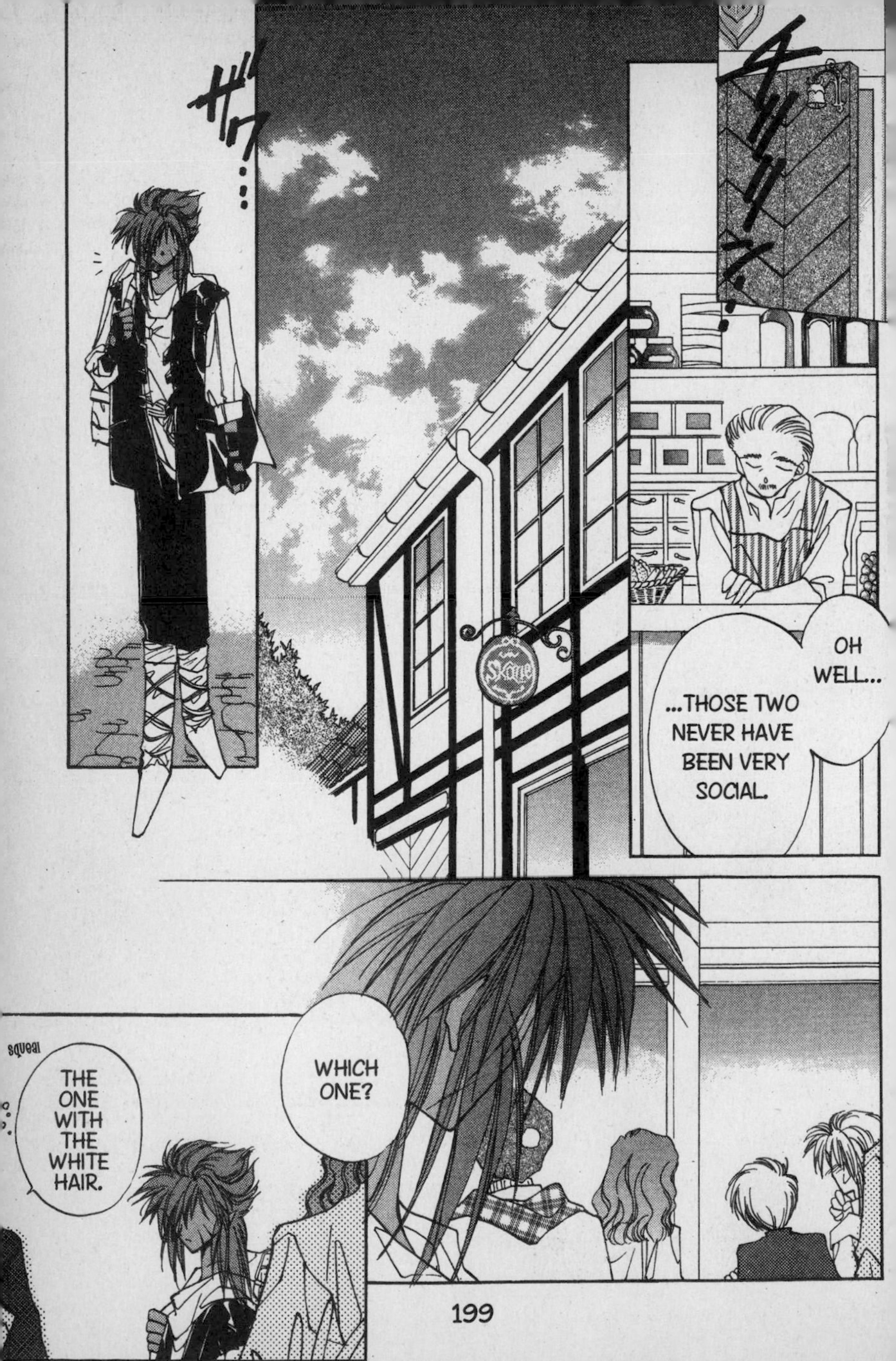
OH WELL...
...THOSE TWO NEVER HAVE BEEN VERY SOCIAL.
WHICH ONE?
THE ONE WITH THE WHITE HAIR.

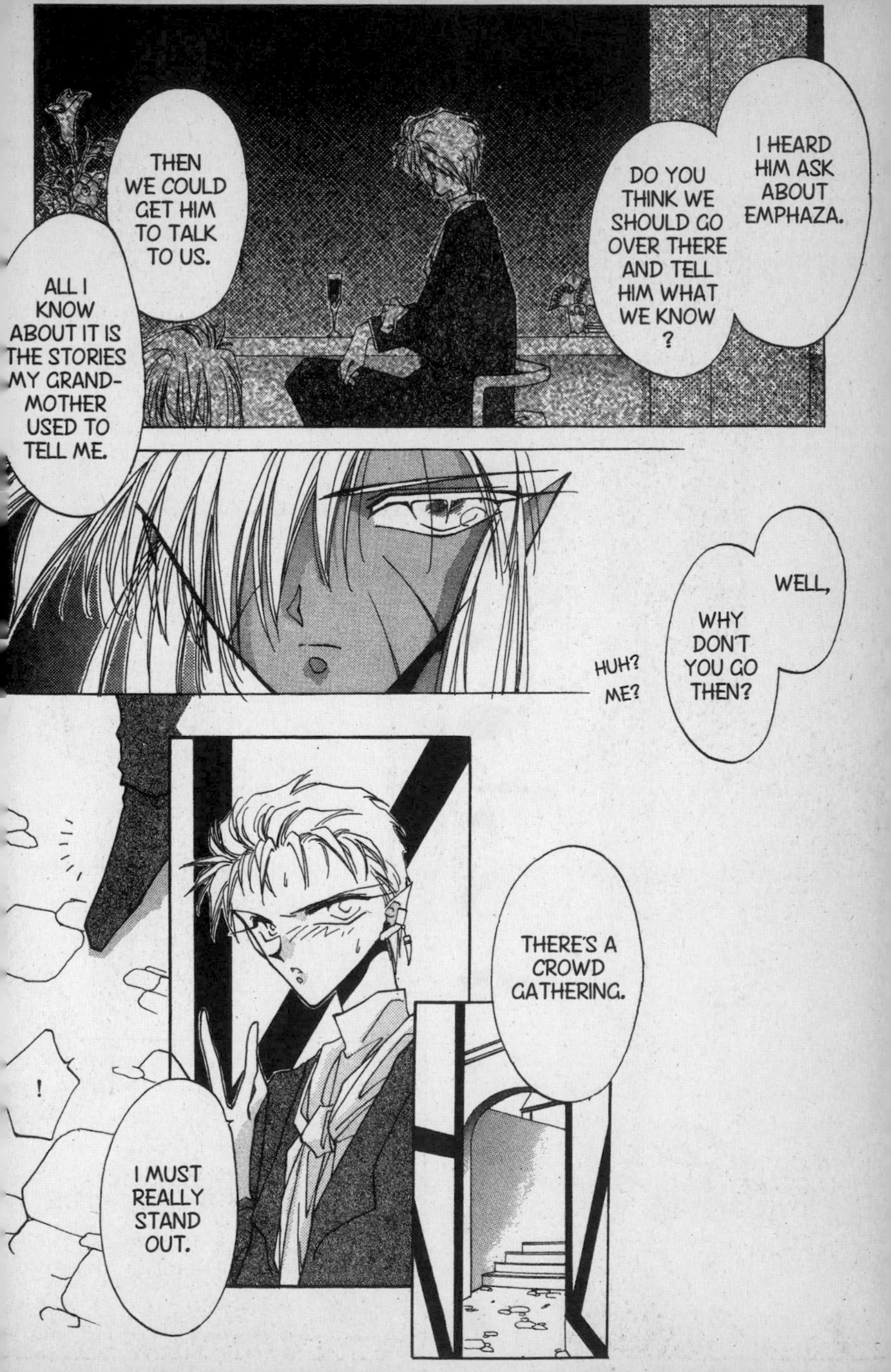
I HEARD HIM ASK ABOUT EMPHAZA.
DO YOU THINK WE SHOULD GO OVER THERE AND TELL HIM WHAT WE KNOW ?
THEN WE COULD GET HIM TO TALK TO US.
ALL I KNOW ABOUT IT IS THE STORIES MY GRAND-MOTHER USED TO TELL ME.
WELL,
WHY DON'T YOU GO THEN?
HUH? ME?
THERE'S A CROWD GATHERING.
I MUST REALLY STAND OUT.
!

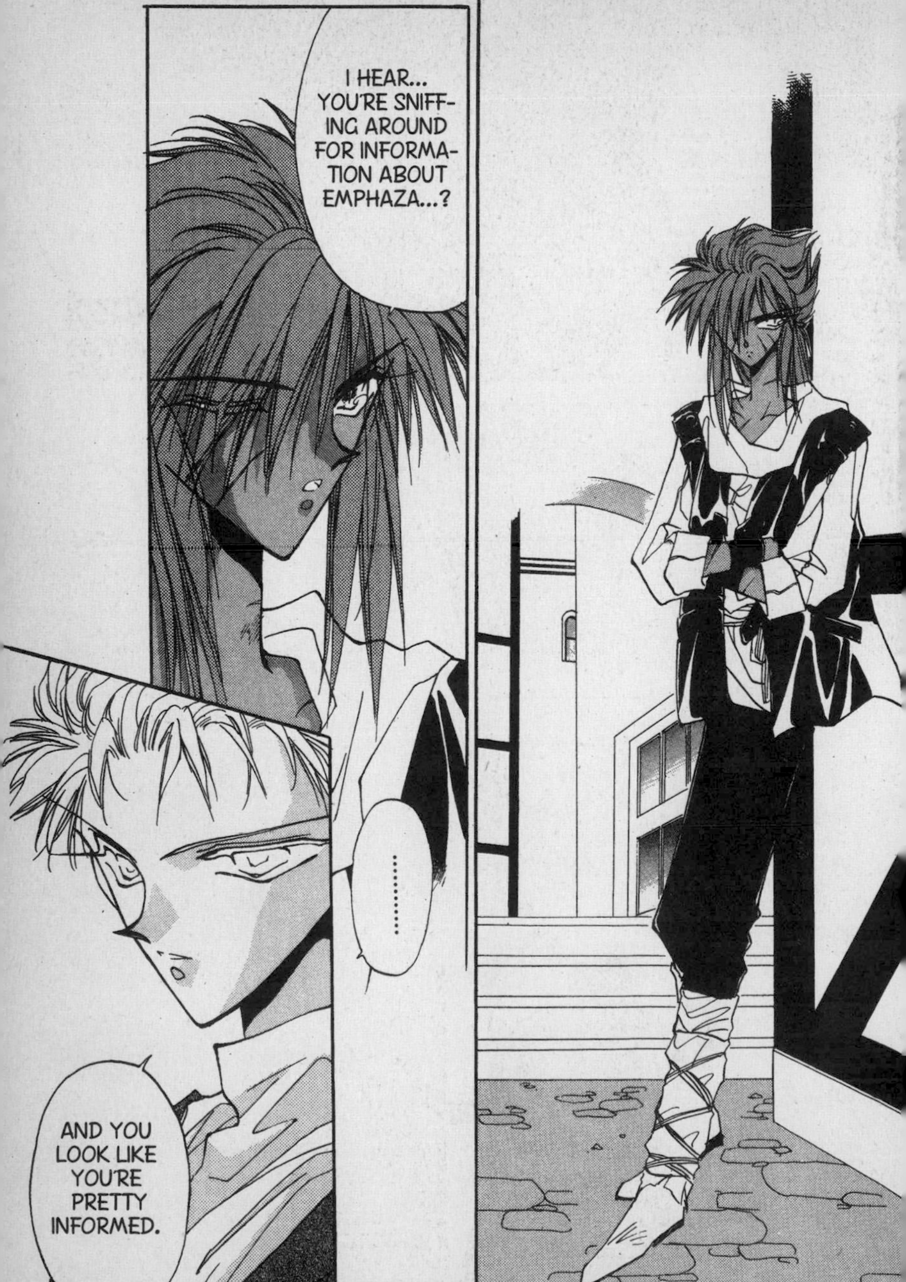
I HEAR... YOU'RE SNIFF-ING AROUND FOR INFORMA-TION ABOUT EMPHAZA...?
....
AND YOU LOOK LIKE YOU'RE PRETTY INFORMED.

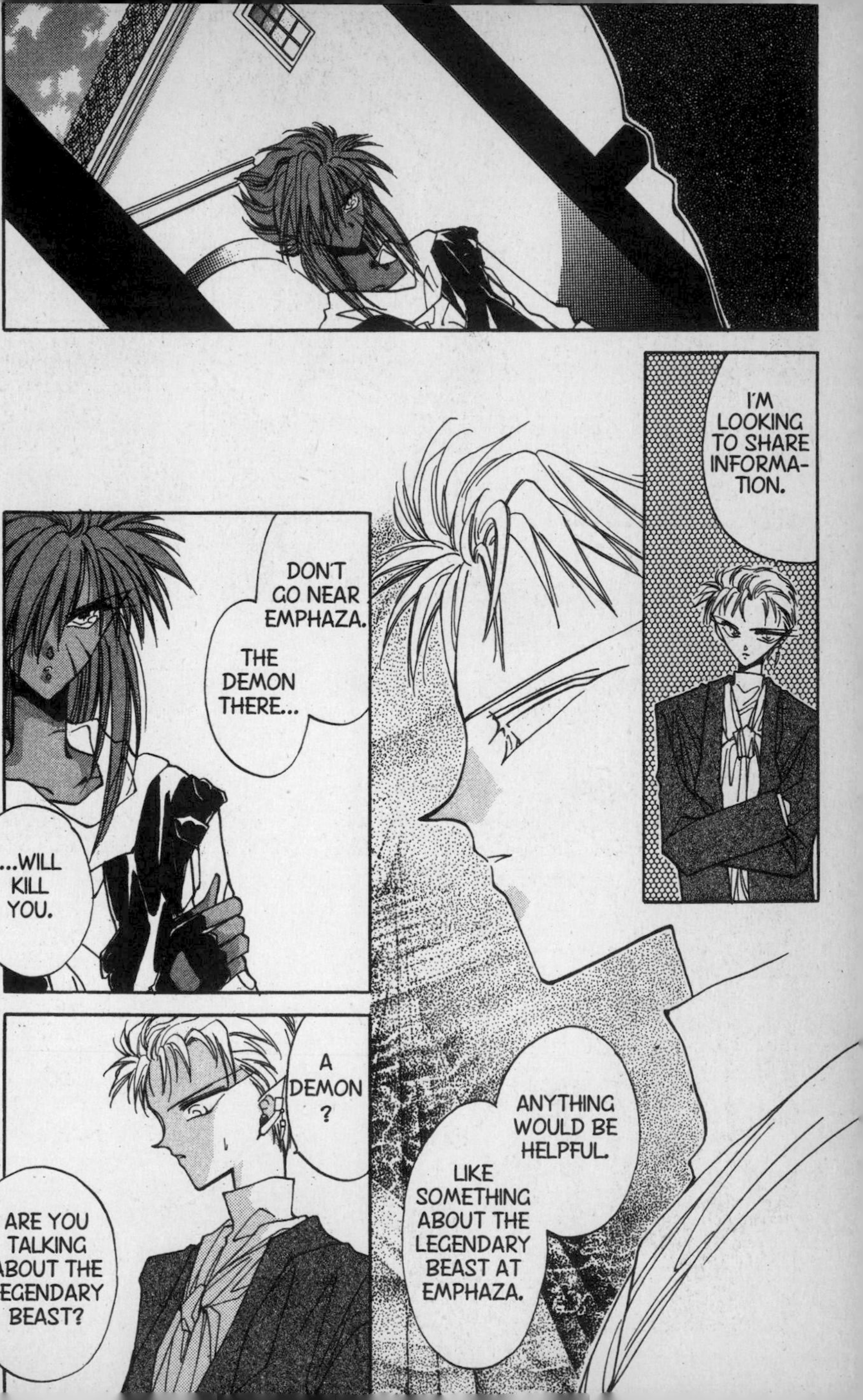
I'M LOOKING TO SHARE INFORMATION.
ANYTHING WOULD BE HELPFUL.
LIKE SOMETHING ABOUT THE LEGENDARY BEAST AT EMPHAZA.
DON'T GO NEAR EMPHAZA.
THE DEMON THERE...
...WILL KILL YOU.
A DEMON?
ARE YOU TALKING ABOUT THE LEGENDARY BEAST?

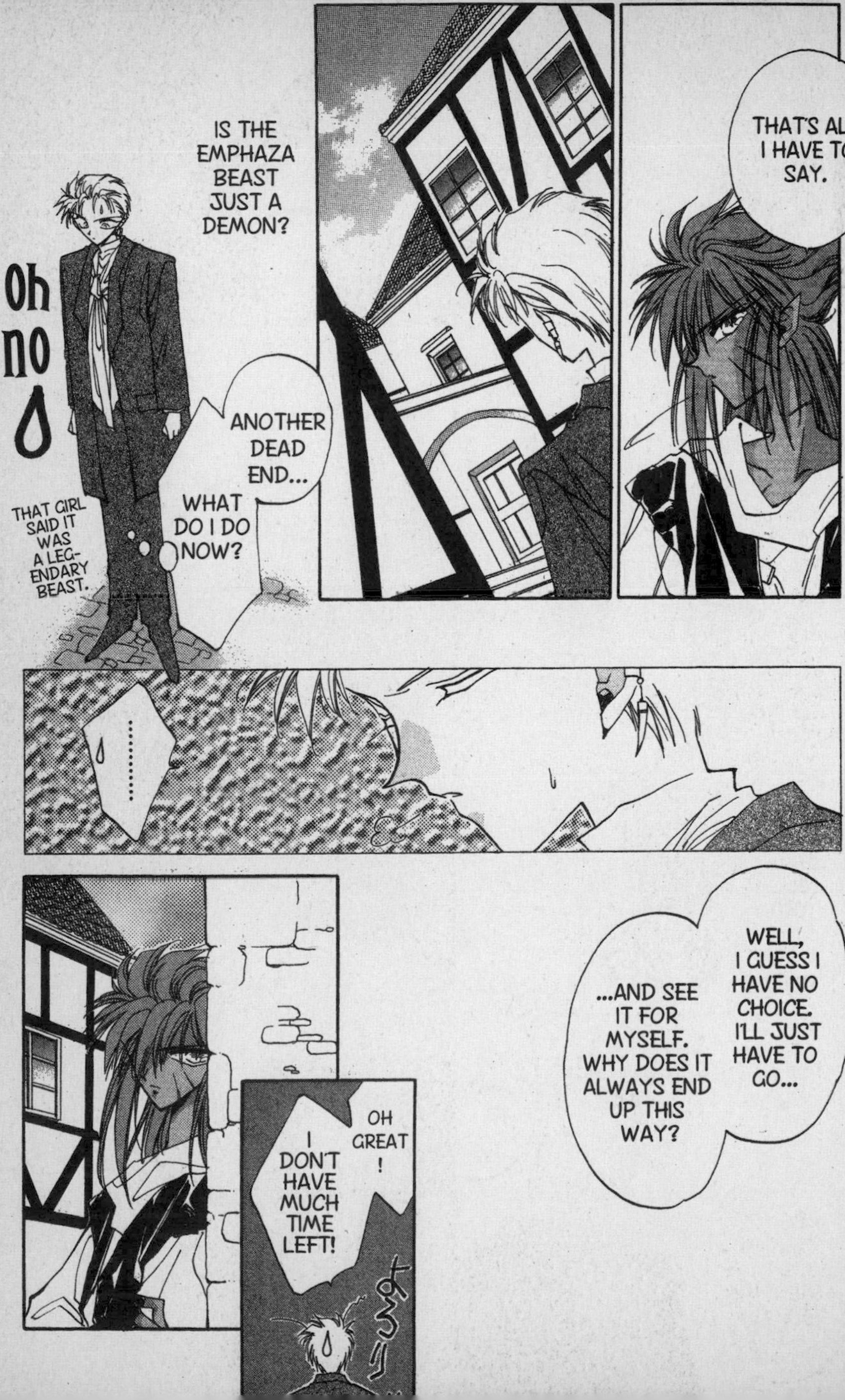
THAT'S ALL I HAVE TO SAY.
IS THE EMPHAZA BEAST JUST A DEMON?
ANOTHER DEAD END...
WHAT DO I DO NOW?
Oh no
THAT GIRL SAID IT WAS A LEG-ENDARY BEAST.
......
WELL, I GUESS I HAVE NO CHOICE. I'LL JUST HAVE TO GO...
...AND SEE IT FOR MYSELF. WHY DOES IT ALWAYS END UP THIS WAY?
OH GREAT!
I DON'T HAVE MUCH TIME LEFT!

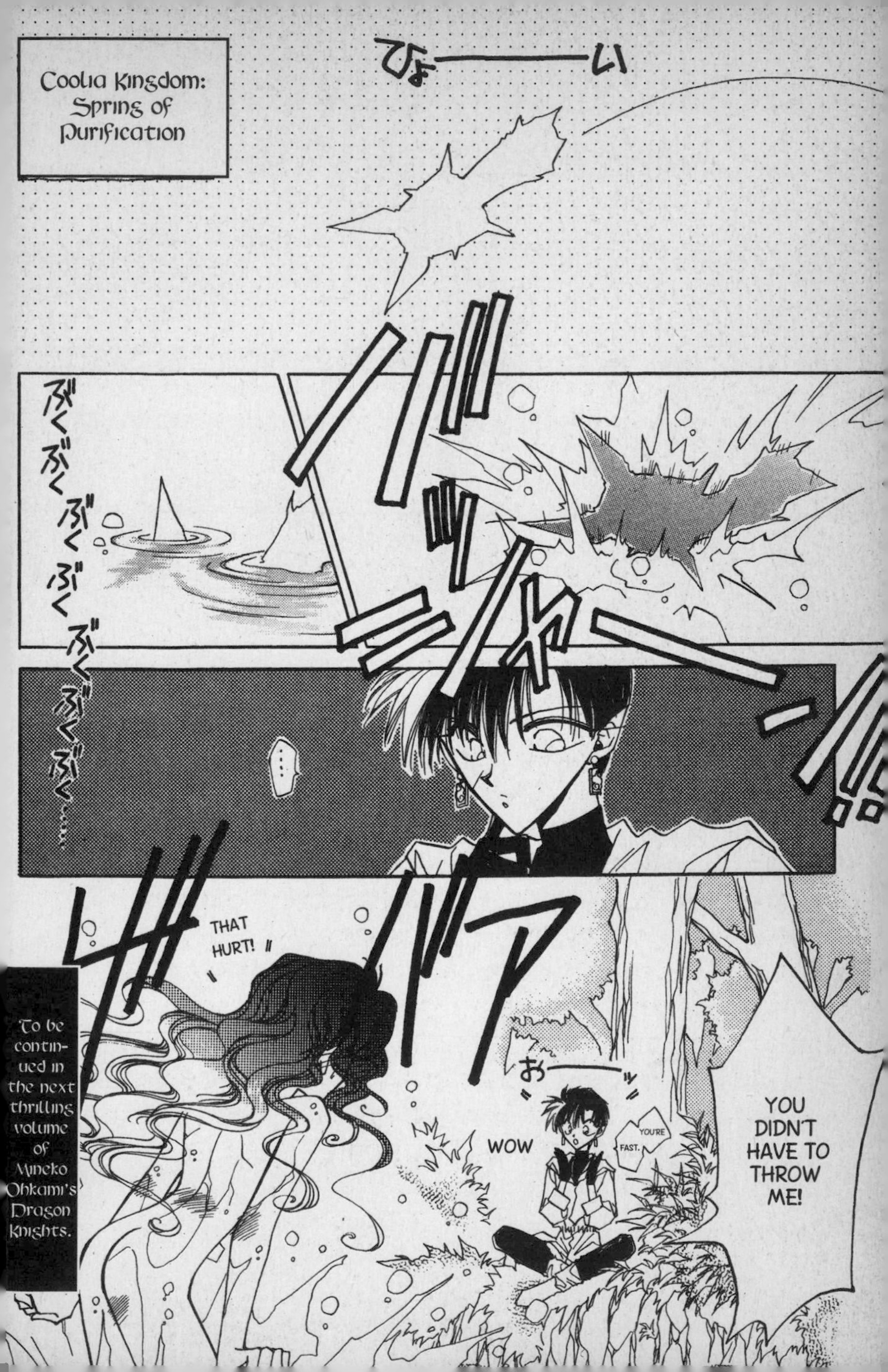
Coolia Kingdom: Spring of Purification
ひょーーーい
バッシャーーー!!
ぶくぶく ぶく ぶく ぶく ぶくぶくぶく……
……
ザバア
YOU DIDN'T HAVE TO THROW ME!
おーーーっ
YOU'RE FAST.
WOW
THAT HURT!!
To be contin-ued in the next thrilling volume of Mineko Ohkami's Dragon Knights.

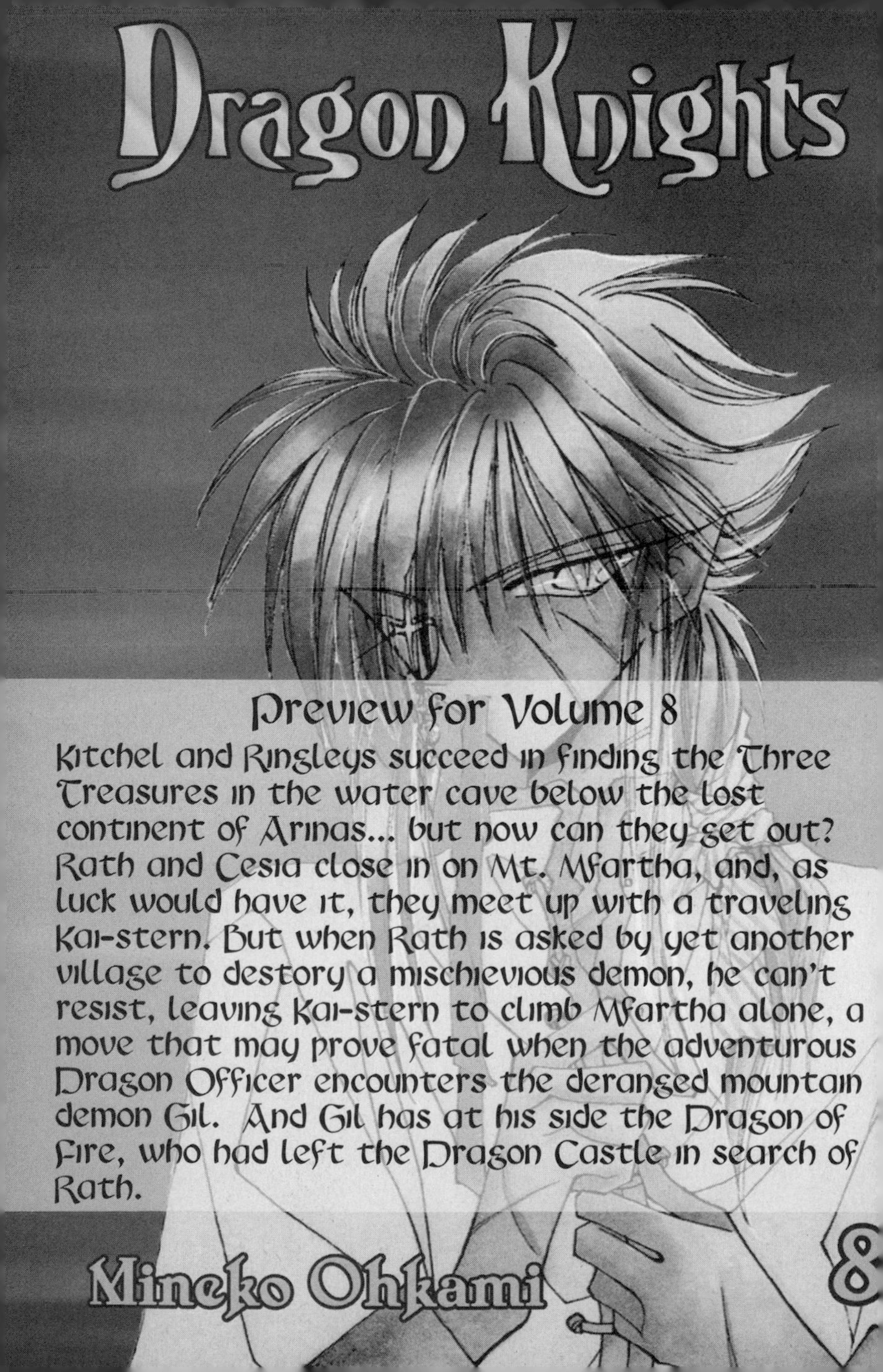

Dragon Knights

Preview for Volume 8

Kitchel and Ringleys succeed in finding the Three
Treasures in the water cave below the lost
continent of Arinas... but now can they get out?
Rath and Cesia close in on Mt. Mfartha, and, as
luck would have it, they meet up with a traveling
Kai-stern. But when Rath is asked by yet another
village to destory a mischievious demon, he can't
resist, leaving Kai-stern to climb Mfartha alone, a
move that may prove fatal when the adventurous
Dragon Officer encounters the deranged mountain
demon Gil. And Gil has at his side the Dragon of
Fire, who had left the Dragon Castle in search of
Rath.

Mineko Ohkami

8

WELCOME TO THE END OF THE WORLD™

RAGNARÖK

Available Now!

TOKYOPOP

DISCARDED

STOP!

This is the back of the book.
You wouldn't want to spoil a great ending!

This book is printed "manga-style," in the authentic Japanese right-to-left format. Since none of the artwork has been flipped or altered, readers get to experience the story just as the creator intended. You've been asking for it, so TOKYOPOP® delivered: authentic, hot-off-the-press, and far more fun!

DIRECTIONS

If this is your first time reading manga-style, here's a quick guide to help you understand how it works.

It's easy... just start in the top right panel and follow the numbers. Have fun, and look for more 100% authentic manga from TOKYOPOP®!

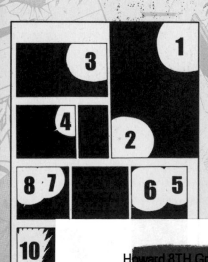

100% AUTHENTIC MANGA